253

Date Due		
AUG 1 1940		
JUL 2 1942		
MAY 1 9 1943		
JY 2 7 48	DEC 2 0 '63	
JA 3 0 '50	FEB 5 '64	
DE 1 0 '52	DEC 1 7 '68	
AU 6 '52		
AG 8 '53		
AG 1 0 '54		
JUL 2 5 '56		
AUG 1 '56		
AUG 9 '56		
AUG 4 '58		
FEB 21 '68		

MUSIC IN AMERICAN LIFE

MUSIC
IN AMERICAN LIFE
PRESENT & FUTURE

Prepared for the

NATIONAL RECREATION ASSOCIATION

by

AUGUSTUS DELAFIELD ZANZIG

With a Foreword by

DANIEL GREGORY MASON

OXFORD UNIVERSITY PRESS
LONDON   NEW YORK   TORONTO

Foreword

M R. ZANZIG has made in the following pages a thorough, timely, and greatly needed study of what may be called, in the broadest sense, the amateur musical activities of America. Such a survey was greatly needed because our American musical culture has always been too passive, too dependent on specialized professionalism, too without roots in the every-day life and feelings of our people, and has of late become so unbalanced in this way that one sometimes wonders whether it can survive at all. In 1929, for example, America purchased only 92,000 pianos — or 238,000 less than it had purchased in 1909 — while it spent 890 million dollars on the passive and vicarious delights of radio. How can such steadily diminishing individual initiative in the production of music be compensated? Obviously only through the means Mr. Zanzig studies: through amateur groups — in schools, colleges, settlements, playgrounds, art museums, summer camps, public libraries, and above all in homes. Only through the activities of such groups can music, atrophied and mummified as it tends to be by exclusive professionalism, remain a living art among us.

Fortunately Mr. Zanzig is not only a thorough and open-minded investigator but a shrewd observer and when necessary a severe but always constructive critic. His pages reveal to us as in a panorama our mixed musical life in its daily cycle, with its strange conventional deadnesses and its occasional thrilling experiments toward new life. Too many of our provincial cities are like the one he describes, 350,000 people strong, where a group of citizens subscribes $200,000 to import a grand opera company for a week's performances, yet where in the schools 70,000 children have only eight teachers of music. On the other hand, there is the detailed account of Flint, Michigan, only 160,000 in population but capable of producing an A Capella Choir considered one of the best in this country, and good enough to be sent all the way to Lausanne, Switzerland, to sing at an International Conference of Educators there. "'The members of this choir," Mr. Zanzig tells us, " are so devoted to it that by their own desire they give up 25 minutes of each day's lunch hour, to add this time in sectional rehearsals to the 55 minutes in full rehearsal which occurs immediately after the lunch hour."

A possible criticism that may be widely made on this book is that now, in the midst of financial collapse, is no time for us to be proposing the investment of money in " non-productive" enterprises like music. The author states this criticism succinctly, and meets it with candid common sense. "We are already suffering," he points out, " from too much productive investment. . . . The romance of riches, of undiscovered natural resources, booming stocks and growing cities has heretofore fired men's imaginations as the stories of Aladdin's lamp excited the dreams of our childhood. Until the crash in 1929, the daily matin of almost everyone, it seemed, from the bootblack to the banker, was said over the financial page of the newspaper. But here in the arts is a new, endlessly rich continent which exists within the minds and hearts of the people and may be realized through such adventuring as is proposed in this book. Here is pioneering and enrichment for everyone, and increasing leisure for it."

Shall we not say "Amen " to that? It seems as if we must, in so far as we are sincere lovers of music and intelligent lovers of America.

DANIEL GREGORY MASON

Contents

Illustrations

Prelude

THE musical scene confronting thoughtful Americans during the last five years has been a very bewildering one; a huge cyclorama as dark with doubt as it has been bright in promise. The most personal and least tangible of the arts, once only a way of worship and of solace and delight to simple folk, and later a crowning grace of the aristocracy, had with advancing professionalism become used as a commodity and often a spectacular display, subject to dickering and ballyhoo. Now to these incongruities are added those of our economic situation with its displacement of men by machines and its high-powered salesmanship to keep the machines running. For, thanks to the radio, music has become a primary factor in big business.

Yet music itself, the best of it, has like a crystal stream flowed through the centuries, a distillate of life, fed by the common loves, faiths, and delights of each people and each period in the history of the human spirit, as well as by the ardors of a glorious succession of great composers. There it is, as fresh and vital as ever, and for an increasing number of people one of the supreme needs of life.

During a two-year national survey conducted under the auspices of the National Recreation Association, the writer of this book followed this stream in all parts of the United States, and he presents herein descriptions and interpretations of what may be seen and heard in the many kinds of places through which it passes. These scenes are shown to be interrelated, from the most lowly to the most grand, and to be even more impressive in the possibilities that they suggest than in what they are at the moment. In other words, the purposes of this book are, first, to show what is being done in all sorts of communities, schools, homes, and other channels of life to enjoy or to provide for others' enjoyment of music; and secondly, using what *is* as a basis, to show what *might be* done in each of those channels of life. In this respect our study has resembled the economic surveys frequently undertaken by government and commercial organizations, for we have made an estimate of our resources, the wealth derived through development of them, and the possibilities of further development. The fact that we have dealt only with human resources for richness of living rather than natural ones for economic richness should not make our survey less important.

Since the field is so large and growth in actual participation in leisure time activities has become increasingly important as a need of the millions of people whose time off has grown in amount and will grow still more, we have given most though not all of our attention to actual singing and playing of music by all sorts of people for the love of it. Listening to music has not received as much consideration, perhaps, as it deserves in such a book as this one. But more is already commonly known about opportunities for listening. Let us observe somewhat more closely the most important aspects of the musical scene surrounding us when our survey was undertaken in October 1928.

Music was pouring from the heavens and flowing through all the highways and byways into almost every conceivable gathering place. It rushed or seeped through apartment halls and walls and was even carried now and then in portable sets on trains and automobiles. The radio shop's loudspeaker was aimed like a hose at the passerby while, still rarely but with promise for the future, a slow-moving radio-equipped airplane drenched him from above.

The radio like the movies had to appeal to multitudes of people in order to bring to each ambitious investor what he expected of it. " Give the people what they want " had apparently become more dominantly than ever the slogan or defense for giving them what was immediately most alluring to the largest possible number. A people disillusioned by the war and its aftermath, and emboldened by the amazing conceptions and mechanical achievements of science, had discarded old standards of almost every kind, it seemed, and had not yet formed new ones. " All *things,* as well as men, are created equal," we seemed to say. There shall be no discrimination as to the qualitative standing of what is looked at or listened to. The worst shall have equal standing with the best, and the people, more especially the people of the cities, shall be without power to choose even when they want to do so.

But in this wilderness there were prophets who interpreted democracy in art differently. " The best is for everyone," was their cry. When quiet was possible and static not too great, one might hear at home Beethoven or Brahms played by a great orchestra; and Mr. Walter Damrosch and other leaders were receiving letters of gratitude from radio listeners in isolated rural places as well as in cities. The Cleveland and Detroit Symphony Orchestras had been giving free concerts to very large audiences in the parks of those cities, and a symphony orchestra under Mr. David Mannes had attracted as many as 11,000 people at a time to its free winter concerts in the New York Metropolitan Museum of Art.

Twenty-five or fifty cents was enough to admit one to concerts by great symphony orchestras in Boston, Portland (Oregon), San Francisco, Los Angeles, the Hollywood Bowl, and the Lewisohn Stadium in New

York. The Goldman Band was setting a superb model for the hundreds of American cities in which free outdoor band concerts were given, and as many as 30,000 people at a time were showing their approval. Many art museums and some public libraries were enabled to give free chamber music concerts. And at all of these free or inexpensive concerts by orchestras, band, and string quartet, trio, or the like, the music was excellent.

Munificent gifts all these concerts were, the radio ones available to almost everyone, everywhere, and the others, unfortunately, available only to the people of a few of our larger cities. But they were, of course, worthless or nearly so to anyone who was without the sensibility and understanding to receive them. What were the prevailing uses of the radio? With what indifference and almost brutal insensitivity was the best music heard in many homes, restaurants, streets, and elsewhere, turned on if at all, amid conversation, street noises, and every other sort of distraction! Phrases like " the depreciation of music " and " music doomed to extinction " appeared in the better magazines and in books. The picture was painted too darkly, but surely something needed to be done about it.

So book after book had been added to those already written, and explanatory talks over the radio were added to many lectures given in public libraries and elsewhere, all to help the musically untrained to choose and appreciate the best music. The interest in providing school and college courses in Music Appreciation, very ably started by Mr. Thomas Whitney Surette, Mr. Daniel Gregory Mason, Mr. Edward Dickinson, and others, was being promoted more vigorously than ever, often against the great odds of musically uneducated teachers. Children's Concerts such as had been given in New York by Messrs. Frank and Walter

Damrosch for many years were being given in more and more cities and schools, notably in Detroit, Cleveland, and Kansas City. By 1928, over 1,500 different cities and towns had carried on city-wide Music Memory Contests.

But books, lectures, courses and contests are not enough. " People themselves must sing or play, however simply," it was said. " Passivity — ' spectatoritis ' — is our disease." " But will anyone take the trouble to learn to sing or play when canned music is so easily obtained, and when ' sound pictures ' and the radio will soon force thousands of professional performers out of the theatres and hotels? "

Two great endowed music schools, the Juilliard Graduate Music School and the Curtis Institute, had been added to those already established, and the number of talented young men and women who were attaining admirable heights of musicianship was greater than ever. Moreover, with great improvement in the quality of music and performance in college glee clubs, the number of students in such clubs had grown. Led by Dr. Archibald T. Davison, the Harvard Glee Club had shown that, credited with as much intelligence and love of excellence in the superb sport of singing as they have for generations eagerly exhibited in the usual college sports, students will sing the best choral music with great delight to themselves and to their audiences. And through the opportunities provided by the Intercollegiate Glee Club Association's concerts, this faith and delight had become more and more generally known and adopted by other colleges. That Association, starting with four glee clubs in 1914, had by 1928 an affiliation with 90 such clubs.

Nineteen music school settlements in various parts of the country were providing first-class, inexpensive music instruction to about 5,000 individuals, mostly children. These schools, ideal in purpose and spirit, were administering to the social as well as (or by means of) the musical needs of their pupils, and seemed surely to be making true musical amateurs, who would sing or play the best music for the love and joy of it, and for no other reason. In many of the 140 other settlements in which there were musical activities of one sort or another, inexpensive lessons were given in playing or singing.

In some ways most impressive of all, a National High School Orchestra composed of from 250 to 300 high school students from 30 to 39 states, which had been formed in each of three years, commencing in 1926, had given performances of great music that in skill and insight had passed beyond the highest expectations ever held for public school music. That orchestra, at first a forecast, soon became a token of what was being done in an increasing though small number of high schools in all parts of the country. In a survey made by the Federal Office of Education in 1927–1928, the numbers reached in this development were impressively shown; 3,935 out of 14,725 high schools reporting courses in instrumental music in which a total of 132,468 boys and girls were enlisted. Public school classes in piano-playing as well as in all the instruments of band and orchestra were growing in number though they were causing much head-shaking among earnest musicians. In 1928 the Flint (Michigan) High School A Cappella Choir appeared with Bach, Palestrina and others of the best composers before 2,500 public school music supervisors gathered in Chicago from all parts of the country, setting an amazingly high and very much needed standard of music and performance destined, we hope, to give new life and growth to choral music, which was being more and more overshadowed by the music of instruments.

We had to remember that with the exception of a

few promising endeavors, notably in Iowa, Wisconsin, and Ohio, little musical opportunity outside that of the radio was being provided for the rural schools representing about one-fourth of our total population. And we had to observe that our great conservatories of music tended strongly to conserve music and all our musical talent for a few large cities. Dr. John Erskine, whom, very fortunately, the Juilliard Musical Foundation has for its president, was striving valiantly against that tendency, but with what results (at that time) the following excerpt from an address made by him will show:

What would we think of Germany if it didn't have an orchestra or opera house in it, or an important center where concerts were given? What would you think of Italy or France if you could say that of each of them? But our states are just as large as those countries and far wealthier, and we have two opera houses. And there are many states in the Union, and groups of states, in which there is no really first-rate orchestra. A consequence is, that when we hold competitions in the Juilliard School every year for the fifty candidates for whom we usually have a place, we get about seven hundred applications from all over the United States. And when we have chosen the best, they are from every state in the Union. We have taken the best out of the state. And you couldn't blast them back! We have tried to pay them to go back. We have tried to bribe them and threaten them. They would rather starve competing with Paderewski and Kreisler than to go back. The reason is that there are not enough musicians back there for them to feel comfortable, and there is no particular place to play. The musicians are all somewhere else.

However, the development in the public schools seemed a very bright spot. Might not our high schools in every state in the Union become musical centers, expanding with the age of their students into their respective communities? Seeing or hearing the boys and girls in admirable chorus or orchestra made one very hopeful. " But where will they sing or play after they graduate? " was asked, and this question arose in many lectures and magazine articles; like an evil spirit it shook its warning finger at our great new music schools as well as the public schools, and at all our other advances in musical education. Opportunities for professional performance, except for a very few of the most talented, seemed doomed by the impending " talkies," and by what some concert managers declared was a grave decline in attendance at concerts. And for some reason or other — it was said — very few graduates were singing or playing for the love of it.

No definite information regarding this apparent frustration of the main purpose of public school music was available. The lure of easy, sensational amusements was said to be the main cause of it. Another cause was suggested by the conductor of one of our great orchestras who said that " there are no real amateurs in this country." All performance of music that was at all substantial or required any skill beyond the most elementary had evidently, in the opinion of most people, to be a means to something else — to professional or academic advancement, or at least to giving a concert — never or hardly ever just a way of full, rich living. The trend of music in homes may be estimated from the knowledge that while in 1929 the American people purchased only 92,000 pianos — 238,000 less than were purchased in the record year of 1909 — they spent $890,000,000 for radio sets.

But on the other hand millions of dollars and a great wealth of human possibilities were being spent by cities, by our 232,000 churches, by county and state fair organizations, by clubs and lodges, camps, social welfare institutions, and other privately supported agencies referred to in this Prelude, all for music as a mode of recreation or of worship. In each of several cities a civic organization of some sort had been established for the development of community musical activities of various kinds.

The number of cities observing National Music Week in any one year had grown from 780 in 1924 to 2,012 in 1928, and Spring Music Festivals were continuing to be held in Bangor, Lindsborg, Worcester, Ann Arbor, Cincinnati, Evanston, Spartansburg, and elsewhere. Westchester County (N. Y.), Springfield (Mass.), Raleigh (N. C.), Portland (Oregon), and Harrisburg (Pa.) had recently joined the list of festival cities. Christmas caroling had assumed increasingly large proportions in many cities, and Easter sunrise services and caroling were being tried in a lesser number of places.

Community singing, much less in quantity than during the exciting war days, was evidently being carried on regularly or now and then by almost every group of about 25 or more people in which social feeling was strong or was desired to be so. Outstanding among such groups were the service clubs and the innumerable state and national conventions of all kinds. We seemed destined to have " community playing " also. For the Hohner Company had reported a sale of about 18,000,000 harmonicas — the " pocket companion " — in this country in one year. The ukulele seemed almost equally common and, unfortunately, to be taking the place of its far superior cousin, the guitar.

Very promising was the increasing number of choruses, bands, and orchestras of workers in industrial and commercial establishments. No one knew to what extent the musical heritage of foreign-born Americans was wasting away. International Festivals in Detroit, Boston, Cleveland, and in a few other cities harboring colonies of these people, had proved the great value of preserving and, if possible, disseminating not only the best of their folk songs, but also, and even more importantly, the whole-heartedness and valor of their folk-singing. By no means least in this consideration were our own Negroes, Mountain folk and Indians, especially the Negroes.

Amidst all this activity could be seen traces of the influence and endeavors of various national and other organizations interested in the furtherance of music. The National Bureau for the Advancement of Music, under the direction of Mr. C. M. Tremaine, had given effective support to state and national school orchestra and band contests, music weeks, music memory contests, music in industry, and other phases of community music. The music clubs affiliated in a national federation, having a total enrollment in 1928 of about 300,000 members in all parts of the country, had also contributed to this growth, as had the very large number of women's clubs similarly federated in a national organization. The parent-teacher associations with a total enrollment of 1,275,401 were potentially, through their leadership in the homes where the character and tastes of the coming generation are being formed, the most important force for genuineness and permanency in our musical life. A choral concert of 4,000 men had recently, in New York, represented the Associated Glee Clubs of America with a membership (in 1928) of 543 such clubs enlisting altogether about 20,000 men in all parts of the country.

A report of the Federal Bureau of Education that the number of grown people who attended school during 1928 showed an increase of 30% over the number registered the year before was very significant especially since there was a growing though still small proportion of these adults engaged in choruses, orchestras, bands, and in private or class study of singing or playing in evening schools. Is it possible that as the high school in many a city and town is a vital center of musical culture for youth, so the evening school, perhaps in conjunction with the high school, may become such a center for the adults of the community?

Among professional musical organizations the Music Supervisors' National Conference with a membership of about 5,000 of the 15,000 supervisors and music teachers in the public schools of the country had shown remarkable achievements and possibilities. The state and national music teachers' associations were also capable of providing important help in the promotion of music in American life.

In the tangle of lines in this enormous, changing musical scene rich possibilities were apparent. The challenge that they presented was especially interesting to the National Recreation Association, with its long active interest in the music of the people.

This Association established a Bureau of Community Music during the war. At first its activities were restricted to community singing which was the counterpart in cities of the singing for which the (Federal) Commission on Training Camp Activities had provided in the camps. With the signing of the Armistice and the consequent loss of what had been the primary motive for this singing, the War Camp Community Service song leaders in the various cities soon found themselves obliged to devise musical activities other than such singing. Glee clubs and other choruses, and here and there an amateur community opera company, were organized by them. The Bureau of Community Music became more and more active in providing not only for its own leaders but for many other music workers throughout the country a means of sharing their ideas and experiences and developing musical activities of all kinds in their respective communities. This was done through bulletins, pamphlets and a book, and through answers to thousands of

written inquiries. The Bureau was moreover prepared
to provide for any community desiring it the personal
help of an expert community music worker who would
spend enough time in the community to help organize
musical activities there and to find and instruct local
people capable of carrying them on. With the tremendous growth of interest in, and use of music, as
shown in the musical scene described above, the task
of guidance became increasingly difficult. To help to
discover and interpret the rich possibilities in all this
growth an intensive national study of it was necessary
and was undertaken by the National Recreation
Association as a two-year project commencing in October 1928. The study was made possible through a
grant in 1927 from the Laura Spelman Rockefeller
Memorial.

An immediate motive for this study was the existence in nearly 900 cities of municipal provision for
community recreation, many of the leaders of which
felt strongly urged to make the development of amateur musical activities an integral part of their work.
Some of them, as in Sacramento, Glendale (Cal.),
and Cincinnati, had already provided for choruses,
orchestras, and bands that were worthy of the unstinted respect of the best musicians.

The following excerpt from a statement of purpose
by Mr. Joseph Lee, the President of the National
Recreation Association, throws further light on the
aims of the national music study:

The purpose of community recreation is to liberate the power
of expression of people and communities. What we are trying
to do is to help the men, women and children of America to
find their voice — to set forth in drama, art and music and in
the hundred other forms of play what it is they have all along
been trying to say which could not get itself expressed within
the confines of their daily work.

It is essential to any success in carrying out this purpose
that we should subordinate ourselves and our organization and

make our aid as soon as possible unnecessary. We should not be drawn aside by the desire to make a showing or to get things done. It is not the size of the thing that happens but its expressiveness that counts. If it does not come from the hearts of the people, it is of no use to them. It is to bring out, not to put in or put over, that we exist.

In keeping with this statement the study was much less concerned with the " size of the thing " than with "its expressiveness." That is, we determined to try to find out what in singing, playing, or listening provides the richest satisfaction to people and how the various kinds of musical activity are best started and carried on under the great variety of conditions that exist in different communities. In other words, what can people of all kinds and degrees of musical interest do in music and, more importantly, how can music be made to do its best for them, in all their various moods, and in their homes, churches, recreation centers, industries, clubs, and elsewhere as well as schools and concert halls? Numerous examples of every type of activity have been studied in 97 cities and towns representing every kind of community and all parts of the country, and including musical endeavors that had failed or were failing, as well as successful ones.

Before commencing the study and during its process, the counsel of many outstanding leaders in music and music education was sought and received. An advisory committee was formed, consisting of

Frank A. Beach	Karl W. Gehrkens
Ada Bicking	Edgar B. Gordon
Harold L. Butler	Peter C. Lutkin
Peter W. Dykema	Earl V. Moore
Will Earhart	William W. Norton
Charles H. Farnsworth	M. Claude Rosenberry
John Finley Williamson	

These authorities have through interview or correspondence, or both, given generously of their wisdom.

Chapter XI was written by Miss Rose Phelps of the Music Division of the National Federation of Settlements; and the writing of Chapter XV was in very large measure the work of Mr. Arthur P. Moor. No greater praise of the book could be given than to say that it reflects in every chapter the insight into human nature and recreation that is the freely shared possession of the workers in the National Recreation Association.

Of all the examples of musical endeavor generously described by hundreds of musical leaders and other interested persons in the many cities visited, only a small, most representative proportion can be given. If all the admirable examples were to be given, the book would be much too large, and too unwieldy in every respect. But each example has been taken carefully into account, and it is hoped that the result is a true and adequate synthesis of all the information gathered. Its value will depend on whether or not it can be of assistance to those generous providers of information, to the various national and other organizations interested in music, and to other persons who are or may become interested.

PART I

IN THE COMMUNITY

Introduction

AN American city of more than 350,000 people
that is referred to as the musical center of its section of the country, has had each year a week of grand
opera performances given by one of our great opera
companies. These performances have been gala events
looked forward to and long remembered as marking
the supreme height of the city's cultural and social
life. A group of citizens guarantee the provision of
over $200,000 to make them possible, and they have
been well attended not only by the leading and other
people of the city, but also by large numbers from
other cities and towns in that section of the country.
So far, so good. But in the public schools of that city,
containing about 70,000 children, the entire force of
music teachers has consisted of one supervisor and
her assistant for forty-two elementary schools, one
teacher in each junior high school, one teacher of instruments for all of the junior high schools, and one
teacher in the girls' high school, eight in all. Leaving
out the special teacher of instruments who necessarily
has dealt with only a very small proportion of the
children, there has been an average of one music
teacher to 10,000 children! An orchestra of a sort in
one high school has been in charge of a chemistry
teacher, and a military band in charge of an instructor
in military training.

No matter how many other concerts and other professional musical activities are carried on in that city,
the musical possibilities of its people are far from being adequately provided for.

There are other cities in which every pupil in the
public schools has opportunity to learn to sing or play

as well as his talents will permit, and where there are school choruses, orchestras, and bands rehearsing admirable music daily. But there is very little singing or playing outside of the schools, or if there is, it is confined to formal rehearsals and concerts. Only rarely is music regarded by the people as a mode of play that is free and spontaneous even when most excellent; and persons of lesser talent or training lack the opportunities that would lead them to delight in musical expression. These cities, then, also are lacking in provision for the full measure of musical enjoyment possible for their people.

In no two cities are the conditions for musical development exactly the same. But with very few exceptions, the possibilities are everywhere greater than the actuality. The average community's natural resources in music are vastly greater than the wealth derived from them. What, then, *does* constitute adequate provision for the musical possibilities of a community? And how can such provision be established and maintained?

Answers to these questions must grow out of the following considerations:

1. What are the needs and desires likely to exist among the various people of a community that find enjoyable expression or fulfillment through musical activity of one sort or another? In other words, what does music do to people that makes them enjoy singing or playing?

2. What are the different kinds and degrees of musical ability likely to exist among those people? In other words, what can people do to music?

3. What are the obstacles and the causes of failure, and how have they been overcome?

4. What are the various types of community organization through which provision has been made for musical expression and enjoyment by groups of people?

5. What methods are used in starting and maintaining community organizations for music?

6. What constitutes good leadership for the various types of musical activities, and how can it be secured?

7. How have funds been secured for carrying on musical activities?

These questions can be dealt with best through a presentation and study of actual musical endeavors in various cities and towns. To give at the outset a clear view of our field, let us commence with a survey of all the musical activities going on in a city in which there is organized endeavor to provide for every kind and degree of musical interest and ability.

Flint, Michigan, is such a city.

CHAPTER I

Industrious Music-makers in an Industrial City

IN Flint there is not only generous provision for music in the public schools, but there is also a Community Music Association whose purpose it is "to create community interest (through music) and to develop participation in music" among the people of the city. This city is an especially impressive example not only because of its musical accomplishments, but also because in no other city in the United States is there so large a proportion of people engaged in the making of machines by machines. Surely, if all the children and many hundreds of the adults of such a city have and use opportunities to sing or play admirable music in amateur choruses, orchestras, bands, and smaller groups, the baneful effects of the mechanization of labor and of music and almost all other means of recreation cannot be given as an excuse for the apparently meager interest in, and lack of provision for musical expression in some other cities.

In the Schools

With a population of 160,000, less than half that of the two hundred thousand dollar grand opera musical center previously referred to, it has a full-time teacher of vocal music in each one of its 28 elementary schools, two full-time teachers of orchestra and band instruments, and several part-time teachers of piano serving all of those schools, and seventeen full-time music teachers and leaders, assisted by three junior college music students, in its five junior high schools, two senior high schools and its junior college. Furthermore, it has a supervisor in charge of all the vocal music and piano classes in the elementary schools and junior high schools, and a supervisor in charge of all the musical activities in the senior high schools and junior college and of the orchestra and band music in all the schools. Every child throughout the first seven grades receives from one to two hours' instruction each week in singing, music appreciation, music reading and ear-training. During the past year 650 of the children in these and in the eighth and ninth grades took advantage of the offering of free weekly class lessons in playing an orchestra or a band instrument, and there was an orchestra in each of 18 elementary schools,[1] the best players of which also played in the city All-Grade School Orchestra. In addition, 850 children received weekly class lessons in piano-playing at a cost of 25c a lesson, the entire proceeds being given to the special part-time teachers of these classes as complete payment for their services. There were seven orchestras in the four junior high schools, some more advanced than the others.

Music in the eighth and ninth grades and in the senior high school and junior college is entirely elective. In the three grades of the two senior high schools 400 students were in accompanied choruses, and 160 in two *a cappella* choirs that rehearse for at least 55 minutes every day and sing the best choral music of all time. One of these choirs is regarded as the best high school chorus in the United States and has been invited to sing at the Second International Conference of Music Educators to be held in Lausanne, Switzerland, in the summer. The members of this choir are so devoted to it and its music that by their own desire they give up 25 minutes of each day's lunch hour in order to add this time in sectional rehearsals to the scheduled 55 minutes in full rehearsal which

---

[1] There must be at least ten eligible players before an orchestra is formed.

occurs immediately after the lunch hour. Moreover,
an Alumni A Cappella Choir of over a hundred graduates of this choir rehearses on a Sunday afternoon once
a month for the love of it. Many of the members of this
alumni choir are students in Michigan colleges and
make this their home-coming time in order to sing.
Other members are in business or home-making or
other work in Flint, a small number of them being
mothers or fathers. When money was being sought to
pay the costs of the high school choir's journey to sing
before the Music Supervisors' National Conference in
Chicago, the alumni choir joined that choir in giving a
benefit concert in Flint, and was effective in this and
other ways in increasing the sale of tickets. It is said
that even on recreational occasions, such as a sleigh
ride, a picnic or a banquet, arranged by one or both of
the choirs, the members have spontaneously started
singing such things as Bach's " Blessing, Glory, Wisdom and Honor," and Gibbons' " The Silver Swan,"
and other madrigals and recent choral arrangements
of folk songs that they may have learned and memorized. It is worth while to read the brief story in a
recent concert program of the Choir, which tells how
this development has come about:

The A Cappella Choir of the Flint Central High School is
a product of a cultural emphasis that is not merely on music,
but on all the fine arts: dramatics, graphic and plastic arts,
dancing, and literature, as well as music. Each has achieved and
is achieving distinction in its own right, and is making a tremendous contribution to the cultural life of the student body
and the community as well. Though of a common aim, their
varying media of expression have enlisted the active interest
and participation of from a third to a half of the more than
2,000 students. Each art has reacted upon the others as a part
upon the whole and achievement in one is recognized as a part
of the progress of all. Even the student who is not actively engaged in one or another of the arts must feel their vital influence
in the life of the school.

Nor has all this been the work of a day. . . . Sporadic

efforts to carry on choral work, for the most part as an extra-
curricular activity, prevailed previous to 1921. In that year it
was dignified by a definite place in the curriculum. The mixed
chorus was given one hour a week, the boys' and the girls' glee
clubs each two hours. By 1923 the chorus was a combination of
glee clubs, meeting three times a week. Interest, quality of
talent, and the standard of work done advanced gradually.
State contests inspired great developments. A series of standard
light operas . . . increased local interest, standing, and desire
to participate. The groups became selective, with many appli-
cants failing to qualify. A general non-selective chorus was
created from these in 1925.

By 1926 it had become clear that only the singing of the
best *a cappella* music could rival the great advances being made
in the instrumental field of public school music. In that year the
A Cappella Choir was formed. It was designed to meet five
hours a week, and to receive equal credit. Its primary objective
was to be cultural, to present a cross section of the great choral
music just as the course in English literature gives a cross section of the best in that field. Public appearances were to be a
secondary though highly desirable objective, and the repertoire
was to be chosen so as to meet this dual demand. The members
of this newly formed Choir were to be the most advanced
available.

A special chorus was created of the talented juniors and
sophomores who just missed qualifying for the Choir. A complete voice test of the entire sophomore class was made for this
purpose. This group, meeting three times one week and twice
the next, alternating with gymnasium work, was to review
fundamentals and study and present a standard opera and
oratorio during the year, thus enlarging their experience and
preparing them for the A Cappella Choir in the following year.

The results of this scheme attracted national attention and
resulted in the invitation to the Choir to appear before the
Music Supervisors' National Conference in Chicago in 1928,
subsequently before the North Central Conference in Milwaukee in 1929, and this year [1930] before the National body
again in Chicago. The stimulation arising from these honors
led to such further increase in interest that additional general
choruses, voice classes, and a large selected sophomore chorus
have been created.

In summary, then, the A Cappella Choir is the product of
a three-year graduate course involving two or more general
choruses, a selected sophomore chorus, and a junior " opera

Flint Central High School, A Capella Choir

chorus," the latter admitting also students of the lower classes who can qualify for it. At this point voice culture classes are available. And finally, the best candidates are graduated to the A Cappella Choir, which contains members from all classes, but mostly seniors.

The opera choruses have in the past seven years presented the following excellent works, a record as admirable in its field as any other in the schools or city:

Pinafore	1924
Mikado	1925
Hansel and Gretel	1925
Chimes of Normandy	1926
Hansel and Gretel	1926
Bohemian Girl	1927
Martha	1928
Pirates of Penzance	1929
Ruddigore	1930

The orchestras and bands in these high schools, together comprising 400 students, have had a similar development and are similarly graded. They also have daily rehearsals and equally high standards of choice and performance in their respective fields, and have elicited similar though somewhat less extensive tokens of devotion from present and past members. In 1930, eight members of the orchestras and 20 graduates of them were playing regularly in the city's Symphony Orchestra, and 45 graduates of the bands constituted the entire membership of a community band recently organized. Perhaps most significant of all was the enrollment of 57 students in string quartets and other chamber music groups, and 22 students in similarly small, select groups singing the simpler examples of such music as is sung by "The English Singers," whose performances have been so delightfully and strikingly revealing of a large, rich field of musical experience for such groups. Courses in appreciation and in harmony are also given.

For several years the best of the high school choruses, orchestras, and bands, and recently some of the chamber music groups also, have taken part in district and state contests, almost invariably winning high places in them. The challenge given by each of these contests has evoked arduous work willingly done, and each victory has increased the honor and prestige with which the winning musical organization is regarded by school and community. But throughout the state there is growing interest in minimizing or even eliminating contests and in having festivals instead.

Outside the Schools

Outside of the schools the Community Music Association has provided for almost all kinds and degrees of musical interest and ability.

Community Singing

There is a great deal of " community singing " at meetings of luncheon clubs and other clubs and lodges, of a Chamber of Commerce, of church and parent-teacher associations, of factory workers gathered in their respective factories during the noon recess to hear a speaker provided by the Y. M. C. A., and of other groups. On 56 of these occasions during the year 1930 the leader for the singing was secured through the Community Music Association, but there have been many other occasions when the singing was entirely in charge of members of the groups themselves. A short course in song leading given by the Director of the Association a few years ago enlisted about 40 men and women, many of whom were or became song leaders of such groups as have been mentioned.

Home Music

Effort has been made to suggest and encourage home music. A " home night " on which a program is

given by a number of families has been a feature of
Music Week, and there is a plan by which the city
will be divided into five sections in each of which there
will be provision for four concerts a year to be given
by musical amateurs who live in that neighborhood.
These concerts, it is hoped, will include performances
by family groups. The twenty such concerts that will
occur in the city in a year will be so timed that one
will occur each fortnight, except in the summer, and
interchanges of performing groups or individuals can
be made between neighborhoods now and then.

Foreign-born Groups

Foreign-born groups or individuals have taken part
in performances on " Cosmopolitan Night " in Music
Week, and a chorus and an orchestra of Polish people
have been formed by a Polish musician employed for
a time by the Community Music Association. But the
requests for assistance from foreign-born groups, and
the rich possibilities in aid aimed not only at fulfilling
immediate desires but also at discovering and developing as far as possible the folk music and especially
the characteristic ardor and sincerity of folk singing
and folk playing, are far from being adequately provided for because of a lack of appropriate leadership.

Industrial Groups

The Industrial Mutual Association of workers in
the automobile industry has a men's glee club of 50,
and a women's glee club of 60 members, both established by the Community Music Association. The
Men's Glee Club, started seven years ago, " for our
pleasure and the pleasure we can give to others," is
one of the best of such groups in the United States. It
sings admirable music, and is generous in performing
without charge at churches and elsewhere. It accepted
invitations to sing for the Music Supervisors' Na-

tional Conference in Detroit in 1926, and for the Associated Glee Clubs of America in Philadelphia in the same year, and in 1929 it won fourth place in a national contest conducted by the latter association in New York City. The funds for travel and maintenance in these ventures of the club, gathered mainly through the Industrial Mutual Association, were doubtless given because of the resulting indirect advertisement of Flint and its main industry as well as for reasons of loyalty and of devotion to music, but the feelings prompting the latter reasons must have been aroused or expanded in thousands of the people of the city by the honors given to what must seem *their* " I. M. A. Glee Club."

Church Music

Twenty-eight of the city's 39 churches have choirs, each having from 15 to 60 members, almost all of whom are unpaid. Ten of these choirs confine themselves largely or entirely to *a cappella* singing, a condition evidently due to the development of such singing in the high schools, and to the effect of several concerts of such singing given in Flint by the leading *a cappella* choruses of the United States and some of the European choruses that have toured this country. Many of the members and graduates of high school choruses sing in church choirs.

One of these *a cappella* church choirs is an especially impressive example of the effects of religious devotion coupled with the choice of excellent music. There are 40 American men and women in this choir, all of them volunteers and all of them working people. The choirmaster himself, a man of about 35 years of age, was for a number of years a worker in one of the automobile factories. He sang in the Industrial Mutual Association Glee Club there and studied singing. Failing health forced him out of the factory into more intensive study of music and a position as choir-master. His wife attends every rehearsal though they have five children and she does all the housework. When commended for the devotion that brings her to the choir despite all that she has to do, she said, " Why, that's nothing. There is Mrs. ——, she also has five children. And there is Mrs. ——, who has three children. We all have much to do."

The church building is not at all admirable inside or outside and betokens a financially poor congregation. There is a piano and a small organ, but the choir has no need for either. A rehearsal observed by the writer began promptly at 7:30, every member present, though at that time the choirmaster was engaged in talking to the visitor. Meanwhile a man, a worker in an automobile factory, arose and improvised a prayer commencing:

Our dear Heavenly Father, we thank Thee for the privilege of coming to this place tonight to sing. We thank Thee for the voices given us, and may we use them to Thy honor and Thy glory.

This is a church choir — for the glory of God, as Bach used to say — not a grand opera quartet, or concert chorus.

Then the assistant choirmaster stepped forward, a chord was played on the piano, and the choir sang. The visitor, an itinerant investigator compelled to listen to dozens of rehearsals and concerts in a month, was quite overcome by the beauty of the singing. First came a Stainer anthem, a good one, and then came Bach and the Christiansen " O Beautiful Saviour," followed by one of the mighty Russians in a mood of praise, all without accompaniment and all finely vibrant with the vitality of those deeply rooted impulses out of which music, real music, has sprung throughout the ages. It was not perfect in quality, but it was amazingly good, and the intention, the inner quality of it, was such as is never heard where music is merely entertainment, something superadded to life, not inherent in it. This choir has sung by invitation in churches in near-by towns and in Detroit, and has thereby inspired the ministers and music committees to want a similar choir in their own churches.

A choir festival given in 1930 enlisted sixteen of the choirs in cooperative, not competitive, singing of superb church music by Bach, Handel and like composers — an occasion whose significance and high enthusiasm is or should be to music what Christmas is to the church. The plan for the next festival of this kind included more choirs, and it was held on a Sunday evening so as to be regarded as a religious service, a " union service," emphasizing the idea that the purpose and privilege of a church choir is to worship through music, not to give concerts.

A Community Chorus

A choral union of 200 men and women, 25 of whom are graduates of high school choruses, sings the " Messiah " twice each year, on the Sunday preceding Christmas and on the one following it, and some other oratorio or a miscellaneous program in the spring. The central purpose of the Community Music Association is carried out even to the choice of soloists, at least for the " Messiah." The soloists are all chosen from the chorus, one for each of the twelve solos in this oratorio.

Christmas Festival

The annual " yuletide festival of song " is regarded as comprising all the Christmas celebrations in schools, churches, and in the community during the week or ten days of that blessed season. An eight-page program prepared by the Community Music

Association announces each day's celebrations. These included in one year 35 special musical services in churches and Sunday schools; a high school festival enlisting all the choruses and the dramatic classes of the school and presenting folk carols of all nations; a junior college festival at one of the churches; celebrations by the Y. W. C. A. and the International Institute; the two performances of the " Messiah " by the Choral Union accompanied by the Symphony Orchestra; free concerts by members of the Musicians' Union given in hospitals and other institutions; caroling by the I. M. A. glee clubs and church choirs in hospitals, hotels, railroad stations, at the jail, and the County Farm; caroling at the homes of invalids by eight groups in automobiles of boys and girls from the high school choruses; and caroling throughout the city by about 100 groups of children from the elementary and junior high schools in addition to about 50 groups formed in churches and Sunday schools. The city government provided a Municipal Christmas Tree program on the City Hall grounds.

Opera

In each of the years 1928 and 1929 a grand opera was given by the Choral Union, the Symphony Orchestra, one resident soloist and several soloists from New York City or Chicago. The Community Music Association furnished the plan and the preparatory leadership of chorus and orchestra, and entered into cooperation with the officials of a local theatre for the general management of the enterprise. But the stage director, wardrobe master, advance conductor and all but one of the soloists were engaged through a company whose business it is to supply such aid.

Bands

There are several amateur bands in Flint, together comprising about 225 players: A Post Office Band,

Firemen's Band, Buick Band, Industrial Mutual Association Band, an excellent Salvation Army Band of 60 brasses, a Scotch Band, and the Groves Band of high school graduates already referred to. Band concerts are given in the parks throughout the summer by a band of Union musicians known as the Chevrolet Band.

Harmonica Bands

In 1930 the Rotary Club provided money to engage a young man from Philadelphia to teach harmonica playing. In his stay of eight weeks in Flint, 1,800 children learned to play this instrument, rehearsing before and after school hours and during noon recesses at the school buildings. Several of the "harmonica bands" played at luncheon clubs and theatres.

Symphony Orchestra

The Flint Symphony Orchestra, started in 1922, now has a full, well-balanced instrumentation of 92 players of whom 30 are professionals and members of the Musicians' Union, who, however, like all the other members of the orchestra, receive no remuneration for their playing. High school students who attain "first chair" positions in the best high school orchestras are eligible to play in this orchestra. There is a rehearsal once a week and four free concerts a year of admirable, substantial music. The primary purpose of the concerts is education, "to develop appreciation through definite listening." The programs for each year are interrelated by an idea for the year, such as "Nationality in Music," "Architecture in Music," "The Seasons," and "Favorite Symphonies," and the audiences of from 1,500 to 2,500 that they attract are, judging by the conduct at one concert, exemplary in their attitude, though anyone who will write or call beforehand for a ticket may come to listen. Each concert is sponsored by some worthy social or civic organization of the city. For instance, on the program of a recent concert is the statement,

The Junior League of Flint
invites you to enjoy
The Flint Symphony Orchestra.

The sponsoring organization provides ushers for the concert and sometimes someone to speak briefly during the intermission in appreciation of the work of the players, of the music, or of the work of the Community Music Association. It also pays for the printing of the programs (about thirty-five dollars). Concerts have been sponsored by the Industrial Mutual Association, the Daughters of the American Revolution, the St. Cecilia Society, the American Legion, the Junior Chamber of Commerce, the Council of Parents and Teachers, and several other clubs and societies. At the first concert of each year all of the players are cordially introduced, one by one, to the audience. Each player rises when his name is spoken by the conductor and all receive a greeting of applause.

At least two churches or Sunday schools have orchestras, 40 players in one and 20 in the other, and there are two or three other small orchestras of amateurs that appear during Music Week.

Spring Festival

In each year since 1918 there has been a Spring Music Festival, at first enlisting only the Choral Union and soloists and a small paid orchestra for two or three concerts, but growing with the city's growth in musical resources. Six years ago national music week was for the first time observed in Flint, and the Spring Music Festival was made a part of that observance. Since then there has been less and less distinction between the Festival and the many other musical events of that week. The Festival now evidently comprises all the programs of seven days, 150 of them last year involving all the resources and places included in the Christmas Festival, and still more. The opera or a Choral Union concert is given in this week, and also the Choir Festival, daily brief programs during the noon-hour at factories, special programs at luncheon club meetings, special music assemblies in the schools, city and county contests of various kinds of school musical organizations, an early morning concert and community singing in each of three department stores and five banks, and many other observances in private studios and elsewhere.

*   *   *   *   *   *

Professional Concerts

In each of the past several years a local concert manager has brought to the city a series of five concerts which have had an average attendance of about 1,800. The inclusion among these, at various times, of the St. Olaf Choir, the Westminster Choir, and the Russian Symphonic Choir is said to have had a large influence in the development of choral singing in the community.

*   *   *   *   *   *

All this in one city, and proper direction and growth for it promised by the music director's own comment, " Plenty of musical activity but real appreciation is as yet limited to the groups and a small clientele." By groups he doubtless meant the best of the singers and players. One is tempted to consider now how all this was brought about, through what processes of choice of activity, of publicity, leadership, organization, and financing. But such matters will be presented later. With the evidence collected in Flint to help us to answer, we must now return to the first of the questions that prompted the collecting. "What are the needs and desires likely to exist among the various people of a community that find enjoyable expression or fulfillment through music of one sort or another?" In other words, what does music seem to do for people that makes them want to sing or play or listen to it?

CHAPTER II

What Music Does for People in That City and Elsewhere

MUSICAL activities may differ from each other in kind, in the quality of music performed, the degree of skill required or attained, and in many other respects; but the most important differences are in the quality of experience that the singers and players find in the activity, for this has to do with the fundamental purpose of singing or playing, and determines, at least for amateurs, whether the activity will be continued or given up. Judging from the work of many professional singers or players, and of many an amateur chorus, orchestra, or other group, one would suppose that the sole purpose of any musical endeavor is to get a certain amount of music performed in public. The leader of the group goes at the business as though this were the only motive. True, it may be assumed that people like music and enjoy taking part in a successful social enterprise. But if these motives are merely assumed, seldom felt in full, they may have little force. At their best, they may become the most powerful and rewarding of all impulses to sing or play, but if they are not cultivated, the enterprise may turn out to be only another sort of job or time-filler. It may sometimes be more glamorous and conducive to self-respect than the routine of daily living, but have little or nothing to do with the will to live more fully and richly.

Music itself is of all the arts and other modes of expressing that will the purest and most direct; and the love of it may be sufficient motive for a lifetime of singing or playing. But other fundamental needs or desires of human nature may find satisfaction in the singing or playing. Mere pleasure in music can no longer, if it ever could, keep people singing or playing persistently enough to make a chorus, orchestra, or any other musical enterprise successful or even possible. There are now too many other means of mere pleasure competing for use of our leisure time. But there never was a time when the attainment of joy in music, not mere pleasure, was better worth striving for than it is today, when enormously increased and increasing leisure time provides greater opportunity, and when the prevailing modes of labor and leisure threaten both with mediocrity. Let us therefore consider the variety of vital interests that lead to, or enhance, the various kinds of singing or playing, and how we may make the most of them.

Fooling

We shall observe a certain kind of community singing first, because it frequently rests on what seems to be the lowest degree of musical interest and ability. Here are a hundred men at a luncheon club meeting, or it might be a college class reunion, singing "Sweet Adeline" with superb breath support, complete abandon, and a grand *sostenuto, appassionato* on the word "of" that rises opulently and triumphantly above all restraints, including the tenors' vocal range, and with magnificently daring cacophonies that make even the most modernistic musician wince! Now there is a love of sociability in this, but is there a love of music? "In the name of Bach, Beethoven, and Brahms, NO!" the musician would say. There is probably a kind of love in it of what might be called the "raw stuff" of music, but it is primarily a mode of fooling.

There is no reason to scorn this singing as an evidence of depraved musical taste. It has nothing to do with musical taste. It is non-musical in the sense that the teasing and practical jokes of ordinary fooling are non-moral.

Such fooling requires numbers. Three or four people would be very unlikely ever to sing such a song or any song in such a way, unless they had a good-sized sympathetic audience, or stimulant as well as stimulus. Would even ten or twelve do so? Is this not because where there is no immediate purpose except to be sociable, the larger the group (up to a point beyond which it ceases to be a group) the more strongly does it tend toward complete unity through the elimination of all thinking and feeling that is individual, as well as action that is so? The members of the group are turned, so to speak, toward a level of feeling that is entirely free from any distinctive ideas, attitudes, or abilities possessed by any one of their number. Under the stimulus of good leadership within or outside the group, or of an inspiring occasion — or when there is a purpose other than merely to be sociable — this tendency can be directed toward the highest levels of joy, courage, and aspiration. But left to itself, it is likely to flop to a low level — the lowest common denominator of the human factors present. Is this true? If it is, what place should such flopping have in the life of an individual or a group?

These questions are raised because there are some song leaders and other people who regard the single or repeated gathering and vigorous participation of large numbers of men and women or children in *such* community singing as evidence of great success, as though it were something to be striven for, and as evidence of the social value of music, as though it were not, so far as it goes, diminishing the possible value of social feeling to the lowest point, if not beyond that. Its only excuse from the point of view of social values is that it *may* serve as a starting ground for admirable endeavors by the group as a whole.

Some people do not like to let down at all at any

time, which is unfortunate. But it is a curious fact that many intelligent people who would never be caught being foolish in any other pursuit are almost invariably so when it comes to music. For instance, in summer camps and on playgrounds there is likely to be a fine earnestness and intelligence in all games and sports. " Play the Game! " is the constant motto, and " play it as well as you can." The fellow who acts the clown in a game, even when the game is " just for fun," spoils everybody's fun, and the one who is content to paddle and flop around in the water, instead of swimming as well as he can, is also regarded as a poor sport. The coach or leader will tell him so. Yet when it comes to music, in many camps and playgrounds the same leader or a colleague will seem to say, " Now let's be feeble-minded and sing." And out of the mouths of these fine young creatures will come a lot of hollow-headed sounds about nothing for which they would have any respect in saner moments. Similar conditions exist among adults. There are various ways of fooling, some better than others. The worst of it is that the hollow-headedness may persist even when a fine song is sung. And this is where a criterion of it all is reached. *How far does the individual's or group's range of pleasure and expression in music go?* Can he *play* at music (as he plays at golf or swimming) as well as fool at it? He can flop in music; but can he rise again, enthusiastic, to the meaning of a first-class, simple song of fine feeling, and sing it accordingly? If he can, he is still in possession of his musical birthright and can safely fool now and then. But if he can't, he would better go on a musical diet, quit fooling, match himself with some fine simple songs or choral music and ask, " Are these dull and meaningless or am I deaf and dumb? " The chances are that he is neither, but only diffident about his musical powers.

" A little nonsense now and then . . ." The only

questions are, first, what kinds of nonsense give the most fun; second, how often " now and then " is; and third, whether the fooling tends too strongly to keep the singing from rising much above the lowest level. There is an ample supply of good " stunt songs " and other humorous songs available for the many occasions when such songs are suitable, especially as " icebreakers." The line between fooling and playing is very thin and easily passed over, though the difference between the two is great. There never was a better sport than singing, when the mind as well as the voice is engaged, however simply, and there is the proper spirit. There are many rounds, spirited folk songs with descants, and other first-class simple songs that easily carry any group that is not too large or mobbish victoriously over the line, and there is no end of delight after that.

It is probable that every man or boy who has ever sung at all has many times, when in a group of his fellows, really wanted to sing a good song well just for the love and joy of it, but has joined with the others in turning the singing into fooling because of the reticence and fear of being sentimental that goes with the common idea of how a man should behave. The right leadership would have freed him from this reticence.

Above all, let the leader be especially particular about what songs and attitudes and manner of singing he provides for boys and girls. That they, even adolescent boys, are capable of being led to sing and love the best music of the best feelings is amply demonstrated in Flint. Shall he, then, add his support to such stuff of the cheap vaudeville house as can be heard here and there performed by children at street sings and the like, or even to the distinctly adult kinds of luncheon club fooling that a grown-up of character and established tastes can do with impunity, but a child cannot? There is nothing more pitiful than a child who has been made too sophisticated by adult nonsense to receive youth's heritage of simple joys that are intended by nature to be an inner source of nourishment to him throughout all the rest of his days, a sub-soil where amid the droughts of adult living the roots of his life can always find fresh moisture.

*   *   *   *   *   *

Freedom

The community singing in the luncheon clubs and elsewhere reflects another common interest: it is the deep need to be *free,* to " let go." Even the singing of " Sweet Adeline," whatever else it is, is generous, outgoing, and liberating, not self-centered and acquisitive. The Choral Union's singing of the Hallelujah Chorus is more so, and the bands and orchestras achieve a rich share of freedom also. That violinist or trombonist, or whatever he or she is, may be a browbeaten or machine-beaten laborer or a fretful clerk or bank president. Seeing him at the factory or office, you would never suspect him of being an expansive chap abounding in energy and enthusiasm. But watch him there behind that instrument, or, better still, get behind it yourself and play it as well as he does, and you will come to know what he is and you are at your best. You will realize too that freedom means a great deal more than the right to vote and to do pretty much as you please. The whole personality is enlisted, released from all mental and emotional tensions, and liberated into a wholesome self-forgetfulness and full flow of fresh energy. This is especially true of singing. Of course, other things being equal, the better the music and the performance the fuller and richer the freedom.

The need for, and the possibility of achieving this freedom through music is overlooked by many a musician and pedagog whose ideas of music as an Art and himself as its interpreter are such as to make him set every possible barrier, himself the biggest of all, between the people and the music. The people may gain the satisfactions of feeling cultured, of achieving goals set for them, and of appearing in public, but the joyous sense of being free will not be theirs. To strive for excellence of performance is admirable and very desirable, but excellence of feeling is even more important.

We must decide then that adequate provision for music in a community must include opportunities for as many people as possible to find through music the freedom of spirit and reintegration of the personality that are, after all, what we mean by recreation.

*   *   *   *   *   *

The Joy of Achievement

There are several activities in Flint that show interest in responding to a challenge. The most obvious examples of this are the contests involving school groups and those involving the I. M. A. Men's Glee Club. The vigorous interest and effort aroused by these contests is, of course, due to a desire to win the prize, but it is also due to a desire to conquer difficulties, to excel in something hard to do. Very little interest would be aroused by a prospect of winning first place or any other honor in something easy to do. Of course, there must usually be sufficient interest to start with in the activity itself. But having that interest, just give any healthy individual a respectable challenge to " show his stuff," as the saying goes, and he will be almost bound to do so; that is, if you, the leader, have his good will or at least his respect.

A contest of groups is one kind of challenge. What other kinds are used? The individuals within a group are asked to compete with each other. The members of the orchestras and bands are ranked according to their respective abilities, the best player or leader in each section occupying the first chair in that section and the other being seated in order of rank behind him or beside him. In adult groups, the ranking made at the beginning of the year is usually maintained throughout the year, but in the school orchestras and bands changes in rank may occur at any time. In the orchestra and band at the National High School Orchestra Camp and in some other school organizations there is a formal test of each individual for rank once each week. A portion of the most difficult music being studied at the time must be played by each individual alone. This must give many a heartache, but if the players are not too unevenly matched and good will is maintained, it is a very stimulating challenge which is evidently welcomed.

Other means of challenge used in the schools are the marks, credits, and other honors to be won by attaining certain standards. One of these honors is to gain membership in the chorus, orchestra or band which in skill, not merely in age, is next above the one in which the individual is now a member; or to gain entrance into an all-city group or into the city's adult Symphony Orchestra. This is a very admirable kind of challenge that is, of course, most effective when the more advanced organization has as much well-earned prestige as those of Flint have. Related to this is the challenge inherent in an opportunity to perform in public, a matter that will be considered in another connection later.

The music itself may provide the challenge. Investigation of the likes of established groups of amateur singers and players in all parts of the country has shown that almost all of them, especially the players, prefer substantial, difficult music to the lighter, easier sorts. The leader of the very successful Amphion Club of Seattle says that his men " have got to be

given at least one *pièce de résistance* on each program." The leader of ninety high school boys and girls
who live in or near New York and play occasionally
during the winter and rehearse four times a week during the summer session at Teachers' College, all without credit or extrinsic reward of any kind, says, " I
could not hold them together without symphonies."
So they study the most advanced music, such as the
Brahms Fourth Symphony, the César Franck Symphony, and Bloch's " America." And most other successful school and adult groups of singers and players
have similar ambitions. Conversely, the leaders of
groups at all competent who report that their performers like or should be given only the lighter, easier
music are, with very few exceptions, in charge of comparatively anaemic or otherwise failing organizations.
There are other reasons for the preference for substantial music which will appear later.

   The last kind of challenge to be mentioned here is
the implicit demand for excellence that some persons
give. Their very presence is a challenge of the best
sort. This is often largely due to " personality," but
not that alone. The prestige of position counts, and,
best of all and most effective are expertness, unfailing
devotion to the music and the job, and respect for
the performers as well as self-respect. According to
the informal, spontaneous testimony of two of his
high school seniors, when the leader of the Flint A
Cappella Choir first presented, to what was then a
flourishing opera-performing chorus, the idea of devoting themselves to unaccompanied singing of the
best choral music in the world, there was much reluctance on the part of the students. " We wanted to go
on with the operas," one of them said, " but we were
willing to try anything that Mr. Evanson asked us to
try. We called the new music the ' dry music,' but we
stuck to it. Besides the daily rehearsals, some of us

would stop in when we could at Mr. Evanson's office instead of going to a regular ' study period,' and practice with him. We worked awfully hard, but say — when we learned one or two things so that we could really sing them, they sounded wonderful, and we were ' sold.' " Similar tales could be told about the I. M. A. Men's Glee Club and other Flint groups.

It is evident that most people like to play hard, to enter with full vigor into an activity worthy of their best energies, though the most common conception of recreational music is to the contrary. But they often need a special stimulus, like a challenge of some sort, to arouse their energies sufficiently to do so. In providing for this interest the wise leader will take every opportunity to direct it toward the attainment of better quality and a fuller grasp and enjoyment of the music itself rather than merely toward getting all the notes at the proper time, pitch, and volume. Again there is the question, "How high can you rise in feeling and understanding? " It has been said that " the Prince has always to climb through briers to kiss the Sleeping Beauty awake." The wise leader will as often as possible challenge each performer to climb with a will by persuading him, mainly through glimpses of the Beauty herself, that he is a Prince and she is worth it.

*   *   *   *   *   *

The Noble Order of Craftsmen

The best excuse for having contests and similar challenges in music, which are essentially opposed to the very spirit of real musical expression and enjoyment, is that they tend to carry the performer beyond the inertia and the often uninteresting steps of elementary study to a degree of skill at which he attains sufficient craftsmanship to be " sold," as the Flint A Cappella Choir boy expressed it. We like to do that in which we are skillful, and, given opportunity, are likely to continue in it without artificial stimulus.

The Flint Choral Union and the Symphony Orchestra are made up very largely of people whose present or future vocations or jobs have nothing to do with music or, many of them, with any other enjoyable kind of skill, if skill at all, but these people are, or are becoming, happy members of the " noble order of craftsmen " by virtue of the skill they have gained or are gaining in music. Everyone has capacity for some sort of skill, for attainment of excellence of some sort, by which he or she becomes an upstanding, self-respecting man or woman. But many people nowadays have no opportunity, or have taken none, to attain any sort of skill whatsoever. Their daily work requires none, and mechanically supplied amusements are alluring substitutes in their evening hours. But surely this is not the measure of a man, " made in the image of God," to run a machine for six or eight hours a day which requires of him little more intelligence than is possessed by a horse, and then to attend a movie or ride aimlessly about in his automobile or sit idly at home while a radio pours something or other on him which he has had no part whatever in producing, not even in choosing. He wants shorter hours of labor, more leisure. But for what? Is not his cry, though he may not himself know it, not for less labor but for a better kind of labor more nearly matching his manhood? The rich pleasure-seeker is no better off. As Dr. L. P. Jacks has said:

The only good reason for preferring leisure to labor is because the former gives opportunity for better performance, for the doing of better work. When the hours of labor call for the greater skill, then it will be in labor rather than in leisure that the greatest joy is found. (As by artists, skillful teachers, Edisons, and Fords.)

Labor is a source not alone of economic value, but of all the real values of life, the universal passport of man into whatever kingdoms of the spirit are waiting for him.

Even where skill is only elementary, there may be the attitude of craftsmanship. The best luncheon club singing heard by the writer in two years of travel was by the entire Kiwanis Club of Los Angeles, and the chief reason for its excellence, in addition to other admirable qualities of the leader, seemed to be a sense of craftsmanship that he has succeeded in establishing among the men. Before they sang — the song was The Pilgrim's Chorus from " Tannhäuser " — he said, " Now remember, boys, the five points of good singing," and he named them. Evidently the men have been responding to his suggestions with as much interest as the golfers among them would respond to pointers regarding the best ways to hold and swing a golf club. They are " playing the game " in singing.

Such an activity not only provides satisfaction of the natural desire to be doing something good to do, but it also promotes and satisfies the desire to *be* something good to be.

In Denver, there is a band of ninety boys whose average age is eleven. They are members of the " Highlander Boys," who have two other bands of equal size, one of older boys that is remarkably expert, and the other of beginners. Anyone listening to them is deeply impressed by the quality, precision, and valor of their playing. They are playing an unusually good overture containing a sturdy, exalting tune that is heroism itself. The listener forgets that these are little boys. The music heightens his energies, straightens his spine, and shapes his spirit to its heroic mold. But the conductor lowers his baton, the band stops playing, and one of a whole battery of sonorous trombones is asked a question. Then the listener is disillusioned; for from that section of majestic, deep-throated voices comes the tiny piping speech of a child, saying, " Yes, sir."

These are just little boys after all. But how great they seemed — big souls in small bodies! Most of these boys are very poor and some of them are of the kind who do not shine in athletics or in school work, though they must maintain good records of school attendance and effort or else leave the band. Here is a cure for an inferiority complex! Or protection against one. Playing skillfully in such a band must go far toward giving these boys the self-respect that is essential not only for their happiness but for their right behavior. The same may be said for the best school bands and other musical organizations of Flint and other cities and towns, and also for many a man or woman who is a musical craftsman by avocation. In many amateur choruses and instrumental groups there are rich and poor, bankers and truckmen, university professors and machine workers. In the daily work and other ordinary experiences of life, these men are on very different levels. The truckman would probably be ill at ease in the home and society of the banker, and the machine worker would probably feel very inferior in knowledge and speech to the university professor. But in the group of musical craftsmen, all are peers. Indeed, the truckman and the machine worker may be better singers or players than the banker and the professor, and thereby have the unstinted respect and fellowship of the latter. And another, still richer fellowship awaits them. For it is natural for any devoted craftsman, however humble, to feel a comradeship with all those who follow the same craft, and in lesser measure with all others whose work or play is skillful. In this sense, they will be comrades of the superb singers and players in the great professional choruses, symphony orchestras, bands, and smaller groups to whom they will listen with vastly enlarged sympathy and understanding. Then "*Allons!* after the great companions, and to belong to them!" — to Bach,

Beethoven, Brahms, and the others of the glorious company of supreme craftsmen: to belong to them, too, in the spirit of one's own simple but well-earned craftsmanship.

* * * * * *

Our Greatest " Undeveloped Natural Resources "

The interest in being something good to be, referred to in connection with craftsmanship, may throw light on another interest — a need it is — that persons concerned with planning in music should consider. It has to do with *what* is sung or played. The repertoire of the Flint A Cappella Choir for this year included deeply religious music by Palestrina, Byrd, Bach, and some of the great modern Russian composers, and also a Negro spiritual; some of it mystical and of the loftiest yet lowliest reverence and aspiration, some of it forthright and strong with the Reformation's new faith in the power of the individual human soul, and the rest of it spiritual but with the simple though intense ardors of our most common, childlike yearnings. There were also a half-dozen madrigals, the old " Summer is a-coming in," and a " Chorus of Villagers " from Borodines " Prince Igor." In these are to be found humor, grace, the most lovely romance, and the sheerest gaiety. A third group contains two swashbuckling English sailor chanties; a typical fascinating Spanish folk song; some folk songs of Germany, Ireland, and Wales, each distinctly true to its nationality and beautifully expressive of devotion to homeland or person, and a typical, profoundly vigorous Russian folk dance song.

Now in what other way, save, perhaps, drama, could the ordinary individual experience so fully so many kinds of fine feeling? There is the essence, if not the equivalent in it, for some people at least, of taking part in plays, without any of the self-consciousness and other difficulties that are likely to attend the ordinary person's efforts to " act." For anyone with any imagination at all is almost perforce let warmly into the character of the singer behind the song when he sings it. He *becomes* the medieval monk or the Negro, the Elizabethan gallant or the bully, blustering sailorman, or whoever else text, music, and his adaptable soul make of him. This interest in impersonation, in reaching out thereby into all manner of expansive experiences, is fundamental in human nature — as is shown by the universal delight, as old as humanity itself, in plays and stories, and most obviously by the rapid growth of the Little Theatre movement and of dramatics in schools, colleges, and social centers and the like.[1] " All that Shakespeare says of the king, yonder slip of a boy that reads in a corner feels to be true of himself," says Emerson. To *sing* the king's song, especially in a group (where you can so easily lose yourself — and find it in the king) may carry you even more fully into his character. For it gives him, the shadowy creature that he is, a living voice and body, your own, imbued with full kingly feeling. Or if you are in a chorus, the glorified voice and feeling of the group as a whole are felt by you as his, the king's whom you have become. And every other member of the chorus has become a king. There may be as many kings as there are people — not only one, as there would be in a play.

This is a mode of self-realization. The finer human qualities, feelings, and capacities for joy, enthusiasm, love, reverence, courage, beauty, and the like, may rarely or never be realized in the daily feeding, school mark-getting or world money-getting, automobile driving or dodging, and other self-centered or mech-

[1] See Kenneth MacGowan's " Footlights Across America," published by Harcourt Brace & Co., 1930.

The Bach Choir, Bethlehem, Pennsylvania

German Singing Society in Milwaukee

anized activities. But all of these qualities have found their way into music where the individual may find them, his own, a substantiation of the best that is in him. Talk about oil or coal or precious metals, or the like, and develop them well. We need them. But here are the community's greatest and most precious undeveloped natural resources — these inner qualities or capacities of the people. This is one reason why the boys and girls of that *a cappella* Choir choose to give up half their lunch hour every day for more singing. And this is a reason why the men and women in many another chorus or an orchestra or band — or alone in the privacy of their homes in Flint and elsewhere — will work harder to rise to the full meaning and beauty of a song or a symphony than they do to earn their livelihood, and regard it as recreation.

The members of the Bach Choir of Bethlehem, Pennsylvania, must find satisfaction of this sort in their singing to warrant the very arduous endeavor they have given to it. They are men and women of all sorts of conditions and vocations — steel workers, engineers, stenographers, salesmen, doctors, lawyers, teachers, students, and clergymen — and of various religious denominations. Like the members of every other group discussed, they receive no remuneration whatsoever. After their first performance of the supremely great Bach " B Minor Mass," a newspaper critic said of them:

The loyal tenacity with which they stuck to their self-imposed task was beyond praise. The singers in every part devoted three evenings each week to the study of the work, and in addition to this, many of the better musicians and people of leisure formed classes, meeting at various houses during the day and going over the more difficult passages together. Such whole-hearted devotion was bound to be fruitful of results and it undoubtedly accounted for something which I noticed during the performance and which greatly surprised me at the time.

It was that quite a large number in the chorus appeared to be wholly independent of their copies and were evidently singing the difficult music from memory. . . .[2]

The comment of a man who is himself a member of the chorus reveals the kind of rewards won by such devotion. He said:

The impotence of words is realized when a man tries to describe the climacteric effect of one of these great chorales coming at the end of a cantata, the three hundred voices weaving the harmony of the parts, the strings and the brasses of the great orchestra mingling with the organ's notes, all in a vast and compelling volume of sound, so sweet, so ecstatic, so exultant, that one is sure that until he hears " The harpers harping with their harps," for him it will never be surpassed.

In the process of investigating the musical activities in the largely German town of Irvington, N. J., the writer asked whether the Lutheran traditions of congregational singing with their inclusion of Bach chorales were being followed in any of the churches. " Bach? " responded the secretary of the School Board, " If you want to talk about Bach, you should see Mr.—— in the high school manual training room." That manual training teacher had recently come from Bethlehem where he and his wife had been members of the Bach Choir for six years. After giving radiant tributes to the Choir and its music, he described how earnestly he and his wife considered whether or not they could bear to leave the Choir even to take advantage of the opportunity for advancement which Irvington had offered him. It was evident that the singing had been a means of happiness and spiritual nourishment to him which he was finding it hard to do without.

*   *   *   *   *   *

[2] " The Bethlehem Bach Choir," by Raymond Walters, Houghton Mifflin Co., — The Riverside Press, Cambridge, 1923.

The Festive Spirit

What of the festivals in Flint, at Christmas time and in Music Week? These are evidences of the great influence, first, of music in enhancing the meaning of ideas and occasions and, second, of suitable ideas and occasions in arousing interest in singing or playing. The Christmas festival or festivals — for there are many festive occasions during the week — give especially telling evidences of the first influence. What a loss there would be to the very meaning of Christmas, were the singing of carols omitted! A magic similar to that of the caroling occurs in the singing of May songs, harvest songs, other seasonal and holiday songs, patriotic songs, songs for marching, canoeing, weaving, and other activities, and songs of devotion to college, school, playground, club, team, or to a person. Music enhances the meaning of whatever is fitly associated with it. It is this power of music and of the other arts that John Dewey regards as their primary function in education. " They reveal," he says, " a depth and range of meaning in experiences which otherwise might be mediocre and trivial." They bring ideas from the coolness of the intellect to the warmth of the heart.

The annual Music Week, with its choir festival and many other concerts, is an example of an occasion especially made to evoke vital singing and playing by large numbers of people. It has at its best been invaluable in this, becoming more and more festive in spirit. We all like the expansive " holiday " mood of a festival, when people all about us are agog and aglow over it. The fine light operas in the Flint high schools and the grand operas in the community outside have also aroused this spirit among many people. The pity is that there are not more occasions as vital as Christmas in our American life. The writer heard a

group of Croatian men and women in Detroit — two of the latter with children on their knees — sing harvest songs with fine enthusiasm throughout most of an autumn Sunday afternoon, though the only possible harvest to be garnered within miles of them would have been automobiles. What suitable occasions and other interests are there in homes, settlements, playgrounds, and in the community, that are worthy of being associated with music? And what music is most suitable for each, and worthy? These are important questions.

*   *   *   *   *   *

Social Feeling at Its Best

A perpetual source of occasions for singing or playing is the social feeling existent wherever two or more people are gathered together for a common interest. This feeling is, of course, most strong in established groups like families, clubs, schools, church and other societies, and fellow-workers in an industry. The I. M. A. Glee Clubs and Band; the Post Office, Firemen's, Buick and Salvation Army Bands; the Alumni A Cappella Choir; and the Polish Chorus and Orchestra are all examples in Flint of groups which, though organized especially for music, are the outcome of some social feeling, some community of interests, outside the singing or playing. Here again the relation of music to the other interest — in this case the social feeling — is one of mutual enhancement. This points to two very important opportunities for the music leader. First, that he interest all sorts of religious, educational, social, and industrial groups, already established, in introducing singing or playing into their group life, rather than confine his endeavors to establishing new, purely musical groups; and second, the opportunity to introduce greater social feeling into the musical groups. The banquets and picnics of the

Flint High School musical groups are examples of very effective use of the second opportunity. Social feeling itself, no matter what has aroused it, very naturally finds expression in singing or playing; and the very name, "community singing," betokens the opposite purpose: to arouse social feeling through singing. After all, a community is not *any* group of persons or *any* neighborhood, town, or city. Only where there is a real interest held in common is there a community. Singing or playing has the power of providing in itself alone the real interest as well as an expression of the social feeling arising from the interest. Given a real interest in the singing or playing, no other interests are necessary. But the latter tend to make the purely musical interest still more vital and persistent. In this respect, " the business " of a musical organization — maintaining attendance, providing funds, obtaining new members, etc. — if made interesting to the members themselves, may be a blessing rather than a curse.

It is probable that for certain classes of adults there never have been so many clubs and other groupings, including conventions, as there are now. But there are very few such opportunities for social life and social standing for the working people. The labor unions used to provide such opportunities, but, with some admirable exceptions, they have become almost entirely protective organizations with very little social life. Consider what it must mean to a group of workers deindividualized in a forest of machines to take part in, or to be otherwise identified with, a good chorus, band, or orchestra of their own that has admirable standing in the city or town. " This is our band! This is the kind of band we men at the Smith, Jones, or whatever it is, factory can have! If you like, we'll give you an extra free concert or two in the park next summer (avoiding competition with the paid professional band). We're going to play in the civic parade on Armistice Day and at the community tree on Christmas Eve." The same could be said about a musical group of foreign-born Americans, like the Polish groups in Flint, with even greater emphasis on the importance of opportunities for them to take a happy, commonly appreciated part in the life of the community instead of isolating themselves as foreign-born groups often do. Reference has already been made, in connection with craftsmanship, to the effects of membership in a good community musical organization.

With the large increase in the number of boys and girls who are playing in orchestras, bands, and smaller groups — impressively exemplified in Flint — new emphasis can be given to the values of the team work necessary in such groups. Here are all the citizenly virtues of physical games and sports, but usually without the competitive factor: the ideal society in which each member, be he concert master or the lowliest player of a horn or bass viol, must play his part as well as he can in such a way as to bring out the best that is in every other part.

*   *   *   *   *   *   .

Civic Spirit

Another manifestation of social feeling evoked by music is the very general interest and pride of the people of Flint in the fact that their city has a symphony orchestra, a choral union, and many other rich musical developments. The newspapers have again and again reflected this interest and pride. "Generally speaking," says the Chamber of Commerce booklet, "the cultural development of a rapidly growing city does not parallel its commercial and industrial development. In this respect, Flint is a unique exception." The booklet then describes the purposes and results of the Community Music Association's work, and refers to other musical endeavors also. " Flint is proud, indeed, of her industries," said the manager of the Chamber of Commerce, " but she is also very proud of her musical culture." But the interest and " community spirit " evoked by this musical culture has nowhere been better demonstrated than in the National School Band Contest of 1930 which was held in Flint.

First of all, Flint was chosen as the place for this contest because the community music director received ample financial and other support to give the invitation. There were 45 bands containing in all over 3,000 high school boys and girls who were provided the free hospitality of private homes by hundreds of Flint families. Most of the meals, however, were provided in school cafeterias through funds gathered in Flint for the support of the contest. Through a delay of the special trains, a number of bands arrived at an unexpected time. There were no busses or other vehicles to take the large numbers of players to their respective destinations in Flint. Upon learning of this, the transportation chairman at once issued a call for help through the local broadcasting station. Within thirty minutes over 200 private automobiles had arrived at the headquarters to distribute the players to private homes. The marching contest in the Stadium, after which all the bands played together under the direction of Sousa and others, was attended by about 17,000 people, who paid for admission. A number of wealthy citizens had been prepared to shoulder a deficit for so expensive an enterprise as the three-day national contest, but when all financial affairs had been completed, it was found that there was a net profit of about three thousand dollars, of which one thousand was, by vote of the committee, given for five partial scholarships at the National High School Orchestra and Band Camp.

Bethlehem, Pennsylvania, is also an industrial center. But, as the biographer of the Bach Choir has said, " there shines over Bethlehem with its grimy murky mills, whence so many of its singers come, the lustrous and resplendent star of an idealism not to be quenched without a grievous loss to all America." [3] The pastor of the Moravian Church there said, " All of us throughout the churches and throughout the community feel the effect of this Bach work, not only in the festivals as artistic successes, but in the reflex we are getting in our homes as the result of the choir's singing." [3]

There is no end of additional evidence of such community effects in the many other cities and towns to be referred to in this book. Let us grant the truth of this belief. It is said that the true character of an individual may be known by what he does when he is free from compulsion. So is it with a community also. It is also said that the individual's character is largely the result of the influence, often unconsciously borne, of his home life. But the influences of the community or neighborhood in which he lives are indissolubly intertwined with those home influences. After all, a home is not merely a house and lot, detached in our minds from the city of which it is a part. For instance, Flint's symphony orchestra not only provides a fine sort of expression and recreation for a group of its own citizens, the players; it not only provides the nearest thing to such expression and recreation to the hundreds of its other citizens and children who attend its concerts, including those who have contributed to its support in some way or other.[4] It goes farther, affect-

[3] " The Bethlehem Bach Choir," by Raymond Walters, Houghton Mifflin Co., — The Riverside Press, Cambridge, 1923.

[4] For the sense of possession or responsibility and the feeling of loyalty or neighborliness with which the people listen to their city's orchestra are likely to lead them more fully into the music and the playing of it than the mere paying for an imported orchestra can do. It is their orchestra (of

ing even those who never listen to it. For, given an honored place as it is in Flint — through newspaper, community chest, and other support — it points to the kind of life that Flint is standing for. Like a beautiful park, a fine public library or art center, or one or more stately public buildings, it becomes a token and champion of the dignity and inner life of the people.

*   *   *   *   *   *

Why Give Public Performances?

Next to pleasure in sociability and in music itself, the most common motive for singing or playing is the giving of public performances. This motive is due to any or all of four human characteristics: first, the natural impulse to express or show to others that which excites our enthusiasm; second, the natural tendency or acquired habit of regarding anything that requires conscious effort, like rehearsals, as only a means to an end; third, the natural desire for social approval and standing; and fourth, the need for money to pay expenses. If there is not enough money, or one or more of the other interests already discussed — or the interest in music itself — are not very active and well fulfilled, a chorus, band, or orchestra must, of course, give public performances or else fail. And it is likely for a large group to have to give such performances anyway, because of the strength of the natural impulses favoring such an outcome. But here danger arises. For amidst the vast amount of free music available nowadays through mechanical means, and the high standards of performance cultivated by those means, many an amateur musical group does not at-

course, it must be worthy of possession), playing not merely *to* them as any orchestra might, but especially *for* them and, in imagination, *with* them; that is, as their representative, as though the playing were, in a sense, *their* playing. And this incidentally cultivates more and better listeners who wish to hear imported concerts also.

tract sufficiently large audiences to satisfy any one of the four human characteristics noted. Then, since the hearts of its members were set on achieving successful public performance, they feel that it has entirely failed. The delight in the singing or playing itself and in other features of the life of the group are likely to be overlooked; and one more chorus, orchestra or band fails, and thus makes the formation of another one more difficult than it would be if the first one had never existed.

What can be done about it? This question will be adequately discussed in succeeding chapters. Let us now only turn to Flint again for a moment for an answer or two. To begin with, Flint's community music organizations have the advantages of excellence in choice and performance of their concert music, and both the financial and moral support of the community (see Chapter IV). The concerts of these organizations are free. Furthermore, the symphony orchestra concerts are interrelated in a progressive series, making them appeal more strongly to the widespread interest in education — culture — as well as to the interest in concerts as simply means of delight. And each concert is sponsored by an active club or other association in the city. The Choral Union concerts are given as parts of the Christmas and Music Week festivals, and thereby profit from, as well as add to, the heightened interest in music during those periods. The church, club, industrial, and Polish choruses, orchestras, or bands have ready-made occasions and audiences in the established groups they represent. And the home groups and the small chamber music groups in the schools and elsewhere are usually entirely content without concerts. They are the ideal music-makers, the true amateurs, self-sufficient in every respect.

*   *   *   *   *   *

The Music's the Thing!

" True Amateurs " — this puts us in the key of the last interest to be considered here: the love of music for itself. This is the most important of all, because without it no musical activity will endure; and it is the most delightful of all. The good word, amateur, has fallen into bad company — it has come to be associated only with mediocre or careless performers and their performances — and needs to be redeemed before we can proceed with it. Its true and original meaning is, of course, a " lover " or a pursuit carried on only for the love of it. So it has to do not with a degree of skill — the lowest degree, the next being " semi-professional," and then professional — but with an attitude. It refers, or should refer, to the kind of enthusiasm that Emerson meant when he spoke of the arts themselves as " the daughters of enthusiasm." At any rate, there should be some word to describe this blessed sort of devotion which, like all true love, seeks or strives eagerly for excellence in its object; and some other word for the lukewarm attitude that makes many a chorus, orchestra, band, and music class about as interesting and vital to a red-blooded full-lived man, woman, or child as lukewarm soup would be to an epicure.

We have seen how singing or playing may be aimed at any one or more of a number of interests: at sociability and social standing; freedom of spirit; the joy of victorious response to a challenge; the delight and self-respect of craftsmanship; the realization of all kinds of fine feeling; enhancement of the meaning of ideas, holidays, events, and ordinary experiences; at culture or education in the general sense; at the individual's love for, and pride in his city or town; and at public performance. These interests may overlap, of course. Indeed, they may all be operative in the rehearsals and performance of a single program, and providing that the various interests are felt in proper proportion, the more of them there are the richer will the experience be. But this richness should not be allowed to obscure the end in view. This end, for the true amateur, is experience of the music itself, as music. He needs no other motive. He may even resent the introduction of one.

His best delight is that purest and keenest one of the completely other-regarding, self-forgetful pursuit of a single activity, like the play of a child or the exploratory walk of a nature lover in a chosen haunt. And has he not a rich world to explore? To begin with, there is the sheer pleasure in musical sounds merely as sensory effects: in the tone-quality of voice, violin, French horn — even in a single tone — and in the infinite variety of blended qualities in a good chorus and, especially, in a symphony orchestra: " chords as rich as the eye of a peacock's tail, harmonic passages like sunset clouds, the flow of melodies which, apart from their meaning, are as limpid as a brook among the moorlands."

And there is rhythm, the counterpart of full, eager life itself in its ebb and flow and infinite variety of progressions, the more subtle or sustained of them so often overlooked in the obvious, mechanical " umpahs " of its most common measures. Finally, there are the designs or forms, — from simple song to an hour's symphony, which, even when most fraught with the impulsive, unpredictable urges of life, present a completeness and unity that the mind and whole organism crave but almost never achieve in ordinary life. What more could be needed as a means of delight and recreation?

For many an amateur the ideal musical group is a string quartet or any other well-balanced companionship of a few instruments or voices or both in chamber music. No business of any kind is needed in this; no organization, not even a leader — in the ordinary sense — and, usually, no contests or public acclaim or any other means of artificial respiration. The music's the thing!

*   *   *   *   *   *

Each interest of life is or may be intertwined with so many other interests that the enthusiastic supporter of any one is likely to see in it possibilities involving all the best of the others. Musical performance, requiring — as it often does — a prompt, perfect coordination or series of coordinations of a number of mental and physical activities, is said to be a "mind-trainer." [5] Adequate consideration of this must be left to unprejudiced psychologists. Enough is it for our purpose to remember that the quality and effect of any musical performance does depend on intelligence, and on freedom, control and economy of action, not entirely on feeling or inspiration, and that successful musical leadership depends on the leader's ability to bring those capacities of mind and body into play. But the leader would better let any mind training (if there is such a thing) be gained as a by-product of undivided endeavor to understand and produce the *music*. Music offers physical training, too, it is said. But when mental or physical training is regarded as an aim, not a mere by-product, the activity tends sharply away from the best values of music.

Another claim made for music is that it has curative power for the mentally and physically ill. Everything that has already been said in this chapter has bearing on this claim. Like sunshine, fresh air, and the rhythm

---

[5] The comment on music education that is most often quoted by school music teachers of a certain turn of mind is that made by former President Eliot of Harvard University, that "Music is the best mind-trainer on the list."

of sea, wind-blown wheat field, day and night, enjoyable activity and rest, good music is good for all who
are responsive to it, be they ill or well.

We must now seek a complete answer, fuller than
Chapter I has given us, to the question, "What kinds
and degrees of musical interest and ability are there
through which such values as are dealt with in this
chapter may be realized?" In other words, "What
can people do to music?"

CHAPTER III

What People Do to Music and Where and When

WE can still say with William Byrd that

"Since singing is so good a thing
I wish all men would learne to singe."

And we can, in this more complex life of ours give several other and even better reasons than seven of the eight given by that greatest of all English composers "to perswade euery one to learne to singe." How amazed he would be to see an audience of from 2,000 to 3,000 people listening to one of his madrigals which were made for singing by the family and guests, very likely while they were still seated at the dinner table, after it had been cleared. The merry "Amaryllis" madrigal that was included in the very book — "Psalms, Sonets, and Songs of Sadnes and Pietie" — for which Byrd wrote his eight reasons as a preface nearly 350 years ago, is even now delighting thousands of people, thanks to the "English Singers," as freshly as a bright May morning in merrie England. But in Elizabethan days, when it was written, every lady and gentleman, it is said, was expected to be able to carry a part herself or himself safely through the intricate measures (without bar-lines) of such a song. Now if sweet Adeline had only had *such* music written to her — . But how many of us could sing to her then? That's the question.

"Apt for voyces or viols " was printed on many a madrigal. If you couldn't sing it, you might play it. Or, in 1931, if you are lacking in both of these, you might whistle it, or dance to it, or act out its meaning, and you could doubtless listen to it. Sing, play, whistle, dance, act, or listen — these are the six things people can do to music, six ways of getting at music.[1] What kinds and degrees of ability in each of these are likely to exist among the people of a community, and in what proportion is each kind and degree likely to exist among them? Furthermore, through what channels of group life, and at what times, can they be provided for? A brief but full view of adult amateur singing and playing possible in a community will help further to accustom us to seeing the community as a whole.

Here is a composite picture. In no single community known to the writer is every feature of it present, but each feature can be found in some community.

ADULT AMATEUR SINGING AND PLAYING IN A COMMUNITY

Where?

(By visiting groups or by member groups)

Concert Halls
Over the Radio
Homes
Churches
Evening Schools
Music Schools
Settlements

Community Centers
Clubs and Lodges
Other Associations
Industrial Establishments
Commercial Establishments
Public Libraries
Art Museums

"Little Theatres"
Talkie Theatres
Parks
Streets (carols; "sings")
Hospitals and Asylums
Prisons

In What Kinds of Groups or Activities?

Formal Public Concerts
Other Concerts
Civic Chorus and A Cappella Choir
Civic Orchestra
Junior Civic Orchestra
Civic Band

Other Choruses (Clubs, Industries, etc.)
Other Orchestras (Clubs, Industries, etc.)
Other Bands (Clubs, Industries, etc.)
Family Groups

[1] Reading it silently is too rare a way to be counted here, and so is composing.

Other Small Groups
Church Choirs
Congregational Singing
Glee Clubs
Junior Glee Clubs
High School or College
  Alumni Glee Clubs
Opera
Caroling
Community Singing
Fretted Instrument Groups
Playing Piano or Harp Alone

Playing Fretted Instrument
  Alone
" Acting Out " Songs
Singing Dances
Negro Choruses
Foreign Language Choruses
Foreign Folk Instrumental
  Groups
Minstrel Shows
Class or Private Instruction
Competition (Rare)
Festivals
Choir Festivals
International Festivals

When or on What Occasions?

Rehearsal Times
Grace Before Meals or Starting the Day
Fireside Time
When Friends Gather in a Home
Before or During a Church Service (Playing or Singing)
Holiday, Seasonal, or Civic Observances
Music Week
Evening School Assemblies
At Band Concerts (Choral or Community Singing)
At Organ Recitals (Choral Singing)
Church " Socials "
Meetings of Clubs and Other Associations
Before or After a Lecture or Forum
Before, After, In, or Between the Acts of a Play (Singing or
  Playing)
During a Pageant
Luncheons and Banquets
Picnics and Camp Fire Times
When Hiking, Marching in the Gym, Canoeing, Rowing, or
  Loom Weaving
Water Carnivals
County, State, and National Conventions, Fairs, Institutes
Whenever Else There Is Desire for Beauty, Recreation, or
  Sociability

It should be said at the outset that there is no intention to value quantity for its own sake, an intention that might account for the large number of musical activities and of places and occasions for them that are given in this outline. On the contrary, each opportunity for singing or playing is prized only as a possible entrance to such values as are described in Chapter II; and the large number and variety mentioned are due to the very important consideration that individuals differ greatly in the interests through which they find those values.

Development of the Concert Motive

It is equally if not more important to realize that it is not intended that all these musical activities should include or result in the giving of public concerts. Consider the public! It is well known that the field of successful professional concert-giving has become more and more exclusively confined to the most talented and best trained. The less talented are unlikely to attract an audience. It should be equally well known that the successful giving of concerts by amateurs is also in a limited field, allowing, perhaps, for a somewhat larger number of concerts if, unlike those of the professionals, they are given with a low or no charge for admission, but even then subject to the law of supply and demand and to the higher standards of performance. Consequently, in so far as continuance of their singing or playing is concerned, if the amateurs (so-called) are dependent on concert-giving as a primary motive, they are in the same fix as the professionals. Then, like the latter, they need audiences to satisfy their chief purpose, and failing in this they are likely to disband, to give up singing or playing as a group if not to give it up as individuals also. Yet concert-giving serves very well as an incentive, especially to large groups, and may be hard to do without. What can be done about it?

Fortunately, *public* performances are not the only kind. There could and should be a great many more people taking part in choral and instrumental groups *where music is most needed*. For adults this means in churches, Little Theatres, evening schools, community centers, forums, clubs, industrial or commercial establishments, and the other places shown in the outline. These established channels of life in the community can offer the incentive of concert-giving without the frequently fatal professionalism of the usual sort of public performances. The performances in church, for instance, are or should be a vicarious offering or means of worship for the " audience," not concerts; and those given in evening school assemblies, club meetings, and on similar occasions arising in the other places and activities mentioned should make for a happy submergence of the performers in the social feeling and privacy of the occasion. The performers are among friends. They are, in a sense, members of the audience, not set apart from them; or, even in the Little Theatre or the public forum, they are part of a community enterprise involving a variety of interests. They are not the whole show. And, to get back to our main concern regarding performances, the people are there. You don't have to go out and get them, and stake the very existence of your musical organization on your success in getting them. The art museum or center and the public library are also established channels of life that may serve our purpose especially well. *Every city, town or group of towns of 10,000 or more people should have a good city chorus, symphony orchestra, and municipal band, as it should have at least one beautiful park, a public library, an art center, an admirable city or town hall or county building* — as tokens of the spirit and dignity of its people. The present remarkable developments in public school music are likely before very long to make this possible in all parts of the country. These community organizations should be as capable as the talents and funds of the city can make them, and they should give well planned and prepared series of concerts. They may consist partly or entirely of amateurs. *But good performance of the best music should not be confined to concert halls and broadcasting stations.*

It is true that even the members of the lesser amateur groups like to give a special public performance now and then, a regular concert for the community. This desire is for most amateur groups best fulfilled through participation in a fine-spirited music festival that brings many people to hear it and sends them and the performers happy away.

*   *   *   *   *   *

Now let us examine more closely the possible kinds of, and occasions for, musical activity by children as well as adults in the various channels of life in the community. We shall start with singing.

Singing

Almost everyone can sing. Those who cannot, can learn to do so, say experienced music teachers, unless their vocal organs are badly defective. (We are thinking now only of the achievement of carrying a tune.) If a person cannot carry a tune, it is barely possible that he is tone-deaf, but very unlikely. He may be like General Grant, who knew only two tunes: one was " Yankee Doodle " and the other was every other tune. The general's recognition of " Yankee Doodle " was probably due to memory of its marked rhythm rather than of its melody. But even he would doubtless grow up to be much more capable in music, less general in his responses to it, were he now a boy in one of our best public schools and surrounded, as he could not help being, by singing radios and phonographs as well as singing children, and a teacher of singing.

One may have a good " ear," but lack the natural trick of physiological coordination that turns breath into whatever tone is desired, at the mere thought of the tone. He may thus be in the plight of one of the most enthusiastic singers the writer has ever known. In a regimental or even a company sing it was, in spite of everything, thrilling to stand beside him and feel his ardor. But he would never sing in a smaller group, when he could hear himself clearly, because — he said — " I sing beautiful, but it comes out so rotten ! "

The most common causes of difficulty, however, are insufficient experience in trying to sing or in letting oneself sing, and diffidence, such as troubles a man who never learned to swim when he was a boy and is ashamed to be seen trying to do so now. But no matter what the difficulty, one is very likely to learn to sing if he really wants to do so, and if he will go patiently and unashamed through the first steps. It is perhaps the greatest value of community singing that it frequently arouses the " will to sing " in people who would otherwise go through life musically dumb. The most frequent praise spoken of a successful community singing leader is, " He can make *anybody* sing ! "

It is true that some people cannot or do not sing as beautifully as other people can or do. Perhaps Byrd was right when, for one of his eight reasons, he said that

It (singing) is the only way to know where Nature hath bestowed the benefit of a good voyce; which guift is too rare, as there is not one among a thousand, that hath it: and in many, that excellent guift is lost, because they want Art to expresse Nature.

But it is a very remarkable thing that any person of ordinary intelligence who can make "human sounds in tune"[2] can in a well-led chorus attain a degree of artistic expression and joy that is given only to the most expert instrumentalists and solo singers to attain. Who are the people in the Bethlehem Bach Choir (and many another chorus) who sing music that is as noble and beautiful as anything in the world? We have already seen that they are men and women in the ordinary vocations and jobs of life, not musicians. One of them said, "There are few of us I'd walk across the street to hear sing a solo. But when we sing together, I'd travel a thousand miles to listen." Their conductor inadvertently explains a very important element in his own power as a leader while pointing to the usually unrealized possibilities of the ordinary untrained singer when he says, "You can be a true artist without an exceptional voice, or without a good ear for music, or without sight-reading ability." (Think of it!) "Training and devotion to great choral music will almost certainly enable you to attain the heights of artistic power."[3]

For a few years in the beginning of its career this Choir was accompanied by an orchestra of the best available players in Bethlehem, but these players, despite their probably greater musical talent than the singers', and very much longer and more arduous training, could not perform well enough to be worthy of the chorus. Only the most expert players (Philadelphia Symphony men have for the past several years played the accompaniments) can match a chorus of steel workers, salesmen, stenographers, doctors, and lawyers, if it has been as superbly led in the best music as this one has been.

There is no other art or craft, or any other means of

[2] The sole requirement for entrance into the superb Harvard Glee Club.
[3] "The Bethlehem Bach Choir," by Raymond Walters, p. XVII.

musical expression, in which the unskilled individual can come so near to being an artist himself as he can through choral singing; that is, if he wants to do so. And that usually means if there is a leader who can inspire him through the music to want to do so — perhaps to *surprise* him into *being* so. The music that makes this magic possible may be very simple. Even the kindergarten child's singing of a simple folk song may be as lovely and perfect a thing as has ever been heard or seen.

Let us now consider a plan of provision for singing in a community that will take care of all ages and all kinds and degrees of interest. It is another composite picture: of the best effective endeavors to be found scattered throughout the country.

Singing in a Community

I By children to the age of 18

  A. In schools

    1. Class singing for all children throughout the elementary grades and in the first two years of the junior high school, with occasional general assembly singing, and provision for small, informal groups such as might gather in a home or neighborhood center

    2. Elective or extra-curricular glee clubs or choruses in the upper elementary and junior high school grades, meeting once or twice a week

    3. Singing in the third year of the junior high school and in all the years of the senior high school graded as follows to provide for all degrees of interest and ability:

      a. General assembly singing for all pupils (community singing), and now and then such singing of a song or two in a classroom as a means of recreation between subjects or at other times when better morale or refreshment of mind or body is needed. A special program in observance of a holiday or the like will occasionally involve special singing by the entire school prepared for by brief rehearsals during assembly periods.

b. One or more classes in voice culture in the senior high school

c. An elective glee club for boys and one for girls, or a mixed chorus, for each of these years,[4] meeting two or three times a week in school hours. Such a group is sometimes regarded in at least the earlier years as a class in appreciation meeting daily, the total weekly time being divided between well-planned choral singing and a course in listening.

d. Elective glee clubs or a mixed chorus representing the entire school, meeting from two to five times a week in school hours if possible

e. An *a cappella* choir consisting of the most capable singers in the school. A pre-requisite to it is faithful service in a class or school chorus or glee club. It meets every day and its main aim is to explore some of the best choral music of every period and of every musically great nation. It also, of course, provides opportunities for all other students and for adults in the community to enjoy listening to fine singing of that music.

f. As many informal small groups as can be arranged for, by the students themselves as well as by teachers: duos, trios, quartets, 5- or 6-part madrigal " teams," and the like, such as can have many a happy time singing in the students' homes. There are many extra-curricular occasions, in addition to assemblies, in a school, when good singing by such groups is welcome. There are also plenty of equally suitable occasions outside the schools when such a group is even more welcome. The number of occasions used has, of course, to be limited by the students' need of time for school work and " home work."

g. Provision for granting one or more worthy high school singers the prized privilege of singing in the state, district or National High School Chorus, thus relating the music of the schools to what is or should be the best in school music and giving

---

[4] In many schools the school glee clubs or mixed chorus referred to in d. and e. take the place of such class groups in the last two years.

the pupils an additional stimulus to grow as much and as well as they can in their singing [5]

    h. A good light opera now and then.

B. Out of the schools

  1. *Where* can boys and girls enjoy singing outside of the schools?

    a. Homes

    b. Churches and Sunday schools

    c. Playgrounds and parks

    d. Community centers and settlements

    e. Meeting-places of Boy Scouts, Girl Scouts, and other organizations of boys and girls

    f. Summer vacation schools

    g. Summer camps

    h. Music schools

    i. Hospitals for the crippled or convalescent, asylums, reformatories, and the like (Singing by the inmates of these institutions)

    j. Informal concerts for people at meetings of parent-teacher associations, service clubs, the Chamber of Commerce and other organizations having influence in the home, school, church or community life of the city or neighborhood; for people at civic meetings of every kind, and for people in hospitals and other welfare institutions (but sparing the children from the more depressing sights in such places)

    k. Formal concerts in the art museum or public library, in a public auditorium — probably in connection with a festival — and over the radio

    l. Streets (Christmas caroling and street " sings ")

  2. *When,* or on *what occasions,* can boys and girls enjoy singing outside of the schools?

    a. Holiday, seasonal, and civic observances, such as Columbus Day, Armistice Day, Hallowe'en, harvest time and Thanksgiving Day, Christmas, the New Year, Patriots' Days, Easter, Spring, Arbor Day, and May Day; and visits to the city by dis-

---

[5] Such provision is frequently made by a service club, music club or other civic-spirited organization or individual in the community, or through the proceeds of a school concert.

tinguished persons (e.g. a governor or the President or Lindbergh); also birthdays and wedding anniversaries in homes, anniversaries of clubs and camps, and birthdays of well-known authors and song composers interesting to boys and girls, as Stevenson, Stephen Foster, Field, Blake, Dickens, Barrie, Lewis Carroll, Schubert, Sir Arthur Sullivan, and Mozart.[6] Such observances might well include dramatics, tableaux, pantomimes, or readings, as well as singing.

b. Before, after, in, or between the acts of a play, the songs chosen being in keeping with its content or related to it through its author or nationality

c. Before or during a church service (A church choir or a school, playground, or community center chorus)

d. Festivals (Christmas, Easter, Music Week, or other time)

e. Pageants and playgrounds festivals

f. Water carnivals

g. Picnics and " stunt nights "

h. During rhythmic activities such as hiking, marching in the gymnasium or elsewhere, canoeing, rowing, and loom weaving

i. Praise or stimulation of club or team (club songs and game songs)

j. Greeting to, or praise or bantering of a person — a camp councillor, play leader, visitor, or a speaker

k. Grace before meals

l. In connection with band concerts

m. In connection with organ recitals, including municipal ones as in Portland, Maine; Denver, and other cities

n. Camp fire or fireside time, and good-night time

o. Any other time, especially when there is or may be social feeling

3. *In what kinds* of singing groups and activities can boys and girls enjoy participating outside of the schools?

a. Community singing

b. Church choirs

c. Sunday school or congregational singing

[6] The older children have many additional possibilities.

d. Family groups
e. Other informal groups such as meet in homes, clubs, playgrounds, camps, community centers or settlements
f. Organized quartets or the like, glee clubs, or mixed choruses, connected with the schools, churches, clubs, playgrounds, community centers or settlements
g. An all-city or -town or an all-neighborhood choir of boys alone, girls alone, or one of boys and girls together, formed of the most faithful and capable singers in the city, town, or neighborhood
h. Adult choruses in which high school boys and girls can find sufficient vitality and welcome
i. Foreign language groups (children of the foreign born)
j. Christmas and Easter caroling
k. Singing games, and " stunt songs "
l. Acting songs (ballads and other songs whose texts can be " acted out ")
m. Folk dances in which there is singing
n. Good operettas
o. Contests

II By young people over 18, and by adults

The brief outline of adult amateur singing and playing given earlier in this chapter, and just followed by a fuller description of children's singing, makes such a description of grown-ups' singing unnecessary.

Playing

What proportion of the people can learn to play an instrument? Could one or more orchestras or bands, or both, of children or adults or both, be formed to advantage in the community?

" Everyone can learn to play an instrument," say the enthusiastic music teachers. And considering the fact that special interest, time taken from other studies and leisure pursuits, and encouragement at home are usually required by boys and girls who undertake the playing of such an instrument, one is deeply impressed by the achievements of some of those teachers.

The four hundred boys and girls who play well enough to be members of orchestras and bands in the high schools of Flint are 10 per cent of the total number of students in those schools. In the high school of the much smaller city of Ottawa, Kansas, the proportion of orchestra and band players is 35 per cent, as it is in the consolidated rural schools of Medina County, Ohio. Proportions between 5 and 10 per cent are becoming quite common in American communities, though many a city or town is still below any such stage of development. In 1927–28 a survey made by the Federal Office of Education, gathering statistics regarding all public high school studies, showed that of 14,725 such schools responding to the inquiry 3,935 reported courses involving the playing of musical instruments, in which there were enrolled 77,492 boys and 55,256 girls, a total of 132,648 students. The federal report does not reveal the number of pupils in those 3,935 schools, so it is impossible to compute with certainty the proportion of pupils learning to play instruments. The situation is further complicated by the probability that some schools having band, orchestra, and piano studies reported the total enrollment in each study regardless of whether any pupils were enrolled in more than one of them. But if we cut the reported number to 100,000 and take 600 as the average number for the total enrollment in each of the 3,935 high schools (the average for the 14,725 high schools involved in the survey is only 197), the proportion of pupils playing orchestra or band instruments is still over 4 per cent.

No one knows how many adults can play in an orchestra or band, because no provision half so far-reaching as is commonly made for school children has ever been made for adults. But how many adults would there be in your community who could play in an orchestra or band or other instrumental group if

4 per cent of them could do so? We will be conservative and not speak of the 35 per cent or even the 10 per cent who, in the cities mentioned, represent a cross section of the adolescent community which after all will eventually become the adult community. And we are not counting the large number whose study of instrumental music is carried on without any connection with the schools.

Old Obstacles Overcome

Individuals may not respond to opportunities to play or to learn to do so, because of

1. Lack of interest
2. Lack of sufficient money to pay for worthy instruction
3. Lack of time
4. The idea that adults cannot learn to play, or even to recover skill gained in youth
5. Difficulty in playing in tune or with adequate technique
6. Lack of sufficient money to pay for the instrument

But the first two of these six obstacles are more likely than ever before to be overcome for adults as well as children by new methods of teaching now used in many public schools. Whereas in former times it was usually regarded as necessary to acquire technique through a long period of practicing before any performance of real music could be permitted, nowadays the course of training starts with such music which, even though it must be very simple, may be very interesting and gives vitality to the technical training. Technique, then, under good teachers, is in large measure a natural outgrowth or by-product of the endeavors to make *music*. Furthermore, new, good ways of class teaching of from 2 to about 10 individuals at a time have been developed. Under good teachers these are likely to make the process still more interesting because of the social feeling aroused and the opportunities given from the very beginning to play in parts as well as in unison. And they make the cost of instruction much lower than it might otherwise be. The third obstacle — lack of time — may also be overcome by modern methods. The prevailing methods of the past were devised by teachers of would-be virtuosos, whose ideas of music education were, consciously or unconsciously, all concerned with preparation for professional performance. Those ideas usually called for from 2 to 5 hours practice daily. But while the present standards for professional performance are even higher than those of the past, we now take into account also the needs and possibilities of the amateur who, if given appropriate music and direction, may even in a half-hour's daily practice, soon arrive at ability to play *musically* though with only simple skill.

The fourth obstacle, the idea that " an old dog can't learn new tricks," has been shown to be a superstition, as anyone may see who will read the results of one of Professor E. L. Thorndike's scientific investigations, as presented in his book entitled " Adult Learning." Another means of finding proof is to observe what is being accomplished in classes for adult beginners in evening schools in Long Beach, California; Los Angeles, and elsewhere, and in many music schools.

The fifth obstacle may be overcome by a wise choice of the kind of instrument to be used. Any trouble in playing a piano in tune is no concern of the player at all, only the tuner; and the wood-winds and the brasses — except the trombone — are considerably more likely to emit correct pitches, even when their guiding ear is a poor one, than are the strings. However, the sixth obstacle added to the fifth, plus the non-portability of the piano, may lead the individual to a harmonica, flageolet, ukulele, ocarina, a marimba or xylophone, a bugle or a fife.

The Harmonica, Ukulele, and Other Low Grade Instruments

Now it must be admitted that many musicians and other music-lovers scorn or are indifferent to these instruments, especially the most popular of them — the harmonica and the ukulele. What can be said in defence of these instruments?

(1) Many thousands of boys and girls, and many adults, like to play them.[7] While this fact should by no means be the only criterion for determining the value of any activity, it must be given large consideration. The music chosen to be performed through the simple harmonica or flageolet, or through singing with one's own simple accompaniment on a ukulele, may be as lovely as exists in the world. The player's own delight in it is of much more importance than anyone else's judgment of the sensuous effects of the performance.

(2) They are inexpensive. A good harmonica or a flageolet can be purchased for 50 cents, and a satisfactory ukulele for $2.50 — sometimes for less.

(3) They are easy to learn to play, and yet even that simple effort evidently often carries with it a fuller, keener attention to the music than most persons — even graduates of conventional courses in music appreciation — ever give. To make sounds oneself as well as one can through conscious craftsmanship, however simple, seems often to give them a richness of meaning and delight out of all proportion to their effect on the mere listener.[8] And so, many a person — especially among adolescent boys — who cannot carry a tune or who can carry it accurately but not satisfyingly, and who has never had enough interest to learn to sing well or to play one of the standard instruments, may, through a simple instrument, be led happily into admirable kinds of music to which he had always been indifferent.

[7] In a survey recently made by the National Bureau for the Advancement of Music over 2,000 harmonica bands were found, involving about 100,000 players.

[8] This is, of course, true of any instrumental music or singing that is striven for in this way, and the better the chosen instrument the fuller the delight. The 47-year-old Chicago business man who had only recently commenced learning to play a bass fiddle knew of this keen pleasure when he said, " After drawing the bow across that instrument and making my own noise myself for the first time in my life, I was ' elected ' ! "

(4) They are easily carried about, especially the harmonica, ready for use at any time or place.

(5) The harmonica and flageolet, and with lesser effectiveness the ukulele, may be used for ensemble playing in which there may be not only parts, producing harmony or counterpoint, but also different kinds of instruments — the piano, the fretted instruments, and the various light-toned percussion ones being well suited to a group of harmonica or flageolet players — producing an interesting variety of tone-color.

(6) Having enjoyed playing a harmonica, ukulele, or other so-called " low type " of instrument, the individual may have become sufficiently music-minded and instrument-minded to take up the study of a high type of instrument. There is no definite evidence to show that this hope is fulfilled among the tens of thousands of such players in sufficient measure to be maintained. Personal inquiry in many cities and towns has revealed some interesting instances of transfer from a harmonica to a band or orchestra instrument, but it would be unsafe to say that there are more such instances than there are of boys and girls, apparently no better off financially or musically than any harmonica player, going directly into study of an inexpensive or school-loaned orchestra or band instrument, or the piano, in free or inexpensive class lessons. However, there are probably players of these better instruments who would not be players at all but for having started with a simpler instrument. And if there are not as many examples of transfer from the lower to the higher type of instrument as one would expect, it is at least partly because harmonica and ukulele playing have in most places lacked the kind of leadership and moral support that could have brought about the looked-for outcomes. The scorn or indifference of musicians and music educators has left the lower field of musical interest entirely to leaders who, though often admirable in their attitude, see the hillside beyond only as an avoided course of tedious practice, not as an adventurous climb to fields richer than they have ever seen.

The Piano

The virtue most often claimed for the humbler instruments is that they can be mastered so easily. You can learn in an hour to play a scale and a simple tune or two on a harmonica (if you luckily catch the knack of tongueing in that time), or to play accompaniments involving as many as 4 or 5 different chords on a ukulele. On the simple flageolet you can learn to play the scale and one or two easy tunes in half an hour. But these achievements can be even more easily and quickly gained on another instrument. It is the piano. On this instrument it is not necessary to learn to play a scale, the only time needed being the time that it takes to put down one key after another. And the learning of simple tunes and such chords as are learned on the ukulele is correspondingly easy and rapid. Nothing in the process is one-quarter as difficult as just tuning a ukulele and keeping it in tune. What of the resulting sounds, as compared with those produced through a ukulele? Let the reader answer.

No one could deny that as a single means of getting at music of all kinds, including choral and symphonic music — at all the music in the world — the piano is unsurpassed. Why, then, are the harmonica and the ukulele regarded as so much easier and so much more attractive and effective as introductory instruments for hundreds of thousands of people? Let us leave aside the comparative costs of the instruments — an increasingly important factor when the piano is no longer regarded as an article of furniture indispensable to a " genteel " home, and the money that might be scraped together for it is given for radios or automobiles. The non-portability of the piano has already been mentioned.

There are three other reasons for the greater popularity of those inferior instruments. First, being able to play simple tunes or chords is all that harmonica-playing or ukulele-playing means, but what piano-playing means — as exemplified by expert pianists now heard daily over the radio — makes such simple results seem too meager for any attention at all. The comparison is like that between a proud schooner perfectly equipped for world travel, easy to start in a good wind but hard to direct through all that is expected of it, and a row-boat on a pond. Secondly, like a row-boat, the harmonica or the ukulele offers more direct and intimate handling. Compare the small instrument held in the mouth and played upon by the breath with the imposing array of keys, woodwork, and machinery presented by a piano. And finally, we are only commencing to free ourselves and our children from the kind of piano teaching that starts with notes, counting, position of the body, hands, and fingers, and fabricated preparatory " pieces " or exercises, as though anything more were needed to start the good ship than a good wind and " a star to steer her by " — that is, a desire to play a simple, real tune or accompaniment, and an idea of how it should sound. All power, then, to the teachers who start with the wind and stars, and never lose them completely for us, so that even the piano becomes a direct, intimate way of " singing " ! And an extra blessing on those who can do this well in class-teaching!

The Piano in Chamber Music

In a commonly used book on the teaching of instrumental music it is said that many young people prefer practicing on some orchestra or band instrument to practicing on the piano because " the piano is solitary. The band or orchestra is a social instrument." This unfortunately neglects the use of the piano in chamber music which, after all, is the ideal form of musical expression for amateurs. It is true that most boys and girls like better to play in large groups than in small ones, but that is partly due to the lack of appropriate leadership and suitable, interesting music for all but the most advanced of such groups. Few teachers and other leaders strive to cultivate in themselves or their pupils the true amateur spirit on which chamber-music playing so largely depends.

Orchestras and bands are indeed "social instruments," but they are compelled to have only certain times and places for their meetings. What of all the other times and places when and where one would like to play with others, especially when one is an adult? So far from being solitary, the piano is by nature the most social of instruments. For it is capable of joining agreeably with any other instrument or instruments, voice or voices. The small groups in which it is a welcome and often indispensable companion are ideal social units with need for very little or none of the often large amount of non-musical business required to run an orchestra, band, or chorus. In homes, schools, community centers, and wherever else people gather to sing or play — except in large orchestras and bands and in the still too rare quartets and other self-sufficient groups of strings, woodwinds, or brasses — the pianist has a social part to play. There are many occasions when his part does not demand the intensive team-work needed in the often extremely complicated interplay of instruments in an orchestra or band, but there are duos, trios, quartets and other examples of musical sport that require the most alert and devoted team-work possible of the pianist, even in simple music. The trouble is that the self-sufficiency of the piano has led many teachers to neglect the possibilities it offers for the great fun there is in such playing. However, the best teachers and music schools, including the music school settlements, now not only provide but require ensemble playing of all their instrumental pupils.

Fretted Instrument Orchestras and Chamber Music

The ukulele belongs to a large and ancient family of fretted instruments with relatives in every country. Many Americans who have travelled in Europe know that native orchestras of such instruments in Spain,

Italy, Russia, Czecho-Slovakia, Roumania and elsewhere, play admirable music with good effect, and that frequently their instruments are of many sizes from deep bass to high soprano. It is less well known that there are similar orchestras and smaller groups in this country. An investigation made recently by the National Bureau for the Advancement of Music revealed 237 such groups in 36 of the States.[9] Some of these include among their instruments — besides 1st and 2d mandolins and guitars — mandolas, mandocellos, mando-basses, and similarly varied sizes of the banjo; and a few include piano, flute, xylophone and drums. But many are of chamber music size.

There are undoubtedly thousands of foreign-born Americans or their children in each of whose homes there lies a guitar, zither, balalaika, or other native fretted instrument, abandoned at least partly because its peculiar way of speaking, like its owner's native language, has not been generally understood in this country. The banjo and the ukulele are the most used of these instruments in this country, the banjo often professionally, in dance orchestras, and their most common manner of speaking is with a jazz accent. The mandolin and guitar, very popular in the past, as every middle-aged college alumnus knows, are much less common now, and even the ukulele is evidently losing its hold, which for a few years was phenomenally large. But given the kinds of admirable music that are really suited to fretted instruments — such music as flourishes in the European countries mentioned — players of these instruments may achieve very respectable and enjoyable results. The old guitar — not the modern steel one — when played in the style of its beautiful but difficult ancestor, the lute,[10]

---

[9] See " Fretted Instrument Orchestras," published by that Bureau, 45 West 45th Street, New York City.

[10] The lute, in various forms, is still played, though rarely.

not merely strummed, has a rich store of lovely music written especially for it or for the lute; and it is an ideal instrument, far and away better than a ukulele, for accompaniments to singing or to violin or flute playing. But played so, it is more difficult than the other fretted instruments, each of which, including the guitar, anyone not entirely lacking in " ear " can learn to play. Such an instrument has, of course, to be put in tune, but once it is in tune the player cannot avoid playing it so. However, he must be able to tune it and to know when it has become out of tune again.

Rhythm Bands

The instruments that are easiest of all to play are those used in what are called rhythm bands or rhythm orchestras (sometimes called toy symphonies). These are the small drum, tambourine, triangle, and cymbals — which are diminutive examples of instruments used in symphony orchestras — and any other pleasing means of playing rhythm without melody, such as light sticks struck against each other, castanets, sleigh-bells, oatmeal and ice cream boxes, and horseshoes. Children, of course, delight in playing these, and can, under proper guidance, do so with such discrimination in choice of when to play what and how softly or loudly to do so, in keeping with excellent music being played on a piano or phonograph, that it is quite delightful even to listen to. That " children hear more (in music) by *doing* than by trying to listen " is unquestionably true of these rhythm orchestras, if the music can be clearly heard throughout, and the playing consists of discriminating responses to it. After sufficient progress has been made, simple melody instruments such as water tumblers, xylophones, flageolets, and psalteries can be introduced into this kind of orchestra.

Adults also enjoy playing rhythm orchestras. Many a group of adults has enjoyed taking part in the

Haydn "Kinder-symphonie" and other specially written works for such orchestras, and now that the latter have become so popular and much music and the instruments for them are easily available, more adults are enjoying them, just for fun, in homes, community centers, and elsewhere.

Playing on simple instruments that have been made by the players themselves is becoming somewhat more common, especially in schools, chiefly as a result of the work of Mrs. Satis N. Coleman, represented in her book "Creative Music in the Home." [11]

* * * * * *

We may now proceed to a plan for instrumental music in a community, which, like the plan for singing, is a composite of various kinds of activities to be found in American communities.

Playing in a Community

I By children to the age of 18

  A. In schools [12]

    1. Rhythm bands in the kindergarten and first three or four grades. These progress from consisting entirely of percussion instruments to including simple melody instruments such as small xylophones, tuned water tumblers, flageolets, and psalteries.

    2. Classes in piano playing in at least Grades IV, V, and VI, and very desirably in the junior and senior high

---

[11] Published by Lewis E. Myers and Company, Valparaiso, Indiana.

[12] The provision for instrumental music in schools varies greatly from nothing but an extra-curricular orchestra or band meeting once a week to a system of instruction that is as extensive in subjects and larger in its number of pupils than that offered by any music school. In the light of what is being done in Flint, Cleveland, Milwaukee, Rochester, N. Y., Lincoln, Nebraska, and an increasing number of other cities, a provision such as that outlined here, with the possible exception of the attention given to the fretted instruments and the harmonica, seems likely to become a standard course as common as a standard course in vocal instruction in the schools has been for many years.

schools also, so that pupils in these secondary schools who were unable or unmoved to take advantage of the classes in the elementary schools may still have an opportunity

3. Classes in violin and cello in Grades V and VI and the junior high school with provision also, if possible, for senior high school beginners

4. Classes in the wind and percussion instruments of band and orchestra in the junior high school and for senior high school pupils who wish instruction but were unable to take advantage of the opportunity in the junior high school, or who are needed to provide parts missing in the school's orchestra or band. Eager and ready elementary school pupils might also be given opportunity.

5. Ensemble playing in all the instrumental classes, and opportunities for suitable combinations of instruments not taught in the same class, especially for duos, trios, and larger groups involving the piano

6. Occasionally, instrumental obligatos in class singing periods

7. Continuation of ensemble playing through junior and senior high schools — of strings with and without piano, of wind instruments, and of strings or woodwinds with voices

8. Orchestras, properly graded, for each of the elementary and secondary schools, the senior high school symphony orchestra, rehearsing daily, being the best possible in the school

9. An all-city elementary school orchestra or junior high school orchestra, or a combination of both, consisting of a well-balanced group of the best, most faithful players, formed once or twice a year for a few rehearsals and a performance on some special occasion

10. Bands, properly graded, in junior and senior high schools

11. Provision for granting one or more worthy high school players the prized privilege of playing in the state, district, or National High School Orchestra or Band, thus relating the music of the schools to what is or should be the best in high

school music and giving the pupils an additional stimulus to grow as much and well as they can in their playing [13]

12. Provision for pupils not enlisted in any of the orchestra, band, or piano classes, who may be actually or potentially interested in playing some other instrument (Consider especially the unenlisted " monotones," how they sing not, neither do they play.)

    a. Harmonica classes for Grades V and VI and the junior high school

    b. Fretted instrument classes for junior and senior high school pupils.[14] The ukulele and the banjo will probably be most in demand, and should be included, but effort should be made through demonstrations and explanation to direct such interest toward the guitar and mandolin — especially the guitar — and, if financially practicable, in their larger, more expensive brethren, the mandola, mando-cello, and mando-bass. First-class suitable music should be played in ensemble as early in the process as possible, and the guitar players especially should soon also know the charm of playing lovely accompaniments to singing — no mere strumming.

B. In or out of the schools

    1. Where there is more than one high school, an all-city high school orchestra of the city's best high school players gathered for a few rehearsals once or twice a year for a special occasion, or for weekly rehearsals throughout the school year. This might be directed by the conductor or concertmaster of the adult city symphony orchestra, or an outstanding visiting conductor, or by the school supervisor of instrumental music.

    2. An all-city high school band. All the comments on an all-city orchestra (above) can be applied to such a band.

[13] Such provision is frequently made by a service club, music club, or other civic-spirited organization or individual, or through the proceeds of a school concert.

[14] These classes are made self-supporting by a charge of 25 or 50 cents per lesson.

3. Summer or vacation music school in charge of school authorities or of the recreation department, using school buildings, and providing as far as possible for all kinds of musical activities in which boys and girls are or may be interested

C. Out of schools

1. *Where* can boys and girls enjoy playing outside of schools? In all the places and institutions mentioned on page 75 for singing, and at parades and football and other outdoor games (The bands)

   N.B. Through one or more music schools, music school settlements (partly supported, if necessary, by the community chest or other community agency) or private teachers, there should be good music instruction at a price making it available for boys and girls who wish to progress individually farther in music than is possible in the public schools

2. *When* or *on what occasions* can boys and girls enjoy playing outside of schools?

   a. No occasion need be added to those suggested on pages 75–76 for singing, except

   b. Celebrations of Memorial Day, Fourth of July, and Labor Day (The bands)

   c. Dances, including folk-dancing, modern social dancing,[15] and interpretative or aesthetic dancing

3. *In what kinds* of playing groups and activities outside the school can boys and girls enjoy participating?

---

[15] Orchestras of boys and girls should not be asked or even allowed to accept engagements to play for modern social dances. The dancers should be willing to pay a professional orchestra. Union musicians now need every possible opportunity to help provide a living for themselves and their families, and no encouragement need be given to modern dancing by making it costless. Furthermore, the amateur orchestra should be spared the giving of time that could be better spent otherwise, and the danger of falling into the devil-may-care attitude of jazz which is likely to affect not only all their playing but also their regard for the orchestra and for the best music. A person whose tastes have been formed through full experience of the best music can play and enjoy jazz and yet be able to rise again to the height of the best, but the person of unformed taste and unformed technique is not likely to have this ability.

  a. Accompanying community singing, choruses, glee clubs, or church choirs

  b. Chamber music or an orchestra at church services

  c. Family groups [16]

  d. Other informal groups [16] such as meet in homes, clubs, playgrounds, camps, community centers, or settlements

  e. Organized chamber music groups, orchestras or bands,[16] connected with the schools, churches, Sunday schools, clubs, playgrounds, community centers, or settlements

  f. A city, town, or neighborhood boys' band or girls' band, or one including both boys and girls, organized on the playgrounds, in the community centers, or as a special civic enterprise sponsored by the mayor, the Chamber of Commerce, the service clubs, or a civic music association

  g. Adult instrumental groups in which high school boys and girls can find worthy companionship and music and sufficient vitality of interest and welcome

  h. Groups of foreign born or their children using conventional band or orchestra instruments or their folk instruments

  i. Groups playing independently or accompanying in Christmas or Easter caroling

  j. Playing in good operettas

  k. Playing for dancing of some kind — folk, modern social, or interpretative

  l. Contests

II By young people over 18, and by adults

  A. No places, occasions, or kinds of playing need be added to those given in the outline on pages 75–77 and in the plan for children.

---

[16] Players of fretted instruments, of the harmonica, flageolet, or other so-called low types of instruments, or of rhythm band instruments, are not excluded from this classification. If such groups are not formed and instructed in the schools, they should be provided for by the recreation department or some other outside agency; and even if the schools do provide for them, they should have opportunity to play outside also.

Whistling

After giving earnest attention to really important musical activities; that is, to singing and playing; to turn that attention to whistling seems something of a joke. But a means of realizing, say, the second theme of the Brahms Fourth Symphony's slow movement, or any other tune you like, actually producing its lovely succession of sounds yourself without strain or embarrassment of any kind, is not to be belittled so. In a crowded elevator descending from the 20th floor of a very prosaic business building, a tune that was started by someone on the elevator suddenly stopped. Almost without will, the writer continued it and found himself whistling a tune from the Tschaikowsky Violin Concerto. When we alighted, the first whistler said, eagerly, " Do you know that piece? " And though strangers — he a salesman — we were off on a pleasant little chat about it. (It might, of course, have been Bach or Brahms just as readily.) There we were on that elevator with who knows what thoughts, if any, in the eight or ten heads of us, and up soared a warm, romantic tune as frankly and freshly as a lily in a swamp. (And not from a machine.) What would have happened if the man had sung the tune so frankly, or opened a fiddle case and played it? But would he?

Here is an instrument with a common range of from an octave and a half to two octaves or more that is so easy and natural to play that even the restrained, habitually self-conscious person will play it on the street, in elevators, anywhere, without embarrassment. Why not attain good, firm tone in it, and good rhythm, phrasing and nuance? It is capable of these things, though not for public concerts,[17] thank heaven, but only for getting closely into the tunes you like, into

[17] " Concert " whistlers evidently all go in for warbling and virtuosity, not music.

those you know and those you are trying to recall. Who that goes to concerts has not sometimes whistled all the way home?

The only attempts found by the writer to use whistling in any way outside the almost universal spontaneous use of it were in whistling contests on playgrounds, in which accuracy, quality, quantity of tone, and deportment were the determining factors. Since a chief value of it is its spontaneity, promoters of it will have to be very careful in dealing with it.[18]

Dancing

Dancing, like music, has many kinds of activity using its name, from the most gross, trivial or stupid to the supremely noble, refined, and intelligent. There is the jazz strut, which for a time placed all of us, from the patrons of lowdown dance halls to the girls and young women of our high schools and colleges, in so far as *dancing* was concerned, on the same level: a kind of dancing that even the " dumbest " or most careless person could do. This, like jazz music, is becoming much more refined. There is the ballet which at its best may be a very delightful spectacle, that requires severe training and great skill. It is highly conventionalized and often has very much less to do with the music than with spectacular leaps, spins, and postures for their own pretty or amazing sakes. Someone has said that it aims "to imitate the bird instead of to transfigure the man." Acrobatic dancing is its cousin, quite forsaking music altogether for contortions and other stunts. There is also folk-dancing, ever fresh and wholesome; other old-fashioned dancing, as in the minuet, gavotte, polka, etc.; admirable modern

[18] There is a very delightful " Defense of Amateur Whistling " in the last chapter of Robert H. Schauffler's book entitled " The Musical Amateur " (Houghton Mifflin Co., The Riverside Press, Cambridge), a book which will be completely read by anyone who starts to read it.

social dancing other than the jazz strutting; and other kinds.

But the kind of dancing referred to in the beginning of this chapter has for its sole purpose the realization of the music. It is to come as near as possible to using the body itself as a musical instrument. Music, real music, is not merely sounds sung, played or whistled, something out there in the chorus or orchestra or on our lips or fingers. It is in us, and has its basis in what might be called inner postures, involving muscles, nervous system and other physiological factors. In the full, most satisfying responses to music, even when we are listening quietly, the whole organism is enlisted. To awaken or intensify such responsiveness is the purpose of a kind of dancing (the best sort of interpretative dancing) that is principally a way of making those inner postures outer, of clearing away the physical tenseness or dullness that obstructs them. It is a way of really getting into the music. Thus, the purpose of such a kind of dancing, developed in what is called Eurythmics by Jacques Dalcroze (who is first of all a music teacher), is said to be " to enable pupils to say not ' I know,' but ' I have experienced,' and so create in them the desire to express themselves; for a deep impression of an emotion inspires a longing to communicate it to others." [19]

Now this is an art that we are commencing to discuss, and one to which many a person, including Isadora Duncan, has given genius and a lifetime. Because of the writer's limitations, as well as lack of space for it, we can only hint at its meaning and describe only the simplest applications of its main musical purpose. These can be carried out in schools, homes, playgrounds, community centers, and wherever else there is a piano or a phonograph; and they may well start

[19] " The Importance of Being Rhythmic " by Jo Pennington, published by Putnam's.

with what children and grown-ups already do naturally — namely, walking and running.

For instance, a number of varied simple compositions are played or sung (they may be familiar songs), some for each of these two kinds of motion, and the children or adults walk or run according to what the *music* " says." Skipping and swaying, or swinging the arms and body, may also be included through music suggesting them. With two, three, or four kinds of motion to choose from, a great deal of fine, interesting music can be allowed to say which will be done. And within each kind of motion there are many different speeds, moods, and other characteristics to be responded to. For instance, in walking there is the light, toy-like step of Schumann's " Soldiers' March," the heroic weightiness of his " Northern Song," the swinging gait of his " Happy Farmer," and the very slow pace and benign meditation of the simple " March of the Priests " from Gluck's " Alceste," all of these and others to feel and realize through the walking.[20] (How many people can walk well, anyway, especially slowly and poisefully?) Schumann's " Volksliedchen," in the same " Album for the Young " that contains the others of his pieces mentioned, starts with a slow, quite sad walk and suddenly breaks into a very merry skipping; and then goes back to the walking again. Part of the group may respond to the first section of this piece and to its recurrence, and the rest may respond to the second section, thus experiencing the design of the music very definitely. There may be a change of direction at the end of each phrase, and an appropriate change in some other aspect of the response whenever the next phrase is different from the preceding one, a recurrent phrase, however, being responded to in the same man-

---

[20] See list of suitable phonograph records for such activity on pages 467–468.

ner whenever it occurs. The first theme of Beethoven's Seventh Symphony, which symphony was called by Wagner " The apotheosis of the dance," goes skipping to a climax which asks for a lifting of the head and arms to a posture of joy, and also for a slackening of speed.

So progress is made in responsiveness to the general character of the music, its tempo and volume, and changes in them, to the rises and falls of its melodies, and to its design — including its phrasing — as well as to the rhythm of its measures. Dances like folk dances or freer ones, are improvised or carefully designed by the group in response to the structure and character of the music. The motions become more and more fully in keeping with the music; the emotions and undulating flow of rhythm, harmony, and melody being strongly and wholesomely felt through them. There they go — " monotones," (even the deaf)[21] as well as others — living in the music more freely and fully than many a trained singer or player who has learned only to give lip service or finger service to his god. Of course, it must be free and generous, not awkward or cramped; and be a true, self-forgetful response to the music, not a mere spectacle.

What next? Growth in this free, creative sort of dancing requires the guidance of a person who is something of an artist therein as well as being a teacher. And this requirement should be met. But if it cannot be met, there is still no end of fun and musical experience to be gained through folk-dancing, especially through the English country and Morris dances and some of the old American country dances. Such dancing also is likely to increase the individual's respon-

---

[21] The writer met a young woman this summer who is both deaf and mute, but she could dance beautifully, in perfect keeping with the music. It seemed that her muscles and inner sensibilities could hear the music when she danced to it.

siveness to any kind of music, though not nearly so richly as the Dalcroze Eurythmics or some similar mode of dancing could. And could he later engage in a gavotte, a minuet, a saraband, and the like, a rich field — one of the richest — of beautiful music by great masters would thereby be much more fully revealed to him than they could be otherwise.

The occasions for folk-dancing and for the more musical kind that we have discussed are almost as varied as those for singing and dancing. Almost all school and community physical education and recreation leaders have used folk-dancing in their work, and some have approached the other kind, but usually with indifference to the really musical possibilities of the activity. Since these musical possibilities, conceived and used rightly, have to do with better coordination and freedom of muscles, as well as with fuller responsiveness to the music, physical education leaders should be eager to have them used as well as possible. And music leaders should regard both these kinds of dancing, especially the free, creative kind, as possible phases of the musical culture and recreation of the community.

Acting

Here we invade another art, and again we must be exceedingly modest and brief. There are three kinds of acting that may be considered for our purpose. The first, closely related to dancing, is rhythmic pantomime with instrumental music suggesting fairies or butterflies, slow-moving giants or galloping horses, kings and queens in a stately minuet, mothers rocking their babies to sleep or adventurers on a magic boat rocking on a magic stream, and everything else that can be characterized in music for children or grownups. A whole folk tale or similarly short story may be acted out so with music, the latter being chosen or

composed to fit the successive moods and activities
of the tale. Music is used so in pageants also. Mendelssohn's music for the "Midsummer Night's
Dream" is an example of wise use of music for a long
play.

The second and third kinds of acting to music are
very similar. One is the pantomiming of a song while
someone or a group behind the scenes, or the audience
itself, sings the song. This singing off-stage is, of
course, the only way when the song text tells a story.
"The First Nowell" is an example of this. (There
may, of course, be instrumental interludes to provide
time enough for all the action suggested by the text.)
But even in a dialogue song, like the English "O No,
John" or a song involving more than two parts, like
"My Man, John," the singing may be off-stage. "Good
King Wenceslas" is an excellent example of a song
that has impersonal narration as well as spoken parts.
The first and last stanzas and the latter half of the
third stanza of "Good King Wenceslas" are narrative
and are usually sung by the entire gathering as they
watch the King, the Page, and, part of the time, the
Peasant, carry out their parts. The third kind combines both singing and acting. Opera is or should be
the highest form of this kind, but it enters humbly
and freely into the acting out of songs also. The English folk song "High Germany," for another example
of a dialogue song, is a complete little play in which
each actor may sing his or her part throughout.

This acting out of songs has two advantages in so
far as interest in dramatics is concerned: first, it requires little rehearsing and very little time for presentation; and second, it may bring everybody present
into the play by having them sing.[22] Its musical value
consists in a heightened appreciation of the song and
in possible participation in it through pantomime even

[22] Cf. reference to dramatics on page 50.

by persons unable to sing or play. The writer has observed boys and adults eagerly interested in the acting out of fine old ballads which, merely as songs, could not have attracted them.

Listening

Listening is, of course, the most common means of experiencing music. The radio and phonograph have made this means available to almost everyone, everywhere; and better still, for city people, there are probably more free or inexpensive excellent concerts in libraries and art musuems as well as in concert halls than there ever were before. Munificent gifts these are, both the reproduced and the " living " concerts, but they are worthless until they are turned into gold, of the priceless sort. And only the magic of an inner grace can so turn them. How many have this grace? Apparently almost everyone, perhaps everyone, has it in some measure. What opportunities are there for cultivating it and using it?

Here is another composite plan:

Listening in a Community

I By children to the age of 18

  A. In schools

    1. Kinds of performances

      a. Singing or playing by the teacher

      b. Concerts by professional soloists or groups, sometimes a symphony orchestra, arranged especially for boys and girls

      c. Singing or playing by the pupils' own best choruses, orchestras, bands, and chamber music groups, including vocal quartets and the like

      d. Phonograph reproductions

      e. Radio reproductions

    2. Occasions for listening

      a. Class music lesson periods

      b. Assembly periods

      c. Starting the day in the classroom

    d. Sometimes between subjects or at other times when better morale or refreshment of mind or body is needed

    e. Special concerts by school or outside performers, and through the radio (e.g. the Damrosch school concerts)

  3. Ways of improving listening

    a. Courses in appreciation

      (1) In connection with the regular music periods in the elementary and junior high schools

      (2) Elective courses in the junior and senior high schools

        (a) General course open to all

        (b) Intensive course on a par with a full, daily course in English literature

    b. Preparation for listening to special concerts

    c. Explanatory comments over the radio, in connection with radio concerts

    d. Music memory contests

B. Out of the schools

  1. Kinds of performances

    a. Radio and phonograph reproductions

    b. The other kinds are all represented in the plans, given in this chapter, for singing and for playing in a community.

  2. Where can boys and girls enjoy listening to music outside of the schools?

    a. Homes

    b. Churches and Sunday schools

    c. Playgrounds and parks

    d. Community centers and settlements

    e. Camps and summer vacation schools

    f. Music schools

    g. Theatres

    h. Art museums and public libraries in which concerts are occasionally given

    i. Concert halls

    j. Meeting-places of junior music clubs, 4-H clubs, and other clubs

    k. Hospitals and other welfare institutions

  3. Occasions for listening to music outside of the schools

    a. Starting the day at home

    b. Before a meal, in place of a spoken grace

      c. Fireside and good-night times in homes, camps and community centers

      d. Church and Sunday school services

      e. Before, after, in, or between the acts of plays

      f. Festivals (Christmas, Easter, music week, or other time)

      g. Pageants

      h. Water carnivals

      i. Park band concerts

      j. Indoor concerts and appropriate opera performances

      k. Music memory contests

   4. The ways of improving listening that are given for schools, in A.3. above, can be applied to outside agencies. No way is more effective than the informal adventuring of the members of a family in music that they will later together go to a concert to hear.

II By adults

A. Kinds of performances (See I.B.1., above)

B. Where?

   1. In all places mentioned for children in I.B.2., above, except summer "vacation schools" (Some adults, though few, go to camps for their summer vacations)

   2. Evening schools

   3. Industrial and business establishments (During a brief recess)

   4. At meetings of music clubs, women's clubs, service clubs, Chambers of Commerce, parent-teacher associations, church socials (and other meetings outside of the religious services), grange meetings, fairs, and other rural gatherings, and at conventions

   5. Public forums and the like

   6. In gathering places of Negroes

   7. In gathering places of foreign language groups

C. When?

Nothing need be added to occasions mentioned for children in I.B.3., above, except those times at the beginning or during the process of a meeting when the social and refreshing or inspiring effects of music may be needed.

D. Ways of improving listening

1. All those already mentioned are applicable to adults.
2. Self-improvement through reading of books that give practical guidance to actual listening
3. Special courses or preparatory talks and concerts for Negroes in cities where they are not entirely welcome in concert halls
4. Special aid, and welcome to the city's concerts, to be given to foreign language groups through explanatory talks (with music) given in the native language of the group

There are two things often overlooked that should be considered with regard to this plan. First, the community music leader should do whatever he can to make the most of those opportunities to listen to music that occur or may occur in connection with the common, not purely musical activities of life. For instance, why struggle, and often fail, to gain audiences for excellent choral or chamber music in concert halls, and then provide only a poor quality of music to the people at church services which, despite all that is said about the decline of the church, attain a total attendance of adults each year that is only second to that lured by the movies? If there are any vocal or instrumental groups in the community, or, better still, in the church membership itself, that can perform the best music excellently, including appropriate movements from the best chamber music as well as the most beautiful choral music in the world, how can their art, like the arts and crafts of the medieval cathedral builders and decorators, be brought into the church services?

And what of all the other places and occasions which call for living music and not merely the reproduced variety. What of the homes, the Little Theatre plays, church sociables, community centers, evening schools, clubs and art museums? The music for each place or occasion, like architecture or decoration, may be entirely appropriate and yet excellent and exceedingly delightful. " But where is the payment for such performance to come from? " is asked.

The answer is that improved music instruction at public expense, increasing leisure for many people, and the deep need of almost everyone for creative activity through art of some kind, are or should be conspiring to make skilled musical amateurs of thousands of young singers and players rehearsing daily in an increasing number of our high schools and music schools. They will earn a living by teaching music or, most of them, by entirely non-musical pursuits. May not their singing or playing be without price?

The second thing to be considered is the fact that the most effective means of increasing appreciation of music is through actual participation in it in some way. We have seen that there are five common ways of doing this. But they must be of such quality and musical intelligence, however elementary, as to invite appreciation. Many boys and girls in schools have the confusing and wasteful experience of going from a course in music appreciation in which the glories and delights of music are explained, to a singing or playing class in which there is no thought or feeling for any such glories or delights. The natural desire in singing or playing real music that has a stimulating reach of heart and mind in it, in a class or in a rehearsal of a chorus, orchestra, band or smaller group, is to follow that reach, that is, to feel and understand as fully as possible what is most delightful and otherwise admirable in it. This desire and the possibility of fulfilling it through actual re-creation of the music offer the best possible occasion for a lesson in appreciation, more vital and effective than the special listening lesson can be, though the latter may, of course, be very valuable as a supplement, or as a main means of help to those who neither sing nor play.

Appreciation, like any other enthusiasm, urges us toward expression, to sing, play, whistle, dance or " act "; and if we do so successfully, however simply, our appreciation is enhanced and grows. But if we do not, it is not likely ever to attain the full flowering of power and delight that is its natural destiny.

CHAPTER IV

Common Obstacles

AFTER so extensive a view of musical activity as we have just had, we may well ask why there is so little good amateur singing and playing and intelligent listening in many a community of which we know. The first cause that does or should come to our minds is the lack of initiative and energy or the lack of leadership. But each of several other conditions have in different places been blamed for the often wide separation between what is and what might be. An inquiry to city and town public school music supervisors in all parts of the country brought reports of obstacles from 553 out of 604 of them. The following tabulation shows the obstacles in the order in which they were stated in the questionnaire itself and the number of supervisors in the cities or towns of each population grouping who checked each one.

OBSTACLES TO AMATEUR MUSIC IN COMMUNITIES

POPULATION	1–999	1000–9999	10000–29999	30000–49999	50000–74999	75000–99999	100000–and over	TOTALS
Number of cities reporting obstacles	100	261	94	22	19	8	49	553
Radio because it is easier	21	60	23	9	2	3	12	130
Radio because expert performance discourages amateurs	12	15	3	5	0	0	1	36
Too many other things going on	43	135	53	12	7	6	26	282
Lack of adequate audiences for amateur concerts	25	102	33	12	9	5	18	204
Lack of funds for leadership, music, etc.	44	99	33	14	8	6	23	227
Lack of adequate leadership	26	65	17	8	5	3	14	138

Too Many Other Things Going On

The large number of cities and towns, even the villages, in which it is said that too many other things are going on probably includes many that suffer mainly from a lack of inspiring leadership, but it points strongly to the common lack of purposefulness in leisure. The so-called leisure time problem means for many people precisely the opposite of its intended meaning. For them it is not, " What are we going to do with the extra time away from work? " but " How can we find time enough to sleep and to earn a living? " What with the movies, the radio, the automobile, social and many other sorts of clubs, a flood of rapid-fire novels and of newspapers and magazines competing with one another in allurements, and no end of other raids on people's time and money by advertisers who know their weak points, leisure pursuits (so-called) are very often pursuits *by* rather than *of* means of recreation or amusement. The growth in skill and appreciation that comes through regular attendance and endeavor in a chorus, orchestra, band or other musical group is evidently not regarded by many people as being in keeping with leisure time living.

But there is a growing tendency away from this mere flitting, as shown in the remarkable increase of golfers practicing diligently to improve their game, of amateur gardeners, of men and women attending educational courses of all kinds and making best sellers of important though popularly written books of science, philosophy, and history, and of amateur civic orchestras. The young men and women now growing up in remarkably fine choruses, orchestras, and bands in high schools and colleges have gone deeply into music, finding the gold of it. Will they willingly let it waste away in the years to come? A large majority of them have no intention of becoming professional musicians. May not their interest in music-making turn leisure for an increasing number of them into the most important part of their days, giving to " time off " the inspiring purposefulness that for many can no longer be given to labor?

Too Many Trees in the Choral Forest

In some cities there are many choruses, each one associated with a certain church, club, foreign language group, industry, or a neighborhood, but there is either no civic chorus, none representative of the city, or else there is one that is representative only in name. Its growth in size or quality or in both has been stunted by the competing attractions and needs of the many other choruses. This is perhaps an unsatisfactory condition; like that faced by churches with regard to congregational worship in many a town and city and sometimes resulting in a " community church." A merging of two or more of the choruses, or the attraction into one group of the best singers in each of the choruses, are possible ways of forming or strengthening a community chorus. But each way, especially the latter, may do more harm than good. Will the singing of the community chorus be better and more inspiring to everyone concerned than the singing of the other choruses was? Is there a bond of happy fellowship in each of the smaller choruses that will be lost and not replaced by the formation or reinforcement of a community chorus? These questions should be considered before there is any campaign aimed at such a development.

Two or three good purposes there may be in trying to have a really representative civic chorus as well as or instead of a number of unrelated choruses in a city; (1) the cultivation, by example, of the best standards of singing and musical enjoyment possible in the city, or (2) the provision of opportunity for singers not eligible to the other choruses, and (3) the cultivation of civic spirit. In most cities there are more than enough unattached singers or prospective ones to achieve either the first or second purpose and the third one, or all three of them, in a well-led civic chorus without detracting from any other chorus. And no matter what else is done, a civic festival bringing together most or all of the unrelated groups under excellent leadership can be most effective of all, in itself and also in the impetus that it is likely to give toward the formation or development of a permanent civic chorus. On page 129 may be seen an account of a proposal in this regard made to the members of several choruses in Bangor, Maine.

* * * * * *

The lack of funds and the lack of adequate audiences are frequently interrelated and will be dealt with in later chapters.

* * * * * *

The Radio

The blame given the radio was justifiable in the mid-twenties when listening-in was an exciting novelty finding its way into thousands of homes for the first time, and many a home still suffers heavily from its almost continuous use. But it is probable that life in most of the homes of unbridled radios would be even less interesting without that instrument, and recent experiments in broadcasting introductory lessons in piano and in band instruments give promise of making up in large measure for any decline in amateur singing and playing caused by it.

If adequate facts could be gathered, it would probably be found that this wonderfully improved carrier of an increasing amount of excellent music is now often a means of stimulating interest in good amateur performance as well as in mere listening. It is the combination of good performance over the radio and attractive opportunities to sing or play ourselves, or to learn to do so, that promises to convert an increasing number of us from passivism to self-expression. Part of our gratitude for the support given to the much enlarged provision for music in many public schools is doubtless due to the radio and phonograph that have made thousands of taxpayers and school officials realize the scope and power of music more fully than they ever had before.

Other Obstacles

Other obstacles mentioned by school music teachers and encountered in personal investigations are as follows, stated in the order of their frequency: (1) lack of musical interest; (2) lack of cooperation in the community, due to mere inertia, to rivalries or jealousies between clubs, churches, political groups, or music leaders, or to racial differences and separation; (3) lack of a suitable place for rehearsals or for concerts; (4) the effect, in suburbs, of being too near a large city; (5) the similar effect, in college towns, of too much dependence on college musical activities and events.

Summarizing all the obstacles, we may reduce them to five:

1. Lack of purposefulness in leisure on the part of many people and of adequate conceptions and practices of education for leisure on the part of officials and teachers in many schools.
2. Teacher-training that has not adequately, if at all, taken into account the musical possibilities in life outside of schools.
3. In many communities, a lack of capable leaders.
4. Lack of musical organization or organizing agency or agencies in the community, which could, with necessary adaptations, do for musical leadership outside of schools what the school organizing forces do for it inside of them, including the securing of funds and a rehearsal and concert hall, and the cultivation of musical interest in the community.

The first obstacle has already been discussed in this chapter. Along with the second and third obstacles it should be dealt with by universities, teachers' colleges, normal schools and music schools, not only in their regular curricula but also through extension service to teachers, leaders and to groups interested in furthering music in their respective communities. The second and third obstacles also point to the value of having a musical leader — more than one, in the larger cities — definitely engaged to provide for musical possibilities in the community. The fourth obstacle leads us to the value of community organization for music (discussed in Chapters V and VI) and of effective establishment of musical activities in evening schools, community centers, churches, clubs, and industries.

*   *   *   *   *   *

After so much attention to obstacles it is especially heartening to see reports from school music teachers which show in most cities and towns a marked increase in the number of adults engaged in amateur musical activities. The teachers were asked to state whether in the musical season of 1929–1930 the number of participants in each of several kinds of such activities was larger or smaller than in previous years, or about the same as in those years. Teachers, like other persons of civic pride, are inclined in such an inquiry to overestimate the virtues of their own communities. The reader may make allowance for this and still be cheered. The tabulation given on page 112 shows their responses, the figures in each column referring to the number of teachers who gave the indicated response.

This tabulation incidentally shows the proportion of communities in which, according to the teachers' reports, each kind of musical activity was being car-

SCHOOL MUSIC TEACHERS' ESTIMATES OF PRESENT STATUS
OF ADULT AMATEUR MUSICAL ACTIVITIES

Population of cities reporting	1–999			1000–9999			10000–29999			30000–49999			50000–74999			75000–99999			Over 100,000			Totals		
	*L	S	A	L	S	A	L	S	A	L	S	A	L	S	A	L	S	A	L	S	A	L	S	A
Home and small neighborhood groups	8	2	7	38	7	32	22	·	9	2	1	3	3	·	3	2	·	3	10	1	3	85	11	60
Church chorus	23	3	33	67	17	94	33	5	34	11	1	7	9	3	9	3	·	3	14	·	9	160	29	189
Festival of combined church choirs	10	·	6	26	5	24	14	·	7	5	·	5	3	2	2	3	·	1	10	·	1	71	7	46
Choruses in evening schools	·	·	·	6	2	6	3	·	3	3	·	3	2	·	·	·	·	·	3	3	3	17	5	15
Choruses in clubs	3	·	5	25	4	25	15	3	18	5	1	3	4	·	4	3	1	2	14	1	5	69	10	62
Choruses in industry	·	·	·	1	·	·	4	·	3	·	·	·	2	·	4	·	·	·	5	3	8	12	3	15
Community choruses	6	2	2	31	1	10	17	5	5	4	2	4	5	·	5	1	2	·	4	7	3	68	17	29
A Cappella chorus	·	·	·	9	2	5	7	2	·	·	·	·	2	·	·	·	·	·	3	1	3	21	5	8
Bands in evening schools	1	1	·	10	2	3	4	·	3	·	1	·	·	·	·	1	·	·	3	·	3	19	4	9
Bands in clubs	1	1	·	10	2	6	8	·	8	·	·	·	2	2	2	1	·	1	8	2	6	30	7	23
Bands in industry	·	1	·	5	12	8	6	·	6	·	·	·	3	·	3	·	·	·	5	4	4	19	17	21
Community bands	16	·	6	37	12	46	20	·	14	5	1	6	3	·	3	2	2	2	5	2	6	88	17	83
Orchestras in evening schools	·	1	·	3	1	4	6	1	6	2	·	2	·	·	·	1	·	·	2	·	2	14	3	14

(Top of page, partly cut off at the margin) … ected on. (The list of … was here also printed for checking on each … ment.) Ranked according to frequency, the activities appear as fol-lows:

Activity	C1 (L / S / A)	C2 (L / S / A)	C3 (L / S / A)	C4 (L / S / A)	C5 (L / S / A)	C6 (L / S / A)	C7 (L / S / A)	Total (L / S / A)
Orchestras in clubs	.. / .. / ..	21 / 6 / 7	4 / 1 / 2	1 / .. / 1	1 / .. / 2	2 / 1 / ..	4 / 2 / 3	36 / 1 / 24
Orchestras in industry	.. / .. / ..	6 / 2 / 2	2 / 1 / 2	.. / 1 / 2	.. / 1 / 3	.. / 3 / ..	.. / .. / ..	11 / 3 / 20
Community orchestras	6 / .. / 3	26 / 5 / 14	6 / 3 / 2	2 / 2 / 2	1 / 2 / 11	2 / 4 / 1	3 / .. / ..	64 / 9 / 33
Junior symphony	.. / .. / ..	.. / .. / ..	.. / .. / ..	.. / .. / ..	.. / .. / ..	.. / .. / ..	.. / .. / ..	.. / .. / ..
Orchestra for high school graduates	1 / .. / 1	.. / 5 / 5	2 / .. / 2	1 / 1 / ..	.. / 4 / 1	.. / 4 / 1	2 / .. / ..	17 / 3 / 10
Orchestras in Sunday school or churches	16 / 2 / 3	58 / 41 / 29	13 / 6 / 7	4 / 4 / 6	4 / 4 / 14	2 / 14 / 2	10 / .. / ..	131 / 13 / 80
Luncheon club and other community singing	5 / .. / 4	45 / 41 / 29	15 / 10 / 6	2 / 6 / ..	2 / 4 / 10	2 / 10 / 2	11 / .. / ..	105 / 7 / 85
Totals	97 / 10 / 72	425 / 68 / 379	244 / 40 / 138	68 / 9 / 51	44 / 2 / 35	32 / 1 / 32	127 / 28 / 119	1037 / 158 / 826

*L = larger. S = smaller. A = about the same.

(Bottom of page, partly cut off at the margin) Whatever the obstacle, some form of community organization is itself conducive … more likely to avoid it or overcome them than are … isolated indi-viduals or groups.

ried on. (The list of musical activities here given was printed for checking on the questionnaire.) Ranked according to frequency, the activities appear as follows:

Activity	Total Number Reporting it
Church Chorus Choirs	378
Orchestras in Sunday Schools or Churches	224
Luncheon Club and Other Community Singing	197
Community Bands	188
Home and Small Neighborhood Groups	156
Choruses in Clubs	141
Festival of Combined Church Choirs	124
Community Choruses	114
Community Orchestras	106
Orchestras in Clubs	61
Bands in Clubs	57
Bands in Industry	47
Choruses in Evening Schools	37
A Cappella Choruses	34
Orchestras in Industry	34
Bands in Evening Schools	32
Orchestras in Evening Schools	31
Choruses in Industry	30
Junior Symphony Orchestras for H.S. Graduates	30

*   *   *   *   *   *

Whatever the obstacles, some form of community organization wisely conducted is more likely to avoid or overcome them than are the efforts of isolated individuals or groups.

CHAPTER V

*Various Types of Community Organization for Music
and What They Do*

IT must be remembered that we are now considering
the *whole community*, with all its varied possibilities, as the field of endeavor. Any single musical activity, or even several of them, can be started without
any organization at all. Most of the group singing or
playing in the world, outside of the schools and clubs,
was started through the initiative and energy of individuals, not organizations. Choruses, orchestras, and
bands are organized — simply, we hope — but often
independently, as a result of the inner energy, the
musical interest, of individual members of them, not
of any general community organization. But we are
now considering how a maximum of such energy can
be aroused and expressed amidst the many kinds, ages
and conditions of people in a whole community, with
their greatly varied musical interests and abilities.

In most communities thousands of dollars are
spent annually for music instruction in the public
schools and elsewhere. How can this expenditure of
money and effort be made to yield the richest benefits
to the community in life outside as well as inside the
schools? How can the most be made of the musical
capacities of actually or potentially interested people
now unprovided for? What future uses or improvement of present uses of music, in festivals, civic observances, and in the various channels of social, religious and industrial life in the community, could
be brought about to make living in it richer, more
wholesome, and more socially devoted? Such matters

may well be motives for forming some kind of community organization. What kind? This chapter will present several kinds and, in order to make the picture of each one clear and lifelike, it will also show briefly what it does, important problems it has faced, and, if its origin is especially interesting, how it was started.

A Community Music Association

We have already seen, in Chapter I, much of what the Flint Community Music Association does. This Association is an outgrowth of the Choral Union started there in 1913. For four years the costs of the chorus were entirely borne by a public-spirited citizen, Mr. J. D. Dort, the president of one of the automobile industries then in Flint, whose interest in providing for musical expression and enjoyment in Flint represented one phase of his comprehensive vision of a city providing well for all the needs of the good life. In 1917 he suggested that a Community Music Association be formed not only to take over the support of the chorus, but to regard it as only one channel for its endeavors to provide for all the musical possibilities of the city.

The work of the Association is carried on by a music director who is also general manager, by one full-time assistant director, a part-time assistant director, one or more leaders engaged for briefer services to special groups, and a secretary-office manager who is also an accompanist. The director, besides planning and superintending the year's activities and conducting the Symphony Orchestra and the Industrial Mutual Association's Men's Glee Club, has the responsibility and supervision of all the music courses in the two senior high schools and of all the instrumental music instruction in the six junior high schools and twenty-eight elementary schools. The Board of Education therefore provides without charge an office for the Association in four rooms in one of its buildings and, in addition, contributes $3,250 yearly to the funds of the Association. This payment, however, must appear as compensation made personally to the director for his services in the schools.

The Association is governed through a Board of Directors having seventeen members, three of whom, including the mayor, represent the city government; four are appointed annually by the Board of Education for a term of one year, and the remaining ten are elected for a two-year term by whatever citizens attend the annual meetings for the purpose, the terms being so arranged that five persons are elected each year. All persons interested in making Flint a better city through music are invited to these meetings which occur on the third Tuesday in September, and each one is entitled to a vote. The President of the Association presides and the usual formalities of a business meeting, including reports of officers, are carried on. A nominating committee appointed beforehand by the president announces the names of the five candidates for membership in the Board of Directors, and opportunity is given for other nominations from the floor. Copies of the music director's comprehensive report are offered to anyone who will apply for one at the office of the Association. This meeting is announced in the newspapers on three or four days beforehand, and the first rehearsal of the Community Chorus is held immediately after the business is concluded, so there are always many more people present than the number — twenty-five — necessary for a quorum.

On a later date the Board of Directors meets to elect a president, first vice-president, second vice-president, secretary, and a treasurer, each to serve one year, and an executive committee of seven (in addition to the president, who is an ex-officio member thereof). The officers are usually, although not necessarily, taken from the Board of Directors. The executive committee is responsible for the employment of the music director and his assistants, for determination of the amounts of their respective salaries, and for the general business of the Association. It meets once a month with the director to discuss needs and possibilities and, when the time comes, to determine upon a budget for the ensuing year, which is then recommended to the Board of Directors. When approved by the latter, the amount in addition to the $3,250 expected from the Board of Education, and a small sum given by the Industrial Mutual Association in payment for special services to it by the director, is applied for from the community chest.

In 1929 the chest appropriated $11,000 to the work of the Association. The budget for 1930 was as follows:

SUGGESTED BUDGET

Salaries and Wages

A. Executive and music director (including his services to the public schools) — $6,000

B. Full-time assistant director — 4,500

C. Part-time assistant director and occasional assistants — 1,300

D. Secretary, office manager, and accompanist (all in one person) and occasional additional office service and accompanying — 2,300

E. Out-of-town soloists, judges for contests, and occasional additional players in the orchestra — 250

Communication and Transportation

A. Telephone and telegraph — 70

B. Expense of director's attendance at state and national conventions of music leaders — 200

C. Postage — 200

D. Upkeep of car — 250

E. Freight and cartage — 50

Office Supplies   200

Equipment
  A. Office   150
  B. Music libraries   300
  C. Instruments   100

Fixed Charges
  A. Magazines and bulletin service   25
  B. Dues in state and national organizations   14

Publicity
  A. Printing   200
  B. Music week publicity   200

Miscellaneous   300

Total $16,609

The actual musical activities of such an Association, which are described in Chapter I, are, of course, dependent on a great deal of planning, organizing, secretarial work and other services. A survey of the city's musical resources undertaken eight years ago has been kept up to date. An intensive file contains the names, addresses, telephone numbers, and professional activities of all of the music teachers of the city, all of the leaders of choirs, other choruses, bands, and orchestras, and all professional soloists and groups. It also includes the name, rehearsal and concert times and places, number of members, and requirements for membership, of all amateur groups, and the names of the officers of these groups and all other groups that are or might be served by the Association. These other groups include churches, schools, social centers, theatres, service clubs, other clubs and lodges, chambers of commerce, social service agencies, banks, industries, mercantile establishments, foreign-born groups, labor unions, patriotic groups, and state and national conventions that happen to be held in Flint. At most of the conventions leadership in community singing is provided by the Association, and information is given regarding musical individuals and groups in the city that are available for performance before the delegates. Many churches have been helped to secure good choir directors.

The Association also conducts a free circulating library of music for all kinds of musical groups, and has loaned to schools many used instruments purchased through it at low prices when the instruments were needed. The schools have later bought these from the Association.

The music director gives many lectures on music and its uses in education and recreation. In one year he addressed two of the service clubs, three other clubs, fifteen parent-teacher associations, the Industrial Mutual Association, the General Motors Institute of Technology, and a Christian Endeavor Convention.

Each year a Musicians' Hospitality Dinner is held, its purpose being to welcome into the city all new musical leaders and incidentally to reaffirm the city's appreciation of those already established and active in leadership or teaching. Addresses of welcome are made by representatives of the Chamber of Commerce, the City Council, Industrial Mutual Association, Board of Education, Church Choirs Association, St. Cecilia Society, the Musicians' Union and the Community Music Association.

We must now leave Flint and go to see through what kinds of organizations musical opportunities are provided in other communities. A very impressive feature of the Flint scene was the joint employment of the music director by the public schools and the Community Music Association, offering a vital connection between school-life and life outside the schools that is extremely important. Let us therefore inspect a few other cities in which this feature exists:

*   *   *   *   *   *

A Municipal Department of Public School and Community Music

In 1921 in Winston-Salem, North Carolina, there was established as a part of the municipal government a Department of Public School and Community Music with the supervisor of music in the public schools as director of the department. He was responsible both to the School Commission and to the Civic Music Commission, the latter consisting of seven prominent citizens interested in the development of music in the community, who were appointed by the mayor. In order to relate the community and the school music as closely as possible it was required that the superintendent of schools be a member of this Commission; and, fortunately, another member of it later became chairman of the School Commission. The mayor was a member ex-officio. Only one member was a musician.

The Civic Music Commission was a permanent non-partisan one, serving without pay, but the city's appropriation of funds for its use had to be voted upon each year by the Board of Aldermen and charged to public school expenses. For the first year $10,000 was appropriated, but the director of the department, knowing of the need for economy, asked for less in succeeding years. The appropriation for 1928 was $6,600. However, he continued to spend about $10,-000 each year, obtaining the additional funds through private donations, each given for a special project such as a festival, usually as payment of a deficit.

Under the auspices of the Civic Music Commission there have been music week festivals involving an adult chorus of about 250 — mostly church choir singers — and a children's chorus of about 1000; occasional community singing; a band consisting mostly of high school students and graduates, each receiving $20 for giving 16 concerts during 8 weeks of the summer; a summer music school bringing about 100 adult students, most of them from various parts of the South "for special study with teachers of national reputation" in singing, piano and organ playing, harmony, and public school music, and also bringing from 300 to 400 children of the city to classes in piano or orchestra and band instruments. The presence of singing teachers and students in the summer made possible a season of civic opera in each of two years, but this was discontinued because of the opposition of several local clergymen to opera.

Winston-Salem has one of the most beautiful and acoustically excellent auditoriums in the world, which was dedicated by a four-day Music Festival provided through the Civic Music Commission in 1924.[1]

* * * * * *

An Extension of School Music

Imagine a well-balanced Civic Orchestra of 60 players, their instruments including 4 violas, 5 cellos, 5 string basses, oboe, 2 bassoons, English horn, 4 French horns, contrabassoon, and bass clarinet, in addition to the usual strings, winds, and tympani, *all in a town of 9700 people*. Imagine them playing well, which is a still more impressive and delightful thing to contemplate than their mere number, well enough to attract the prominent Carl Busch, C. S. Skilton, and N. DeRubertis as guest conductors in performances of substantial new compositions of theirs. What sort of town is this, and how has this development been attained?

It is Ottawa, Kansas, 58 miles southwest of Kansas City. It is in most respects like many another city or town of its size. Ninety-nine per cent of its population are native-born Americans (4 per cent are Negroes)

[1] The municipal provision for community music in Winston-Salem was discontinued in 1930 because of the financial depression.

supported mainly through the cultivation and sale of farm and dairy products in the county, through two large tree and flower nurseries and a number of small

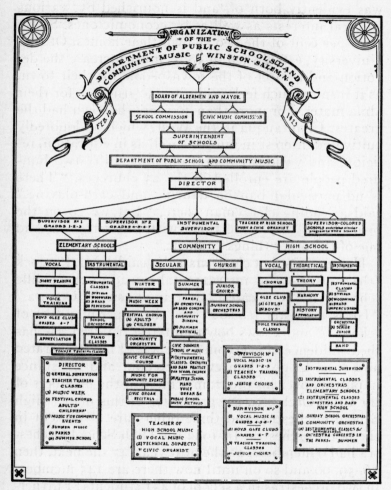

factories, and through employment at the Santa Fe car shops and offices. There are three movie theatres and proportionately as many radio sets, automobiles, and other modern amusement devices as exist in any other community. There is no unusually large amount of wealth or leisure. How, then, can the unusual musical development be accounted for?

To begin with, there is " community spirit " that was evidently born of, and is nourished by, various cultural interests as well as by economic ones. Sixty-eight per cent of the people own their homes. Ottawa University, established in 1865, must increase the devotion and respect of the townspeople for their town, as it inspires such feelings in its 450 students for their alma mater. For more than 30 years the town had the greatest Chautauqua in the West, which undoubtedly cultivated interest in music as well as in education, religion, and various cultural pursuits. Fifty-two hundred people are enrolled in the 23 churches. " There is no particular ban on dancing and card-playing," said a leading clergyman there, " but we go on the principle of displacing them with other things. And one of the other things is music."

However, as that clergyman also said, "Mr. Peacock (the supervisor of instrumental music in the public schools) is the greatest asset in music in Ottawa." " He is a master leader," said the superintendent of schools, " and knows how to interest children. He has the confidence of everyone. The school has cooperated and tried to give him every freedom and assistance in putting over his program." Fifty of the members of the Civic Orchestra are graduates of this man's High School Orchestra, and three others are at present in the latter orchestra. In 1922 the High School Orchestra had 9 members, 22 the next year, 47 the next, then 56, 59, 90 and so on until now there are 145 members in two orchestras in a school of 431 students! Furthermore, there are two string quartets and two trios, and a band of 92 in this school; and there are 65 boys and girls in junior high school orchestras. Outside of the schools there are, in addition to the Civic Orchestra, a Civic Boys' Band which gives one concert a week during the summer and plays on civic occasions throughout the year (there is no musicians' union in Ottawa) ; a band of Santa Fe car shop employees; an orchestra in every church and in the women's club (a community women's orchestra was recently organized) ; a number of informal home and neighborhood playing groups, and many performances by the school groups, small as well as large, in community concerts (for some of which a voluntary collection is taken) given in the admirable Municipal Auditorium seating 1500. School groups take part also in the annual Christmas pageant, and occasionally perform at meetings of the Chamber of Commerce and the service clubs, and at public gatherings of various kinds.

Vocal music has not had so full a development. The College Choral Society of 80, which includes several townspeople, has for a few years sung the " Messiah " at each Christmas time, and other oratorios at other times, the soloists being chosen from the chorus. In 1928 (the first year of the Civic Orchestra then known as the Civic and High School Orchestra), this chorus joined with that orchestra, a ballet from the university, and professional soloists from outside, in a performance of the opera, " Aida." Only three of the churches have choirs, the others having quartets or soloists, and only 40 students are enrolled in the high school chorus. A minstrel show has been given by high school students in each of a number of years.

How has this state of things been brought about? A prominent factor is the success of the High School Orchestra in the state contests. It won fourth place in its first competition in 1923 ; third place in 1924; second in 1925 and 1926; first place in 1927 and 1928, and the highest rating — " highly superior " — in 1929 and 1930 (in a new method of grading contestants). Here are seen the strong, steady efforts of the leader, who has profited from having at one time been a football coach as well as an instrumentalist; and here is seen also the loyal backing of children and adults in Ottawa. One of the greatest difficulties in establishing an orchestra or band is the securing of the less usual instruments which are so necessary to its development as well as its initial pleasures. In Ottawa this difficulty was met by the cooperation of the Chamber of Commerce, the Rotary and Kiwanis Clubs, and the Board of Education. To begin with, the first three gave liberally for the purchase of the needed instruments, and the Board of Education provided the instructor and a place to practice. The instruments were all placed in the care and at the disposal of the Board, which has from time to time purchased additional instruments, now owning three thousand dollars worth of them. Furthermore, the City has purchased instruments to the amount of $4,000. (A small tax is levied for the support of the band.) All of the instruments are loaned without charge to pupils who cannot afford to purchase instruments.

The still greater need, for instruction, has been supplied through classes and, in special cases, individual lessons given without charge for two months — June and July — every summer: this as a beginning for some, and an addition for others, to the daily rehearsals of orchestras and bands throughout the school year. All the instruction and rehearsals are directed by the supervisor. Two hundred and twenty-six pupils enrolled for the summer classes in 1930. Children who have instruments loaned by the school or the city must attend these classes and, in addition, all the rehearsals (two a week) of the beginners' band or orchestra or of the High School Orchestra or the Civic Boys' Band, which are also provided during the two months.

What these musical developments have meant to the people of Ottawa, old as well as young, is, of course, only partly revealed by the many editorials regarding them that have appeared in the local newspaper, by emphatic mention of them in the Chamber of Commerce pamphlets, and by such comments as a mother was overheard making after a concert of the High School Orchestra: "I don't believe there is another man in Ottawa who has done as much for the young people as 'Brick' Peacock (the nickname commonly given in respect as well as good will to the conductor). And they all love him." The community's support is further shown by the inclusion in the new Junior High School building of a completely equipped sound-proof music room planned especially for orchestra and band rehearsals, which is used not only by school organizations but also by the Civic Orchestra without charge. And there is no charge for that orchestra's use of the Municipal Auditorium.

Many communities throughout the state have been given an impetus to emulate Ottawa in its musical development. For in addition to appearing in state contests where it has been heard by school officials, teachers and pupils from all parts of the state, its High School Orchestra and Boys' Band, especially the latter, have played in several near-by cities and towns. Business men of Ottawa regard these excursions as "Trade Trips" bringing valuable prestige to their city, so they provide automobiles and small incidental expenses for them. But something in addition to trade is implied in the remark of the secretary of the Chamber of Commerce, that they "regard the money required for the support of Mr. Peacock's musical 'program' as making the best return of all our tax supported activities." The High School Orchestra recently accepted an invitation to give a concert in Lawrence, the seat of the State University, because the superintendent of schools in that city wished to gain support for efforts toward similar musical developments there.

*   *   *   *   *   *

Another Small City's Achievements

Lest the reader think that in a certain town of about 10,000 people, with which he is familiar, such musical development is impossible, let him consider Springfield, Vermont, a town with a population of 8,000. There is no university, no 30-year old Chautauqua, no victory-laden High School Orchestra (because until 1930 there were no contests), no " Trade Trips," not even a resident orchestra conductor, and the time given to music in the schools is much less than in Ottawa. Yet even here there is a community orchestra presenting all of the conventional symphony instruments except bassoons, in fact an orchestra which is well along on the path trod by the Ottawa one. Of its 48 members, 21 are high school students, 3 are junior high school students, and the rest include the owner of a meat market, three machinists, the superintendent of a machine shop, a truck driver, the postmaster, a textile mill superintendent, a housemaid, clerk, teacher, and mothers. A father and his two sons, and a mother and her son and daughter are among them. Their excellent leader is a superb young cellist recently graduated from Harvard, who even as a student had much experience in orchestra conducting as well as playing. His long bi-weekly journey to Springfield from his home near Boston and his services as conductor are made financially feasible by the securing of ten cello pupils for him there as well as remuneration from the orchestra's funds, and by his eager interest in the orchestra and the community. Here, too, however, there is active cooperation between the public schools and the community, the supervisor of music in the schools giving support to a civic-

minded woman in the town whose vision and everlasting endeavor to secure interest and funds have made
the orchestra possible. A fifty-cent fee collected from
each member in the beginning, and never again, increased a little the modest sum gathered from a few
donors, and in due time a free concert was given on a
Sunday in a local theatre. Seven hundred people attended and were so pleased that at the next Town
Meeting, when one of them asked that the town give
aid to the orchestra, it was promptly decided to contribute $500 of town funds each year to the support of
the orchestra for three free concerts during the winter
and spring. The same amount is given for the support
of a band of 20 amateurs who give about 15 outdoor
concerts during the summer.

*   *   *   *   *   *

An Annual Festival Holds Its Own

Bangor, Maine — its present and largest population under 30,000 — presents a record of musical development that is in some ways the most admirable of
all. For 34 years there has been an annual music
festival in that city that has ranked among the best
in America. A proposal regarding the relation of these
festivals to music in the community made in 1927 by
the then newly appointed conductor of the festivals,
who had been for several years the assistant conductor
and an honored musical leader of the community, is
well worth quoting at length:

My proposal, which met with the unanimous and hearty
support of the joint committee, is that the various church choir
singers, and all who are in a position to study and produce
choral music, form an amalgamation and all work unitedly for
these objectives: assistance through concert participation in the
erasure of the festival deficit, in which all of our musical people
should have an interest, and the study of the masterpieces of
choral music.

The instrumentalists of Bangor have, during the period

of more than thirty years, been developing an orchestra for the study and performance of symphonic music. All the lesser organizations, from the schools up, have constructively, and with purpose, contributed to that idea. Now is presented an opportunity for the singers of Bangor to do the same service. Only by such union can the larger aims be accomplished.

The existence of several choral interests and the accompanying demands upon rehearsal time have defeated many praiseworthy projects. One organization has been carrying on an ambitious plan to study for two seasons, but it has been unable to command sufficient attendance at rehearsals actually to prepare a program for public performances. This difficulty is essentially due to the fact that most of the singers belong to two or more organizations.

I realize that the amalgamation suggested might mean the loss of identity of the existing interests, but if these interests are unable under present conditions to accomplish their purposes, names and titles are empty. A fresh name, such as Bangor Choral Club or Choral Art Society, might give new vigor to the cause of music. The important point is not who the persons or what the organizations are, but rather it is the study and production of beautiful and inspiring music.

Bangor should have a chorus of fully 300. Plans are already in hand to reduce or to abolish for the year, if possible, membership dues. Let us get together and show the Festival Association that the singers of Bangor are solidly behind their effort to lift the debt, and then give to Bangor music-lovers the results of our study as our rehearsal efforts crystallize. The instrumentalists have already voiced a willingness to cooperate through their participation in the joint committee.

The orchestra referred to is the Bangor Symphony Orchestra of 65 members ranging in age from 17 to 74, which gives five symphony concerts a year that are in every way exemplary of the fine possibilities in a well-conducted American community orchestra. Forty-four of the members are graduates of the High School Orchestra, and the conductor, who is the conductor of the Festivals, is also conductor of that High School Orchestra. Even the graduates of the latter orchestra who do not attain to the standards for entrance into the Symphony Orchestra are provided for by the privilege of playing in the so-called Junior Federation Orchestra. Furthermore, the conductor directs a high school chorus that joins the city's festival chorus, under his leadership, in rehearsals and participation in the festival. His direct musical and amalgamating influence goes still further. He also directs the students' chorus of the University of Maine — 10 miles away — and combines it and Bangor's choruses with smaller choruses from seven near-by towns, all joining to form the festival chorus of 400 voices. Of not less importance, he is conductor of the Bangor Band of 46 members, representing, as do the members of the Symphony Orchestra, many kinds of vocation, humble and distinguished, and all ages from youth to " threescore and ten." Twenty-one of the members of the Band are graduates of the High School Band.

There is no single community organization governing all these various activities. Each has its own organization. However, they have been vitally interlinked by the good leadership of one man, by an interlocking membership among them, and by devotion to the yearly festival which is governed by a community organization. The following excerpts from the Bangor " Daily News " of February 12, 1929, tell of the attainment of another very important amalgamating influence, and of some important considerations regarding it:

One of the most important moves ever made in Bangor in the cause of music has just been consummated in the purchase of what is known as Stewart Hall, the former college of law of the University of Maine, at Union and Second Streets, by the Bangor Symphony Orchestra, with the Bangor Band cooperating to its full ability in furtherance of the splendid enterprise.

The purpose is to convert the property into a community music center.

Opportunity will be offered to the permanent musical organizations of Bangor to share in the privileges and obligations of the enterprise. Permanent rehearsal and library quarters will be provided on the third floor for the Symphony Orchestra itself and for the Bangor Band, which latter organization has already registered a desire to cooperate in the undertaking by renting quarters. In order to meet the costs of maintenance, private studio rentals will be offered on the first two floors.

It is the hope that ultimately the Bangor Public Library will install in the building its music department, to be administered by a musically-equipped deputy librarian. Genuine musical service cannot at present be offered by the library because of lack of proper facilities. Such service demands the use of a piano and opportunity for actual performance in music study and research.

The securing of this beautiful building is the realization of a plan for several years entertained by the active musical organizations of Bangor, the need of permanent quarters for the Symphony Orchestra and Bangor Band having first been urged by Conductor Sprague at the annual meeting of the Symphony Orchestra Corporation in the spring of 1921.

Committees of both these organizations have worked on the problem at different times, two ideas having been advanced: one to purchase a lot and erect a rehearsal and concert hall, the other to secure or erect a building, part of which might be used for the organizations, the rest to provide studio and other rentals to meet the cost of maintenance.

The new quarters offer many fine prospects for the future, and many hope that in time Bangor will have a conservatory of music there, with the advantages which go with such a project, and the bringing of many pupils to Bangor from far and near.

The orchestra has certain funds available and will at an early date take possession. The balance will be solicited, and sufficient promises by interested persons encourage the orchestra to hope that the building will be occupied without indebtedness. The success of the enterprise as a public benefit will depend largely upon the ability of the organization to occupy the property free of debt.

The building possesses dignity and architectural beauty, which in itself should be no small contributive factor to artistic achievement.

Such a building will be valuable not only in fulfilling the need for an adequate and attractive rehearsal place, but also in being a substantial symbol, " a local

habitation and a name," for the musical life of the city — an attainment especially valuable to an art which, though powerful and indestructible, is yet so intangible.

* * * * * *

The city plans for music thus far discussed are indicative of an interest in making the musical life of children and adults of one piece and an integral part of the city's provision for the welfare and happiness of its people. Among school officials in many cities and towns a similar interest is represented in what is called adult education, which is coming more and more to mean education for all adults, not only for those who are recent immigrants or otherwise backward in understanding of American customs or language, or who are interested only in the vocational uses of education. In an increasing number of evening schools there are choruses, orchestras, and bands, as well as courses in music, usually in charge of high school music instructors. As these become less instructional and more recreational so they will become more really educational, attracting all kinds of grown-ups and affording them a fuller measure of those satisfactions and delights described in Chapter II of this book. What is needed are the ideals of the best leaders in the recreation movement which is most impressively symbolized by the municipal commissions or departments of public recreation now established in many American cities and towns.

Municipal Recreation Departments

These municipal agencies, though still mainly and properly concerned with physical games and sports, are being turned more and more toward the arts, especially music and drama. Provision through them of adequate musical opportunities for adults and chil-

dren in the life outside of school only awaits adequate
purposes, leadership, and methods. In a few cities these
are in process of being realized. For instance, in Irvington, New Jersey, such a Municipal Department is,
outside of the schools, the chief source of support for
the music of the city's 55,000 people. Organized and
maintained by this Department are a Community
Chorus of 146 men and women ranging in age from
18 to 70 and representing all vocations and conditions
of life in the city; a very admirable civic symphony
orchestra of 76, likewise widely representative of vocations and ages (including four high school students
and several graduates) ; a Boys' Band of 45 who range
in age from 12 to 18, including several who have
graduated from, or otherwise left the schools, which
gives two free park concerts a week in the summer and
plays on civic occasions during the winter; a Boys'
Harmonica Band and a Girls' Ukulele Club; Christmas caroling; occasional community singing, and the
annual observance of Music Week which in 1930 enlisted the Elks', Police, and Boys' Bands, and individuals and groups in schools, churches, and theatres.

There are exemplary methods shown in the origin
and maintenance of these musical activities, such as
will be discussed in the chapters dealing with the various kinds of activities. Three outstanding features
must be given emphasis here. First, all the musical
developments mentioned, including the symphony
orchestra, are an integral, highly valued part of the
regular work of a municipally supported recreation
department, a model, therefore, for each of the many
other cities possessing such a department, and for all
other cities and towns that should possess one. Second,
the symphony orchestra and the boys' band are directed by the director of music in the public high
school. And third, the net expense for all these endeavors, not counting the incidental time and energy

of the superintendent of recreation and his secretary, was in 1929–30 only $1,760, about six hundred dollars having been received through voluntary contributions at concerts.

* * * * * *

We have thus far observed various situations in which there is a very close connection between school and community musical endeavors. With the exception of Springfield, Vermont, the principal community music leader in each of these cities is also a leader in public school music. There are many other cities of which this is true, though the number of them is very small in comparison to the number in which the school musical leadership is completely confined within schoolhouse walls and hours and within the brief period of life from 6 to 18 years of age — often principally because it is so fully occupied there and no organization or individual outside of the schools is prepared to initiate or support any community music projects. Let us now observe a few different situations in which there are organizations and individuals outside of the schools actively engaged in such projects, but without direct, if any, relation to the work of the public school music leaders.

* * * * * *

Other Municipal Recreation Departments

In Cincinnati the director of recreation, Mr. Will Reeves,[2] was himself an expert choral conductor. He directed the Mothersingers of Cincinnati, a remarkably fine chorus of 140 representatives of the mothers' clubs in the city, whose two public concerts a year are among the important musical events in the city. He also organized and conducted a mixed chorus of

[2] Deceased June, 1931.

about 200 young men and women from the Y.M.C.A., the Y.W.C.A., the Junior Chamber of Commerce, and from four other young people's social organizations, whose weekly rehearsal was followed by dancing. Moreover, to him was due the formation each year of a chorus of 450 boys and girls from the public and parochial high schools of the city who, after preparation by their school music teachers during six weeks of their regular music periods, followed by four joint rehearsals on Saturday mornings under his direction, gave a Christmas concert which in 1929 was sponsored by the Institute of Fine Arts and included also the Mothersingers, the University of Cincinnati Men's Glee Club, the Catholic Women's Choral Group, and the Y.M.C.A. Glee Club. This was a model achievement, especially valuable in the variety of people it brought together — high school students, college students, young men out of school, mothers and other women, and Catholics and Protestants.

Mr. Reeves also brought about the organization of several choruses now independent of the Recreation Commission, and provided for the employment of a full-time supervisor of community music and four part-time music instructors, the latter being especially engaged for choral and instrumental groups in community centers. In the summer of 1930 a well-balanced band of 29 boys, and two orchestras — one of boys and one of girls — whose 38 members later combined, were started on playgrounds; and in the autumn a community orchestra was formed.

The Los Angeles Department of Playground and Recreation has a Division of Musical Activities in charge of a supervisor who with four special directors of musical activities have all been full-time, year-round employees of the department. One of the special directors, a man, has been in charge of a Boys' Band and a few harmonica bands, and acting in a sub-supervisory capacity with respect to the work of the other directors, visiting their groups now and then and helping to see to it that they are properly provided with equipment, time, other necessary conditions for good rehearsals, and with encouragement. The other directors are women. One of them specializes in the production of operettas, a second one specializes in small orchestras and rhythm bands, the third is especially interested in singing by groups of children, but each is able to sing and play the piano adequately, and each directs a variety of musical activities. The Division also employs a full-time secretary and from 8 to 25 part-time accompanists, the number depending on need, each receiving 75 cents per hour with a minimum of two hours per assignment.

The supervisor has been almost entirely confined to the business of organization, for he has aided in organizing many outside groups having their own leaders, as well as the large number of playground and recreation center groups of all kinds that are directed by the Division's leaders. Furthermore, the Division was in 1928 responsible for a great Festival of Music enlisting several thousand children and adults in connection with the World Sunday School Convention held in Los Angeles in that year, and for the annual Christmas caroling in which, it is said, about 15,000 persons have been actively engaged at one time.

The possibilities in so large a provision by a municipal recreation department are great. The desire for, and faith in them, is further demonstrated by the fact that in the year 1929–30 the cost of maintaining this Division of Musical Activities with all its expenditures for equipment and transportation as well as for personnel was $29,345. The results in delight and deeper satisfactions to children and adults of the city depend, of course, on the qualities and methods of the

supervisor and his assistants, and on their understanding of the real needs, desires, and best possibilities of the people in their charge. This understanding
requires among other things knowledge of the musical
activities in the schools, and some measure of cooperation between school and recreation leaders. Does it
also require direct supervision aimed at finding the
greatest possible effectiveness in carrying on each
activity?

The Los Angeles supervisor believes that his whole
business should be that of organization, publicity, engaging accomplished persons as leaders, and enrolling
as many people as possible as soon as possible in every
kind of musical activity on his extensive list — in all
of which he has had remarkable success. There are
others who believe that without his or someone's direct, expert supervision and persistent search for ways
and means of making the most, in durable enjoyment
to the individuals enrolled, of the talents and efforts
of his assistants, and the situations in which they find
themselves, the numbers will soon dwindle and be
harder than ever to build up in future endeavors.

However, Los Angeles has established a very com-
mendable high-water mark of provision for music by
a recreation department.

* * * * * *

The generous provision for musical activities made
by the Los Angeles Recreation Department has already influenced the recreation departments in several
other cities, outstanding among which is San Francisco. The Supervisor of Music for the Playground
Commission of this city is a woman who with the assistance of only an accompanist and a part-time
teacher of harmonica is herself starting and leading
groups of children and adults in several recreation
centers. She is building gradually but firmly from the

bottom, and gives promise of bringing about a continuous growth that will be lasting. In its first year, 1928–29, the music department of which she is in charge started and maintained at playground centers fifteen children's choruses, three rhythm bands, three harmonica bands, three adult choruses, and one playground orchestra, with a total enrollment of 553 persons. Furthermore, the supervisor of music worked closely with the supervisor of educational dramatics and together they produced two large city-wide festivals of fine quality that are expected to be precedents for annual presentations of this kind, one in the autumn and the other during Music Week. By the end of 1930 there were added to the groups of the first year two children's choruses, a young men's glee club, a mothers' chorus, and a Junior Civic Symphony Orchestra. And more importantly, the first year's gains have been held and developed.

The city government itself, through the Music Committee of its Board of Supervision, has provided for a superb and large community chorus under a great leader, and for many inexpensive concerts by its excellent symphony orchestra. With steady growth of the Playground Commission's Music Department, realization of the sought-for development of music in the schools, and maintenance of the present standards and activities of its Conservatory and its Community Music School, San Francisco will be well on the way toward answering our question regarding adequate provision for the musical possibilities of a city.

* * * * * *

Another way in which recreation departments may serve in the development of community musical activities is through taking charge only of the general management and secretarial work of chorus, orchestra, band, or other group. This is true in Glendale,

California, where the leaders of the community's symphony orchestra and its chorus are paid directly by the city, and the establishment and present executive management of each organization are the work of private individuals, but the business management by the Recreation Department is felt as a steadying influence often lacking in such organizations. This is true in several other places also. "Let us start and run the musical end of this game," the singers or players seem to say, "but you, the recreation people with your special training and experience in organization, run the rest of it for us. That is, you help us get organized, get more members and perhaps a place to rehearse, and either show us how to provide for regular attendance, social life, opportunities to perform and adequate audiences to listen to us, and efficient maintenance of our music and other equipment, or else do these things for us."

*   *   *   *   *   *

A Privately Supported Community Arts Association

Another type of community organization for music, resembling somewhat the Flint Community Music Association, but supported through private funds and having no connection with the public schools, is exemplified in the Santa Barbara Community Arts Association. This Association was formed about ten years ago to supply those elements of the arts — graphic, plastic, architectural, dramatic, and musical — that make for a rich community life. "To afford individuals the opportunity of self-expression, training and education" (in the arts), said its charter, "and to aid in the cultural improvement of the people." The representative of a large Foundation that contributed to its support said of it that "the various divisions of the work appeal so directly to various groups of the population that one may well hope that this experience will constitute a demonstration of what can be done in enlisting the interest of a whole community in the cultural possibilities of art."

Many wealthy people have come to live in this city because of its agreeable climate and beautiful natural setting, and it is their wealth and their desire to make the city as fine a dwelling-place as possible in every respect that have brought about establishment of the Association. A superbly fine result of their interest is the unforgettable beauty of the city's court house, its public library, various public places, and of many of its homes. But there are a large number of quite poor people there also, many of them Mexicans.

The musical activities of the Association have in the past included a music school employing 18 teachers and providing from 15 to 20 scholarships per year; the bringing of symphony orchestra, chamber music, and other concerts and recitals to the city, some of them at popular prices, and some designed especially for children; a community chorus and a small orchestra of local professional musicians and advanced students; free band concerts in the summer; a children's chorus, and provision of music for various events such as Members' Meetings, the Community Christmas Celebration, and the annual Fiesta. Seven public school teachers were paid to give special training to children's choruses which were combined in a festival and directed by Arthur Bliss, the composer, who was then music director for the Association. Furthermore, the supervisor of music in the public schools was invited· by the Association to attend, at its expense, a well-known summer music school 3,000 miles away, so that the music teaching in the schools might be as good as possible.

During the past four years, however, all the musical activities except the bringing of concerts and recitals, the management of the band giving free summer con-

certs, and the dispensation of from 12 to 15 scholarships for study with local teachers, have been given
up. This is evidently because the majority of those
now responsible for the Association's policy with regard to music estimate the value of any musical activity only according to the conventional professional
standards. Support of the community chorus and the
local orchestra was given up, it is said, mainly because
they did not perform well enough and did not attract
large enough audiences. The free music instruction
granted through the scholarships has provided only
for the more talented pupils who have not been permitted thereafter to play in their respective public
school orchestras, though no other experience in orchestra or small ensemble playing has been provided
for them by the Association.

The present policy of the Association seems to be
to bring music *to* the people — and not *from* them.
It brings excellent symphony concerts, including some
especially arranged for children, and it has brought
many concerts of chamber music, but it does little
to encourage singing or playing by the children or
the adults themselves. For example, despite the dozens
of chamber music concerts, of which many were given
by a great string quartet whose members were engaged for two years to remain as residents of the
city, there is apparently very little or no chamber
music being performed by the people themselves, for
the love of it. The writer was told by an official of the
Association that a similar policy has been pursued
in the Art School that is affiliated with the Association. Only unusually talented individuals are given
scholarships in that school, it was said, and all pupils
are given the professional point of view in their studies.
That so apparently perfect an agency as the Community Arts Association — like a happy dream come
true — for administering to the universal need to

create, should leave many people inexpressive, merely receptive, apparently unfired by any sort of urge to sing, dance, draw, *anything* to express the best that's in them (even whittling a stick well would be a beginning), is evidently due to the prevailing policy among those who direct it.

Any criticism of what has been so promising an enterprise should be followed at once by constructive suggestions. What could be done by this Association, in addition to preparation of the annual Christmas pageant and the Fiesta, and the bringing of good concerts to the city?

First of all, its policy with regard to music might be made educational in the broadest sense, providing opportunities for development of the latent talents of as many people in the community as are interested in music and can be provided for. A return to endeavors to help in the music teaching of the public schools might be very beneficial. If the Association does not allow its scholarship pupils in music to play in the public school orchestras, it must be that these orchestras are for some reason regarded as harmful in their effects on the players. Since there are 110 children in elementary school orchestras, about 100 in the high school orchestras, and 70 in classes learning to play orchestra instruments, any aid that the Association could give in helping to improve the work in these orchestras and classes would be valuable to a large number of individuals. Moreover, there might well be a music school having the ideals and purposes of the best music school settlements and providing for a large number of children and adults.[3] The aim of this school would be to provide music education for amateurs with all that that implies of emphasis on music as music, not as a means of public performance or professional advancement, on ensemble singing and playing, and

[3] See Chapter XII.

on every other means of gaining a rich experience of the best music. Such a school, amply supported as it could be by the Association, might be of great service not only to Santa Barbarans but to people everywhere, by being a means of discovering better ways of teaching children and adults to be good musical amateurs.

A second kind of endeavor that the Association could carry on is to provide for vocal and instrumental chamber music by amateurs outside of the music school. By providing a quiet attractive place, excellent suitable music, and effective coaching, some of the admirable interest in chamber music that has been aroused by the many chamber music concerts might result in actual singing or playing rather than mere listening on the part of many people. Occasional informal concerts might be held at which in addition to time for listening, a half hour or so would be given to what might be called exploratory singing by the audience of fine, simple choral music. On some of these occasions various local groups grown capable might appear, such as a group of Madrigal singers who have been meeting at a home or at the Association's Music School, a string quartet that has had similar preparation, a group of Mexican folk singers, worthy groups from the public schools, and perhaps even the Community Chorus or the small orchestra, both of which, no longer supported by the Association, but still aided by some of its members as well as by other contributors, are being carried on independently.

There might well be an orchestra for amateurs, especially for the young people who have graduated from school musical organizations. An attempt at providing such an orchestra was recently made, but little response was given to it and it was abandoned. This brings us to the suggestion that the Music Committee of the Association be made representative of, or at least unmistakably cooperative with, the music department of the public schools, the Board of Education, and the Public Recreation Department, as well as with the best musicians and musically interested leading citizens of the city.

* * * * * *

A Music Week Become a Year

How a Music Week may become a year has been demonstrated in Denver where a Music Week Association of several hundred members, organized twelve years ago for a Music Week observance, has a permanent office in a downtown business building and is responsible through its Board of Directors for Christmas caroling, for special concerts now and then, and for encouragement to, and planning by many groups for the next Music Week. The Board has eleven representative members, only two of whom are musicians, and it meets once a week at luncheon time from October to May. Usually only six or eight of the members attend, some of them having often to be out of town, but they keep their hands on the pulses of organizations who have participated or will participate in Music Week, including those (and also individuals) who might be available or suitable for the performance of the opera (a different one each year) that is an outstanding event of Music Week. The city contributes $4,000 a year to the Music Week Association, and the members pay one dollar a year, which entitles them to two tickets for the opera. The entire expenses of the Association amount usually to between twelve and fourteen thousand dollars a year.

* * * * * *

A Municipal Bureau of Music

What of our largest cities? How can anything like adequate provision be made for a gigantic, disjointed megalopolis like New York, Chicago, or Philadelphia, or for Cleveland, Detroit, Los Angeles, and other cities nearly as large? Chicago has a Civic Music Association whose support through private contribution, and whose good work in connection with a civic student orchestra and with choruses of children on playgrounds, will receive attention in later chapters.[4] But it has not anything like the scope of the Flint Community Music Association, for instance. Los Angeles has already been referred to. With the possible exception of Los Angeles with its phenomenal civic enthusiasm, the largest cities are, of course, much less likely to develop the community spirit that is sunshine and rain to the community music tree.

But Philadelphia is showing a way for these large cities to make more of their musical resources than is commonly made. That city has a municipal Bureau of Music in its Department of Public Welfare, which with a budget of $90,000 [5] has accomplished much in its first two years that gives promise of making it a very worthy example of what every large (or small) city could do.

This Bureau of Music is a successor to the Philadelphia Music League which was itself started mainly to arrange for the city's first Music Week observance in 1922. The League did much more than this, however, providing throughout the entire year such services as are now in charge of the municipal Bureau. The city contributed $10,000 a year to its support, and about $15,000 was secured annually through membership dues and donations. Additional funds making possible a budget of about $50,000 were secured through proceeds from sales of tickets and programs for Music Week, from fees for open air dances, and from other special offerings. The following articles from the By-Laws of the League are especially

[4] Chapters VIII and XVII.
[5] Lessened in 1931 because of the financial depression.

revealing as to the form and the mode of support taken by that organization:

ARTICLE III. MEMBERSHIP

The organization shall have the following classes of members, viz.: (1) individual members; (2) contributing members; (3) supporting members; (4) patrons; and (5) member organizations. All persons engaged in the practice of music or who are interested therein shall be eligible to membership of the first four classes after they have been elected to membership by the Membership Committee and upon payment of the annual dues.

The following organizations shall be eligible to membership of the fifth class, viz.: orchestras, bands, musicians' unions, choral clubs, community singing clubs, conservatories, colleges, music clubs, composers' societies, musicians' societies, choirs of churches, religious societies, operatic societies, organists' societies, music manufacturers, publishers and dealers, and organizations shall be entitled to voting representation as follows, viz.: an organization consisting of 50 members or less by its President and one delegate; an organization of not less than 51 and not more than 100 members by its President and two delegates; and for each additional 100 members belonging to an organization one additional delegate shall be added to those above prescribed, provided no organization shall be entitled to more than five representatives.

ARTICLE IV. DUES OF MEMBERS

Annual dues shall be at the following rates: individual members, $2; contributing members, $10; supporting members, $100; patrons, $500. The dues of member organizations shall be at the rate of $2.00 for each representative of said organization entitled to vote at annual meetings.

Its membership in its first year amounted to 363 individuals and 60 organizations.

In 1926 a suit brought by a taxpayer against the city for contributing $25,000 per year to the Civic Opera Company which, it was alleged, was not a public service but a ticket-selling private organization and was thus opposed to the city charter, resulted in a similar action against the League, on the ground that

the City Council had no authority to appropriate public funds to any private corporation for its distribution
or use. This action intensified interest in the prospect,
which had already been talked about, of establishing a
municipal Bureau of Music; and before the suit could
reach trial, definite steps were taken toward realization of the prospect. The present Mayor of the city,
then engaged in the campaign for his election, included
among his pledges the establishment of such a Bureau.
After his election he called on the President [6] of the
League to prepare proposals for its establishment. The
following " Preamble " was the result, the form and
every item of which is worthy of consideration by anyone concerned with organization of any kind for music
in a community:

PREAMBLE and PROGRAM

Prepared by Committees appointed by Dr. Tily
in preparation for the public meeting
Tuesday, March 13th, 4:30 P.M., Bellevue-Stratford
in behalf of the
PROPOSED MUSIC BUREAU

PREAMBLE

Prepared by Mr. William O. Miller

*   *   *   *

A MUNICIPAL BUREAU OF MUSIC

Hon. Harry A. Mackey, Mayor of Philadelphia, in his inau-
gural address pledged himself to strive to make adequate provision for the artistic, aesthetic and intellectual development of
the city. He stated that he would outline and persistently advo-
cate a constructive musical program. He declared that municipal
aid is necessary for the proper development of music, in the
belief that music thus fostered would make for better citizenship.

In line with this announced policy, the Mayor has requested
that recommendations and proposals looking to the creation of a

[6] A musician, Dr. Herbert J. Tily, who is president of one of Philadelphia's largest department stores.

Bureau of Music should be submitted to him for his consideration and guidance. As a result, at the call of Dr. Herbert J. Tily, President of the Philadelphia Music League, the following organizations interested in the musical life and development of Philadelphia sent representatives for a conference on this all important subject:

American Guild of Organists, Penna. Chapter

Art Alliance of Philadelphia

Associated Glee Clubs, Phila. District Council

Board of Education, Division of Music

Boy Council of Philadelphia

Bucknell Alumnae Club of Philadelphia

Choral Art Society

Choral Society of Philadelphia

Civic Club of Philadelphia

Emerson Club

Falls of Schuylkill Male Chorus

Gimbel Choral Society

Hathaway-Shakespeare Club

Lit Brothers' Chorus

Matinee Musical Club

Mendelssohn Club

Modern Club

Musical Club, University of Pennsylvania

Musical Coterie of Wayne

National Council of Jewish Women, Phila. Sec.

Orpheus Club

Penn Mutual Glee Club

Pennsylvania Grand Opera Co.

Philadelphia Chamber of Commerce

Philadelphia, City of, Welfare Department

Philadelphia Civic Opera Company

Philadelphia Club of Advertising Women

Phila. Federation of Women's Clubs, etc.

Phila. Festival Chorus, Central-South Unit

Phila. Festival Chorus, Germantown Unit

Phila. Festival Chorus, Northeast Unit

Phila. Festival Chorus, West Phila. Unit

Philadelphia Interstate Dairy Council

Philadelphia Mothers' Club

Philadelphia Music Club

Phila. Music Section, Wildwood Civic Club

Philadelphia Music Teachers' Association

Philadelphia Operatic Society

Presser Music Foundation

Republican Women of Penna., Phila. Section

Rotary Club of Philadelphia

Service Clubs, Executive Council

Society for Contemporary Music

Soroptimist Club

Strawbridge and Clothier Chorus

Temple University Glee Club

Temple University Woman's Club

Tioga Choral Society

Treble Clef Club

United Singers of Philadelphia
Women's Club of Frankford
Women's Club of Overbrook
Women's Club, Society for Ethical Culture
Women's Symphony Orchestra
Women's Welsh Club
Wynnefield Women's Club Chorus
Young Women's Christian Association
Women's Committee for the Phila. Orchestra

Several meetings of this Conference Group have been held, as a result of which the following recommendations have been formulated and approved for presentation to His Honor, the Mayor, as a basis for the formation of a Bureau of Music in one of the existing departments of the City government.

City Support of Arts and Letters

The City of Philadelphia is becoming more and more recognized as one of the great centers of cultural and artistic interest in the country. Citizens of Philadelphia have been lavish in placing in the custody of the city great collections of paintings and sculpture. The noble Museum of Art which dominates the Parkway is already known as one of the architectural masterpieces of the world. The collections to be housed therein are valued at many millions of dollars. Elsewhere throughout the city private philanthropy has added to the city's art assets by gifts of sculpture, statuary or monumental objects which have become the property and heritage of the citizens.

Similarly, in the field of literature, the city has provided generously for the needs and cravings of its citizens by the erection of the magnificent new Public Library on the Parkway; and by the maintenance of branch Libraries in various sections of the city so that the people have ready access to works of scientific, cultural or inspirational character.

It will thus be seen that in two of the three great fields of aesthetic and cultural development the city has provided generously and efficiently. As a result the confidence of persons of large means and public interest has been aroused with the gratifying result that collections of inestimable value both in art and literature have been acquired by the city under permanent trusteeship.

The Sphere of Music

Music alone of the great arts that affect the spiritual life of a community has heretofore been given but meager recognition and support by the municipality. Of all the arts, music most vitally enters into the life and daily activities of our people, and the cultivation of an interest in music upon a wider scale, and with public direction and support, cannot but make for better citizenship, as the Mayor has declared.

The creation of a Bureau of Music, under one of the existing Departments of the City government, will give to music that security and opportunity for Public Service now enjoyed by the sister arts, and should create among persons of means who recognize the potency of music as an agency in developing national and civic ideals, a desire to supplement the municipal grants with private gifts and endowments, through which the love and knowledge of music may be more widely disseminated among all classes of the community.

It is conceivable that when such a Bureau is firmly established and functioning, private philanthropy may provide a Temple of Music comparable to the Art Museum or the Public Library, in which may be housed orchestra, operatic and other essential phases of the musical life of the community. If once Philadelphia's civic consciousness is stirred in recognition of the ministry of music, it is confidently believed that abundant resources will be made available to bring to the people of Philadelphia all the enriching and ennobling influences of music. The time may not be far distant when, with the efficient organization and administration of these three intimately related factors of cultural and aesthetic influence, the city might further recognize their importance in civic life by creating an independent city department of the fine arts. In view of the enormous investments which ultimately will be made from public or private funds for these activities, expert direction thereof will become imperative.

The Mayor, happily, and with extraordinary intuition, has pointed the way to the larger cultural life of the community through his efforts to promote civic support of music, and to place it on a parity with the other arts as an instrument of public service.

FUNCTIONS OF A MUSIC BUREAU

A Bureau of Music organized under the Department of Welfare would immediately undertake two primary functions, first to coordinate and bring under a single administration all those musical activities which now receive grants from the city treasury; second, to promote and stimulate musical activities whereby individual and group self-expression of the people may be achieved. Among the many practical services of such a Bureau may be briefly enumerated the following, although these by no means represent the extent to which the public usefulness of such a Bureau may grow:

1. To stimulate music for the people and by the people of the City of Philadelphia to the end that through its activities there shall be larger opportunities for hearing good music and more definite ways of developing individual and group expression through the medium of music.

2. To build up philanthropic activities to assist in carrying music to the institutions of the City: hospitals, prisons, etc.

3. To advance the standing of Philadelphia as a music center.

4. To foster public and private support of opera so that the people may more generally have the benefit of this inspiring form of musical culture.

5. To be a clearing house to foster worth while musical movements.

6. To encourage choral and orchestral activities in industrial plants and other establishments.

7. To be responsible for all Municipal Bands, Orchestras, and other musical activities undertaken by the municipality and to assemble and maintain a Musical Library.

8. To organize Municipal Choruses in various branches to be used on festival occasions, and provide such training facilities as may be necessary.

9. To promote the organization of a Municipal Orchestra of professional musicians; one or more Civic Orchestras composed of amateurs; and one or more Junior Civic Orchestras.

10. To organize music and dance, folk and interpretative, for the Municipal Recreational Parks and Playgrounds; fostering and developing racial group programs for the many nationalities incorporated in the population of the city.

11. To utilize as far as possible, the public libraries for lectures on Music Appreciation.

12. To encourage private citizens to foster musical activities of value to the community.

The administration of the Bureau obviously becomes a municipal activity. The objects and ideals which the Mayor has in mind by the creation of a Bureau of Music can be further promoted with the counsel of an Unofficial Commission appointed by the Mayor, and made up of public-spirited citizens interested in the principal fields of musical expression.

A Pledge of Support

In conclusion, the conferees in subscribing to these recommendations individually, desire to express to His Honor, the Mayor, their pride and gratification at his courageous and far-sighted policy in respect to music; and to pledge to him their whole-hearted and enthusiastic support in carrying through this program. This preamble and program will be submitted by representatives to their respective organizations for action in all cases where authority is not given to act for such organizations.

Respectfully submitted,

(Signed by all Conference Members)

Preamble Committee:
William O. Miller, Chairman
Robert V. Bolger
Harvey M. Watts

The proposed Music Bureau was favored at the public meeting for which the Preamble was made, and eight months later, in November, 1928, the proposal was formally presented to the City Councils and, enthusiastically pleaded for by representatives of organizations mentioned in the Preamble, it was approved. An appropriation of $90,000 was voted for the first year's work of the Bureau, which included provision of summer band concerts that had for several years been paid for by the city. But this act of the Councils had to be referred to the city budget officials, and another taxpayer's suit against the city, opposing the appropriation, had to be answered. The City Charter of 1919 gave the City Council the right to establish additional bureaus, but that taxpayer alleged that the purpose of the Music Bureau was not a public or civic one. Before the suit was heard and before the city solicitor approved the application for funds for the purpose of the Bureau, the Legislature of the

State of Pennsylvania approved the action of the City
Council by proper enactment. But the taxpayer per-
sisted. He contended also that the Music Bureau
might become a channel for graft, but the court
pointed out that such fear might be felt toward all
governmental agencies in charge of funds or powers.
He was rebuffed by decision of the Court of Common
Pleas. The Bureau was established with a staff consisting of the director (formerly director of the
League) an assistant director, and four clerks. Special
part-time musical leadership is also engaged, including the director of the Municipal Amateur Symphony
Orchestra, the director of four sight-singing classes
held in different sections of the city, and other musicians engaged for shorter periods. An honorary Music
Commission of eleven citizens in addition to the director and assistant director of the Bureau appointed
by the Mayor, meets three times a year to consider
the work of the Bureau. This commission is made up
of representatives of the public schools, the University
of Pennsylvania, and of the American Federation of
Musicians (the Union), and outstanding citizens interested in music as a cultural force.

It should be frankly stated that the staff of this
Municipal Bureau have been left entirely free to carry
on their work without any political interference. The
honorary Music Commission, consisting as it does
of outstanding citizens, is itself sufficient safeguard
against such interference, and is to be further strengthened by being made self-perpetuating, not subject
to changes in political administration in the city. This
assurance against the fear of " politics," added to relief from the sometimes very arduous and unpleasant
task of seeking contributions and other means of
financial support has made the evolution from the
League to the Municipal Bureau a fortunate one.
There are sometimes " politics," arising from jeal-

ousies between supporting groups, even in a privately sustained organization.

* * * * * *

Community Organization for Professional Concerts

A city in which there is not a series of well attended concerts of the best music performed by great artists is musically somewhat like a country without great men. The emphasis throughout this book on the singing and playing of amateurs, of the people themselves, is aimed at fulfilling a still greater need than there is for such concerts, a fulfillment on which the continued success of concerts as well as the enjoyment and deeper satisfactions of large numbers of people depends. But we must give some attention to the business of bringing the musically great to our cities; and so we should include among community organizations for music the so-called civic music associations or community concert associations whose purpose it is to enlist enough members at five dollars a year to insure beforehand adequate support for a series of concerts which the members will attend. They are all alike, these associations, and represent an idea that in the ten years since it was employed in Battle Creek in 1921 by a Chicago concert manager has been adopted with success in over 200 cities of all kinds and sizes. Thus far this type of organization has gone no farther in support of local singing and playing than to have supplied soloists for civic orchestras in a few cities, but once well established in a community, its scope might be enlarged to include support of good amateur music also. [7]

* * * * * *

The various community organizations described in detail in this chapter may be classified in four divi-

[7] See Chapter VIII.

sions: (1) those in Flint, Winston-Salem, Santa Barbara, and Philadelphia, each of which was especially
designed to provide for the year-round musical possibilities of a city; (2) that in Ottawa, and those referred to in the comments on newer ideas in adult
education, which are public school systems extending
their services; (3) those in Irvington, Cincinnati, Los
Angeles, San Francisco, and Glendale, which are
municipal recreation departments, and (4) those in
Bangor and Denver, each of which is the outgrowth of
an organization in charge of an annual festival. But
within each of these four divisions there are important
differences in sources of leadership and of financial
support, and in purposes and methods. While the
accomplishments of each organization are admirable,
they are not given here as the "adequate provision"
which in the introduction to Part I of this book we
set out to find. Rather are they to be regarded as in-
dications, as promises, of what might be done if vision,
common sense, leadership, and moral and financial
support could all be what they should be. Moreover,
there are several other cities admirable in this regard,
whose community endeavors for music are not mentioned in this chapter mainly because they are not
different in any important particulars from those mentioned herein. But we shall now and then take a hint
from them also as we go along.

CHAPTER VI

What Can Be Done in Your Community?

WHATEVER kind of organization is formed or whatever else is done, its purpose is to help provide musical opportunity for the people *of a particular community*. It should therefore be an outgrowth of that community's own conditions and possibilities. In other words, what is done must depend on what is already being done and on available leadership, musical interests, leisure, community spirit, financial support, and civic, social, educational, and other organizations or institutions which might help in musical developments. So first of all we should find out what resources of these types in the community can be used and what developments are most needed and practicable. How can this be accomplished? There are three ways.

The Festival Reveals

One way is through a community observance of Christmas, National Music Week or some other occasion to which people of all kinds and conditions can give interest and whatever musical ability they possess. Music Week may have an especially broad appeal, bringing out every possible kind of musical activity. Though not primarily intended to be so, it is in a sense an exposition, a kind of Fair in which not farm products but the musical products of a community are placed on exhibition. But for this very reason, in a city or town in which the musical products are not likely to be anything for even the musically untrained to be proud of, a festival in which the singing and playing are primarily a way of celebrating something outside of music, like Christmas, is likely to be safer and more valuable *as a beginning,* than a Music Week observance would be. In one the people's attention is focused *on* the musical performances, and in the other it is focused *through* the musical performances; and yet the latter may be made to reveal the community's resources as fully as, and perhaps more truly than, the first.

The Informal Survey

A second way is what might be called an informal survey.[1] Information regarding musical activities in the community can be obtained through interviews with the public school music supervisor, other outstanding music teachers and professional and nonprofessional performers, the librarians of the public library, recreation directors, choirmasters, other music directors, newspaper editors or music critics, music clubs, other clubs (including parent-teacher associations), music dealers and officials of industries and department stores. Through these interviews and also actual observation of as many as possible of the musical activities revealed by them, a good working knowledge of the resources, needs and possibilities in the community may be obtained.

An excellent immediate motive for this kind of survey is the desire for information by people of the community with regard to opportunities available to them to take part in musical activities. The recreation department or some other agency should see to it that anyone who might like to sing or play can easily obtain information as to the choruses, bands, orchestras and music schools in the city, what the entrance

[1] It was largely through this kind of survey, though often necessarily very brief, in many cities and towns, that the national study of which this book is an outcome was carried on.

requirements are of each, when it rehearses or gives instruction, what other activities are carried on in it, and where, when and how a person can join it. Information regarding opportunities to listen to music should also be available. It should be a living survey, always kept up to date.

The Formal Survey

The third way might be called a formal survey, a more intensive and thorough-going study than the second way. It is designed to give a disinterested view of the whole situation, with a minimum of dependence on mere opinion; to clear the way of all obstacles, actual or potential, that are due to short-sightedness or to personal ambitions, animosities or inertia. It is to make clear and whole what is or might become muddled and divisive, to lift vision from what may be worm's-eye views to a bird's-eye view.

Now — how can each of these three ways of finding out a community's musical resources and needs be carried out most effectively? A festival or a Music Week may be a very effective way and should not be overlooked, but they and modes of organization for them are dealt with elsewhere.[2] Let us proceed to the two kinds of surveys.

Making the Survey

It is well for both the informal survey and for the formal one to have the backing and counsel of an admirable committee representative of the civic, religious, educational, recreational, business, and musical organizations and institutions that are fitted to give at least moral support to the practical endeavors that will be suggested by the results of the survey. This committee might be constituted as follows, and per-

[2] Cf. "Community Music," a book obtainable from the National Recreation Association.

haps be a natural outgrowth of a previous cooperative
endeavor in a festival or Music Week observance:

> A representative of the City government
> The Public School Music Supervisor
> The Superintendent of Schools
> The Superintendent of Recreation
> Two leading churchmen or choirmasters representing re-
> spectively the Catholic and Protestant churches, Sunday
> Schools, and related organizations, and a cantor or other official
> representing the Jewish Synagogue and its related organizations
> A representative of the City's social workers
> A representative of Music Clubs and Women's Clubs
> A representative of Men's Clubs
> A representative of the Community Chorus [3]
> A representative of the Community Orchestra [3]
> A representative of the local Musicians' Union [3]
> A leading business man, probably an official of the Chamber
> of Commerce
> Perhaps one or more interested men or women of leisure,
> wisdom, and influence.

A small committee selected from this larger one
might be appointed to formulate the subjects and
methods of the survey and then, after having tested
and possibly changed them in discussion with the
larger committee, make the survey. But to bring in an
expert from outside the city to make or direct the
survey is likely to be a better way, even though the
small executive committee has an important supporting part in it. This is especially true of a formal survey. For such an individual has, or should have, the
great advantage of being expert, uninvolved in any
local " politics " of any kind, unbiased, and impersonal — though warmly interested and courteous —
and therefore he can move freely and innocently in
situations that might be explosive to a local person.
He should, as far as possible, himself make all in-

[3] These and some other organizations referred to may, of course, not
yet exist.

vestigations directly, though receiving much assistance in finding where and when there are musical or related activities that he should observe or persons with whom he should confer. He will subject his interpretations of data to every possible test, including frequent preliminary discussions with the small committee and final discussions with the large one, but the clear, accurate, and comprehensive view that is expected of him requires that he be as little dependent as possible on reports of other people's investigations.

The surveyor must carefully avoid stirring up old antagonisms or causing new ones. He must be as innocent as a lamb with regard to any ill will between leaders or groups, keeping all remarks arising from such feeling in strictest confidence, and refusing to be drawn into any controversies. It must be clearly understood that his purpose is only to be helpful, not to be meanly critical. Yet he must not be blind to defects. He should deal only in verifiable information, treating all hearsay evidence as clues to such information, not as conclusive in itself. He must be respectful, earnest but good-humored, confident but modest, efficient, and appreciative of whatever musical efforts have been made. If there is a chorus, or any other musical enterprise by amateurs, the mere fact of its existence is proof of interest and initiative which are far and away more valuable than any amount of talk and writing about choral ideals could be without them.

The most important consideration in a music survey is the quality of the music and of people's experiences of it, but this would better be dealt with indirectly. The surveyor should find out from each leader what music has been performed and which pieces have evidently been most enjoyed and are most lasting in interest, and publish that information in his report, without condemnation where poor taste is shown but with simple praise wherever the best is shown. In his recommendations his plea for the best music should be made through the lists of additional music that he suggests for each group as delightful compositions which the group has the good fortune of now being able to perform or learn or otherwise enjoy. And if his service to the city is wisely planned, it will include at least two meetings with each group of music leaders of the city at which, among other things, much of the music suggested will be available not only in notes but in sounds, with some skilled musician at the piano. Moreover, during the survey one or more local newspapers will welcome write-ups from the surveyor, and these may well include interesting and accurate accounts of admirable musical organizations that he has found in other cities, and of the fine and much enjoyed music performed by them.[4] A survey may thus become an occasion for a forceful educational campaign, through carefully edited newspaper articles whose human interest and humor carry the moral of the tale quietly and welcomely to its sought-for destinations. *No conclusions or even guesses regarding the City's musical activities should be published until the survey has been completed and adequately considered in private.*

Do We Want Such an Investigation?

There are various ways in which interest in having a survey is aroused. Some person or group of persons interested in music or education or in the leisure time problem, or in all three, may be possessed by the old urge toward a better-than-what-is in the community, and seek to answer it with music. He, she, or the group, talks about it to friends and acquaintances. "What can be done about it?" becomes a more and more pressing question. Before long, enough interest is

---

[4] This book contains many examples of such organizations.

aroused in this question to bring together a group of
representative citizens for the purpose of answering
it definitely. They, perhaps, invite an expert who is
familiar with the best that is being done in other communities to make a brief informal survey and then to
present a well-founded and practicable prospect of
possibilities to the people of the city or town, at regular meetings of men's clubs, women's clubs, parent-
teacher associations and the Chamber of Commerce,
or — in a small city or town — at a mass meeting.
Carefully edited newspaper accounts also help. The
mass meeting might be primarily for some other purpose, but before it is over there can be community
singing and discussion of the musical possibilities of
the community and how they might be fulfilled. Or it
might be a special meeting for the musical purpose
alone. The procedure at regular meetings of established organizations could be similar.

What is even more likely, the individual or group
whom we first found possessed of the urge has come
upon, or will gather, information regarding admirable
developments in other cities and towns. " If ———
can do this, why can't we? " will then be the question.
Then the group — perhaps it is the municipal recreation department,[5] the parent-teacher association, the
Board of Education, or a music club — might itself
invite the expert to make the brief survey and present
the possibilities. A more thorough and comprehensive
survey might then be desired and made under the
auspices of the community itself or of its representative and appropriate organizations, or immediate steps
might be taken toward carrying out those possibilities
in chorus, orchestra, band, festival, or other activities.

[5] It should be not merely an added service but a positive regular function of a recreation department to bring about some sort of music survey,
just as it should find out what play spaces are available in the city.

Time and Money for the Survey

Let us assume that sufficient interest has been aroused in having a more thorough survey and that a good, widely representative committee has been appointed to put it through. We have now to consider how much the survey will cost in time and money, and where and how a surveyor can be secured. The amount of time will, of course, depend on the size of the city, the diversity of its musical activities and its social and educational conditions, and on the degree of thoroughness desired. If a compact schedule of appointments has been made beforehand, a week may be enough time in which to gain a good working knowledge of the outstanding possibilities and needs in a moderate-sized community — even less time for a small city or town — but two weeks would, of course, be better, even for an informal survey. A formal, thoroughgoing study in a city of from 100,-000 to 500,000 people should be given at least three weeks or a month after all preparations have been made. The surveyor, experienced and capable in conducting many kinds of musical activities himself and in training others to do so, should have time allowed him for unpredictable needs in his survey, including, perhaps, informal experimental endeavors made by himself or under his supervision, with various groups. Furthermore, he should remain in the city long enough to supervise the first steps to be taken in carrying out his recommendations, and, if need be, to find and develop leaders for the various phases of the work that is to follow. Give him plenty of time.

The cost in money will depend on the time and extent of the study, the amount of printing of questionnaires, the amount of secretarial work, including tabulation of data, as well as the remuneration and travelling expenses of the surveyor and his assistants, if, as in a large city, he needs some. A group of local volunteers may make the survey, or a resident of the city — perhaps the public school supervisor of music — may be capable of acting as an expert music surveyor, either giving his services or charging little for them. If the school system of the city, or of one near-by, or the state university, has in its employ a person especially trained to conduct school or social surveys, the resident music surveyor or group might receive much help from him not only in gathering the facts but also in being fortified by the scientific, unassailable spirit of his help as against their own disadvantage as resident investigators.[6]

The obvious need to determine exactly what information should be sought and what questions should be asked is, we hope, provided for by the topics and discussion chosen for this book. Chapters II, III and IV should be especially helpful.

* * * * * *

Let us assume that a survey has been completed. What next?

Arousing Interest in the Results

With the completion of the survey the group which is working to weave music into the warp of community life, has only begun its work! The findings of the study — needs which have been brought to light, musical assets which the community has been found to have, recommendations for future developments — all these must be brought to the attention of the public. And here local newspapers can be powerful allies by publishing the findings of the study as well as stories

[6] Information with regard to securing the services of expert surveyors can be had from the National Recreation Association, 315 Fourth Avenue, New York City.

of what other communities are doing. Newspapers may also be counted on to help in such possible beginnings of community musical activities as a Learn-a-carol-a-day campaign at Christmas or Easter, a Music Week celebration, a music memory contest, or a music festival. Very often such an activity or a successful orchestra or choral group may lead to full and continuing provision for music in the community.

Always there must be a group of individuals acting as the leaven, the motive power, keeping the idea before the public and striving for permanent organization.

What Kind of Organization Shall We Have?

As we have pointed out, the organization adopted must be the outgrowth of the community's own conditions based on existing assets and community needs. In Chapter V we have discussed some of the types of community organization for music which are now operative in various cities. These include a community music association, a municipal department of public school and community music with the supervisor of music in the public schools serving as director, organizations resulting from a music festival, municipal departments of recreation that are promoting musical activities, a community arts association, a music week association, and a municipal bureau of music. There can be no standard kind of organization. In your community the best kind may be one or a combination of those described in Chapter V, or a very different kind may be desirable.

Relating the Schools to the Community

The need of providing opportunities for high school graduates to continue their participation in music is a good point at which to start. The most important need next to the provision of good leadership is likely to be for intelligently planned cooperation between school music leaders and those outside the schools. In some of our smaller cities and towns an effective plan would be to have a city director of music who would superintend the development of musical activities in the schools and in the community and direct the city's best chorus or orchestra or both.

Where there is a municipal recreation department — and such departments are increasingly taking responsibility for musical development — it might assume the place taken by the Community Music Association of Flint. The resulting plan would be somewhat as follows:

CITY DIRECTOR OF MUSIC [7]

In the Recreation Department

Conduct city chorus and *a cappella* choir
Conduct city symphony orchestra
Superintend work of a full-time
    Supervisor of vocal music [8]
    Supervisor of instrumental music [8]
Advise or supervise in the provision of summer band concerts
Advise or supervise in direction of junior symphony orchestra
    (This may be conducted by the director of instrumental music in the public schools, or by the concertmaster of the city orchestra — who may be this instrumental director in the schools.)

In the Public Schools

Conduct or supervise direction of
    All-city high school chorus
    All-city high school orchestra

[7] Responsible to an honorary music commission representative of the city government, the public schools, and the recreation department as well as of the city's best musically interested citizens.

[8] Only one full-time supervisor may be sufficient for both the vocal and instrumental music. He will provide and assist one or more full-time or part-time leaders, if any are needed, in addition to leading the various kinds of groups of his own. He is to the musical activities of playgrounds and recreation centers what a public school music supervisor is to the musical activities in the schools.

Superintend work of
  Supervisor of instrumental music
  Supervisor of vocal music and appreciation
Advise or supervise in the
  Providing of children's concerts, some of which may be
    given by the city symphony orchestra itself
Supervise planning and direction of choruses, orchestras, bands,
    chamber music, class lessons in instruments, and apprecia-
    tion courses, in evening schools
Superintend advisory and demonstration service for any out-
    side music leader or group wishing help. There may be
    leader-training institutes also.

In the Community

Provide encouragement and welcome every possible assistance for the commencement and maintenance of all such musical
endeavors mentioned in Chapter III as are feasible in homes,
churches, clubs, industries, foreign groups, institutions, etc.,
and in independent musical organizations (including glee clubs
and junior glee clubs) in the city; and to help as far as possible
in the provision of good, not too expensive music instruction by
private teachers, and, if possible, by a music school settlement
or community music school for children and others wishing to
continue study beyond what it is possible for the public schools
to provide.

Note: Much of the city director's supervisory and advisory
duties could be carried out through staff conferences and demonstrations, but he should occasionally observe directly the
work of each leader and of each kind of activity. The whole
instrumental staff of the schools should play in the city orchestra, and the vocal staff should sing in the community chorus,
each of these teachers acting as a " coach," if needed, in his
or her section of the orchestra or chorus.

Can Education and Recreation Join Hands?

Such a plan appears all the more feasible when one
can see how nearly alike the two agencies are in form
of organization, as the following description of the
duties of each member of a recreation department's
personnel will show:

The Superintendent of Recreation

In relative importance this position is similar to that of superintendent of schools. Its duties include the organization and administration of the recreation system; the selection, training and direction of play leaders; the purchasing and installing of apparatus and the laying out of playgrounds; the planning of buildings for recreation purposes and the securing of the use of the school buildings and other centers for use as community centers; the organization of neighborhood groups, cooperation with all community organizations, and the encouragement and development of recreation in the community. It is his task to see that holidays and special days are appropriately celebrated; that dramatics are developed; that community choruses, orchestras, and bands are organized; that all other suitable arts and crafts as well as physical games and sports are made available; and that new Americans are helped to become a part of the community. Finally he should lead in arousing and maintaining community interest and support for all this work.

Supervisor

This term is sometimes used to designate the worker directly in charge of all the playgrounds of a city, but it is also generally applied to the worker in charge of a special activity on the playgrounds or at the recreation centers, such as music, dramatics, athletics, folk-dancing, story-telling or handcraft. A recreation department supervisor, like a school supervisor, is responsible for organizing and supervising the special activities of his kind at each of the various centers, and for training leadership to carry them on.

Recreation Director

This is the name given the worker in charge of an individual playground or recreation center who, like a school principal, is in charge of the equipment and buildings at the individual center, and cooperates with the supervisors of special activities in seeing to it that the activities deemed advisable are carried out as well as possible by the play leaders and assistants.

The Play Leader and Assistant

These correspond to the classroom teacher and his or her assistant.

It is plain that so far as processes of administration are concerned there could be perfect unity for the director of music between his duties inside the schools and those outside the schools. If he is as broad-minded as anyone should be to be entrusted even with a single group of children or adults, he can achieve what is sadly lacking almost everywhere. That is, he can inter-relate school music and recreational music, bringing to one a working conception of what music may be in the leisure-time, self-propulsive life of all kinds of people, and to the recreational endeavors an equally work-able conception of how people grow in music. And if he is as finely musical as he should be, he will bring to both the tonic of beloved excellence, of what is in truth the amateur spirit which the professionals of the city may have lost or have kept hidden away. Each section of our fractional musical life tends to be carried to an absurd extreme, professional music becoming exotic, school music academic, and recreational music trivial. All hail, then, to the professionally skilled music lover who, through such a position as has been suggested, could make three thirds equal one, instead of three!

However, a suitable person to undertake the posi-tion of city music director may not be obtainable, or the policies or personnel of the schools or the recrea-tion department, may be contrary to the needs of such a plan. They frequently are. But even then a commis-sion such as is suggested in the plan (a small one will do) acting only as a discussion group under the chair-manship of a capable person who is not a musician, may be the best means of providing for the desired broader vision and mutual understanding of the school and the community music leaders, without endanger-ing the freedom of choice which each one prizes so highly.

Other plans for bringing the best obtainable leader-ship into effective service to people of all kinds and degrees of musical interest and ability may be suggested to the reader by study of Chapter VII. The size and the present musical development of the city, and especially the quality of leadership available, are, of course, the most important determining factors in working out a plan.

Lessons from a Musically Backward City

The need for capable leaders in any plan cannot be overemphasized. Consider the following abstracts from notes written in 1929 in connection with a brief survey of a city of about 60,000, of whom 25,000 are Negroes and about 15,000 are, as the writer was told, "mill people" (white), the latter a separate community:

MUSIC IN THE SCHOOLS

There is no music supervisor or systematic course in the elementary schools. Until four years ago there was a supervisor, an elderly woman who is said to have been incompetent. As a result of a need for money for a new building, both music and art were dropped from the curriculum. But two years ago, because of a demand made by the principal of the Girls' High School, a music course and a teacher were provided in that high school. The Boys' High School has no music except a band which is small and inferior. The lack of training in the elementary schools makes teaching in the Girls' High School difficult and not very productive. Of 850 girls only six girls have studied or are studying violin and only one of these is capable. There is one saxophone player, and many ukulele players. The music teacher has attempted to have a small orchestra but with little success. She has done nothing to capitalize the interest of ukulele playing. Almost every girl "takes music" outside, by which is meant piano lessons, but the principal says that not one of them plays well enough to play a march or a song accompaniment in school.

Reasons given for lack of music instruction in elementary schools, the Boys' High School, and the Junior College:

1. From the music teacher: Lack of interest.
2. From the High School principal: Politics. The superintendent is expected to keep the school budget as low as possible

and he is afraid to raise the issue of more expenditure for music. Last year a few members of the School Board asked that music in the Girls' High School be dropped for the sake of economy. The principal, whose wife is musical, fought this, speaking to the Board and writing editorials for the newspaper; and he won.

3. From the superintendent: He gave no reasons except economy, saying that several years ago the schools were spending more than their income but now, under his economy, the Board has a surplus to carry the schools through the lean months. I spoke briefly of the belief that modern conditions of labor, etc., require education for leisure, and asked him whether there was a trend in that direction in his city and others in that section of the country. He then spoke of the shop work for boys and sewing and cooking for girls, but agreed that these were vocational rather than avocational in spirit if not in intent. "This city is musical," he said. "The children study music outside the schools. And the movies take care of the leisure hours of the 15,000 mill people." I asked him whether he referred to "Synthetic Sin," the movie then being given at a leading theatre. He smiled. He knew of the failure of the two concert series given in the city, but offered no solution of the problem. He heard the National High School Orchestra at Dallas and thought it remarkable, but when asked whether music of that sort would not be valuable in his city, he referred to the band at the Boys' High School! When told about the piano teaching in the city, and asked whether it wasn't the business of the schools to help in every way possible to provide better standards of instruction in piano as well as in other kinds of music instruction, he said that as superintendent, he is the field agent of the schools, the intermediary between the schools and the people, and that he has not time to keep up with methods of teaching! "It's up to the supervisors to look after methods." (But he has no supervisor of music.) The arts depend upon individual impulses anyway, he said. The people who pursue an art as an avocation do so because of their own interest. The schools can do very little, if anything, to persuade children to cultivate an art as recreation. He supposed that most people listened only to jazz over the radio because that is what they want. When asked whether environment has not something to do with the pursuit of an art by any individual and whether the schools should not provide a suitable, adequate environment, he asked me again what my mission was and where I came

from. Being told again, he suggested that I see a local under-
taker who is in charge of the playgrounds.[9]

INSTRUCTION OUTSIDE THE SCHOOL

Almost every child of the more cultivated white families receives piano lessons. "Millions of dollars are wasted on such
lessons," said the High School Principal. There is no one to set
good standards.

There is a teacher of violin, also evidently inferior. There is
no cellist in the city and no trained teachers of other orchestra
and band instruments.

LISTENING

Two years ago a local music merchant organized a concert
series, expecting the cooperation of the Women's Club. Through
lack of understanding by the Club of their responsibility to purchase and sell tickets, and through lack of interest, the merchant lost $1100 in the venture. Last year a wealthy citizen un-
dertook the financing of another series, including Max Rosen,
Mary Lewis, and the Flonzaley Quartet. The audiences were so
small that he will not undertake another series. Mary Lewis
drew the largest audience. The local theatre manager explained
this failure as due to "too high-brow" music. So he engaged
Paul Whiteman's Jazz Orchestra. That, too, was a financial
failure.

CHURCH MUSIC

Methodist Sunday School

There are about 1000 members, including 150 in a men's
Bible class and about the same number in women's classes.
They are divided into seven groups which are never all together, for there is no place large enough. So each group has a
volunteer song leader and volunteer pianist. The children use
a hymn book containing many inferior tunes, with words correspondingly insipid. The adults use the Cokesbury Hymnal.
When asked why the church hymnal is not used by adults in
the church school, the lady in charge said that the hymns in the
Cokesbury book are brighter. People don't want in Sunday
school the solemn hymns used in church services. The leader
of the singing said that Sunday school hymns have to be " short
and snappy." " Do they have anything to do with religion? "
was asked. " The words are religious," he said, " and the tunes

[9] This discussion was entirely courteous and kindly.

mean whatever you take them to mean. 'Abide With Me' and
the other good hymns are all right for church, but not for Sunday school. They are too doleful." "Maybe they are sung too
dolefully," was said. "Oh, no, I pep them up."

Sale of Music and Instruments

The man who seems to be the most important music dealer
says that his sheet music sale had a severe drop a few years
ago and is only slight now. The radio may have caused this,
but most if not all of the sales of popular songs are now due
to the hearing of those songs over the radio. Piano sales are
rare, as are phonograph sales. People are turning in pianos and
phonographs in exchange for radios. The dealer said that this
is because the radio does not require any effort whatever,
whereas, you have to put on the records, change needles, and
wind up a phonograph. (A new automatic victrola is being
featured now.) Furthermore, people like the element of surprise in radio programs. You never know what is coming next,
and you don't need to choose.

Considerable piano teaching music is sold.

Factors Unfavorable to Music

1. The incompetent teaching of the former Supervisor of
Music in the elementary schools. This probably has given a
false impression of the place of music in schools.

2. Incompetent teaching and playing of the piano which,
again, gives no realization of what the best music is, and of the
delight possible in performing it well.

3. The plague of trivial hymns. The high school principal
says that church music in the city is " rotten."

4. Recreation has probably been sorely limited by the
churches with their prohibitions and lack of positive direction
in this regard, so that in the present age of greater need for
recreation and tremendously increased facilities for gaining one
or another sort of recreation, there is little or no power of choice
or initiative, no taste, no traditions, guiding the individual. Evidently the movies and the radio are for most people the sole
indoor means of recreation. A complete survey of recreation in
this and similar towns for many years dominated by such
churches might be very valuable.

5. The idea of paying for music of any kind or form, except
for piano lessons as a sign of "culture" for girls, is evidently
foreign to custom and interest.

Now what type of organization for music is needed in this city? It is obvious that what is chiefly needed is leadership. Even one good leader could be a Godsend,[10] though amidst the musical inertia and all the competitions of modern life — the " Synthetic Sins," automobiles, etc. — the support of a group or groups of influential citizens, as well as adequate financial and other assistance, would be extremely valuable, and probably indispensable, in clearing the way for his efforts and strengthening them.

The Power of Good Leadership

What may happen when the kindling musical spirit of even a single individual is set down in the midst of a community is impressively exemplified in Billings, Montana. A cellist of the Minneapolis Symphony Orchestra, being in poor health, resigned his position about nine years ago and came to Billings to live and teach. Being warmly disposed toward orchestra and chamber music, and there being no provision for developing players of such music, he taught violin, viola, and bass, as well as cello, and did so not only for individuals but also, later, for classes in the public schools. The sum of all these facts is now a well-balanced orchestra of 35 high school students; a " Ladies' Ensemble " (established in 1922) of 6 first violins, 6 second violins, a viola, cello, and bass, a flute and clarinet, a harmonium, harp and piano, which ensemble rehearses twice a week and gives at least one concert of excellent music each year, always including in the program one or two performances by a string quartet composed of its members, 180 pupils in public school classes in the various string instruments; and a goodly number of private pupils.

*   *   *   *   *   *

[10] The public school music supervisor might be this leader or else find and assist one or more actual or potential leaders in the mills.

Most impressive of all in this regard is the following report of a single year's work by an excellent musician, a young woman, who was commissioned by the Juilliard Musical Foundation to establish a music center in Atlanta, with the promised cooperation of musically interested people of that city. The report is here given exactly as it was written in the midst of great activity.

Appeared before:
  The Standard Club
  Atlanta Women's Club
  Atlanta Junior Music Club
  Atlanta Music Club
      (2 programs — lecture — recital — modern composers — Lieder)
  DeKalb County Teachers' Forum
  DeKalb County Parent-Teachers Ass'n — "Music as a necessity in Public School programs"
  Fulton County Parent-Teachers Ass'n — "Music as a necessity in Public School programs"
  Alliance Française
      (2 programs — old and modern French Song literature)
  Decatur Fine Arts Club
  Atlanta Rotary Club
  History Club — (Russian Song-literature)
  Griffith-Dobbs School of Music
  Morgan-Stephan School of Music
  West End Women's Club
  Quota Club
  Georgia Federation of Music Clubs Convention, Tifton, Ga.

Assisted Mr. Hudgeson at the University of Georgia for 10 weeks, on evening programs in Public Music Appreciation classes — also worked with the Glee Clubs.

Gave 20 opera lectures, in preparation for Opera Week — and 5 radio talks.

Gave 6 lecture-recital programs on Song Literature at WSB. These were very successful and will be continued in the fall.

Visited 7 Atlanta Schools and gave class instruction in tone work and diction at the request of the Supervisor. Lectured on "Class-room Singing" at the regular Teachers' Forum, and will appear at 2 Forum meetings next season.

Formed a Teachers' Forum for teachers from 35 rural schools in DeKalb County — where music has never been entered in the curriculum. Will continue this work next year, as it is most successful and there is a possibility of giving units for it.

Opened National Music Week Program — May 1st.

Visited the southern part of the state, and was successful in organizing 7 towns into the " South Georgia Music Festival Association " which presents its first May Festival at Albany, Ga. in a series of 4 concerts. Hope to start a " Students Concert Series " next year as these towns have had very little good music.

Cooperated with the Schubert Memorial Inc. in presenting their concerts.

To close the season — am holding a Memory Contest for the Schools in DeKalb County under my supervision, covering the work done in the Teachers' Forum.

My program for next year will be somewhat different and more definite.

Have chosen 5 Sub-centers in which to present talks on general Music Appreciation next season. Will appear once a month in each of these 5 places giving the same lecture and covering a period of 9 months, thereby making the work fairly consistent.

Will have an announcement column in each of the Sunday papers " Music Events of the Week " — in an effort to assist organizations presenting artists, and to give information concerning the Music Center and its activities.

Will give Music Appreciation talks twice a month in the Decatur Schools. This can be accomplished through assembly work, as there are 7 schools to be reached. The appropriation is now being raised for a regular supervisor, and it is hoped that one can be secured by May 1930.

Establish a music center? The young woman who made this report is herself the music center. Wherever she is, it is; which describes an indispensable characteristic of all real music centers. They are *persons*.

Quantity vs. Quality

Each person in a singing or playing group may also be a music center whose interest or enthusiasm, kindled by the leading music center, will in turn incite other persons to sing or play. Music organizers forget this. They wish to engage the whole community at once. Nothing less than hundreds or thousands of people to start with will interest them. By modern supersalesmanship you may succeed in getting a great community flare-up of a sort of musical interest, but unless you have also provided well for the perhaps small but steady and spreading light of real music centers — of *persons,* not crowds — you will soon find yourself in darkness. About two years ago the National Community Foundation employed two persons to supervise the organization and maintenance of social and cultural activities, including choruses, orchestras, and bands, under local leaders, in 29 towns with population ranging from 100 to 2662 in New Jersey, Delaware, Maryland, Pennsylvania, and Virginia. In addition to regional conferences held with delegates from the towns at the beginning and at the close of the year's work, the two supervisors visited each town about every three weeks. The following statement from the report of the Foundation bears directly on our question:

We have not undertaken to interest the whole community in anything cultural. It seems to us that such effort is unwise. The whole community must be stirred to insist on pure water, pure milk, etc., but for cultural matters the approach is the small group — even 3 or 4 people. Only persons with common interest are to be brought together. This makes for coherence and progress, and longer life for the activity. Communities must be won to this point of view, for they are accustomed to judge any activity by the number enrolled.

It is possible to interest the whole community, or most of it, when it is not too large. A festival may do so, and with superbly valuable results, especially when it is associated with so universal an interest as Christmas or, in agricultural communities, with a grange meeting, a county fair or the like. Provision of a wide variety of musical activities may go far toward doing so. The more people who can be interested, the better. The defense made by a certain community music association which has interested only a very small proportion of its people — that it is seeking quality, not quantity — is as sadly mistaken as the assertion of some other such organizations that they are seeking quantity, not quality. The place to seek quality is in every individual in the community who can be interested, which is to say every individual who can be led to do his own seeking, with whatever help is available and necessary. Confining one's efforts to a few choice ready-made music-lovers is a very near-sighted, wasteful seeking. Were our natural resources sought in that way, most of us would starve. What of our human resources?

No organization, however large or well-intended, can be substituted for the powers and devotion of one or more gifted leaders, and no organization plus any number of leaders can successfully substitute publicity, pep, and bigness for the genuine, lasting interest and satisfactions of Mary, John, and whoever else is led. But its purpose must be to provide for the best quality of *experience* attainable by each of as many individuals as can be interested.

CHAPTER VII

Leadership: Its Kinds, Methods, Sources, and Costs

A CHORUS in a southern city was directed by an expert musician with an attractive enough personality — a promising enterprise, but it failed because the warm blood of social feeling and loyalty was not in it. After nearly a year of rehearsals, the conductor knew scarcely a name among his singers. His only relation to the members was as instructor, and there was no one to cultivate a sense of fellowship among them. It lacked what may be called social leadership. In another city the writer attended a rehearsal of a community orchestra, then a few months old, at which nearly twenty-five minutes were spent in tuning and in distributing the music for the first piece. The conductor himself gave out the music amidst a great deal of chatter and inattention, and the tuning was equally disorderly. This orchestra lacked what may be called executive leadership, which sees to it that all the preliminary and extra-musical needs, including finances, attendance, equipment, and the general conduct of rehearsals and concerts are efficiently cared for.

A large proportion of the successful music leaders have in themselves these two kinds of leadership also, depending for the details of each on worthy, willing members of the group. Or the city recreation department, or whatever organization or institution the musical group is affiliated with, may take over the responsibility for much or all of its business or executive management, and perhaps even for much of its social life also. But music is itself so conducive to good fellowship that it must be a cold-blooded conductor who can deprive it of that power. And out of that fellowship will readily come other social activities, if there is need or desire for them, such as suppers, dances, and other "parties" that enhance it. We will confine ourselves now to musical leadership.

The Range of Musical Leadership

A glance at the lists of activities given in Chapter III will remind us of their very wide range, from the often careless and crude singing of some "community singing" groups to the fervent and superb singing of an *a cappella* choir, and from the harmonica playing of street urchins to an orchestra's excellent performance of a symphony. Can the leader of the highest be expected to lead the lowest, too, and all the kinds and degrees between? We say that the most valuable trait in a leader is the love and enthusiasm which he himself feels for the music. Can his love have so very wide a range? If it cannot, can he be successful beyond its limits? Music, especially to a musician worthy of leading a good chorus or orchestra, is so intimate and direct an expression of himself. Must he do himself the injury of being insincere when he leads a playground group of boisterous boys or an untrained group of adults? Let us refer to some actual experiences.

(1) In order to provide for a good amateur civic orchestra and a chorus, as well as playground music, in a southern city, an excellent musician experienced in conducting was engaged by that city's Recreation Department at a yearly salary of $5,000. But he apparently had no interest in, or talent for cultivating or supervising, the cultivation of any sort of musical activity suitable for any of the thousands of children and adults not in the orchestra or chorus. He was forced to resign.

(2) The superintendent of recreation in another city, who is himself an expert choral director, has provided for much community singing in community centers, parks, and on the streets

(in connection with a travelling theatre), but he will not lead any of this singing himself because as director of a women's chorus that has an honored place among the musicians of the city, and of a festival chorus of boys and girls that is honored in both the public and parochial schools of the city, he feels obliged to avoid being directly associated with any musical activity that is so much below the standards of the musicians and the schools. Not only his own reputation but also the reputation of his two choruses would suffer by such association.

(3) The conductor of one of the somewhat lesser of our twelve or thirteen great symphony orchestras is very much interested in education and would like himself to direct regularly an orchestra of high school graduates which some influential people of the city would be much interested in forming and sponsoring.[1] But he fears that it would dull the edge of the powers which the symphony orchestra requires in him.

These instances are sufficient to exemplify the three kinds of obstacles to a wide range in leadership. The first one, a lack of interest, was rightly condemned. The second one, a matter of reputation, must be respected, because the community singing in question — at least that in a street " sing " observed by the writer — was not of a high type. The third, a matter of energy and sensitivity, is also worthy of respect when it refers to persistent work with musically inferior groups. Even Knute Rockne could not have been expected to be the superb football coach he was if he had had in the midst of the season also to coach young " dubs " on playgrounds. Real, adequate conducting of great music involves tasks of intellect, eye, ear, and body, all coordinated in the often extremely sustained act of creative imagination that requires the freshest possible energy, insight, sensitiveness, and impeccable taste.

However — and this is a most important point — the best in music is not exclusive. It is natural and true to impulses fundamental in human nature. The es-

---

[1] This does not call for nearly so low a " drop " as we have been considering, but it serves well as an example in our consideration.

sential qualities that make a Brahms' symphony or the irrepressibly gay movements of Beethoven's " Seventh," or the devout Bach " B minor Mass " beautiful and worthy of the best possible leadership are to be found in the best music of each kind and degree of musical interest, even the lowest. For example, consider the hundreds of folk tunes, of every mood, including those used by Bach, Haydn, Beethoven, and Brahms themselves; the many universally lovable composed songs like " Who is Sylvia? " Brahms' " Der Schmied " and " Vergebliches Ständchen " (both translated) as well as his well-known " Lullaby," and not excluding modern popular songs as good as the best Victor Herbert ones and " Ole Man River "; an increasingly large supply of simple and delightful choral music like the old English " Come Again, Sweet Love " by Dowland, and our own Clokey's " Kye Song "; and no end of excellent lasting pieces and tunes for even the most elementary instrumental performers of all kinds. Can a city or any other organization outside of Tin Pan Alley afford to spend money for any musical activity that is persistently so coarse and cheapening that even a very social-minded music leader must shun it?

The most harmful obstacle to our musical progress has been the common idea that all music, musicians, and music-lovers are either high-brow or low-brow, classical or popular, and " never the twain shall meet." The next most harmful obstacle, a corollary of the first, has been the common idea that the best musicians and the best music well sung or played are for professional performances in concert halls and sometimes in schools, but not for any of the many occasions and places at which music is most needed.

The New Type of Community Music Leader

The radio broadcasting of excellent music everywhere, and the remarkable progress being made in school music reaching millions of the coming generation, are now making wise leadership by excellent musicians for all kinds and degrees of musical ability, in recreation as well as in education and in professional concerts, not only possible but necessary, unless we are to waste golden opportunities for the increasing number who can respond to such leadership. It is very pleasing, therefore, to see the superb musician, Ernest Schelling, at one of his orchestral concerts for children, leading a large assemblage of the children and their parents in singing " The Blue Bells of Scotland " or some other simple song, to read of community Christmas caroling on the Plaza in Philadelphia under the direction of the great conductor Stokowski, and to see some of our best musicians teaching or conducting at the National High School Orchestra and Band Camp, and acting as guest conductors of all-city high school orchestras. Most gratifying is it to picture the greatest of all, Bach, teaching boys in the St. Thomasschule in Leipzig to sing.

Plainly, a new type of community musical leader is needed in the community, one who combines professional expertness and good taste with the amateur spirit and a large breadth and depth of interest in people, and who will supervise many lesser musical activities in addition to directing the city's best chorus or orchestra or both.

Supervision

Supervision, referred to in the foregoing, is frequently brought about through inviting outstanding leaders from outside the city to hold institutes or to observe and give advice concerning various musical activities and the plans for them. In Philadelphia the Director of the Municipal Music Bureau has arranged for several such institutes, one of them eight weeks in length, to which teachers and leaders, together reaching thousands of people, were invited. This means of help, commonly used in all kinds of educational and recreational service, is most effective when the visiting leader actually demonstrates the leading of such groups as the students in his institute are expected to lead, and gives each of them opportunity to practice under his helpful supervision. It must be remembered that the chief purpose of supervision (or of an institute) is to develop powers of self-directive leadership in those being supervised. Merely telling people what to do may do more harm than good. The following recommendations made to the Playground Association of Philadelphia after a survey of possibilities in the community centers of that city in 1928, suggests a type of supervision (it might be adapted to an institute) that might be effective in the reader's own community:

Suggestions for Musical Endeavors in the Settlements and Other Recreation Centers of Philadelphia

1. That a musician with love and understanding of the best music, preferably one who plays the piano and sings freely and well, who has himself the true amateur spirit and the other qualities necessary to leadership of uncultivated groups, be engaged as supervisor of music in the settlements, recreation centers, playgrounds, and Smith Memorial playhouses of Philadelphia.

2. That he (possibly she) work intensively (with assistance, if necessary, in instrumental music groups) at starting and developing at Funfield Center whatever musical activities can be lastingly delightful to the various people who come or can be attracted to that Center. He will keep in mind not only the purely musical interests of people but also their interests in dramatics, holiday ob-

servances, and other activities at the Center in which singing or playing may be integrated. Any one or more of the following musical activities are now possible:

Informal group singing
Adults' chorus
Boys' glee club (ages about 13 to 18)
Girls' glee club (ages about 13 to 18)
Children's chorus (younger children)
Orchestra (adults and capable boys and girls)
Chamber music and less pretentious home-size instrumental groups
Harmonica band
Orchestra of fretted instruments
Concerts at the center, and
Preparation for listening to them and to other concerts, including Philadelphia Symphony Orchestra broadcasts

His work there, while being of the utmost value for the people of the center, should serve as a demonstration of the possibilities in other centers as well.

3. That, as far as possible, each settlement, playhouse and recreation center have one of its workers assigned either partly or entirely to developing one or more similar activities at his or her center, and that all such workers gather once or twice every week for two or three hours to discuss with the supervisor of recreational music the problems and possibilities of those activities and to learn suitable music for them. Much of the time of these meetings should be spent in actual singing and, if possible, playing of music to be used in the centers, and some of this performing should be directed by the workers themselves. Furthermore, provision should be made for periodical observation by each of the workers of the work being done at Funfield Center, and for occasional observation by the supervisor himself of activities at each other center, one or two evenings a week being kept free from Funfield for him for this purpose. He should be available for a limited number of special conferences or " practices " with workers in the mornings and early afternoon.

4. That the supervisor of recreational music keep informed by frequent observation as to what music children are singing or playing in the public and parochial schools,

for the purpose of helping to have school music, in so far as it should be, carried into life outside of the schools, and also for the purpose of discussing with the school music officials what the effects of the school music and of the outside recreational music are and what they might be. He should maintain very friendly but sincere and frank relations with the school music teachers, especially with the director of public school music.

5. That all the work suggested above be regarded as sufficient for a full time position. The supervisor should have leisure to study, plan, and re-plan. He should be a student as well as an executive. What he accomplishes and learns may be of great value not only to hundreds of people in Philadelphia, but also to people in many other cities and towns. He should receive a salary making possible for him a simple but full living free from financial cares. He should not have to seek extra employment to eke out a living.

Four kinds or phases of leadership have appeared in our discussion: namely, social, executive, the purely musical, and supervisory leadership. Such a discussion quite unavoidably touches upon qualities of leadership also. We shall now attend to the question of what qualities, skills, and methods are most to be desired in leaders in music.

* * * * * *

Qualities and Methods of Leaders

Obviously, a group leader should have health, a likeable and forceful personality, enthusiasm, skill, sympathetic understanding of people, alertness, confidence, devotion, dependability, patience — but not too much — a sense of humor, tact, and, above all, a character in his general life as well as in his musical loves and expression that is worthy of emulation.

A *music* leader should, of course, *know music*. He may know very little of it and yet succeed as a leader in community singing, but even in that his success will be greater if he has intelligently experienced to the full a great deal of the best music; and such experience is indispensable to a really successful conductor of a good chorus or orchestra. For music, like religion, is at best more than a profession; it is a *possession*. The " do as I say " sort of leadership is far from being enough. Indeed, a very large proportion of the leader's " saying " can only be done through gestures, postures and other still more subtle but strongly telling signs that depend almost entirely on his feelings and intuitions, on what he *is* at the moment. And these depend almost entirely on his past experiences, on his possessions in music and life. The chief purpose of conducting, like the minister's " leading in worship," is to put each individual in the fullest possession possible of his own capacity to feel and understand and to express himself; and that is done mainly through example or contagion. The trouble often is that professionalism in music, as in religion, tends toward a mere presenting or telling that exhibits the leader's knowledge and skill but does not bring the other fellow any nearer to possession of his own possible share of musical or religious power. Still more often the trouble is that the leader doesn't possess enough himself to be worth all the effort through which he puts himself and his followers.

We must observe some living leaders, not only hypothetical ones, but before doing so let us consider what a Committee (of outstanding recreation leaders) on Training and Experience in Community Recreation Work regard as the special qualifications needed by a director or supervisor of music in a recreation department:

Broad appreciation of recreational values of the many forms of music which have a place in the recreational life of the people, including the simple and sometimes crude forms of musical expression as well as the more highly technical forms; personal skills in one or more forms of musical activity, including especially piano and voice; ability to organize and direct musical groups, especially bands, orchestras and choruses.

Minimum Age: Cities under 100,000 — 23 years
100,000 to 500,000 — 25 years
over 500,000 — 25 years

Experience: Previous experience as a teacher of music or conductor of choruses, bands or orchestras.

Minimum experience in years:
Cities under 100,000 — 1 year
100,000 to 500,000 — 3 years
over 500,000 — 5 years

Education: Equivalent of university graduation with major in music and preparation for teaching.

The following questions included in a Cincinnati civic service examination devised in 1927 are indicative of other qualifications that recreation leaders have sought in music leaders:

EXAMINATION No. 3294
MUSICAL DIRECTOR

1. Outline a tentative plan of municipal provision for musical activities in a city.
2. List the existing organizations in Cincinnati which might be expected to assist in such a plan, and state what should normally be the contribution of each.
3. What is the value of music as a leisure time activity? Explain briefly — not more than 250 words.
4. Is community singing an end in itself, or may it lead to other phases whose values are equally if not more important in cultivating musical appreciation and citizenship?
5. (a) Name five characteristics you consider necessary in a good community song leader.
   (b) Name ten songs best suited to the average adult community group.
   (c) Name the keys in which they should be sung.
   (d) Name three rounds that are adapted to the average adult community group for community singing.
   (e) Name three play songs that are adapted to the average mixed group (children and adults).
   (f) Name three singing games that are adapted to children under the age of 12.

6. Given an average community where interest is expressed in regular choral singing, name chronologically the steps you would take to organize a community chorus.
7. Name four group musical activities that are adapted to playground use.
8. Name three city-wide musical events that would foster musical appreciation among the people.
9. Name the successive steps you would take in organizing a glee club in parent-teacher associations.
10. Give two reasons why community singing with the foreign born has citizenship values.
11. (a) What is the value of volunteer leadership in community musical activities?
    (b) Describe briefly how you would interest and train volunteer leaders.

Evidently, a chief requirement of the music leader is a broad vision of the many various musical possibilities in a community, and another chief one is that insight, foresight, and firm grasp of details by which he is enabled to plan and start a musical enterprise, taking it step by step from its beginning to its fruition. Many a finely intended enterprise has failed because it was not timed correctly — like a child forced to do long division before learning the "tables" or kept at "tables" when he should be going beyond them.

The Community Song Leader

The foregoing questions also show the importance given to community singing in recreational music. The community music leader of whatever sort is very likely to be confronted again and again by opportunity to lead in this informal kind of singing — at luncheons, banquets, socials, club meetings, conventions, band concerts, and other occasions.

The social qualities of sincere good will, enthusiasm, personality, and humor are so important in this leading that the musician without any one of them is likely to be less successful in it than the musically untrained person who has them all and is able to sing accurately, freely, and dominantly enough to be a stimulating model. But, of course, the better he sings and the more musical he is, the better model he will be, and the more satisfaction will the people have. Furthermore, he should know by heart many songs of all kinds, including rounds and such others as are most likely to free the group from the inhibitions of formality and shyness.

But endeavors to bring about this freedom are often misdirected. Who has not seen the " pep " leaders who in an honest endeavor to arouse as much energy as possible in the people, make a show of a great deal in themselves that is trumped up and artificial? It elicits only the same kind of pseudo-enthusiasm in the singers. " Sing out! " the leader yells, and the singers sing themselves out of the song. The energy needed is that which can be generated by music itself, if it is given a good chance. Let the song itself — born as it was, or should have been, of the fullest sort of real enthusiasm — carry the leader most winningly into his job. The scientists know, by actual experiment, that the mere presence of attractive music produces an increased flow of energy in the individual. *Why assume the attitude of a pugilist or a football coach?*

Related to this mistaken attitude is the sort of time-beating in which each tone of the tune is poked at, and also the sort in which the conventional notions of conducting — down and up for two beats; down, out, and up for three; down, in, out, and up for four; and so on — are carried out stiffly and mechanically. The most freeing thing in the world is rhythm, in which we feel the flow of time, like a deep current, carrying us along, and in which the single tones of the tune compose a line, not a series of points to be poked at. Sometimes single tones need emphasis,

which is signified through an appropriate extra motion for each one by the leader, but even then the
flow of the rhythm is maintained through the manner of his motions, felt as a whole. He is always indicating the progression of the music through each
phrase, and from phrase to phrase. Music is always
going somewhere, until it comes to a closing cadence.
So the conventional motions given freely and, in
a simple sense, expressively, always in keeping with
the character of the music, are the best. Of course,
no amount of mere description can teach one to beat
time effectively, any more than swimming can be
taught so. There are other analogies, as to coordination and balance, between conducting and swimming.

Another quality of leadership implied in the foregoing paragraph is a combination of imagination and
sensitiveness — the ability to " feel into " the mood or
possible and desirable mood of the singers, likewise
to feel into the mood of each song, and similarly to
be fully conscious of the emotional needs and possibilities of the total situation at a given moment. The
last of these three abilities was indicated by the lack
of it when, after a very inspiring address that left at
least one of its hearers in a fine, lofty mood, a song
leader chose the song " Smiles " !

It is interesting to try to determine to what extent
the success of a community sing is dependent on the
leader's actions and remarks. Apparently the main
basis for the high opinion in which some song leaders
have been held has been their funny antics and remarks or their phenomenal show of energy. That is,
the singing is a minor part of the show in which the
leader is the star actor. Now there is, of course, nothing wrong in enjoying such a show. As we have said
before, a little fooling with music, especially if it is
foolish music, may be a very wholesome and pleasurable thing; and it may through skillful leadership be

followed by fine singing of great songs. But it is the singing itself that we have in mind when we speak of the value of community singing; and that value is to be estimated not alone by what happens at the sing, but also by what each individual takes away with him and may live on, so to speak, when the leader is not present. Some of the best community singing observed in a two-year jaunt around the country was carried on with the leader at the piano, merely singing and playing with all the love and delight that is expected of the group — this, of course, being less effective for large than for small groups.

In any event, the leader in community singing ought to let the song itself go as far as it can in doing the trick. There is a lyrical strain in most people, perhaps in all, as old as the race but covered over with the many concerns and cultivations of a more and more complicated and materialistic world. Reach that strain — like a lost river — and the people will sing for hours, as the simple farm folk of European countries do, and our unspoiled Negroes do, without wearying, and go home refreshed in body and spirit — recreated.

Conduct of Rehearsals

Now let us observe some of the more formal endeavors of music leaders, in organized choruses, orchestras and bands. First of all, there are attendance, distribution of music, and other introductory matters to be attended to. Attend a rehearsal of a national or any other high school orchestra under Mr. Joseph E. Maddy who with remarkable effectiveness and amazing simplicity has organized and led more orchestras than anyone else ever has done. Mr. Maddy's own account[2] of the initial processes of such a re-

[2] From "All-State, County, and City High School Orchestras," by Joseph E. Maddy. Published by the National Bureau for the Advancement

hearsal is as clear and effective as the processes themselves:

ATTENDANCE

Calling the roll is past history as far as orchestras are concerned. Armed with a seating chart with removable cards on which appear the names of the players, any member of the orchestra or each section-head can take the attendance in a few minutes, turning the cards of the absent players, to be listed in the classbook after the rehearsal by the director or librarian. These charts may be purchased from the Board of Education, Minneapolis, Minnesota, at a nominal fee.

Attendance should be taken one minute before the rehearsal begins, all the players being required to be in their places five minutes before time for the rehearsal to begin. The tuning bar is struck five minutes before the rehearsal starts and this time is spent in tuning.

At the moment for the rehearsal to begin, the players move forward, filling up all vacant chairs in front of them. Tardy players take the rear seats, unless excused by the director. The director must not be lenient in this matter or the morale of the entire group will suffer. The person taking the attendance changes the cards when the players move up and this promotion stands.[3]

START AND STOP ON TIME

The leader who starts one minute late will find the players two minutes late the next rehearsal, and so on. Running overtime is an admission of weakness and an injustice to the players who have other calls upon their time. One hour's rehearsal containing sixty minutes of actual rehearsing with the full group will accomplish wonders. It is not fair to the group to spend as much as five minutes of the full rehearsal drilling one section or a few players.[4] The leader must keep in mind that every minute he wastes must be multiplied by the number of people in the orchestra. The conductor who talks five minutes to an orchestra of 200 players has talked away 1,000 minutes of time.

---

of Music with the cooperation of the Juilliard School of Music. (Quoted with the kind permission of the publisher.)

[3] The promotion in rank (shown by order of seating) stands until the next try-out for rank. Where there are no try-outs for rank, the promotion may stand only through the rehearsal. But other disciplinary measures may be decided upon as regulations by the group as a whole.

[4] Special sectional rehearsals are held for this orchestra.

TIME SAVING

A blackboard placed so it can be seen by all of the players is a most valuable asset if used properly. It should contain the rehearsal program and all announcements that are necessary. When a blackboard is used the director should never call the numbers or repeat the announcements. The players will never look at the blackboard if the announcements are made verbally in addition. Teach them to get their directions from the board, always.

DISCIPLINE

There is no more difficult group to discipline than an orchestra and the larger the orchestra the more difficult the task, for every player holds a noise-maker which is likely to " go off " at any moment. This difficulty is reduced to a minimum if the following rule is rigidly adhered to: *Perfect silence when anyone is on the conductor platform.* If this is done at the first rehearsal it will not be necessary again, providing the conductor keeps off the platform except when silence and perfect attention is needed. It is always necessary to drill the players on this rule until they hush instantly when the conductor or anyone else steps upon the platform. Whenever the players begin to get lax it is only necessary to say, " Too slow," step down, and try again. This reminds them of their carelessness and they are most anxious to improve.

This form of discipline may seem irksome to some teachers, but it is exactly what the young players relish most, for by means of perfect attention they accomplish many times as much as without it and there is no joy like the joy of accomplishment. Likewise there is no disciplinary trouble in any group which is kept busy and interested all of the time.

TUNING

Tuning means tuning, not practising. The way to tune correctly is to tune softly. Orchestras usually begin softly and increase until bedlam ensues and tuning is impossible. Here is the National High School Orchestra's tuning routine: (1) Concertmaster stands and sounds A by striking the tuning bar. (2) Violins, violas, and cellos tune softly, drawing the bow full length on two strings simultaneously. (3) Violins, violas and cellos stop while basses tune, using harmonic unisons, the usual way. (4) Concertmaster, still standing, sounds A again and first oboe player stands and remains standing while the woodwinds and horns tune; then sits. (5) Concertmaster sounds A again and first trumpet player stands and remains standing while the brass and timpani tune. When the trumpets have tuned the first trumpet player sounds B flat (C for B flat trumpet) and trombones and tuba tune to this tone then the tuba gives the proper tones for the timpani player if necessary. (6) When the timpani are tuned the first trumpet player sits; the concertmaster sits; the conductor steps upon the platform and the rehearsal begins instantly without a word.

It is difficult to keep the wind players quiet while the strings tune and vice versa. It is less difficult if the players are taught to tune quickly and softly, and to *stop the instant they have tuned*. The tuning of the entire orchestra should not take more than two minutes.

Position of Players

The playing position of orchestra players is very important — and almost never good. The wind players should sit so they can use their back rib muscles in breathing and string players must sit so their shoulder blades do not touch the backs of their chairs. It requires constant vigilance to maintain correct playing position.

Librarian

The music should be passed out, in folios, at least fifteen minutes before each rehearsal and the librarian should keep a close check on every sheet of music at all times.[5] Probably the best and most efficient music library system in America is that developed by the University of Illinois Band. It was borrowed bodily and put into effect at the National High School Orchestra and Band Camp. An empty manilla folder, slightly smaller than the folio, is placed inside each folio. When a player wants to take the music home for practice he merely dates and signs the folder, takes the folio and leaves the folder on the stand. (He is not permitted to take any music from the folio but must take the entire folio or none.) The librarian collects the folder and places in it any additional music which may be passed out between rehearsals. The folio is returned to the librarian at least 15 minutes before the next rehearsal; the librarian date-stamps the folder, replaces it in the folio, and passes out the folio as usual. If any music is missing from the

---

[5] Special folios, designed for the National H. S. Orchestra, are obtainable from the Educational Music Bureau, Chicago.

folio it is charged to the player who had it out. This takes practically no time and keeps the music in excellent order.

The following form appears on the folder:

LIBRARY FOLDER

Part .... No.........................

Rack...................................

.............................Folio

I, the undersigned, do hereby agree to take full responsibility for the return of the music and folio from which this folder was taken, to the library desk at least 15 minutes before the next rehearsal

Date Taken Out	Name	Date Returned

Now some of the disciplinary injunctions and regulations given by Mr. Maddy would have to be modified for an adult amateur group, and perhaps even for a group of boys and girls that is unattached to a school. But there is no reason, except a lack of orderliness and self-discipline in the conductor himself, why all the effects of discipline obtained in the National High School Orchestra should not be obtained as well by a recreational musical organization. It must be remembered that the purpose of such discipline is freedom, freedom to sing or play without distraction, without waste of time, and with the utmost effectiveness and satisfaction. There is in such orderliness and economy of effort an enjoyable kinship to the same qualities in excellent music. It is one sort of craftsmanship, or of "playing the game" of which every

member is capable, no matter how poorly he sings
or plays, and once inured to it, he will himself be offended by a violation of it. But observe a rehearsal of
the Bethlehem Bach Choir, as described in the following comment:

> Now, the discipline of the Bach Choir is different in kind
> from that of a company of soldiers or even of a professional
> orchestra. Before rehearsals and after, and during the brief
> intermissions between choruses, the singers relax into laughter
> and chatting — yea, gossip. Dr. Wolle himself contributes many
> an atrocious pun. His talks to the Choir have a delightfully
> cheery tone — a kind of vocal handclasp for every one. When
> later his words of reproof leap forth, lapsing singers know the
> utterly impersonal intent and they are not offended. Similarly,
> because no element of friendship could extort it, his praise for
> work well done is intoxicating.[6]

The value of discipline depends very largely on its
spirit. Its regulations and methods should as far as
possible be the result of unanimous agreement and of
initiative on the part of the members, determined upon
after free, thoughtful discussion by them. And they
should be carried out with zest, not with solemn vir-
tuousness.

In this respect music is a sport. The notation of
pitch, rhythm, phrasing, and dynamics; the conductor's notions; and the total effect of the quantity and
quality of sound into which the individual must fit his
own contribution: all these are to be observed with
eyes and ears both (the rhythm urging him on) as
alertly as ever a man watched a ball in tennis or hand-
ball. The best of sports it is, of the spirit as well as of
mind and body.

Getting into the Music

But we now have only the framework. What will
be put into it? Music! Here is an orchestra or chorus

---

[6] From "The Bethlehem Bach Choir," by Raymond Walters —
Houghton Mifflin Co. — Riverside Press, Cambridge, 1923.

confronted by a composition new to its members. They commence the first phrase, but they are stopped, because a trumpeter played a wrong note or the sopranos left off a " t." They commence again. They may this time be allowed to finish that first phrase, though under many a conductor this would scarcely be possible. There may be a month or two of rehearsals before, if ever, any member attains anything like a feeling for the whole composition, as music; and by that time the meaning and glow of many a fine phrase may have been dulled or destroyed. The leader should bring the performers to the heart of the music by the most direct way in the very beginning, overlooking for the time being such errors as do not mar the total effect too severely. Or if it is a large work, he should deal so with enough of it to make the rehearsals of details musically significant and inspiriting. Probably most of the errors made the first time through will be corrected by the performers themselves the second time.

Depend on their intelligence so that they will use it. " Teachers should teach less and let the children learn more," said the wise Comenius. So should conductors — with adults. Have especially significant portions or all of the music played for them beforehand, if necessary, and then start " climbing through the briers," [7] commencing, perhaps, as Dr. Wolle of the Bethlehem Bach Choir does, with the last phrase and working backward, thus often, even in the first rehearsal, reaching a satisfying cadence. Anyway, begin with a feeling for the music and then work outward (or upward) from that. And still expect intelligence from the performers.

It must be remembered, however, that good musical performance and musical experience require freedom and serenity of spirit, and time and some guid-

[7] Cf. page 45.

ance for the performers to grow in understanding of it. Though a maximum proportion of the time of the rehearsal must be given to actual singing or playing, the conductor's value will be very much enhanced by an ability to speak well, to present in brief, telling remarks such ideas as escape the notation and his baton, gestures and facial expressions. Whether he has such ability or not, he should be able to sing or play well enough himself to say what he means through demonstration, when that is necessary.

Contrary Methods

Unfortunately for the ideas just set forth, there are some conductors who are apparently very successful though their methods are entirely contrary. For instance, the leader of a civic symphony orchestra of 65 unpaid players in a southern city, their ages from 16 to 60, conducts rehearsals mainly through shouted warnings and criticisms, the latter the harshest heard by the writer anywhere. Yet though in addition to this inefficiency and harshness he subjects those men and women to two rehearsals a week, outside study of the music, tests of individuals called for without warning during rehearsals, and does not provide any social life for them outside of the playing, they are faithful in attendance, and many of them have been so since the formation of the orchestra six years ago. It must be said that the playing was quite coarse, sounding somewhat like the conductor's voice. But it is the city's orchestra, sufficiently though not generously supported at its concerts. The most important explanation of its success is the fact that most of the players are or have been pupils of the conductor, who is a violin teacher and capable of teaching other instruments also; and he labors with utmost diligence and effectiveness to make players of his pupils. Many, possibly inclined to be even less energetic in study than are most young people in northern cities, have arrived at praiseworthy achievements under his mental lashings and infinite helpfulness, and that has given them a self-respect that is proof against the harsh criticisms, and a respect for work that welcomes the arduous and frequent rehearsing. Here again is the joy of achievement. Almost everyone wishes that he could be more accomplished than he is, be it in football, bridge, music, or in some other interest. And whoever can make him strive sufficiently to reach the goal, will win his loyalty, even though the method be a harsh one.

But, the question is not under what conditions, however bad they are, a group can be kept going and made to accomplish things, but what conditions can be brought about that will make it possible for the singers or players to attain the richest experience of which they are capable. There is altogether too much dependence on the idea that "leaders are born, not made."

Of the methods or lack of methods of leadership that are evidently mistaken, the following are the most common ones:

(1) *Temperament or affectation, which is it?* A chorus leader in one city makes himself appear extremely sensitive, with frequent grimaces, remarks, and stroking of his forehead showing how very deeply he feels the music and how very trying is the task of a genius to cultivate the ordinary people of a chorus. And when they achieve something that pleases him, his praise is honey sweet and extravagant. From petulance to flattery, he is a "show" all by himself; and the whole enterprise seems centered in helping him stage himself. A leader should feel deeply, when the music warrants it, and when he does he may at times be extraordinarily demonstrative, but if it is mainly himself he feels, not the music, he is out of place among amateurs.

"In such a climax as the 'Superbos mente' in the 'Magnificat,'" said a newspaper critic who had sat on the choir platform at a Bethlehem Bach Festival, "his (Dr. Wolle's) face is a map of fighting emotions, his eyes support the ancient Baconian superstition of actual 'ejaculations,' his whole being vibrates. . . .

. . . It is a leadership men and women are bound to follow

with all their might, if they have an interest in life superior
to the material phases." This sort of leadership is from an ordinary point of view strangely demonstrative, but it is utterly
sincere and self-forgetful, as all musical leadership should be.

(2) *Poor seating, balance, or acoustics.* The writer has sung
among the basses of many a chorus at whose rehearsal he could
hear very little or nothing of any part except the bass part. The
conductor could probably hear all the parts, and at a concert
the audience probably will also, but the experience of the singers
(or the players), especially in an amateur group, is, of course,
the most important consideration. How many of the very large
number of choruses that disband after a year or less would be
flourishing now if the members could have had the intense
pleasure of hearing their respective parts blended into the
whole?

(3) *Anti-musical gestures and remarks.* A chorus practicing
the Praetorius "Lo, how a rose e'er blooming" was yelled at
many times in a coarse, rasping voice whose owner's motions
were those of a pugilist. He thereby forced the chorus into the
very soft singing he wanted. His powers in developing wonderfully controlled *a cappella* singing, especially among high school
boys and girls, has made him famous. But here again, is there
not a great distinction between getting things accomplished
and attaining a true conception and experience of the music?
Excellence is the goal, but excellence in feeling and thinking as
well as in performance. Many leaders would profit much from
a thorough-going physical culture (not calisthenics) like the
Dalcroze Eurythmics, and practice in speaking impressively
and yet quietly and sincerely.

(4) *Lack of sympathetic understanding.* A chorus which had
been getting on well under a public school music supervisor
commissioned to prepare it to participate in a concert of one
of our great symphony orchestras, was turned over to the orchestra conductor. Accustomed to professional players, he expected the chorus to give him whatever he demanded of it. He
did not start where they were in interest, insight, and skill, and
lead them forward from there. This requires another sort of
imagination, an ability to put oneself in the place of the singers
or players in front of one. The chorus was soon disbanded.

"Start Where They Are"

This last need — to start where the people are, and
to continue to be where they are as they go forward —
which is a fundamental one, is frequently urged with

regard to the quality of music to be used. Let us observe a few instances of effective dealing with it:

1. When the present director of instrumental music in the public schools of Ottawa, Kansas, started his work there, the members of the then small high school orchestra wanted to play only jazz. He agreed, but every note had to be correct and handsome. In the process of refining the jazz, the boys and girls heard themselves making sounds of such admirable quality as they had never fully heard before. From such quality of performance to quality of music more worthy of it was a natural step for them.

2. Here are some notes written after a visit in one of the Smith Memorial Society Social Centers in the poorest section of Philadelphia:

A MOTHERS' CLUB

About 35 mothers attended a weekly meeting, their ages ranging from 25 to 80, almost all of them Irish. They were laughing, fooling, and displaying funny prizes won at some game they had been playing. Quite suddenly they swung as merrily as could be into "We've got a new pig in the parlor," not in the least abashed by a male stranger escorted by the head worker of the center. Then as suddenly they formed for "Three deep," which they played amidst shrieks of laughter. The head worker invited them and me to have some singing. Some copies of the "Twice 55" Brown Book were there. They chose "When you and I were young, Maggie" and then "Onward, Christian Soldiers," each sung very loudly and shrilly.

But these women are Irish, inheritors of some of the most beautiful folk songs in the world. "Do you know this one?" I asked, and played for fun "The Irish Washerwoman," which set them all a-laughing and clapping the rhythm, while the oldest lady there (80 years old) stepped to the middle of the room and jigged. Then she sang a long humorous Irish song, the rest joining heartily in the chorus.

"Do you know this one?" This time I played the "Londonderry Air," quietly and as well as I could. Evidently most knew it. Some hummed along. It's quiet they were for that one. It was not in the book and no one knew the words. But "Believe me, if all those endearing young charms" is very near to it in spirit. They sang this with remarkably pleasing quality. Then someone asked for " If a body meet a body." It started quite well, but it soon became shrill and loud. However, I played it still more softly then, though with evident animation. Missing the sound of the piano, more and more of them quieted to listen. At the close of the second stanza I half-humorously spoke of the Scottish lassie's secrecy ("But what's his name . . . I dinna choose to tell") and incidentally sang the third stanza through in that spirit, not overlooking the climax and the changes in tempo in the refrain, which had not been felt by them at all before. Their own singing of it was then very gratifying. " Drink to me only with thine eyes " was just above " If a body " in the book. We closed with it, giving an unintended victory to the British, but also to the inherently musical natures of the Irish.

3. A student at the National Recreation School was placed in charge of a group of " rough-neck " Italian boys in a settlement on the lower east side of New York. His efforts to get them to sing resulted only in the worst sort of yowling of popular songs, sometimes accompanied by cat calls and the like. But he was able to interest them in forming a club, a sort of social club, meeting three times a week for various activities, including play in the gymnasium and listening to stories of adventure. Such a club should have songs of its own, the leader suggested. They started with the good, hearty " We're all together again " borrowed by scout organizations in this country from the British Boy Scouts. Then came the Cornell Alma Mater Song — a college song if you please — with the words changed to fit the club. This song of sentiment needs, of course, to be sung quietly though fervently, which need even these boys could appreciate. Other good songs have found a place, including some sailor chanties which the leader said were sung by the very sailors who took part in the adventures of the sea of which he tells.

4. A Rotary Club in a mid-western city, whose members were accustomed to a meaningless but free

sort of singing, mostly of trivial songs, admitted to their membership a man who is a professor of music in the state university in that city. Having no official song leader they asked him to take that position. His first task was to preserve, despite the leadership of a professor, the freedom with which they had been singing. He was able to do this and to get some pretty good singing of the best folk songs they knew. But the time was always short and the interest was not great enough to lift the singing to a level on which it would have been very interesting. So at one of the meetings the leader asked each of eight men whom he had chosen for their voices, to stay a little while after the meeting. They then had their first rehearsal as a Double Quartet singing " Sailing " and " Carry Me Back to Old Virginny " in the four parts, the melody of each being familiar to the Club. After three more such meetings, the last one just before the other club members arrived, they sang the two songs to the surprise and great enjoyment of the members. The Double Quartet became a small Glee Club. But the leader's main purpose was different. He had the chosen singers seated where each could be most helpful, and the whole Rotary Club sang in parts now and then. The most important result was an increased interest in singing well. The sense of craftsmanship, however simple, was developed. Even in the unison singing there was better sportsmanship, more zest and more meaning.

There are many other instances, but these will do to exemplify the following ideas:

A. Get people to realize the delight of singing or playing well by leading them through their own interests into doing so. Surprise them with it. Don't preach. (Cf. Examples 1 and 2.

B. The central need in getting anywhere from where you are, in anything, is, of course, striving of some sort. Striving is first of all an attitude. Obtain the attitude. The best way is through a love for the better music or better performance, and that must enter the enterprise sooner or

later or else the main source of delight will be lost. But
lacking that, arouse interest in some related form of
excellence. Any of the various means of orderliness
suggested earlier in this chapter may be effective. Memorizing the music to be sung is another means for a
chorus. The success for 13 years of a large chorus in a
western city is evidently largely due to the excellent
procedure of its rehearsals and to the striving and sense
of achievement involved in the requirement that all
music for concerts must be memorized. Striving for excellence of any sort is a tonic. (Cf. again Example 1.)

C. Bring about moments of quiet listening, of contemplation.
A good, informally presented performance of good
music, simple and universal in spirit, will arouse a feeling of beauty in almost anyone. In this mood a group
otherwise careless and unresponsive is likely to sing or
play better than any amount of mere coercion could
have made them do. Usually this mood is most readily
attained after a period of animated singing or playing.
(Cf. Example 2.)

D. Provide real motives for the better music or performance,
as did the student leader referred to in the third example. This is an especially valuable way.[8] One of
these motives is group feeling, a pooled self-respect.

E. A model of admirable performance given to a group for
its pleasure, without any preaching, by a few of its own
members, as in the fourth example, is likely to give the
other members, too, a stimulating sense of fine possibilities. A whole group may do this for other groups of
the same kind. A famous example of this is the effect
that the splendid singing of the best music by the Harvard Glee Club has had on the singing of many other
college glee clubs. There are other examples on every
level of musical interest and ability.

F. Another idea not represented in any of the examples given
is with regard to the importance of environment in
bringing about growth. The atmosphere of some places
makes them more conducive to the realization of fine
feeling than others are. This may account in part for
the kind of songs and singing that often occur in hotel
dining rooms. Meet in a lovely home, a tastefully
planned room in a community center, a public library,

[8] Compare what was said about holidays, festivals, etc. on pages 75–77.

an art museum, or in any other place where a person may be reminded of the best that's in him, without feeling constrained.[9]

Plainly, "*Start where they are*" is important advice, and it requires a large breadth as well as depth and height of musical taste on the part of the leader. Unfortunately, with very few exceptions the leaders of musically backward groups have not this requirement. Wherever there was such a group, the writer took especial care to engage the leader in an informal chat about music and particularly about compositions and collections known to musicians as suitable for such a group as his. Most of these leaders were ignorant of this music. For instance, having been asked by a leader to say a few words to his church choir after a rehearsal of some trivial music, the writer told, among other things, of the promise shown by the Flint High School *a cappella* Choir and by the choir referred to on page 28 in this book. Simple mention of the Bach chorales and other models of church music brought from the leader, "What are these numbers you're talking about?" There is a good deal of supposed starting where they are that is really a starting where the leader is, with no place to go — unless the leader himself by eager striving progresses in a good direction while trying to lead others to do so.

* * * * * *

Long Life and Loyalty

To continue is more difficult than to start. The main factors on which it depends have already been

---

[9] Miss Edith Rhetts, whose faith and good work have brought thousands of children voluntarily from all sorts of environments to listen to the Detroit Symphony Orchestra in the handsome Orchestra Hall, has told of " a dirty and very sad-faced little lad " who at the close of the Andante of Beethoven's Fifth Symphony sighed, " Gee, that just makes me feel like I was rich! "

amply discussed in this and other chapters. The feeling
of loyalty to the group and to the leader is another
very valuable factor. Fortunate is the group that has
a nucleus, however small, of unfailingly devoted members. Their example to the other members is invaluable, for the talent of faithfulness is in many people
frail.

At the 25th Anniversary Concert of the Salt Lake
City Orpheus Club, one of the charter members was
able to say of three other charter members, " I am
convinced beyond doubt that but for the unfaltering,
never-ending patience and energy of these men, we
would not tonight be celebrating the 25th anniversary. . . ." A large percentage of the Bethlehem Choir
have taken part in all the festivals since 1912. In the
Cincinnati Orpheus Club fifty per cent of the men
have been members for ten years or more, one member
having a record of 36 years. One charter member of
the Bangor Symphony Orchestra, started in 1896, is
a business man whose work sometimes takes him to
Boston. He has on some Sundays gone to Bangor,
about 250 miles away, just to attend the weekly rehearsals on those days, though he had to be in Boston
again the next day. The new members coming into an
organization blessed with such loyalty are likely to
inherit not only the opportunity to sing or play, but
also the loyalty of its older members.[10]

[10] Following are the attendance records of a number of men's glee
clubs affiliated with the Associated Glee Clubs of America:

Number of clubs reporting	Number of members	Average percentage of year's attendance at rehearsals
6	16 to 20	88
25	20 to 30	83
27	30 to 40	79
23	40 to 50	77
24	50 to 60	80
19	60 to 75	78
14	75 to 100	79
6	100 to 180	74

21 clubs have an attendance record of from 90% to 100%.

The leader should make it part of his business to cultivate such loyalty. The payment of dues may add to a member's incentive to be regular in attendance, especially when the resulting fund is used partly or entirely to defray expenses of social affairs for the members. In the San Francisco Municipal Chorus, a model of good spirit, a charge of 25 cents a month is made for this purpose. And rules of attendance, sometimes, perhaps, accompanied by coveted recognition for good records of regularity, are likely to help. But after all, loyalty is largely due to contagion, starting with the leader himself. There will be times when he and the members will have their loyalty tested by needs for extra rehearsals or for attendance under difficulties. Let his own response to the test be a model, and let him have gathered about him a group of officers or ordinary members whose response is equally exemplary. But let him beware of asking for more time, energy or sacrifice from the members than their regard for the organization can stand. A show of disloyalty should be avoided as a plague.

The leader's loyalty to the group should make him forgetful of his own personal advancement in so far as they are concerned in it. The first leader of the Glendale Symphony Orchestra, who had labored hard for a number of years to get it established, freely and unurged declared that the orchestra had become ready for a better leader than himself, and he played in it under the new leader. The contrary of this sort of devotion is far too common.

Loyalty should also include the community in its regard. A leader should not only be willing but eager to have his organization and himself contribute in every good way to the musical life of the whole community. This thought leads to consideration of the value that the interest and moral support of the community has in maintaining loyalty among the members of any group. We all like to belong to something that has good standing in the community.

A Summary of Qualities

No summary of the most important qualities of leadership in music could be more fitting than that given recently by Professor James Mursell of Lawrence College before the Public School Music Supervisors at their National Conference. " The central, the vital force in music education is the sacred flame of artistic love and enthusiasm in the heart of the teacher. You cannot light anything at all from a lamp that is not burning, no matter how beautifully constructed and planned it may be. Is the teacher's musicianship a growing musicianship? For a musicianship that is not growing is dying. Is the teacher's musicianship a humane musicianship? For a musicianship that will not transmute into human and humanizing values is deeply defective. Is the teacher's musicianship an apostolic musicianship? For a musicianship that has no message of beauty and inspiration is not worth while. These are the questions that determine the value of his instruction."

Who May Be Leaders?

Wishing to start a chorus, orchestra, band, or other group musical activity for amateurs, where shall we look for a leader? The proportion of leaders of such groups who are professional conductors making that their vocation, is very small, as the remuneration given for their work is usually small. The development of music among our people would be greatly enhanced if adequately remunerative positions could be provided for excellent conducting of amateur groups. However, in so far as receiving little or no money for the work is conducive to growth of the amateur spirit in the entire enterprise, it may be a virtue — if the best available leaders can earn a satis-factory livelihood in some other good way.

The other good way is most often through teaching. Among teachers of singing or playing, public school music supervisors, and college or normal school music teachers, are some who are very capable of the leader-ship desired. Many choruses and at least one good civic orchestra are led by church organists or choir-masters. The more mature of capable students in music schools, and the best of those preparing in col-leges and normal schools to become school music teachers should welcome opportunities to lead a group appropriate to their talents, if they can do so per-sistently for at least a year; and they should be given appropriate academic credit for doing so. One of the best adult bands in Flint has been directed by a talented and well-trained high school student. The training in conducting given to him and many other high school students at the National High School Orchestra and Band Camp is happily promising of a fuller and much-needed supply of leaders, when they have matured, in many cities and towns in all parts of the country.

Most of these boys and girls, it is hoped, will be amateurs whose interest in leading is not due to "baton fever," but mainly to their desire to provide opportunity for themselves and others to sing or play together for the love of it. Amateur leaders as well as performers in admirable choruses, orchestras, and bands, reserving for the professionals the field of re-munerative performance, and enlarging that field by the increased general musical interest aroused by such organizations in a city — this is the prospect. Observ-ing its full significance, we are once more set on the path to chamber music, *haus-musik,* of all kinds, which needs only a quiet room and suitable music (which the public library might supply) and perhaps some coaching. There are many musicians, professional or amateur, incapable of conducting, who are very well able to coach small groups.

The Costs of Leadership

The remuneration of leaders of adult amateur choruses, orchestras, and bands ranges all the way from $5.00 to $55.00 a rehearsal depending largely on the experience, standing, and demand of the individual leader, and the standing and standards of the group. The most common rates are between $10.00 and $25.00. Concerts are usually either rated a little higher or are conducted without charge, but in some groups they are rated the same as rehearsals. Part-time leaders of playground and recreation center groups receive from $3.50 to $5.00 per evening and from 52 cents to $2.50 per hour. The national Committee on Training and Experience in Community Recreation Work recommends the following salaries for supervisors of music in municipal recreation departments:

Cities under 100,000	$1800 to $3500
100,000 to 500,000	2100 to 4500
over 500,000	2400 to 4500

CHAPTER VIII

Government Aid and Other Kinds

The recently established French National Committee for Musical Propaganda in Paris has just opened an inquiry regarding all musical organizations, orchestral and choral societies, existing in France, which will be aided financially.

COULD three words have been appropriately changed in this notice appearing in a May, 1931, issue of the *New York Times,* what eager expectations it would have aroused among the members of a great many American musical organizations perennially pressed for funds! For what are these funds needed? What are the necessary expenses of musical enterprises?

Material Needs

For an organization aiming to provide for the various musical possibilities of a whole community, the budget of the Flint Community Music Organization, given on page 118, will be adequately suggestive of the needs and expenses that may be incurred in such an enterprise.

The costs common to choruses, orchestras, and bands usually involve the following items:

> A director
> Music
> One or more music stands
> Rental of a rehearsal hall
>   and a concert hall
> Secretarial work
> Programs
> Advertising

These and other items and their costs appear in the chapters dealing with each kind of organization and, with respect to the director, in the chapter on Leadership. We wish now to point out that some of these needs may be partly or entirely fulfilled without cost. The public library may already have suitable music for free circulation or, as in Bangor, Maine, it may purchase excellent music when it is needed, and care for it as it cares for its books. The high school or some musically advanced adult group in the city may be willing to lend suitable selections from its own library. Many a movie theatre formerly blessed with a substantial orchestra may have a store of good music from which scores and parts may be inexpensively purchased.

High school and city or city hall auditoriums have been used at little or no expense, sometimes fully equipped with music stands. So have auditoriums or smaller halls of Chambers of Commerce, churches, community centers, public libraries, art museums, clubs, and industrial plants. The fine Chicago Business Men's Orchestra rehearses in a department store, the Kalamazoo Symphony Orchestra had its start in an automobile sales room, the Salt Lake City *Tribune* gives the use of its small auditorium without charge to the Civic Orchestra of that city, and not a few choruses and orchestras of moderate size have the drawing room of a spacious home in which to rehearse.

Recreation departments are often well equipped and eager to provide all the secretarial or managerial services necessary, as the people of Irvington, New Jersey; Sacramento; Jacksonville and other cities know. And they can go far in providing publicity for concerts and for the membership committee.

The cost of printed programs is often defrayed through sale of advertising space in them, this practice sometimes being so profitable as to help defray other expenses also. The cost of simple but dignified programs has been borne for several organizations by local music or other merchants who are allowed therefore to have an unostentatious reference to themselves on the back page. In Flint the club sponsoring the orchestra concert pays the cost of the programs.

* * * * * *

So the common needs of musical endeavors may be directly supplied. But almost always money is required for other needs if not these. How shall this money be secured?

Government Aid to Music

There is no American national bureau to buy the surplus products of singers and players as the Farm Board purchases surplus wheat, and no federal Department of Fine Arts to give official recognition to the fact that the character of a nation is measured not alone by its trade balances, but mainly by its culture. This is perhaps fortunate because art is so personal an affair, to be governed for each individual or group by his or its own tastes and intuitions, not by popular vote, by ex-cathedra rulings or through congressional debates. But it is possible and very desirable for a government to support music and yet leave the direction of it entirely in the hands of the most capable and politically disinterested persons. A finely motivated and responsible music commission such as we found in Flint, Winston-Salem, and Philadelphia, matching with moral support the city's financial support, keeps the administration of the latter safe for the best interests of everyone concerned, and makes it a boon indeed.

Unfortunately, municipal support for music, unlike support for sanitation, must depend for its continuance on strong personal interest in the art on the part

of one or more of the most influential government officials, or on sufficiently impressive and persistent demands for it on the part of private citizens. A newly
elected set of city officials, if insufficiently urged or
impressed by popular interest, may discontinue even
the most meritorious musical support given by their
predecessors. A mere frill, they may call it, or they
may ask why the unmusical taxpayer should have to
bear any of the expense of providing pleasure for the
musical ones, forgetting the use of city funds for the
provision or support of public libraries, parks, monu-
ments, municipal architecture, golf courses, and other
" frills " that make for the happiness and otherwise
good behavior of only parts of the total population.

Let an amount equal to but ten per cent or even one
per cent of the hundreds of millions of dollars being
spent yearly for overcrowding the jails be most strate-
gically applied to development of such musical activities as we have referred to in Chapters II and III.
Might not so much governmental recognition and
the resulting opportunities for the best sorts of musical
experience and growth among the people be as long a
single step as could be taken toward better morale in
our cities? [1] They might also bring nearer the time
when a general realization of the supremacy of human over purely economic values will make possible
the changes of purpose necessary for intelligent direction of our overgrown material powers that, like wild
horses, have pulled us into a dangerous morass.

The catch-phrases of " prosperity " that have fired
our grown-up imaginations as alluringly as any story
of Aladdin's lamp ever fired the dreams of our child-

---

[1] What is known as " police power," that fundamental function of
state and municipal governments, has to do with the " health, morals, and
well-being " of the people. It is reasonable to ask why wisely directed support of music might not be as effective a means as some other provisions
made under this power, though it would better not be regarded as an
application of police power!

hood are proving themselves just as unreal. No glow, no romance whatever have they for the seven million unemployed, and even the "bigger and better" winners in the game must be weary of it. When we have recovered sufficiently from the present depression, there will probably be greater support than there has ever been before in this country for cultivation of our greatest undeveloped natural resources, of all those human interests and capabilities that make for fuller, richer living. There could be no more encouraging sign of this than the generous support already being given to public school music in many cities. But as things have been, the teachers and leaders have sent rank after rank of musically trained boys and girls out into the world only to be in large measure defeated there by the contrary pressures and lures of an acquisitive society. What aid to after-school musical endeavors may we look for from city governments?

Municipal Funds to the Rescue

Of the 767 cities and towns represented in the report of a survey made by the National Bureau for the Advancement of Music in 1925, 327 answered affirmatively the question, "Does your municipality make an appropriation for music for the people?"[2] A total of $1,254,481.17 was given for music by these cities in 1924, exclusive of the sums appropriated for public school instruction in the art. For what sort of music? Nearly a million dollars of the total were spent for band concerts, doubtless because they often attract a larger number of people than could be gathered for any other sort of concert unless it were a free or popular-priced performance by an excellent symphony orchestra or a very famous soloist, either of which would be more costly. From this it will be seen that a

[2] See "Municipal Aid to Music" by Kenneth S. Clark, National Bureau for the Advancement of Music: New York, 1925.

primary consideration with respect to government aid to music has commonly been the number of people to be affected by it, and this usually results in bringing music *to* the people rather than *from* them. This is a good purpose, as millions of people would affirm who during each summer gather in the parks of their respective cities to listen to band concerts and, whether they come prepared for it or not, to enjoy the feeling of being a member of the community. There is always, for most people, a pleasant neighborliness in such a gathering, and sometimes something deeper than that. The large gathering of people and the place — often a beautiful park — are idealized by the music, if it is good enough, as though it were their spirit, the spirit of the city, finding a voice: gay, heroic, tender, triumphant, or whatever it may be at the moment, but always good-willed and expansive, a very good antidote for the cynical and belittling voice of the city that blats out at us from the pages of many a newspaper. If the band is good enough, we said; and we should add that no radio or other device can ever take the place, in this situation, of a good band actually present; nor can any microphone be adequately substituted, in the experience of the band, for a live, responsive audience.

In most cities and towns appropriations for band concerts may be made directly from the municipal treasury or from funds collected through a special tax varying in different states from one-half to three mills. Frequently, however, the appropriation is included in the budget for maintenance of the parks. Recreation departments, bureaus of public welfare, and municipal publicity bureaus are also channels for such funds. Among smaller cities and towns there are many in whose charters there is no permission to grant municipal funds for music. But by 1925 each of the following states had achieved legislation giving specific

The Hollywood Bowl

statutory permission to its cities and towns to appropriate funds for free public concerts:[3]

Alabama	Montana
California	Nebraska
Colorado	New Hampshire
Illinois	New York
Indiana	Ohio
Iowa	Pennsylvania
Kansas	South Dakota
Massachusetts	Texas
Michigan	Utah
Minnesota	Vermont
Mississippi	Wisconsin

In twelve of these states the law specifies *band* concerts. The Nebraska law would include every sort of musical organization capable of giving an enjoyable concert. It authorizes all incorporated cities to levy a tax not exceeding one mill " to establish and maintain a vocal, instrumental and amusement organization for the purpose of rendering free public concerts, music festivals and entertainments." Utah's law governing the provision for recreation in its cities goes still farther, authorizing recreation directors to organize and conduct " pageants, festivals and celebrations, community music, vocal and instrumental." West Virginia authorizes all municipalities of less than 2000 inhabitants to submit to vote the proposition of levying a tax for maintenance of a municipal band, but each larger municipality is incorporated by a special act of the legislature; and whether or not it has such authority depends on whether special provision is made for that authority in its charter. From Virginia comes the report that " while the subject of band music is not specifically mentioned, . . . under the broad language of the law an appropriation for the hiring of bands or the maintenance of a local

[3] See " Municipal Aid to Music " by Kenneth S. Clark, National Bureau for the Advancement of Music: New York, 1925.

public band would be proper and permissible;" and this doubtless describes the situation with respect to municipal concerts of any kind in many other of the states not included in the above list. For example, in 1886, before Massachusetts had any law authorizing its municipalities to appropriate money for music, the Supreme Court in the case of Hubbard vs. City of Taunton upheld the right of the city to pay for band concerts on the basis of a state law permitting towns and cities to appropriate not over one-fiftieth of one per cent of the proper valuation for armories, celebrations, and for other public purposes. "Other public purposes" was construed as admitting music.

State permission or absence of prohibition for municipal support of free concerts may not be enough. The city or town fathers may wish to do in this regard only what they must do. There is a very interesting account in Mr. Clark's book of the establishment of special Band Laws making it possible for a majority of the voters themselves to enact a tax levy for band concerts if petition is made for it by a small proportion, varying in the different states from five to twenty per cent, of the total number of legal voters as shown by the last regular municipal election. Following the petition, a proposal to levy a small tax (usually not to exceed two mills) for provision of band concerts must be submitted to vote of the people. Iowa, Illinois, Kansas, Michigan, Mississippi, New York, South Dakota, and Texas were reported in Mr. Clark's book to have enacted such a Band Law. Since the publication of that book Arizona, Georgia, Idaho, Maine, Maryland, Minnesota, Missouri, Nebraska, and North Dakota have done likewise.

The amount of municipal aid for band concerts undoubtedly increased in the years between 1925 and 1930, though it is impossible now to tell what effect the present financial depression has had upon it in many cities. For example, by 1930 San Fransisco had doubled its annual appropriation from $25,000 to $50,000; Baltimore had added over $12,000 to the $37,000 reported by it in 1925, and Long Beach, California, had brought the record for this sort of municipal generosity from $128,000 to $133,000 for free band concerts all the year round.

Municipal Organs

Through the generosity of Mr. Cyrus H. K. Curtis, who presented one of the world's best organs to the city in 1912, Portland, Maine, was able to establish a model of municipally supported organ recitals that has been emulated by at least ten other cities and one county. They are Denver, San Diego, St. Paul, Minneapolis, Dallas, San Antonio, Atlanta, Atlantic City (in a high school), Springfield (Massachusetts), San Francisco, and Westchester County (New York), the last having an organ installed in a large new County Center auditorium which is under the auspices of the county's Recreation Commission. New York City may be said to have a municipal organ and a municipal organist though they are both under the auspices of the College of the City of New York. Public organ recitals have been given there twice a week for many years. Pittsburgh is similarly but doubly blessed by having such recitals in its two Carnegie Halls. The famous Tabernacle organ recitals in Salt Lake City are to all effects municipal though they are an offering of the Mormon Church. Cleveland, Toledo, and Detroit each provide public organ recitals in the fine settings of their art museums. The city of Portland appropriates $12,000 a year to be used by the Portland Music Commission of three prominent citizens, which is a regularly constituted department of the municipal government, "to make it possible for every resident of Portland and the visitors within the city to hear the finest of music produced by a master on the finest of musical instruments, and to encourage general musical activity." [4] Twenty Sunday afternoon concerts are given by the city organist with soloists from November to April, and five such concerts are given each week — Monday to Friday inclusive — during July and August, all of them in the splendid large auditorium of the city hall.

It is not essential, though desirable, to have a permanent city organist. The series of recitals may be given, as in the Westchester County Center, by a succession of guest organists. But then there will have to be an individual or committee capable of choosing the players very wisely; and even so, there may still be the disadvantage of having a series of programs unrelated to each other.

It is a fine thing for a city to be represented, so to speak, by the king of instruments, and such a stroke for music arouses a good deal of interest and, doubtless, pride among the people. Unfortunately, the audiences, quite large at first, have dwindled in at least seven of the cities mentioned. Evidently the usual sort of organ recital becomes a pretty dull affair to many people, and the number of unusual, top-notch recitalists among organists is even smaller than the number among the players of the piano or violin. Solo singers and instrumentalists — especially of the violin or cello — often add much interest to an organ recital, and should be allowed to do so quite often; but they have to be very capable to do so in these days, and their fees may be high. Why not give good amateur instrumental and, best of all, choral groups a chance to play or sing with or without the organ? Of course, the chorus should be one that sings musically and has the joy of life and beauty in it —

---

[4] From a statement by William S. Barnard, Jr., of the Portland Music Commission, quoted in " Municipal Aid to Music " by Kenneth S. Clark.

not the inane or sanctimonious sort of choir that some
organists love.

Portland has tried this with much success. The
organ concerts of one season enlisted, in addition to
soloists, the Portland Orchestral Society, now a full-
fledged symphony orchestra, the Women's Choral Society, the Polyphonic Society, and at Christmas time
a large mixed chorus in a performance of the
" Messiah."

Municipal Support for Orchestra Concerts

At a cost of $30,000 to the city treasury, the Detroit
Symphony Orchestra, reduced to about 55 players, has
each year since 1925 given a free concert every evening for eight weeks during the summer at Belle Isle,
a Detroit park. The shell in which the concerts are
given was paid for through subscriptions from the orchestra's patrons. The average attendance is about
5000. Every Wednesday evening a foreign-born group
in costume (residents of Detroit) is given the second
half of the program for singing and dancing, and other
special programs are given from time to time. For
example, three performances of the " Midsummer
Night's Dream " were given one summer with the
city's Civic Theatre Company, the orchestra playing
Mendelssohn's incidental music for the play.

The Cleveland Orchestra has, since 1927, followed
a similar plan, with almost exactly the same conditions, including the support from its city's treasury.

The entire financial support of the Baltimore Symphony Orchestra, beyond the receipts from the sale of
tickets at from twenty-five to seventy-five cents each,
for 14 years has been given by the municipality. The
appropriation for it in 1930 was $29,500.

San Francisco has shouldered the deficit, about
$8,000, for an annual series of five Municipal " Pop "
concerts, each of which attracts about 8,000 people; it

has appropriated $15,000 for each of a number of years for a series of popular priced symphony concerts in the summer, equally well attended, and in 1930 it gave the same amount to aid in the support of the regular series of winter concerts. This generous support is said to be given for the delight and edification of the permanent residents of the city, not for the attraction of tourists.

The city of Denver contributes $1,000 a year and the free use of its city auditorium to the support of the Denver Symphony Orchestra.

Other cities could be included in this roster. But with mention of the Denver orchestra we have struck upon another purpose of municipal aid to music, which has not been apparent in our discussion thus far. It is to bring music *from* the people, the non-professional people, not only *to* them.

Music from *the People*

To give concerts is only half the purpose of the Denver Orchestra. The other half is to provide opportunity for capable players, regardless of profession, to take part in the performance of great music. While 80 of its 110 members are or have been associated with the musicians' union, even they for the most part earn a livelihood in other pursuits, and the remaining 30 members are, though capable, entirely innocent of professional intentions.

The main value of having foreign-born groups take part in the Detroit and Cleveland summer orchestra concerts is for those amateur performers themselves and for the listeners who may be stimulated by attractive amateur performances to do likewise, though it be only in their own homes or clubs.

Other examples of municipal aid for musical expression, not *im*pression alone, are the community sings held in connection with municipal band concerts, notably in Milwaukee, Minneapolis, and Chicago. We must bow again to San Francisco as we tell of the superb large chorus there that is supported entirely with city funds, $5,000 a year going to the director alone. A similar chorus in Glendale, California, is supported by the city with the proviso that it give a free, outdoor concert in the summer.

Glendale's city fathers have a similar arrangement with the Glendale Symphony Orchestra asking for two free concerts in the summer, $1200 going to the conductor and $300 for the purchase of music, the players receiving no remuneration. Long Beach, not content with its munificent support of a fine band, in 1929 and in 1930 appropriated $5,000 to the Long Beach Symphony Orchestra, by which, in 1929, two free performances — with the city's Handel and Haydn (Choral) Society and the Choral-Oratorio Society, respectively — were given in return. The reader may remember that the town of Springfield, Vermont, appropriated $500 for three free concerts by its good amateur civic orchestra.

Many an amateur band owes its life to opportunities to give concerts under municipal auspices and thereby to receive sufficient funds as well as incentive to carry on. Of course, this kind of municipal support should not be given where it causes unemployment of vocational musicians. There are police, fire, and street cleaning department bands that subsist at least partly on municipal funds even when they give no concerts.

Music Weeks

Still nearer to the idea of government aid for musical expression by the people is the support that has been given to Music Week observances in many cities. In Boston; Virginia, Minnesota; Pueblo, Colorado; Dallas; Denver and doubtless in some other cities this support has included municipal funds, Denver maintaining probably the highest annual contribution, of $4,500. But the value of enthusiastic moral support by municipal, state and national government officials must also be counted here for its power of inducing private organizations and citizens to contribute money and effort. The Honorary Committee for National Music Week, including, as it does, the President of the United States and the governors of nearly all our states and territories, is not merely a nominal one, as the following proclamation will show.

MUSIC WEEK IN THE STATE OF NEW MEXICO
A PROCLAMATION BY THE GOVERNOR

National Music Week is now being observed in nearly all the states of the Union. The custom has been established for the purpose of focusing public attention on the importance of music in individual and group life. Music in its varied forms, vocal and instrumental, is one of the greatest contributing factors to human happiness. Its study and practice should be encouraged in families, schools, state institutions, church organizations, cities, towns, villages and rural settlements.

Our Creator has made music available in some form or another to all of His children, from the baby cooing in the cradle and the barefoot boy whistling in the fields to the world's greatest master of instrumental technique. Community singing and song-fests bring great spiritual inspiration and joy to whole communities; patriotic music thrills us with love for our country; songs and melodies bring cheer to those suffering from illness and other misfortune.

Now, THEREFORE, I, ARTHUR SELIGMAN, GOVERNOR OF THE STATE OF NEW MEXICO, do hereby proclaim the week beginning Sunday May 3rd and ending May 9th, 1931 as

MUSIC WEEK

in the State of New Mexico.

I respectfully suggest that citizens in general, especially all school authorities, formulate musical programs for the week and map out some plans whereby such programs may be extended throughout the year in the hope that song and music may become a daily habit among the children of the state. I especially urge that good programs be provided in our State Penitentiary, Reform School, Girls' Welfare Home and the various state hospitals.

Done at the Executive Office
this 23rd day of April, 1931
Witness My Hand and the Great Seal of
the State of New Mexico
ARTHUR SELIGMAN
Governor

Attest:
MARGUERITE P. BACA
Secretary of State

In 1930 twenty-seven of the governors each issued a proclamation or gave a newspaper interview in endorsement of the interest in Music Week. In Wyoming the local Music Week chairmen are appointed by the Governor in consultation with officials of the State Federation of Music Clubs. Mayors, too, issue proclamations, and in many instances serve as chairmen of their respective Music Week committees, for some of which the members are appointed by the mayor. The reports of persistent musical activities and support of one sort or another growing out of all this interest are very promising. Excerpts from them have been published by the National Music Week Committee at 45 West 45th Street, New York City, in a booklet which is sent free upon request.

Civic Music Organization Again

A very striking example of the extent to which music may be regarded as a civic enterprise is Philadelphia's Municipal Bureau of Music, which has been fully reported upon in Chapter V of this book. Especially notable is the fact that the mayor made municipal support of music one of the planks of his pre-election platform. Baltimore, with its municipal director of music, its generous appropriations already referred to, its community singing and, in 1931, the establishment of a City Colored (People's) Symphony Orchestra, is equally admirable, and it deserves additional praise for the steady growth, through fourteen years, of its musical support and achievements. Incidentally, it may be interesting to know that part of this city's annual expenditure of approximately $100,000 has been derived from a special tax on transit facilities. This assignment to the higher purposes of *living* of part of the money spent for *moving* suggests other possible transferences of power from flourishing physical interests to those often undernourished ones having to do, at least more directly, with finer living. Think of having some of the bellowing ardors of prize fight and football crowds converted in this way into the joys of singing, playing, or listening to first-class music! — And without any decrease in the bellowing, which is also good.

*   *   *   *   *   *

We have seen that a very large proportion of government aid to music outside of schools and colleges has been directed at bringing concerts to the people. But the recent large developments in musical expression in the schools and colleges, especially in the former, are begging for extension into adult life, to say nothing of the great need for expressive activity among all adults in these times. The examples we have seen of municipal support for music *by* the people, notably in Philadelphia, Baltimore, and San Francisco, may be regarded as precedents for provision of such extension by any other city. A still more direct precedent, keeping the schools in mind, is Milwaukee's yearly appropriation of $3,500 for the support of a junior symphony orchestra that is expressly for the purpose of providing for graduates of high school orchestras. In connection with special services to agricultural folk, funds from county and state bureaus and the federal Department of Agriculture are being used in a measure to help advance musical expression among rural adults as well as children.

Aid through Municipal Recreation Agencies

The Utah law enabling cities, towns, school districts, and counties to appropriate funds for the conduct of recreation suggests a way for any such governmental unit to provide legally for musical activities even if for any reason no direct appropriation can be made for them. By 1928 the following states had passed a "home rule bill" authorizing the cities, towns, villages, and counties to operate systems of public recreation and playgrounds:

Connecticut	New Hampshire
Florida	New Jersey
Georgia	New York
Illinois	North Carolina
Indiana	Ohio
Iowa	Pennsylvania
Kentucky	Rhode Island
Louisiana	Utah
Massachusetts	Vermont
Michigan	Virginia
West Virginia	

Even though the law make no mention of music, there is evidently no reason for excluding musical activities. They also are, after all, ways of recreation. And it may be possible for a city to support music in this way even in a state which has not yet passed a home rule bill.

"It is not to be inferred," says Dr. Andrew G. Truxal,[5] "that the states which are not included among those having specific home rule enabling acts legalizing municipal recreation have not permissive legislation. . . . In states such as California and

[5] In "Outdoor Recreation Legislation and Its Effectiveness," Columbia University Press.

Texas, where rather broad interpretations have been placed by the courts on the powers granted under constitutional home rule, a number of cities have included recreation departments as separate departments of their city governments in the making of their charters." In other states " when a city has wanted to establish a recreation system, the state has assumed the power not to exist, but has delegated the power by ' special legislation.' Such legislation often takes the form of so-called ' class ' legislation in which the law is made applicable to a certain class of cities within the borders of the state, of which class there may be only one or two cities."

According to reports received by the National Recreation Association, in the year 1930 municipal funds were used to provide recreation in 781 American cities, representing together every state except Nevada. In 189 of these cities private funds were added to those contributed by the municipality, and in 222 of them receipts through charges for use of recreation facilities helped to defray the costs. Forty-nine cities and towns had the benefit of county funds. "The total expenditure for public recreation reported in 928 cities (including privately supported community recreation agencies) is $38,518,194.88. This is $5,000,000 more than the largest amount previously reported spent for public recreation within a single year and represents an increase of more than 100 per cent during a five-year period. Although most of the increase over the previous year (1929) is in expenditures for land, buildings and permanent equipment, it is significant that the amount spent in salaries of recreation workers exceeds by more than $1,000,000 the amount reported spent for leadership the previous year." [6]

[6] From the 1930 "Community Recreation Year Book" published in the magazine "Recreation" for June, 1931.

It should not be inferred from this very impressive statement that large support for choruses, orchestras, bands, and festivals is or can be made available at once wherever there is a municipal recreation department. The following summary of reports from recreation officials is indicative — though many correspondents did not answer this part of a questionnaire — of the comparatively slight though impressive amount of attention given to music in the nation's "recreation program" as a whole:

Activities	Cities Reporting
Orchestras [7]	104
Bands [7]	150
Light Opera Groups [7]	21
Band Concerts (Amateurs)	161
Band Concerts (Professionals)	179
Christmas Caroling	185
Community Singing	180
Choral Groups	103
Harmonica Bands	123
Music Memory Contests	27
Music Week Activities	92
Quartets	61
Singing Games	287
Toy Symphonies	100
Ukulele Clubs	59
Whistling Contests	33

One deterrent is the fact that only 282 cities report full-time, year-round recreation workers. Another is the lack of mutual understanding between recreation leaders, music leaders, and citizens generally as to the possible scope of music as an integral part of the work of a recreation department.

However, we have seen in Chapter IV the admirable extent to which some municipal recreation departments have gone in support of amateur musical

[7] Doubtless many of the groups represented by this item were composed of children and many were small. But as we have already seen, a few cities can report full-fledged adult orchestras and choruses.

expression, and we may justifiably look forward to increasing support for it by such departments everywhere, remembering that in some cities the park department, the board of education, or the department of public welfare — not a recreation department — is the agency at present holding this destiny. An especially impressive token is the persistently generous effort of the National Recreation Association in behalf of music.

Aid through the Board of Education

When, as at present, a life of rich significance, rather than the mere accumulation of facts, is more generally than ever the chief aim of education, music should receive generous support in the education of adults as well as of children. Undoubtedly, in more cities than any one person knows of there are choruses and orchestras in public evening schools as well as in the day schools. Minneapolis, Milwaukee, St. Louis, and Los Angeles and other California cities have been exemplary in this regard. But evidently this sort of municipal aid to music is still very sparse, and in some places where it exists it is unfortunately affected by the small salaries given for leadership and by the custom in those places of regarding the entire faculty of an evening school as *teachers,* in the academic sense, not as *leaders.*

It is not unreasonable to imagine a neighborhood chorus in each of several evening schools in a city, which choruses would join in a city festival in the spring, all under the auspices of the public schools. The orchestra for the festival would be made up of players from the several evening school orchestras. Many of the singers and players would be parents whose gatherings in the school would make that place and the life that goes on in it all the day more significant and attractive for their children as well as for themselves. And it might well be that some entire families, including high school students, would be members together of chorus or orchestra. The old, original People's Choral Union organized and so long directed by Dr. Frank Damrosch in New York City was made up of several choruses, each meeting in a school building; and the present People's Chorus of that city is in these respects a direct descendant of the Choral Union. The large chorus for the recent Philadelphia Sesquicentennial Exposition was formed in the same way. But the funds for support of these choruses had or have to be secured from sources outside of the schools.

However, Winston-Salem's generous expenditures for adult singing and playing were made, as we said in Chapter V, through the School Department, and that chapter also showed the director of instrumental music in the schools of Ottawa, Kansas, achieving a very stimulating model of the direct extension of school music into adult life. Most impressive of all is the engagement of a music leader at a salary of $5,000 a year by the Madison, Wisconsin, Board of Vocational Education, for the development of an avocational civic orchestra and chorus in an evening school, as well as for teaching a class there in music appreciation. There are precedents enough.

* * * * * *

Before leaving the subject of government aid, it should be said that it is well to have an effectively representative music commission even where support is secured through the recreation department or the board of education, if only to ensure persistently adequate endeavor amidst the many other interests of the department or the board.

Other Sources of Aid

Through the Community Chest

Among the five kinds of service commonly supported through community chests is the provision for wholesome leisure-time activities — the other services being aid to dependents, aid to delinquents, the promotion of health, and what is known as "common service" such as is given by the community chest organization itself. It is not surprising, therefore, to see the Flint Community Music Association included among the beneficiaries of its city's chest.[8] But the only similar aid to music found in one hundred cities was the $425 allotted in 1929 to the West Chester (Pennsylvania) Community Music Fund through the chest of that small city, in which support for community celebrations and for a recreation department is also secured through the chest. However, the Community Music School of San Francisco in that same year received in this way $11,875, about 60 per cent of its total income; the Music School Settlement of Syracuse received $1,440 and the Cleveland Music School Settlement $19,677, about 72 per cent of its total income.

Evidently, as is to be expected, leisure time activities to be supported through a community chest must be especially or entirely for underprivileged children or adults, or have as a purpose the development of character or health or both, as in the Y.M. and Y.W.C.A., and the Boy and the Girl Scouts. But though the Flint Community Music Association serves many a person who could easily pay for the privilege, it makes as justifiable though not so obvious a claim to developing his character as do the Scouts or the Y.M.C.A. And this cannot help but be the

[8] Cf. page 118.

contribution of any community or other organization for group singing or playing of good music as a means of recreation. As musical expression comes to be generally recognized as the superb means of recreation and morale that it may be — not merely as performance, a means of display, or as a mere diversion — the people will be likely to support community provision for it through taxation or through community agencies as readily as they now support some other modes of recreation and social service.

Private Support for Civic Music Associations

The Philadelphia Music League, as was noted in Chapter V, secured about $15,000 in its first year through membership dues and donations from 363 private individuals and organizations. It received similar amounts in this way in succeeding years, always bolstered by the city's annual appropriation of $10,000. But the Civic Music Association of Chicago, organized in 1912, long before the many purely concert-bringing organizations of that name were thought of, receives only a small sum from the city — $450 in 1930 — which is to pay for summer-time community singing once a week on the Navy Pier. All the rest of its own income — it also takes care of the Chicago Orchestral Association's financing of the Civic Orchestra for students — is secured through memberships of private citizens and organizations. Its report for the year ending May 31, 1930 is shown in the table at the top of page 236.

This represents the substantial total of 611 memberships, and in a poor year. The preceding year brought $15,997 from 715 members. This Association's excellent work in maintaining playground children's choruses that join annually in Christmas caroling and a Spring Festival is described on pages 495–498 of this book. It also manages the Civic Orchestra and pro-

Memberships		*Totals*
4 at	$500.	$2,000
10 at	250.	2,500
1 at	125.	125
16 at	100.	16,000
19 at	50.	950
41 at	25.	1,025
224 at	10.	2,240
155 at	5.	775
121 at	2.	242
20 at various sums		272
Total income from memberships		$11,729

vides from 10 to 15 Free Artist Concerts, as they are properly called, some of them combined with community singing, in park recreation centers during each year.

The Reading (Pa.) Musical Foundation is a somewhat similar organization supported by about 400 members, each subscribing $25.00 or more and receiving two tickets to each concert of its symphony orchestra and its chorus. Civic organizations in Newark, N. J. and White Plains, N. Y. are similarly managed, the latter's orchestra and chorus, however, being made up entirely of amateurs.

But these three cities bring us near to the plan of the new sort of civic music association or community concerts association described in Chapter V, whose sole purpose is to bring professional concerts to the city. Milwaukee's Association of this sort had a membership in 1930–31 of 3,875 at five dollars each; and that of the smaller city of La Porte, Indiana, had 1428 members at the same rate in the same year: nine per cent of the total population of 15,575! Over 200 other cities now have such associations. This support for music is very impressive, especially in a year of financial depression; and when coupled with the fact that in some cities such an association has offered in its series of concerts one in which the local civic orchestra has been combined with an important soloist, there is basis for supposing that this new concert-bringing plan might gradually be enlarged to include opportunities for people of the city to sing or play as well as to listen.

Perhaps the first step in this development might be the offering of a festival for which the association would enlist one or more local amateur choruses and a civic orchestra or, if necessary, form a new chorus and orchestra. This festival would be the climax of the series of concerts, and the association might engage for it not imported soloists but a great leader whose prestige and whose ability to lift the chorus and orchestra to an inspiring level of expression would make the lure of imported soloists unnecessary. But such a development will require very capable as well as enthusiastic direction, and would perhaps better not be undertaken until the present plan that is proving so successful is well established.

Aid from Foundations

Among a number of foundations and endowments from which generous contributions are made for the support of important musical endeavors of various kinds, the five that evidently have the widest scope are the Juilliard, Presser, Eastman, and Curtis Foundations, and the Carnegie Corporation. But of these only the Juilliard, Carnegie, and Eastman endowments have given aid to community musical endeavors. The report given on page 176 from the music leader whose services are contributed to Atlanta by the Juilliard Foundation is exemplary of what this foundation has done in a number of other cities, notably in the Pennsylvania cities of Harrisburg and Reading, and in El Paso, Texas. That is, its aid to communities is being given through providing leadership of one sort or another, not funds.

The Carnegie Corporation's grants have included some to outstanding community choruses, and one to a Music Week association, but all of these have been in its own city of New York. On the other hand, it has been very generous in giving aid for music education in schools, colleges, and music schools, to several of the most effective national organizations for the promotion of music in American life, and to a community arts association in a western city.

Through the generosity of Mr. George Eastman has come the establishment of a great music school, the support of a civic orchestra, and greatly enriched musical opportunities in a public school system; but all of this has been done in the city of Rochester, New York.

PART II

In Various Centers of Life in the Community

Introduction

IN Part I we dealt with achievements and possibilities viewed as components of the total musical activity of the community. It was as though we were looking down from an airplane at a city or town, with its homes, schools, churches, and other centers of life all blended in the single vision. Now we shall come down and go in turn into each of those centers, observing it at close hand while still remembering the vision we had of the entire city from above. Not only will the features and activities of each center stand out much more clearly than they have before, but the larger vision's blending of all the centers into a whole will be seen to have basis in practical interrelationships between them.

We start with various kinds of schools because they are the fundamental means of advancement in musical expression, enjoyment and taste; and we must include among them the colleges, conservatories, and other leader-training institutions which may be outside of the community and yet have a vital bearing on its life.

The remaining chapters might very well include one on each of several other channels of life in the community — on industrial and commercial establishments; clubs, lodges, and other associations such as the Y.M.C.A., or the parent and teacher associations; hospitals, prisons, and other welfare institutions; the public libraries; the theatres; Negro groups; and foreign-language groups. As the index will show, these have each received some attention in various parts of the book. Moreover, much that is said elsewhere in the book is also applicable to them. The necessity of keeping the size of the book within moderate cost has made fuller treatment of them impossible. A second volume may be issued before very long. Our bibliography refers to other books and to magazines that may be helpful.

Further mention must be made, however, of the musical activities of various clubs and federations of them. The National Federation of Music Clubs has taken under its care the promotion of every kind of musical endeavor, for people of all ages, professional and amateur, in all sorts of places, and composition and music appreciation as well as performance. Its first concern is or should be with the musical development of its own 400,000 or more members in their 4,762 clubs (1931). Courses of music study based on six books, of which five were especially written for the Federation, have been issued for the use of club members. Effort has been made through choice of music for club programs, through contests, and through magazine articles, speeches and other methods of publicity to give aid and encouragement to American composers and performers. And many of the individual clubs have helped very much in achieving more or better music in schools, churches, fairs, and communities. Most of the state and national gatherings of the clubs have been occasions for a music festival of one sort or another as well as for addresses by outstanding musicians and educators. The initiative and support that music clubs can give to community, state, and even national musical endeavors are very important and, when carried out intelligently and without bias, very valuable. The more compact and better focused organizations of music teachers, public school music supervisors, organists, and of other people vitally concerned in our musical development need in every community the support of such individuals and groups as are to be found in the best music clubs. But the greatest possibilities seem to be in the cultivation, especially among the club members themselves, of small vocal and instrumental groups — not excluding men — such as are described in our chapter on home music.

The General Federation of Women's Clubs is even larger, a very large proportion of its 14,500 clubs sponsor choruses or orchestras or both, of their own members, and many of them have given support to musical endeavors outside of their own member-ship.

There is scarcely a Rotary, Kiwanis, Lions, or other service club among the thousands in the United States that does not have general singing at each of its meet-ings. The singing of the Los Angeles Kiwanis Club is example enough of what can be done under good leadership where the members are genuinely interested in making the most of the opportunity.[1] Many of the songs commonly used by service clubs seem child-ishly sentimental in words and music, especially those giving the members a laudatory pat on the back, but apparently more and more men are revolting against them. Several clubs, including the Rotary of San Diego and the Kiwanis of San Francisco, Worcester (Mass.), and Mobile (Ala.) have admirable glee clubs comprised of their members, which lift the general singing in quality as well as enthusiasm. The definite moral and financial aid given by service clubs for the formation and development of boys' bands, school orchestras and bands, music festivals and contests, and other community musical enterprises has in many places been far more helpful than the activities of some other organizations whose members have much to say about music but do little more than form com-mittees and hold meetings. Many lodges, notably among the Elks, Masons, Shriners, and DeMolays,

[1] Cf. page 47.

have flourishing bands, orchestras, or choruses that are outstanding factors in the musical life of their communities, and some of these lodges have also given aid to musical activities outside their own membership. With greater knowledge and appreciation of the possible uses and values of the best music of various kinds, the clubs, lodges, and Chambers of Commerce will be even more effective musically than most of them have been, both within their own membership and in the community.

The increasing interest in music is nowhere more clearly shown than in the public libraries. For example, the number of registered readers in the reference music room of the main New York Public Library has grown from 5,598 in 1911 to 17,098 in 1919, to 28,976 in 1925, and to 39,687 in 1929, an increase of 132 per cent in the last ten years. The following paragraph from the annual report of the Director of the New York Public Library for 1929 comments upon an especially interesting aspect of this growth:

The most striking feature, however, in the general character of the work done by the users of the music division is the new and lively interest in the historical aspect of the art. This does not mean the actual study of music history, pure and simple, which of course is being pursued now, as in the past, as an academic subject by a well-defined class of readers, but a practical, specifically musical, interest in historical questions, which is made to have a bearing upon actual production and performance. The desire for authenticity, for genuine local color, the striving for accuracy and historical truth is spreading far beyond the circle of more or less professional students of music history. It is beginning to interest and influence a type of musical worker who in the past was content to adapt to his purpose the thing that lay nearest at hand, with no question as to its genuineness, its stylistic truth or the real fitness of his choice to the desired end. This indifference is being replaced by a more critical attitude and a willingness to work harder and seek farther for the things that will fit properly into a preconceived musical plan or project. Theatrical producers, stage managers, motion picture and radio directors, concert managers, teachers who are planning a concert or a dramatic performance with their pupils, and even solo recitalists, come for aid in finding genuine material for the music that is to accompany or enliven their performances.

This phenomenon is evidence not only of increasing interest in music, but also of greater enlightenment and better musical taste among a large proportion of the millions who listen to music only in theatres and over the radio as well as among those who attend the concert halls. More and more people are becoming capable of recognizing and enjoying what is true, authentic, and fitting in the music presented to them. The common range of musical interest is evidently growing horizontally, backward in time, as well as vertically, in taste.

The circulation music departments of public libraries confirm the evidence from the reference department. In 1920 the average number of volumes per day loaned by the Music Branch of the New York Public Library was ten; in 1930 it was over 200. This branch in 1930 contained about 13,000 volumes, including many scores, with parts, of concerted instrumental music. The estimated size of the Cleveland Public Library music collection is as follows:

2500 books about music in circulation
 650 volumes for reference
5000 volumes of vocal and instrumental music
2000 pieces of sheet music
1500 volumes of music and musical literature in the John G. White Collection of Folk-lore and Orientalia, also available for students of music.
 600 standard orchestral scores with parts

The Detroit Public Library in 1930 contained scores and parts for 138 works for full orchestra, 378 for small orchestra, 21 for string orchestra, and 614 for instrumental trios, quartets, quintets, sextets, septets, octets, and nonets, and 7 works for slightly larger combinations, all in addition to a large stock of choral music in multiple copies, and music for piano, organ, and solo or unison singing. Chicago, San Francisco, Philadelphia, Indianapolis and doubtless several other cities are nearly or equally well equipped to loan music to professional or amateur groups of all kinds. Evanston, Illinois, has, in proportion to the size of the city, an excellent collection, especially of chamber music.

The free circulation of music to be sung or played seems as important a contribution as can be made in providing for more and better music-making by all sorts of people; but unfortunately, the use made of it is still quite small, though growing, and most of what circulation there is of orchestra and chamber music is among professionals, it is said. This is partly because much of this kind of music has been acquired by the libraries through bequests from deceased professional musicians or patrons of music; it has not been chosen to include the lower degrees of skill among amateurs. Moreover, until recently there has been very little chamber music and worthy orchestra music published that has not been quite difficult, and the number of skillful amateurs has been very small. If the libraries could purchase excellent music carefully chosen by a committee familiar with the needs and interests of amateur groups, the growing quantity of such music now being published and the increasing number of young people acquiring admirable skill in schools and colleges would be likely to bring about a gratifyingly large circulation of the music. It is encouraging to know that there were 1,444 borrowings from a total of 609 chamber music volumes — with parts — in the New York Public Library Music Branch in 1929. It is believed that many of the borrowings were by individuals, not groups, for the purpose of preparing to listen to a professional concert, but many of the works are too difficult for any but professionals. One of the largest library collections of choral music for circulation has been amassed through the kindness (?) of choirmasters and other church officials whose music shelves were evidently too small to hold all their trivial music.

Efforts have to be made to interest people in taking advantage of the music for circulation. Besides the usual sorts of publicity through library bulletins, special notices on the library bulletin board, and reports in the newspapers, the Cleveland, Philadelphia, and doubtless some other libraries have one or two sound-proof rooms containing a piano for the use of people who wish to try over music before borrowing it. It might be very effective to have a meeting once a month or more often to which people would be invited to come free of charge to hear music that is available for circulation. The performance might be by a small chorus and a chamber music or *haus-musik* group or — for the vocal music — if there are enough copies to go round, most or all of the assemblage might themselves sing. Even a good piano performance of the music, vocal or instrumental, would be inviting and helpful, especially if accompanied by enlightening comments. If the library building or personnel cannot provide for such meetings, they might be arranged for another building by the recreation department or the adult education authorities of the city. One or more members of the city's library staff should be an active member of the governing body of any organization for music in the community.

There are encouraging developments in the rural communities of some states, notably in Iowa, Wisconsin, Michigan, Ohio, and New York. Eleven states now have State Directors of Public School Music (six employed since 1925), whose principal duty it is to introduce and advance musical instruction in rural schools. County music contests and festivals have also been effective in this regard. In Michigan 27 counties each had a music festival in 1930–31, involving school choruses, orchestras, and bands from rural schools and, in a few instances, from adult communities also. It is, perhaps, the radio's most appreciated and effective musical mission to bring the best music to rural homes. If through the State Home Demonstration Agents, the Farm and Home Conventions, Grange meetings, and fairs, as well as through the schools and county festivals, the avidity of many rural folk for knowledge and culture could be answered in suitable ways, presenting music for what it really is — not enmeshed in professionalism — a musical culture might arise among country people that by its genuineness and spontaneity would be a model for the people of the cities. This book, it is hoped, might help in such a development.

CHAPTER IX

School Music and the Community

SCHOOL officials and teachers in many cities have long expected every child in the elementary grades to acquire as much of some sort or sorts of skill related to vocal music as time and his talents have permitted. While participation in church choirs and, where there was one, in the city choral society, has always been regarded by the best of these officials and teachers as the ultimate and, in the earlier days, often successful purpose of this skill, the immediate aims and methods have often been such as later to cause the saying, though not always justly, that "there are two kinds of music: school music and music." But the phenomenal developments in many public schools in the last ten years are making even the man on the street expect a respectable measure of real musical skill for every child and a large measure for many of them, from the schools.

Indeed, life is now so full of things and subjects of interest and means of pleasure, for children as well as for adults, and immediate interest rather than future happiness is so strongly in the saddle, that few of the thousands of children who are learning to play as well as sing in the schools would " take lessons " and " practice " if these had to be done outside of the schools. Urged by the social and educational pressure of school life, they *begin*, and most of them go on, and once they pass sufficiently through the necessary initiation to hold even the simplest privileges of membership in the noble order of music-makers, they are, we hope, likely to continue to go on, despite all the counter-attractions, taking lessons and practicing — or at any rate singing or playing — outside the schools when they have gone as far as they can or wish inside of them. So the music teaching in our public schools, so long regarded — at least by musicians — as having little to do with the real musical life of the individual and the community, has become the chief possible means of that life for almost all individuals and all communities. We say a *possible* means because its efficacy is, of course, dependent on its quality, quantity, and the directions it takes.

The admirable quality and skill of musical performance now being attained in some high schools is impressive enough in itself, but it becomes especially significant when we remember that the high school period of life is the most crucial one so far as music education is concerned. The new impulses and powers of this often turbulent period are at their best the very essence of music, literature, and the other arts, as well as of idealism and worship, though they may frequently not appear so. Roots of adult life are growing with great, new energy and they seek their soil. What they will find most suitable to grow in will depend, of course, largely on the past experiences and likes and dislikes of the individual, but whatever it may be, it is likely to be a consciously used source of nourishment throughout manhood and womanhood. A love of music established during this period is likely to be a lasting possession. The high school stage of life is also one in which an adequate foundation of skill in choral singing and in playing may most readily be established, though the beginning may best be made in earlier years. It is a " confirmation " period in music as well as in religion.

Until recently musical performance had no place in a large majority of our high schools, except in a short period of general singing now and then, and some special singing at commencement exercises. There are now about 5,000,000 boys and girls in the high schools, fifty times as many as there were in 1880, and the proportion who enroll in elective choruses, orchestras and bands, many of which rehearse daily, seems to be increasing. This is something new in education, and no one knows to what extent it may go in enriching American life.

An inquiry made of school music supervisors in all parts of the country in 1930 brought 604 responses to a question regarding the enrollment in elective musical activities. The following table is a summary of those responses.

COMPARISON OF NUMBERS OF PARTICIPANTS IN SCHOOL MUSICAL ACTIVITIES IN 1929–30 WITH THOSE OF PREVIOUS YEARS ACCORDING TO ESTIMATES OF 604 SCHOOL MUSIC SUPERVISORS

Activities	None Reported	Participation in 1929–30 Larger	Smaller	About the Same
Elective high school choruses [1]	164	275	22	143
High school *a cappella* mixed choirs	554	39	1	20
High school vocal chamber music groups	496	61	7	40
High school classes in voice culture	531	40	7	26
High school orchestras	223	229	31	121
High school bands	360	157	19	68
High school instrumental chamber music groups	525	53	4	22
Classes in orchestra and band instruments	415	141	8	40
Classes in piano	509	57	9	29

The surprisingly large figures in the column " none reported " are partly due to the fact that 100 of the replies came from towns of less than a thousand peo-

[1] Many schools have general or compulsory singing but no *elective* choruses.

ple, whose high schools are likely to be very small in enrollment and in financial support. Those figures indicate, however, the large extent of progress still to be made before the impressive new developments to which we have referred can be regarded as common. Yet there is the evidence of increased musical activity, which is indicated also by the growth in the number of school music contests and especially by the increasing number of students entered in them. When the first State School Band Contests were held in 1924, only five states were represented and 30 bands entered. In 1931 there was such a contest in every state except Alabama, Georgia, Louisiana, Nevada, and Wyoming, and 1,100 bands strove for honors. In that year there were also about 700 orchestras which, together with the bands, presented a total of 72,000 high school players. The total number of choruses, chamber music groups, and soloists competing in the 42 states was not known, but reports from several states indicate equally impressive increases in each of these musical fields. The national contests of school bands, held annually since the first one in 1926, and of school orchestras, held annually since the first one in 1929, give similar evidence.

Knowing of all these accomplishments, we can readily understand why the question as to their effects in life outside of schools has become so insistent. The promise is so great. One leader in public school music has gone so far as to say that if in the next ten years those accomplishments have no greater effect outside the schools than they now have, municipalities will refuse to continue the present provision for them. But while this warning is justified, the prophecy it gives should never be fulfilled, even if in our adult life we do not make any greater progress than we have in using the musical wealth stored up in our youth. We must remember that even now there are in a few cities community musical developments resulting from school instruction that make the latter richly deserving of even stronger support than has been given for it anywhere. To realize this, the reader has only to recall accounts in Chapters I and V of what is being done in Bangor, Ottawa, and Flint. There are other cities nearly or equally as admirable. What one city or town can do can at least in large measure be done in any other city or town.

Indeed, so long as education is regarded as having to do with the whole man — with his spirit, emotions, imagination, and his capacities and need for beauty, as well as with his intellect and body — so long should every boy and girl have the right to music instruction fully commensurate with his capacities and needs, even if there were never a sound of amateur singing or playing outside of the schools. Youth should have its way in this, at least.

I must laugh and dance and
   sing.
Youth is such a lovely thing!
Soon I shall be old and stately;
I shall promenade sedately
Down a narrow pavement
   street
And the people that I meet
Will be stiff and narrow, too,
Careful what they say and do.

It will be quite plain to see
That they were never young
   like me.
When I walk where flowers
   grow,
I shall have to stoop down low
If I want one for a prize.
Now I'm just the proper size.
Let me laugh and dance and
   sing,
Youth is such a lovely thing! [2]

However, if conditions outside the schools are not opposed to singing and playing, the presence or absence of it there is the most important criterion as to whether the school musical training *is* commensurate with the children's needs and possibilities. And since it is in the days of manhood or womanhood, in the

[2] A poem written by one of the children in the Lincoln School of New York City, and appearing in " Creative Power " by Hughes Mearns, Doubleday, Doran & Company, New York.

making or preserving of "the good life," that singing or playing is even more valuable than it is in childhood, the growing concern as to the relation of the public school to the musical life of the community is doubly justified.

The effectiveness of that relationship depends largely on such provision of opportunities in the community as we have considered in Part I of this book, and on intelligent cooperation between all who have to do, or might have to do with singing or playing in the community — in homes, churches, music schools, community centers, and playgrounds, as well as in the schools. But even more largely does it depend on the attitudes toward music that are developed in the schools. Are singing and playing merely school subjects taking place at stated hours in the curriculum, or are they also used as wished-for means of recreation or of enhancing the real occasions for music? In other words, is music being integrated in the real, self-propulsive life of the pupil, so that it will not be something super-added like a coat or dress to be worn only in school, but a way of life itself? Perhaps the children are always *preparing* to sing, *learning* to sing, or learning only *to read the notes*, but never really *singing* with the kindling imagination, love, and joy that put to shame all the dull, waterlogged or artificially lighted songs and singing — like gas logs — and the other pedagogical obstructions that more and more teachers are casting away. If this is so, must it be allowed to remain so? It is not enough to cultivate knowledge and skill that are applicable in real life in the community. We must also cultivate attitudes, use motives, that are applicable there.

But before observing ways of doing this, let us consider what constitutes adequate provision for the attainment of knowledge and skill in music.

Quantity in Music Instruction

In 1921 the Music Supervisors' National Conference unanimously adopted a Standard Course in Music prepared by its Educational Council. For the information of readers not connected with school music we quote some of the recommendations given in that course.

Music must be given a reasonable and fair amount of the time of the school day, not only as an art subject both beautiful and useful, but as a subject broadly educational. In a daily schedule of 300 or more minutes, music as such should be allowed not less than 15 minutes daily in primary grades, not less than 20 minutes daily in intermediate grades, and not less than the equivalent of 25 minutes daily in grammar, junior high and high school grades. The time assignment is not to include the valuable functioning of music as an ally in Physical Culture, English, Festivals, Pageants, etc. In upper grades this time allotment may include one period of Glee Club practice or orchestra rehearsal. All other periods of instrumental music (piano and orchestral instruments) should be additional.

Music work meeting the present day requirements necessitates in every city, town, and county a thoroughly well-trained director of music, and a sufficient number of able assistants to permit a trained supervisor to visit each classroom not less than once each month. A visit twice each month is highly desirable.

The demands upon the classroom teacher in carrying on the daily work make it absolutely necessary that every Normal School shall require for graduation at least 24 weeks of daily lessons in the study and practice of music under practical and musicianly instructors who have had experience in school work.

The increased wide-spread use and enjoyment of instrumental music and the undoubted highly educative value of the subject when properly pursued, make it imperative that the schools offer instrumental courses open to all children, in school time, and largely or wholly at public expense, exactly as has been done in Science, Physics, Manual Training, Domestic Science, etc. Systematic effort should be made to discover and encourage children possessed of special talent in any and all fields of music.

The equipment necessary to make music effective must include a keyboard instrument available for each class, pianos of good grade for piano classes, recitals, etc., and a good phonograph and carefully selected library of records. A player-piano would also be distinctly helpful. There must be an ample supply of text-book and supplementary material for carrying on the proper procedure in classroom vocal music and also ample material of real musical worth for bringing music to the service of the school, the home, and the community. . . . The Conference recommends the following summary of music accomplishments as a standard of attainment for the end of the 6th year.

1st. Every child shall have acquired the use of his singing voice and pleasure in song as a means of expression.

2nd. Every child shall have learned to enjoy music as something heard as well as something expressed.

3rd. Every child shall have acquired a repertory of songs which may be carried into the home and social life, including "America" and "The Star-Spangled Banner."

4th. Every child shall have developed aural power to know by sound that which he knows by sight and vice versa. Every child shall have acquired the ability to sing at sight, using words, a unison song of hymn-tune grade, and the easiest three-part songs; these to be in any key; to include any of the measures and rhythms in ordinary use; to contain any accidental signs and tones easily introduced; and in general to be of the grade of difficulty of folk-songs such as the "Minstrel Boy"; also knowledge of the major and minor keys and their signatures.

5th. Every child talented in musical performance shall have had opportunity for its cultivation.

6th. The children shall have developed a love for the beautiful in music, and taste in choosing their songs and the music to which they listen for the enjoyment which only good music can give.

7th. The children shall have acquired the ability to appreciate the charm of design in songs sung; to give an account of the salient features of structure in a standard composition after a few hearings of it; to identify at least the three-part song form from hearing; and to recognize and give titles and composers of a reasonable number of standard vocal and instrumental compositions.

8th. Above all, the children shall have arrived at the conception of music as a beautiful and fine essential in a well-rounded, normal life.

The composite plans in Chapter III of this book indicate much of what the high schools can do.

In the reader's own community, what provision in leadership, time, activities, equipment, and school credits is made for singing, playing, and for listening in the elementary schools, the junior high schools, and the senior high schools? How often do the classes and extra-curricular groups in elementary and junior high schools have direct help from music teachers? What proportions of the students are enrolled in elective choruses, orchestras, bands, chamber music groups, appreciation courses, and in extra-curricular musical groups of other kinds? Are there good, suitable rooms in which to rehearse, with an ample supply of vocal and instrumental music worthy of being sung or played by boys and girls whose musical tastes and abilities are now being formed? Are there enough good pianos, in tune, and good phonographs and a treasury of the best recorded music suitable for boys and girls? Is there at least one radio set in each school? What living concerts (not reproduced ones) especially suitable to the pupils have they had opportunity to hear? Is there an ample supply, loanable to students, of the less common but indispensable instruments of orchestras and bands? To what extent can pupils progress in the instruction provided in the schools?

These are questions which can be answered with pride in an increasing number of cities, some of which have already been referred to, and the largest proportion of which are in the north central states. In Detroit, for another example, in 1930 there were 167 special teachers of music in the elementary schools; 41 in the intermediate or junior high schools, of whom eight were confined to teaching instrumental music; and 52 in the senior high schools, of whom 24 were instrumental music teachers. Sixty to sixty-six minutes a week are given to music for all pupils in elementary and intermediate schools. In the senior high schools music is elective and classes meet daily. Instrumental instruction, introduced into the elementary and intermediate divisions in 1923, was in 1930 being received by 5,000 pupils in those divisions. Orchestras, balanced in instrumentation, had by that year been organized in 80 elementary schools, 15 intermediate schools, and 15 high schools; and bands in 2, 12, and 15 of these three kinds of schools respectively. These three divisions were further represented by three all-city orchestras and two all-city bands, the latter from only the elementary and intermediate schools. District orchestras and bands were organized in four of the fifteen elementary districts into which the school system is divided.

In Minneapolis there is an elementary school — the Cooper School — in which 115 pupils out of a total of 282 in Grades III to IV were in 1930–31 given instruction in orchestral instruments, and 54 in piano-playing; a proportion of 60 per cent! An orchestra of 61 was adding to the interest of these children, and ownership by the school of 51 loanable instruments was relieving poorer parents of any economic obstacle to allowing their children to learn to play.

But between these high degrees of provision and that reached by the city referred to on page 171 there is a long scale in which many cities and towns have not yet progressed beyond "do, re, mi." For instance, in a New England town of 45,000 people who deservedly pride themselves upon having one of the best school systems in the United States, with a remarkably fine corps of teachers and a high record of achievement made by its graduates in colleges, the total amount of time per week given to music in school hours in the entire four-year Senior High School is 80 minutes. This time is divided equally between the entire Freshman and Sophomore classes, each having about 500 students who are compelled to have chorus once a week in a beautiful big auditorium in which they cannot hear the effects of their part-singing! In the elementary schools of that town every class has at least fifteen minutes of singing or listening every day and is visited by an expert music teacher once every week. But in the High School, where all this training and experience should find its fullest flowering and promise of still richer fruit to come, there is only the weekly " sing " of those two large classes, and as much of an orchestra, a band and boys' and girls' glee clubs as the sing leader can gather to meet once a week after school hours without school credit. The silent shadow of the college is on that high school, and it is further limited by the fact that, unlike the high schools of the middle and far west, its day closes at 1:30, only 4½ hours of school time each day. It should be said, however, to show what might be done if there were adequate provision, that it has had a good school orchestra of 35, a band of 25, and larger glee clubs.

When our great eastern colleges offer entrance credit for music, as it is expected that they will do, this New England high school will undoubtedly offer adequate courses in preparation for that credit. The following resolution adopted by the Department of Superintendence of the National Education Association at Dallas in 1927 is also promising:

We would record our full appreciation of the fine musical programs and art exhibits in connection with this convention. They are good evidence that we are rightly coming to regard music, art, and other similar subjects as fundamental in the education of American children. We recommend that they be given everywhere equal consideration and support with other basic subjects.

Quality in Music Instruction

Quality in this regard is usually thought of as having to do with the character of the music used and of the performance of it. These are of great importance, but the following episode will illustrate another kind of quality for which the first two are the means or tokens, and without which they would be of little value.

One day the writer visited a school in a large city and in two hours heard six separate classes sing with such accuracy, unanimity, and purity of tone that had he been asked to mark it all, he would willingly have said 95 per cent. But when he was about to leave the building, the principal invited him to observe the work of a class in Americanization, a group of 19 children from nine to seventeen years of age in which five nationalities were represented. A few minutes after he entered their room the teacher called on two French children, a sister and brother, to sing one of their native songs. Then came a family group of three Croatian boys who did likewise. After them a little Russian Jewish boy sang.

By this time the walls of the school-house had disappeared for the writer. If he had been asked for a "mark," he would have been not only impotent but offended. This was real singing, the first he had heard all day, that took hold of him and seemed somehow so natural and essential as to be the very life of each child re-embodied in the song. The little Russian boy's singing was especially deep-rooted and moving, though free as a lark's. When asked where he learned the song, he said in broken English, " I heard a Christian girl sing it on the street in Russia." One thought of some of the Christian girls who teach singing in the schools, and of those two hours (and dozens more in some other schools) spent listening to 95 per cent " singing," often of 2¾ per cent songs. But there was little time and no need for reminiscence. The teacher, with obvious pride and patriotism, called on the entire class to sing " America, the Beautiful." She had full right to be proud of their diction, and their faces showed a docile eagerness to please her. But how different it was from the singing of their own songs, the songs that they had appropriated, taken to themselves, from someone who had himself or herself done likewise, instead of having merely imitated someone who evidently was herself only an imitator in music, not an appropriator. Though well-intended, it was only a kind of lip-service.

Now it must be admitted that a song beloved by one's own countrymen and friends, sung in a strange land far from those friends, is likely to be more significant and moving to the singer than it would be were he in his native home; and it must also be admitted that there is likely to be for the listener a glow of romance associated with a song and singer from a country foreign to him. But these factors do not account for all the difference. And it was not due to any qualities merely of their voices or voice-production. The children of the six classes heard earlier in the day would have sung those lovely native songs with qualities of voice that, objectively considered, are more admirable. The difference then was in the quality of *experience* of the singers, what the songs and singing meant to them. This seems too obvious an idea to be mentioned, but it is evidently forgotten or overlooked by many teachers and leaders.

The quality of the performer's own state of mind and feeling determines the value of the whole enterprise to him, not only for the present but also — and this is now our chief concern — for the future. The most perfect automobile will not go any farther than it can be pushed without the spark of expanding life in the fuel. To get singing and playing beyond the school door we will have to make them so full of genuine meaning, so fused and blended with the expanding interests of real life, that they will become as natural and essential to the individual as the little Russian boy's singing was to him. One hint as to how this may be done in this fearfully distracting environment of ours in which music is so often "put on," [3] may be taken from the fact that the school and community singing in this country that comes nearest to being so fused with life is our Christmas caroling. If the reader has read Chapter II and studied the plans presented in Chapter III, he has other hints even if he had none before, and we may now consider some of the difficulties under which school music is carried on, some or all of which the reader may help to overcome.

(1) *Subjected Music*

The very systematizing of music in schools, so valuable in making sure that every child of a certain school, and the twenty million or so enrolled in village, town, or city elementary schools, shall have carefully planned music instruction, tends strongly to make it a *subject*, another compartment in the fractional cubby-holed school life, instead of being a way of expression integrated in the whole life of the individual. Here is a class of sixth grade children who have this morning had a period of arithmetic, one of social science, and then one of English composition of some sort. It is now 10:30. The music teacher has come. Now this is a wonderfully potential combination of forces — a group of expansive youngsters who for the past hour and a half have been pressing their energies first into one shape and then into another (at best somewhat unnatural and constraining) confronted by a music-loving musician come to sing, play, or listen with them. Here is stuff of which the richest living is made, and the richest learning, too.

But hold on! Music is a subject, just as important as arithmetic. This is another "Christian girl," in school. Hasn't she had to take a four-year course in

[3] We talk about "putting on" a concert, and the phrase seems often to fit the enterprise perfectly.

Public School music methods and everything else necessary to get a college degree and a job, in which course, having perhaps had previously little musical training and little talent, she was obliged to turn all her singing and playing into laborious practice? Hasn't she a course to follow, made out by the far-off editors of a series of books or by her superior officer down in the Board of Education building? And isn't she being paid for doing so? " Defer! Defer! to the Lord High Executioner! " She's " got 'em on the list " — the songs — and " they never will be missed."

Now it would be grossly unfair and untrue to say that all or even most music teaching in schools can be so characterized. The writer has visited elementary school music classes, sometimes in obscure places, whose singing and attitude it was a benediction of joy to hear and feel. Almost every teacher wants with all her heart and mind to win the love of children for music. But it is no easy task to maintain their love for it throughout the daily, weekly, monthly and yearly endeavor to have them, all of them, grow to the musical stature that in the past was vouchsafed only to the few whose exceptional talent or cultural homes and wealth made it possible. This is no mere " community singing." Growth, the utmost growth possible for each one — poor, rich, the vulgarly or barrenly brought up as well as the well brought up, and the one-talented as well as the ten-talented — this is the task!

We are only pointing out a damaging tendency, overcome by the most gifted teachers, that is mainly due to the enormous weight of our whole educational machinery, employing over a million classroom teachers (about 17,000 music teachers) in a work in which many are called but few are chosen. However, we must not forget that even the least gifted teacher has resources that do not appear on the surface, and at the crucial moments she is only one, not a million.

Moreover, she is confronted by only one group of children, whose expanding energies are a "new-created world" which "springs up at God's command," at whatever of God — in freedom, joy, beauty, and wisdom, as well as skill — is in her.

(2) *Competition from Tin Pan Alley*

The artificial motives for singing or playing in schools, which are likely to be the only ones in music thus "subjected," are opposed by another, more alluring sort of more or less artificial motives outside. The use and dissemination of new songs in the talkies, music shops and elsewhere, has become an enormous business aided by garish color and other ulterior lures in the theatres and on the covers of the printed songs. The songs themselves are designed to make immediate appeal, following the emotional and sensuous paths of least resistance.

During three weeks spent in one of our largest cities the writer was able to compare children's singing in the schools with some of their singing in the recreation centers of the same districts early in the evenings. The school singing was all light and smooth, according to the most admired traditions of school singing, and the songs were such as are made especially for children. The recreation center singing was heavy, harsh, almost cynical in its ugly hardness, according to the choices of the children, and the songs were those of the talkies. The writer was informally introduced to small groups of children of from about nine to fourteen years of age in these centers as a man who plays the piano and likes singing. "Would you like to sing? " "What would you like to sing? " These were the questions. After playing with complete acquiescence whatever he could of their choices, he told them of his own two children who, he said, sing or hum at home many songs they learn at school. " I wonder if you learn the same songs. What songs do you learn in school?" With the exception of some favorable responses from the youngest children and a few vain attempts on the part of older ones to remember the words and tunes of school songs, they were either unable or unwilling to answer his questions. But there was persistent enthusiasm for popular songs, both the words and tunes of which most of the children knew very well.

In seven of the centers each child who visited the center during two or three days was asked by a worker to write on a slip of paper, without communication with anyone, the name of a favorite song. It was explained that the song might be a school or patriotic or church song, or any other kind. This was not intended as a thorough, dependable test of children's tastes. Such a test would require other conditions. But the 1,055 responses may be interesting to the reader. The order of preference started as follows:

Sonny Boy [4]	378
America	100
Rainbow Round My Shoulder	87
Lilac Time	76
Star-Spangled Banner	73
Ramona	73
Blue Heaven	41
That's My Weakness Now	39
The Red, White, and Blue	22
Sweet and Low	13

The rest of the songs were mostly popular ones, the total number of votes for such being 799. Of the additional school songs, almost all were well-known real songs including " Old Folks at Home," " Old Black Joe," and " My Old Kentucky Home," and four

[4] Al Jolson was then " teaching " this song through a talkie in one of the city's theatres, and there were doubtless other " teachers " of it being heard over the radio.

Christmas songs, it being early in December when the vote was taken.

Artificiality and Its Cure

One wonders how the unadorned school songs learned and sung in the simple, quiet schoolroom ever compete successfully with the endless, rapid flow of garishly presented popular songs of which the best as well as the worst pass quickly away. When the school singing is all confined to light, pretty tones, the same for all songs regardless of differences in meaning, and the conscientious teacher stands constantly over the children, correcting or approving throughout the lesson, is not a totally artificial situation likely to result? Even if this is pleasurable and the children welcome it, what has it to do with the lasting human qualities and needs for expression to which real music and real singing administer? Is it not another kind of " Sunday religion," or like working-clothes or a pretty decoration that are worn only in school?

Again, our hope lies in arousing and using naturally the natural motives for singing or playing such as holiday spirit, social feeling, the need for real freedom of spirit and re-creation between subjects and at other times, the impulse to sing arising from rhythmic activity as when the children are marching in the gymnasium, the impulse to have fun, the love of beauty, and the happiness of occasional quiet contemplation, and other interests discussed in earlier chapters.[5]

(3) Individual Differences in Children

In any one elementary school class there may be degrees of musical intelligence or talent ranging from

[5] See especially the reference on pages 53–54 to the effects of associating music with otherwise ordinary experiences. Is it not probable that the capacity for enthusiasm, for prizing many of the everyday experiences of life that otherwise seem trivial or inane, is itself cultivated through real singing?

moron to genius. Yet the entire class is to be taught, usually the same thing at the same time. Every child is expected to learn to read music at sight with the taxing variety of capacities and skills involved in the process, and to participate in part-singing, listening, and the study of musical theory. Obviously, those of greater talent are likely often to be bored, and the least gifted discouraged. What strange, almost incredible perversions of the values of music and of the conscientious teacher's own purposes occur because of this condition and mistaken procedure in it! The writer has visited many a class in which a good song beloved by him — say, a part song — well introduced by the teacher, presented a prospect of a happy quarter of an hour; but from the moment the children tackled it until it was either given up or merely intoned in despair, they were driven farther and farther away from it.

However, it is now quite generally believed that individual differences in talent must be provided for in music as well as in other subjects. Some junior and senior high schools have long been providing for a wide range of individual differences. Music supervisors are only commencing to solve the problem for elementary schools, but the following comments may safely be made:

(a) The social and inspirational powers of music for the whole regular class are to be increased, not lessened, by any provision for individual differences. Let special provision be made for the more talented children, and let every other child have attractive opportunity to rise to his own highest level of possibility, but let there also be provision for the richest possible musical life of the class as a whole. How can it be made possible for every child, no matter what his talent, to have a real, enjoyable part in the class musical life?

First of all, through real singing of first-class simple songs learned in the most direct way possible, some of them with parts or descants matching the various talents of the children; through playing, even if it be a drum, tambourine, triangle or other respectable rhythm band instrument which, if appropriately played, may be happily used singly or in any combination with or without singing, and by quite big children as well as little ones; through dancing of some sort; through acting out songs or instrumental music; or through quiet listening. There may be more than one boy or girl who will find a way to music through making a drum, a marimba or some other simple instrument that he or she will be proud and happy to play. And the collecting instincts of other pupils may help music win them through keeping scrapbooks of pictures, comments, and even, perhaps, the copied notation of themes.

(b) There are extra-curricular activities even in elementary schools such as choirs, orchestras or smaller playing groups and music appreciation clubs, meeting usually after, but sometimes during school hours, that can be made to provide for individual differences. In Seattle, for instance, there are 63 elementary school orchestras of from nine to thirty members each, and an all-city elementary orchestra made up of 65 of the best players in those schools. There are 80 such orchestras in Detroit. In Detroit, Rochester, Pittsburgh and other cities that have a plentiful supply of special music teachers, usually one in each elementary school, the formation or occasional informal meeting of such elective and sometimes selective singing, playing or listening groups gives especially good opportunity to provide for individual differences. In Kansas City, Missouri, where there is an orchestra of from 10 to 25 players in each of 50 elementary schools, special part-time leaders are employed to take charge of weekly rehearsals in the schools in which there are no teachers capable of doing so. These leaders are paid two dollars an hour.

(c) Classes in piano and in other instruments are usually formed in such a way as to have children of like degrees of talent or learning power working together and progressing at their own rate of speed.

(4) *Another Kind of Artificiality*

There is some dissatisfaction with the prevalence of made-to-order songs that are in most of the series of school music books. Made to teach something by, to provide additional practice in reading or to give novelty to the books, they seem rarely to contain the incalculable quality that makes music real and lasting. In some of these books there are many folk songs and other real songs, but even if the singing of them is real, which is even more important, is it so diluted by much singing of vacuous songs that the total experience resembles watered milk?

Enough has been said about this with regard to children in Thomas Whitney Surette's " Music and Life," in Archibald T. Davison's "Music Education in America," and in other books and articles. Let us consider also the effect on the teachers, of singing and listening to pretty or dull little made-to-order songs day after day, year in and year out.

It seems a remarkable token of the durability of the spirit that there are so many school music teachers who despite such songs maintain superb eagerness and devotion to their work. But evidently most teachers use them only for practice in sight-singing, going quickly from one to another, and they doubtless enjoy the sense of progress which comes of having children go through a book so. This may be valuable. It certainly is safer and easier for the teacher to follow a book than to follow and lead the children. When we do the latter, we bring about a series of real musical experiences which, while coherent and progressive, are fitted to, or enlist the vital interests of Mary, John, and the others — each a unique individual as well as a social being: experiences that will arouse and develop in them, with their particular powers and interests, in their particular school, home, church, and other situations, the natural will to sing or to make or respond to music in some other way, for the love and inner need of it. And we lead them to gain skills as a means to, or a result of that singing, playing, dancing, or whatever is done. We frequently have in education to choose between safety and real growth.

But what is the effect on you, the teacher, of the music and singing you teach? What does it do to you? Let your own real attitudes and feelings with regard to music be a barometer to you of the quickening pressure that is in the classroom when you are teaching. No amount of dull, fabricated music or singing, no matter what technical progress it inveigles children into achieving, can be exchanged for the quickening musical spirit of a teacher, without penalty to everyone concerned. One can see, with Blake, the angelic host

> throw down their spears
> And water heaven with their tears.

*   *   *   *   *   *

Whither Instrumental Music?

What about the quality of instrumental music in schools? The stupendous and almost sudden achievements in this field, as represented by such superb high school orchestras as are in San Diego, in Lincoln, Nebraska, and elsewhere, by excellent symphonic bands, and by the phenomenal National High School Orchestra and Band, dispel all thought of handicaps. Yet anyone who has heard many other school orchestras and bands and visited normal schools and other teacher-training institutions knows that much of the playing and many of the courses for teachers are lacking in adequate leadership. The very speed of the growth in school instrumental music has naturally brought about a great deal of superficial and unmusical teaching and preparation of teachers. Many teachers who have not learned to play any one instrument very well are expected to teach all the members of a prospective orchestra or band, or of both, all the instruments; and their achievements are amazingly large, but not always musical. In at least eight of the cities visited by the writer, classes in one or more band or orchestra instruments were in charge of classroom or vocal music teachers whose preparation consisted only of a few lessons from the city supervisor of instrumental music or from a supervisor giving class instruction in a university or teachers' college summer session. Some of this activity might more justly be regarded as being in the manual training department.

The state and national contests, so effective in arousing and maintaining interest in the development of orchestras and bands, have brought about abnormal progress for some individuals. Excellent but very difficult compositions have been chosen as contest pieces. In one of the large eastern states Liszt's " Les Préludes " was chosen as the contest piece for Class A Bands. The leader of the band that won first place (the contest took place in May) told the writer that since four horns were required, he secured funds to purchase four French horns in January and assigned them to boys who had never played any such instrument before. By arranging frequent lessons for them with a horn teacher in the city, and almost daily sessions of practice with himself at the school, he succeeded in getting those boys to learn in four months to play the difficult parts of that Liszt virtuoso piece well enough to take part in winning first place. But they learned nothing else. Knowing of the victory of the band, the writer visited its city in the summer and listened to one of the few band concerts given in the parks there by adults. It was a very feeble band. " Why doesn't the prize High School Band give some concerts in the summer? " he asked. " They have worked so hard learning the contest piece," replied the supervisor, " that they haven't had time to learn anything else. It's all we could do to learn four marches for the football games, and that contest piece. Anyway, they need a rest in the summer."

Another extreme kind of perversion of the good intentions of the leading school music supervisors is exemplified in an otherwise musically admirable school system in the Middle West. About 1,700 children are receiving free class instrumental instruction at a cost of about $7,000 a year to the city, a notable generosity. But no child receives more than one semester's instruction, after which he or she is placed in an orchestra that, in all but the Senior High Schools, meets not more than twice weekly. The children are urged to continue their study with private teachers, but many of them do not because of the cost of such lessons. The reader can perhaps imagine the welter of sound in which many an unfledged fiddler finds himself, especially in the larger of the orchestras. He can neither hear nor see what he is doing. It must be to the pianist and perhaps one or more valiant trumpeters and drummers, with their assertive and fairly accurate execution, that his continued interest and the citizens' approval of the enterprise are due. But is this not bad for the character of the individual as well as for the powers of ear, mind, and spirit, by which music might become to him what it is at its best?

To the adult, at least, there seems to be a kind of dishonesty in playing false notes and omitting others without correcting the errors some time. Applause is, of course, freely given and evidently freely received every time there is an audience, regardless of the errors and poor quality.

There should be no objection to having beginners play in an orchestra or, better, a smaller ensemble of like instruments. It provides incentive and the group idea. But the music as a whole, and the requirements of each part, must be suited in every way to the individual performers. And surely there ought to be good, inexpensive instruction available after that single semester is over. A music school settlement or a community music school should be established or the public schools should make a slight charge for further instruction, if free lessons cannot be afforded.

These extreme perversions are described here, despite all the good work that is being done, only to point the more emphatically to the need that will always call for special attention in school music instruction, especially in orchestras and bands. It has been demonstrated that youth with its abounding energy plus daily rehearsals and every conceivable kind of challenge and other stimulus, can achieve orchestra performances of the world's greatest symphonies. The National High School Orchestra Camp, directed by a man with genius for the work and assisted by some of our great conductors, achieves a complete symphony concert every week of its season such as is given by our greatest symphony orchestras. But now and always we need very much to have demonstrations in high schools everywhere of the kind of steady, thorough inner growth that is not overbalanced by outer stimulation and virtuosity.

Instrumental music, so far advanced technically as it now is, tends away from the fundamental musical impulses of the individual. Even children with prodi-

gious talent — some of our musical prodigies — have
not been able to sustain their inner energies in the
midst of that tendency and stimulation. They grow
stale. What is going on in the minds and spirits of the
thousands of less talented boys and girls who are being so valorously led into public performances and
contests of the music of the most mature artistry and
mature feeling?

They evidently love it — those who, like the National Camp players, are skillfully led, and are not
lost in a maze of bombastic fiddling, blowing, and
pounding — and the fuller and richer in feeling and
color it is, and the harder it is, up to the last notch of
their energies, the better they like it. Two of the works
that the writer has heard most often in high schools,
some of them in places never yet reached by a great
symphony orchestra except by radio, are the slow
movement from Tschaikowsky's Fifth Symphony, and
Sibelius' "Finlandia." But, as almost every radio listener must know, complete symphonies of Beethoven,
Brahms, Franck, Dvorak, as well as Tschaikowsky,
and Wagner preludes and overtures, are the magnificent substance given to and by those nearly three
hundred boys and girls at the National High School
Orchestra Camp. And the Band out there is equally
valorous.

There is no patriotism, no thrilling sense of values
and of fine possibilities in American life, more moving
than when one hears the Camp Orchestra play such a
work as the first movement of the Beethoven *Eroica*.
Here is youth at its best, one feels: expansive, liberating, the whole personality given generously and, in
a true sense, heroically, to what is of most worth, most
lovable; to what it chiefly needs and desires but often
vainly seeks in the stuff offered to it by the commercial and other dispensers of mere diversions.

They love it. But some leaders and other musicians

believe that more of the sweet reasonableness and naturalness of the best choral singing, and a more leisurely though animated and thorough growth, must enter instrumental music, or else it may in adult years fade away like the glories of a sunset, because it was too dependent on very stimulating outer influences that do not exist in adult life.

This brings us to the third very important consideration, after quantity and quality, regarding music in schools: namely, the directions it takes, or the purposes cultivated in the pupils engaged in it.

Pupils' Purposes in School Music

As was said earlier in this chapter, we expect the schools to cultivate skill in music. We also expect them to cultivate desire to use that skill for the love and joy of the music. Possessing adequate skill is itself likely to be a cause of such desire, for we are all prone to enjoy doing what we can do well. The converse of this — that we do not enjoy what we do poorly — has become an increasingly potent factor in these days of radio-raised standards of performance. But the purposes or incentives cultivated in what we have referred to as the social and educational pressure of school life may be such as cannot be carried out or maintained in life outside the schools.

For instance, the present unemployment of thousands of professional performers is evidence enough that the purpose to become such a performer is very unlikely to be successfully fulfilled by any except the few who have highly superior talents. In this regard, the following summary of responses to inquiries addressed to high school students is interesting:

In 1928, of 306 members of the National High School Orchestra
  58% purposed to be professional players, and
  16% to be music teachers.

In 1930, of 293 members of the National High School Orchestra

    38% purposed to be professional performers, and

    10% to be music teachers.

In 1930, of 249 members of high school orchestras and bands in Flint, Michigan,

    16% purposed to be professionals, and

    13% to be music teachers.

In 1930, of 689 members of orchestras and bands in the Emporia, Kansas, School Music Contest

    11% purposed to be professional performers or music teachers.

In 1930, of 1,120 members of orchestras and bands in the schools of Westchester County, New York,

    15% purposed to be professional performers, and

    8% purposed to be music teachers.

In 1930, of 433 members of high school orchestras and bands in Milwaukee, Wisconsin,

    21% purposed to be professional performers, and

    16% purposed to be music teachers.

In 1930, of 124 members of school orchestras and bands in Tipton County, Iowa,

    15% purposed to be professional performers, and

    3% purposed to be music teachers.

What other purposes or incentives are used to motivate the work of gaining skill? In Chapter III we mentioned the challenges given through group and individual contests, of which there have been many, through competition for individual rank in orchestras and bands, through the awarding of marks and credits in a course, or honors for achievement, through the giving of public performances, through the personal force of the leader, and lastly through the appeal of the best music itself which makes those who are responsive want to strive to achieve full participation in it. Now which of these motives are operative in adult life?

There have been many contests of adult choruses, mostly of men's glee clubs; and now and then at a Shriners' or American Legion Convention or the like there are band contests. But the opportunities for musical competition by adults are very much fewer than they are for boys and girls. One reason for this is that many men and women cannot leave their work and homes, as children can, to take part in a contest in some distant city, and there are not likely, except in large cities, to be enough groups of any one kind, size and degree of skill to make a local contest feasible. Competition for individual rank in an adult amateur orchestra or band is even more rare. Some evening school choruses, orchestras and bands have something of the spirit of a course, the leaders of them frequently being public school music teachers who almost unavoidably give the performers the educational, step-by-step attitude. And in some adult groups medals or other tokens of esteem are given for regular attendance. But no system of credits such as is common in high schools exists for any such groups. The only common musical incentives for adult amateurs are those mentioned in Chapter II, especially the giving of public performances, the personal force of a leader, and the appeal of the music itself.

Of the latter incentive, which is the most rewarding, enough is said elsewhere in this book. Of good leaders there are far too few. By many school music supervisors it is said that graduates of their schools do not continue singing or playing because the leaders in the community and in its various channels of interest are not good enough. It is the supreme task of the best music schools, such as that of the Juilliard Foundation and other private institutions, and those of the best universities and teachers' colleges, to develop good leaders whose personal and musical force will be given to amateur music-making by adults as well as by children, or only by adults.

To the concert-giving motive we have already given consideration on pages 68–70, which the reader is urged to review with special reference to its relation to school music. In pleading for entry of the skilled singer or player into the life of the community, Dr. John Erskine recently said, " Perhaps he would prefer to give a rigid program in a large hall, beginning with Bach and ending with a Hungarian Rhapsody. But if his neighbors prefer to listen to their music at a church sociable, then he is something of a fool if he lets what he calls his professional ideals prevent him from making the church sociable of some musical importance." He may earn a living partly or entirely through teaching or conducting or both, or through a non-musical vocation.

*   *   *   *   *   *

Youth's Equivalents of Successful Adult Motives

The equivalents for boys and girls of the motives and activities that make adult singing and playing flourish in the community are good performances by them for their class-mates, for assemblies, in school plays and dramatic festivals, at suitable meetings of school clubs and in school music festivals. In every city and town in which any school instruction is given at all, classes or other school groups perform now and then for a church, a parent-teacher association, a welfare institution, a luncheon club or chamber of commerce or the like, or for a holiday or civic occasion attracting people of all ages. In 1929–30 the school musical groups of Detroit provided over 400 concerts of varying length for various adult organizations of the city. In what cities and towns do not groups of school children go caroling on the streets, in the hotels, hospitals, and elsewhere on Christmas Eve and sometimes on the days before? Moreover, there are junior choirs and orchestras that participate in Sunday school or church services, and there are in many cities informal performances by various kinds of groups in settlements, community centers, playgrounds, and other organizations or institutions attractive to youth.

In most of the outstanding adult music festivals — in Cincinnati, Ann Arbor, Bangor, Spartansburg, and elsewhere — one concert is given by a chorus of school children. A chorus of 500 junior high school boys sang specially arranged, unaccompanied four-part music well enough to have an honored place in the great annual North Shore Festival at Evanston, Illinois, in 1930; and in Westchester County (N. Y.) Festival, of equally high standard, an afternoon concert in that year included an All-County School Orchestra as well as a chorus of 2,500 boys and girls.

Now amidst so many opportunities to perform for people, there is no lack of incentive such as teachers seek to give to their pupils, yet it may be so used as to spare the pupils from the professionalism that we are or should be trying to avoid, and at the same time associate their school musical training with lasting community interests. But the utmost care must, of course, be taken to protect each pupil or group from the harm of too many performances. Singing or playing and quiet growth in music that is without any audience or prospect of one should be maintained as a simple, daily means of grace. Exhibitionism and overstimulation should be avoided as a plague. Only someone who feels the importance of preserving the self-forgetful play-spirit, and who understands boys and girls well, should ever be permitted to arrange for performances by them.

School Music Festivals and Operettas

Every two years there is given in Milwaukee a two-day Public Schools Music Festival that brings several thousand adults to the city's large auditorium. In 1927 the programs enlisted, in addition to children selected from all the grades and high schools, the

Minneapolis Symphony Orchestra, a chorus consisting of the famous Lyric Male Chorus of Milwaukee business and professional men, and the Girls' Glee Clubs of the high schools. The men and girls together sang the "Elijah" with the orchestra. But in 1929 the programs were given entirely by public school pupils with the exception of a baritone soloist and the local State Teachers' College Orchestra, the latter used only for accompanying. On a Tuesday evening in April the Grade School Band, the Grade School Orchestra, a Seventh Grade chorus, an Eighth Grade chorus, and the two choruses in combination, gave a program on which appeared the names of Beethoven, Schubert, Mendelssohn, Weber, Cherubini, Brahms, Grieg, Saint-Saens, Tschaikowsky, Rachmaninoff, as well as lesser names, each composer represented by one brief composition except Beethoven, whose Larghetto from the Second Symphony was played by the Band, and Mendelssohn, whose Wedding March from "A Midsummer Night's Dream" was played by the orchestra. Each of the four groups was an all-city one representing many schools of its kind in the city. On Wednesday afternoon the program was divided between a demonstration of class instrumental instruction in which a string ensemble and a woodwind ensemble played, among other things, some music of Schumann and Beethoven arranged for them, and a first performance of a cantata composed and dedicated to the children by a beloved composer of the city, Mr. W. Otto Miessner. An All-City Sixth Grade Chorus performed this, aided by the director of the Lyric Male Chorus as soloist, and the orchestra of the State Teachers' College as accompanist. The high schools had their inning on Wednesday evening when their All-City Band brought Gounod in the Marche et Cortège from "La Reine de Saba," and Tschaikowsky in the Andante from his Fourth Symphony; their All-City Orchestra played the Mozart "Marriage of Figaro" overture and Beethoven's Allegro from the First Symphony, and their All-City Chorus sang "Hiawatha's Wedding Feast" by Coleridge-Taylor.[6] The tenor soloist was a student in one of the public prevocational schools, and the accompanying group a combination of the orchestras of two high schools. In addition a harp ensemble played among other things a beautiful Sarabande by Handel. Each of the all-city groups was organized between three and four months in advance of the Festival and rehearsed once each week, after school hours or on Saturday mornings. The Grade School Band was made up of 130 boys and girls chosen from 46 schools (there is also an All-City Grade School Second Band), and the High School Band of 95 represented nine senior high schools and two junior high schools.[7] The Seventh and Eighth Grade Festival Chorus contained 20 per cent — 2,016 boys and girls — of the total number of children in those grades, the songs having been learned by all as part of their regular work in the music course. The Grade School Orchestra's 158 members, chosen from 41 schools, were able to present the following instrumentation:

> 49 first violins, 55 second violins, 5 violas
> 14 violoncellos, 3 string basses, 15 wood winds
> 12 brasses, and 5 percussion instruments

The 107 players in the High School Orchestra had the instrumentation of a professional symphony orchestra, including 18 violas and 7 string basses. At the time of the festival there were 2,182 boys and girls in public school orchestras.[8]

[6] Each group brought other lesser but respectable composers also.

[7] The total number of pupils enrolled in public school bands throughout the city was 1150.

[8] The numbers in bands and orchestras added to the 600 in violin, viola, cello, and string bass classes and the 1600 in the piano classes (a three-

After having heard such a festival, with its stirring sights and sounds of exuberant youth enthroned before its multitude of once-youthful admirers — parents, most of them — one does not expect to find another such musical holiday-making for many a moon, certainly not when he is crossing the viaduct that looks down on the unavoidably ugly stockyards which with the river separate one Kansas City from the other. But arrived on the Kansas side on another April day, he had once more, like the cow who will never be caught under that viaduct, to jump over the moon. For there in that lesser Kansas City [9] he found a seven-day music festival, the third annual one, being presented by the public schools; and because of certain extra-musical considerations, in addition to the pleasure of the music, it was as stirring as the Milwaukee affair. First let us go quickly through the programs: Monday evening, Grades V and VI and a High School Band; Tuesday evening, Grades VII, VIII, and IX in a girls' chorus, boys' chorus, the two combined, and in an orchestra; Wednesday evening, the senior high schools and Junior College in exactly the kinds of groups given for Grades VII, VIII, and IX; Thursday evening, the schools for colored children in choruses, their colored teachers also in choruses — one of men and the other of women — and a colored Parent-Teacher Association Chorus (those extra-musical considerations are commencing to appear); Friday evening, the Junior College Orchestra, two choruses of white teachers, one of men and the

---

year course at two dollars a semester is offered in this instrumental instruction) make a total of about 5,500, nearly 10% of the total number of children in the grades and schools to which instruction is offered.

[9] An admirable and musically more ambitious May Music Festival enlisting choruses and an All-City Orchestra and Band, all from the high schools, in one evening's program, is given annually in Kansas City, Missouri.

other of women, 180 altogether;[10] a white Parent-Teacher Association Chorus of 60 mothers, and the teachers' choruses combined; Saturday afternoon, the kindergarten and Grades I, II, III, and IV (nothing, not bridge or Lindbergh, or even Amos 'n' Andy in person could keep away the parents, most of them anyway, of these little children up on the stage of the handsome auditorium); and on Sunday afternoon, still "presented by the public schools," the Civic Choral Club of 100 men and women closing their eighth season with a free performance of "The Messiah." Now for other extra-musical factors in making this a peculiarly valuable festival:

1. About one-sixth of all the children in the schools took part in the festival, a quota from every school.
2. While some consideration is given to musical ability in choosing the children an effort is made to distribute the opportunities from year to year among as many children as possible, so that those who perform one year are likely to be displaced by others in another year. (This, of course, calls for music both simple and real, an often supremely beautiful combination of traits; for no matter what the circumstances, the music of a festival should be important and the performance admirable.)
3. For the next festival it was planned to have, in addition to the Mothers' Chorus, a Parent-Teacher Association Fathers' Chorus, a quartet of fathers representing each school.
4. Ten cents is charged for admission to each concert except that given by the Civic Choral Club, which is free. The audiences are large. Despite the cost of the additional printed music used, and the rental charge of $500 for the auditorium, a profit of $876 was made in the first year, $993 in the second year, and $1,590 in the third. These profits are devoted to the purchase of music and instruments for the schools.
5. *In neither the Milwaukee nor the Kansas City, Kansas, festivals was there a single competitive event,* and yet

[10] Formed especially for the festival six weeks in advance of it.

there was apparently ample interest and striving for
excellence.[11]

A single concert may be made a festival, by its spirit.
Especially festive are concerts given by one or more
groups from a nearby town or towns in conjunction
with local singers or players.

Operettas

Much more common than festivals of these kinds,
but not nearly so common as brief performances for
adults, are operettas given by high school and junior
high school groups. Reference has already been made
in Chapter I to the fine adventures in this field by
students of Flint's high schools. Music may be all the
more substantiated, its place in life made broader and
more secure, by the possibility — often the necessity
— in operetta-giving, of enlisting the workers in every
other art and craft, and even, perhaps, the classes
in physics and chemistry (the latter for problems
with regard to special lighting — electricity — and in
the making of dyes for costumes.) There is scenery to
be designed and made, posters, as well, costumes also
requiring art and craftsmanship, special devices for
lighting, business management, and, of course, dramatics and dancing.

In the Ethical Culture School in New York the entire libretto of an operetta based on the story of Dick
Whittington and his cat was written by the students
of a seventh grade class, the music consisting partly
of original music, some of which was made by the
pupils, but mainly of English folk tunes and one Moor-
ish one. This project involved a study of verse, practice
in English composition, and even a simple study of
dramatic technique. The question of how to tell the
story through a play, effectively and delightfully,

[11] In Milwaukee there is competition beforehand in the choice of members for the all-city groups.

caused several discussions and eager perusal of ways used by a certain William Shakespeare in telling the story of the Merchant of Venice. The need for information about the customs and costumes of the time of Edward IV in England made the reading of history a very vital activity.

All of life, it seems, may go into the preparation of an opera, even eating (for every venture holding people together in so long and arduous an undertaking should be followed by a special supper and merry-making for the cast and all). But how sadly wasteful is all this in an appalling large proportion of the operetta-giving in our schools! At least 30 per cent of the performances encounterd by the writer in all parts of the country were of stuff that seemed to him so trivial in words and music as to defeat every good purpose of music in schools or anywhere else. The singing and acting of one good ballad after an hour's preparation would be much more delightful and nourishing than all the four months of preparation given to mere glitter. But there is growing opposition to all this, well epitomized by the Board of Education member who, after such a show in a school, said heatedly, " Are we turning our schools into debilitating ' show ' places? "

It is especially delightful now to give a report of excellent lasting work in operetta-giving. For the past twelve years Gilbert and Sullivan and a peer or two of theirs have each year taught delight to high school students in Lewiston, Maine. The writer joined a large audience there in enjoying " The Gondoliers " performed by adults (for an amateur company of adults also does homage to the writers of first-rate light operas each year) and found that fourteen of the performers were graduates of high school companies, and that the school supervisor of music was himself a principal member of the community adult company.

It hardly needs to be said that adult concerts of all kinds by children (a logical converse of "children's concerts" by adults), when they are genuinely and generously *for* the adults, not contests or mere exhibitions, must tend strongly toward giving the music of the schools a bright and lasting place in the whole, not merely the school fraction, of the lives of the boys and girls, to say nothing of its effects on the adults with whom they live at home and on whom they must depend for continued and further support of music in the city.

The School Music Teacher as a Leader of Amateurs In and Out of the Schools

Whatever the purpose or occasion, the conduct of any school musical enterprise should be entirely amateur in spirit. Even in some superb concert-giving groups of adult amateurs the rehearsals are conducted with all the single-hearted devotion to the music, as music, that any small *haus-musik* group could feel, as though neither time nor space (seat-space at the concert hall) or money, existed. Like the best professionals, the members of these groups would probably continue singing or playing — in some group or alone — even if there were no audiences. That spirit is essential to school music, and whether it exists and persists or not, depends almost entirely on the qualities and attitudes of the leader.

Are school music teachers themselves amateurs in the true sense? No one who has heard or, better still, joined the hundreds of those teachers gathered informally in the hotel lobby for the best kind of community singing, from 10:30 to midnight or later, after a very busy day at one of their District or National Conferences, can doubt that there exists among them generally a real love of music for its own sake. But it must be admitted that school music teaching itself still suffers in many places from being professionalized, which is to say that it is, in those places, more or less subject to artificial standards as to methods, quality of tone, and choice of music. This must be said though purposeful freedom from it all is spreading very encouragingly, especially among the new generation of teachers who will, in turn, be joined by young people of whom many are now singing and playing excellent real music in superb high school choral and instrumental groups. The National High School Chorus is in itself alone sufficient token of what we may come to in all school music if the normal schools and colleges and book publishers will let us.

It must also be admitted that personal inquiry made of many teachers and supervisors indicates that only a small proportion (including some fine chamber music " fans ") sing or play for the love of it after school. True, they need recreation through other pursuits, their school work may not leave time or energy for beloved musical expression of their own, and they may find such expression in ample measure through leadership in real music at school. But is there not danger that because of contrary pressures and attitudes they will themselves lose the amateur's urge and delight that they are or should be trying to communicate to the boys and girls?

This may account for the fact that in many of the 97 cities and towns visited by the writer for the purposes of the national survey, the school music teachers knew very little about musical activities going on in the community. They in whose hands lie the chief possible contributions to the musical life of the community were too hard-pressed by their school work or too lacking in interest to know into what present and future non-professional musical activities their pupils might be going when they leave the school either for a day or forever. The answers to the question, " What are the graduates of your school musical organizations doing in music? " had again and again to do only with professional attainments — " So and so won a scholarship," or " He is now playing in such and such a professional symphony orchestra," or the like. Admirable attainments these are, very much worth having a part in; but so far as the main aims of school music are concerned, they are exceptional, to be eagerly welcomed but regarded as beside the main line of endeavor.

Many teachers, evidently, are too school-minded.[12] For example — an unusually bad example — the director of music in the schools of one of our large cities knew nothing about the valiant but feeble or misdirected musical efforts being made, mostly with children, in recreation centers in all parts of the city, and evidently cared less. His interests in music were definitely confined to its uses in education and in public performances. Later, a well-financed city organization for furthering music was created and one of its first purposes was to provide better opportunities for music in the recreation centers. But though the school director of music accepted membership in the organization, he has objected to that purpose in so far as it involved singing by children, because it would be trespassing on what he holds to be exclusively the function of the schools.

Even within some schools it frequently happens that when music is really needed, as in class socials, school club meetings, rallies, and the like, it is of a very poor sort poorly performed that can give little real pleasure. The school music teachers in those schools seem to disregard these very important opportunities for the desired carry-over of music into leisure-time life, and the students seem carefully to avoid what they would

[12] There are very admirable exceptions, some of which have been fully described in Chapters I and V.

regard as interference from the teachers. True, the students should manage such affairs entirely themselves. They should start to do so when they are in the kindergarten, and throughout the grades there should be such occasions when, if the teacher is a participant at all, she is just one of the singers or players, listeners or dancers or actors. But if she or he has no feeling and no musical and other resources for the spirit of such occasions, and does not often invoke that spirit, at its best, even in the regular lesson-periods, the singing, playing, and listening that she brings about are likely to be associated only with school work, something apart from leisure time living.

The vicious cleavage represented by the terms " high-brow " and " low-brow " that commonly separates education or culture from recreation, impoverishing both, will under those conditions have been well established by the time the students leave high school. One can sadly imagine them after the last school rehearsal putting away the books and parts that bear all that is left of the blessed ardors of Bach, Handel, Schubert, and the others to whom music was a way of full, happy living, and saying "Good-by to all that," while the teachers proudly repeat the often-quoted " Music is the best mind-trainer on the list! "

But of all the companies of musicians, the 17,000 or more school music teachers and supervisors in the United States possess among themselves the largest measure by far of the existing potential capacities for leadership of musical amateurs in our communities. To what extent are their capacities so used? Of the 604 supervisors who responded to the questionnaire already referred to, 73 are engaged in directing amateur musical activities outside of schools. They together are leading a total of 14 bands, 14 orchestras, 3 string ensembles, 54 choruses, glee clubs, and choirs, and 2 organizations of combined choirs.

When one thinks of the 604 cities and towns, this record seems small. But again we must remember that after a full day of school work, many a supervisor is too needful of recreation in non-musical activities to be a music leader again in the evening. Moreover, in some cities the various fields of community musical endeavors were already in charge of leaders when he or she came to take up the school work in the city. The number of teachers who are taking part in community groups led by others is evidently also small, but they should be honored as much as those who lead. It is probable that more and more school systems will allow sufficient time in the music supervisor's day to make leadership in the community possible for him.

Evening Rehearsals

It may be very effective to hold a rehearsal in the evening now and then in addition to, or in place of some of the rehearsing in school hours. This as a training for leisure has the advantage of employing what are the normal and most challenging leisure hours of adults and of every young man or woman who has escaped from so-called home work. Many a school music teacher has been forced to hold some or all rehearsals directly after school hours and has rightly protested because the students were too tired then or were unwilling to give out-of-school time to the work. But the evenings find them rested again, and it is precisely their willingness to sing or play in out-of-school time that we wish to cultivate. There should certainly be sufficient rehearsals in school time to ensure attainment of satisfying skill. But would it not be more in keeping with all the talk and writing about education for leisure if during some of the normal leisure hours, in the evenings, there could be good, voluntary choral singing and group playing instead of home work or instead of whatever else young people may fill their evenings with? The Inter-High School Orchestra in Yonkers, N. Y., that rehearses every Tuesday evening from 7:30 to 9:00 throughout the school year is surely preparing its members more fitly than the school-confined rehearsals alone can do for rich, leisure time living. Such rehearsals as are held by the Bangor (Maine) High School Chorus on one evening each week in company with the Bangor Festival Chorus of adults may be still more effective in this respect, to say nothing of other values possible in joining two or three generations in a common civic enterprise.

Cooperating with Parent-Teacher Associations

There are other ways, besides actual conducting, in which school music teachers can exercise leadership in the community. Probably in every city and town where there is a parent-teacher association and a school music teacher, he is asked at some time to address a meeting of that Association. Such meetings usually consist of a description of the music curriculum in the schools, and demonstration by one or more groups of children of various phases of the work being done. This is very valuable and is made more so when in addition the parents themselves sing two or three real songs from each of the principal song books used in the schools, the songs being chosen to show not only the developments from grade to grade, but, more importantly, to suggest family singing at home. The writer, as a school music teacher, has frequently on the days soon after conducting such a meeting been gleefully greeted by individual children with " My mother (or father or both) learned some of our songs at your meeting! " or " sang out of our book last night," or the like. Related to this is performance by one or more family groups of singers or players at such a meeting and at school assemblies or class parties, enhanced, perhaps, by a brief explanation of how the family got started making music together and when and what they like best to sing or play at home. Similar meetings might well be conducted for the Chamber of Commerce and other men's organizations. Lists of the best suitable music for various activities by family groups of various sizes and kinds are, of course, very helpful.

Cooperating with Sunday School Music Leaders

In Kansas City, Kansas, the school music supervisor has held one or more meetings with Sunday school leaders of singing to let them know what is done about children's singing in schools and to discuss ways and means of making the most of the opportunities offered by the Sunday schools. In the other Kansas City, the school music supervisor herself directs a boy choir that is a worthy model of church and Sunday school singing. The music in more churches and Sunday schools would be better if in more public schools the children could through their manner of singing good suitable hymns realize simply and naturally the feelings expressed in them and the beauty possible in them, instead of using them merely for additional practice of one sort or another or for a thoughtless kind of assembly singing. For instance, contrast Bach's Passion chorale set to the words beginning " In Heavenly Love Abiding " with his " What Tongue Can Tell Thy Greatness, Lord? " the first trustful and serene, and the other full of fine enthusiasm and, near the close, of wonder and reverence. Even fourth grade children can in simple manner achieve a true singing of such superb hymns, and there are now published some excellent collections for children in which even the youngest singers of the kindergarten may begin making music " for the Lord to hear," to which

Bach and any of his fellows, as well as ordinary folks, would be delighted to listen in the Sunday school.

Connections with Recreation Centers and Settlements

Such connections as we have described between the schools and the homes and churches have all too rarely been made with organizations of private music teachers and of recreation and settlement music leaders. Assistance in preparing school children to take part in festivals, plays, parties, and other occasions requiring music in recreation centers and settlements is, however, a somewhat more common means by which school music teachers have related their work to the life of those outside agencies.

Pupils' Playing Outside of Schools

We have been considering to what extent school music teachers exercise leadership in music outside of schools. It will be interesting now to see to what extent the pupils' musical interests are carried outside. This is important because the question as to what is to happen to all the school-grown skill and knowledge after the pupils graduate depends largely on what happens to it before they graduate.

To gather more information in this regard, copies of the following questionnaire addressed to the boys and girls in school orchestras and bands were sent to the music supervisors of a variety of communities and of a State and a National Contest.

AN INQUIRY TO MEMBERS OF ORCHESTRAS AND BANDS

Name _____ Age _____ City or Town _____
Instrument you play _____ Your position in the orchestra or band _____
For how many years have you received instruction in this instrument? _____

Do you expect to make music your means of making a living? _____ If so (1) as a public school music teacher (2) a private music teacher, or (3) a professional player? (Underline your answer)

Do you ever play in any orchestra, band, or small group outside of school? _____ If so, in which of the following kinds? (Please check) Family Group? _____ Friends' or Small Neighborhood Group? _____ Dance Orchestra? _____ Sunday School Orchestra? _____ Larger Neighborhood or Community Orchestra or Band? _____ What other kind? (Such as a Scouts' or Club group or one in a music school or a private teacher's studio) _____
_____

If a Family Group —
  1. With what members of your family? _____
  2. What instruments? _____
  3. About how many times in a month does the group play?
     _____
  4. Name three or more pieces that you have played with your family: _____
     _____
     _____

If a Friends' or Small Neighborhood Group
  1. How many persons are usually in the group? _____
  2. About how old is each person? _____
  3. What instruments? _____
  4. About how many times in a month does the group play?
     _____
  5. Name three or more pieces that you have played with the group: _____
     _____
     _____

If a Sunday School Orchestra —
  1. In what church? _____
  2. How many persons are usually in the orchestra? _____
  3. What instruments? _____
  4. Name three or more pieces that you have played with the orchestra: _____
     _____
     _____

If a Larger Neighborhood or Community Orchestra or Band —
1. What is the name of the organization? _____
2. What is the leader's name? _____
3. Where do you rehearse? _____
4. How often do you rehearse? _____
   On what day or evening and what hour? _____
5. About how many, if any, concerts does the orchestra or band give in a year? _____
6. How many persons are in it? _____ How many adults? _____
7. What instruments? _____
8. Name three or more pieces that have been played by the orchestra or band: _____
   _____
   _____

If a Dance Orchestra —
1. How many persons are usually in the orchestra? _____
2. How many of them are also in a school orchestra? _____
3. What instruments? _____
4. About how many dance engagements does the orchestra have in a school year? _____
5. Do you receive pay for these engagements? _____
   If so, what is the rate of payment? _____
   Are you a member of a Musicians' Union? _____

In comparing the pleasure of playing in a small group — like a string or brass quartet, wood wind ensemble, or a duet or trio — with that of playing in a large orchestra or band, I think that the small group gives:
      1. Less pleasure
      2. More pleasure
      3. About the same amount of pleasure
        (Underline your answer)

The proportions of those boys and girls who perform in groups outside of school rehearsals, and the kinds of groups in which they do so are indicated in the following tabulation of their replies, which were made under the supervision of their instructors:

Organizations	Kansas[13] Contest	National[14] Contest	Flint Jr. High	Flint Sr. High	Milwaukee	Iowa (Tipton Co.)
No. of students reporting	689	216	372	249	433	124
No. who play outside schools	70%	57%	56%	67%	66%	63%
No. playing in family groups	14%	13%	33%	17%	20%	22%
No. playing in small groups of friends . . .	59%	12%	19%	16%	25%	14%
No. playing in Sunday school orchestras . . .	42%	23%	15%	31%	6%	12%
No. playing in community bands and orchestras .	29%	12%	3%	13%	27%	48%
No. playing in dance orchestras	9%	16%	3%	15%	17%	2%
No. playing in other groups, in clubs, music schools, etc.	12%	19%	5%	15%	9%	2%

WESTCHESTER COUNTY, N. Y.

Organizations	Yonkers Pop. (134,646)	Mt. Vernon Pop. (61,499)	New Rochelle Pop. (54,000)	White Plains Pop. (35,830)	9 towns Pop. (5000–17000)	13 towns Pop. (under 5000)
No. of students reporting	104	129	103	214	245	322
No. who play outside schools	79%[15]	51%	63%	61%	67%	53%
No. playing in family groups[16]	12%	19%	23%	21%	26%	23%
No. playing in small groups of friends[16] . .	20%	17%	19%	12%	30%	18%
No. playing in Sunday school orchestras[17] . .	3%	5%	6%	2%	11%	10%
No. playing in community bands and orchestras .	10%	5%	16%	0%	9%	8%
No. playing in dance orchestras	7%	11%	15%	18%	13%	13%
No. playing in other groups, in clubs, music schools, etc.	24%	12%	8%	14%	11%	10%

[13] State Contest, Emporia, Kansas, 1930.

[14] National Orchestra Contest, Lincoln, Nebraska, 1930.

[15] The larger proportion of Yonkers students who play outside is partly due to the existence there of an Inter-High School Orchestra and Inter-High School Band, both of which are regarded herein as outside organizations

One can easily forgive the player of a bass viol or bass horn for not playing in any group requiring the moving of his instrument from the school. Sixteen per cent of those who reported no outside playing were wedded to one of these weighty instruments. But of the rest who reported so, 34 per cent were players of the violin, 3 per cent of the viola, 3 per cent of the cello, 25 per cent of one of the wood winds, 3 per cent of the trumpet, 2 per cent of the French horn, 4 per cent of the trombone, 3 per cent of the alto horn, or the mellophone, 5 per cent of percussion instruments, and 2 per cent of a saxophone. The number of years that had been devoted to study of the instrument was a negligible factor in this regard. Many mere beginners reported playing in an outside group, usually in a family group, and many veterans did not; and vice versa.

Money-making in Dance Orchestras

Many a boy has earned his way through college by playing in a dance orchestra, and many a high school boy has started study of a musical instrument with the hope of doing likewise. It is interesting, therefore, to learn that despite the unemployment of thousands of professional musicians, 137 out of the 2,171 pupils answering our inquiry in Flint, Milwaukee, and Westchester County, reported receiving remuneration for dance orchestra playing — that is, one out of every sixteen members of school orchestras and bands in those cities and the county. Their rates of payment vary

---

because they rehearse weekly after school hours throughout the school year and membership in them can be held only by students who also play in their own school's orchestra or band.

[16] Many family groups and a few friends' groups consisted of only one other person besides the pupil reporting, the size of the ensemble making no difference in its standing in our estimation.

[17] Many Westchester County towns doubtless suffer in this regard from being in the shadow of New York City.

from 75 cents an hour to $10 an evening, the largest number reporting from $3 to $5 an evening. The quantity of engagements vary from one a year to three a week, the largest number reporting about one a month. If a boy who is worthy of it gains in this way a college education that he might not otherwise have had, we may rejoice; but aside from any question of the effects of such playing on students, we must decide that except where there is real financial need students should be led away from accepting paid engagements that adult professional musicians might otherwise secure. Only four of the 137 boy professionals were members of a musicians' union.

What Music Is Played by Family Groups?

In showing the relation between school training and the musical life outside of schools, nothing is more revealing than the choice of music played in the various groups, other than dance orchestras, mentioned in the above reports. Each pupil was asked to name three pieces played by each group of which he is a member. The most revealing with regard to children's tastes are the groups in which choice is made by the players themselves, not by a leader; that is, in family and friends' groups. However, some of the friends' groups are, like community groups, subject to individual leadership, and among those that are not under leaders the predominance of dance and other popular music is doubtless partly due to something like the gang spirit and the hope, perhaps, of playing for dances. Twelve out of 221 pupils in friends' groups report chamber music, ten in string quartets and two in violin duos, including such music as a Haydn Quartet and the Bach Double Concerto — inspiring reports — but most of the rest of that total are in quite different boats. The fairest measure of tastes can be got through the family groups, though even in those the influence of adults, the parents, may be potent.

Every piece or general classification (e.g., "sacred music" or "popular music") mentioned by more than one of the pupils in family groups in two cities is given in the following list. It was impossible to classify all the pieces mentioned, as popular, standard, dance or folk music, so they are given in order of frequency. The two cities chosen are among the first in the nation with regard to the quality and quantity of music instruction in their schools.

MUSIC PLAYED IN FAMILY GROUPS IN TWO CITIES
Pieces Mentioned By More Than One Pupil
Popular Numbers [18] — 15

America — 13

Marches [18] — 10

Happy Days — 9
Springtime in the Rockies — 9
Stein Song — 9

Old Black Joe — 8

Blue Danube — 7
Barcarolle — 7
Stars and Stripes Forever — 7

Betty Co-ed — 6
Home Sweet Home — 6
Over the Waves — 6
On Wisconsin — 6
Star Spangled Banner — 6

Humoresque — 5
Sextet — 5
Spring Song — 5
Serenade — 5
Sacred Songs [18] — 5
Tannhäuser — 5
Largo — 5

Angel's Serenade — 4
Christmas Music — 4
Folk Songs [18] — 4

[18] This represents only the reports giving this term instead of the names of pieces.

Pieces Mentioned By More Than One Pupil (continued)

Kiss Me Again — 4
Londonderry Air — 4
Marche Militaire — 4
Nearer My God To Thee — 4
Song of India — 4

Ah, Sweet Mystery of Life — 3
Cavalleria Rusticana — 3
Carolina Moon — 3
Director's March — 3
Love's Old Sweet Song — 3
La Paloma — 3
Melody in G — 3
Minuets — 3
Moments Musical — 3
Old Oaken Bucket — 3
Poet and Peasant — 3
Pilgrims' Chorus — 3
Red Wing — 3
Rosary, The — 3
Silver Threads Among the Gold — 3
Whispering Hope — 3
Gavotte — 3

Aida — 2
A Perfect Day — 2
Andante — 2
Annie Laurie — 2
Anchors Aweigh — 2
Adoration — 2
Ave Maria — 2
Around the Corner — 2
Booster March — 2
Diana — 2
David's Dream — 2
Down the River of Golden Dreams — 2
Dance Music [19] — 2
De Beriot — 2
Flag Day March — 2
Gypsy Love Song — 2
Glow Worm — 2

[19] This represents only the reports giving this term instead of the names of the pieces.

German Songs [20] — 2
Hungarian Songs [20] — 2
Indian Love Call — 2
I Ain't Got Nobody — 2
It Happened In Monterey — 2
Liebeslied — 2
Let Me Call You Sweetheart — 2
Liebesfreud — 2
Melody in F — 2
March Romaine — 2
Martha — 2
Negro Spirituals [20] — 2
Onward Christian Soldiers — 2
Old Time Pieces [20] — 2
Pagan Love Song — 2
Scotch Pieces [20] — 2
Swanee River — 2
Saxophobia — 2
Trios [20] — 2
Welsh Airs [20] — 2
Waltzes [20] — 2
Yankee Doodle — 2

In addition to the compositions mentioned by more than one pupil, there were 274, of which each was mentioned by only one pupil. The reader will congratulate himself on not having to hear as well as see all of this list. It is an impressive token of the enormous variety and range of qualities in music, a cross-section of the musical tastes of families in American cities that rank high in musical interest and opportunities. It must be admitted that the boys and girls who play instruments do very likely as a whole represent a larger proportion of musical and otherwise cultured families than any other group of children do; and that in selecting three pieces to be named in the questionnaire it is probable that many of them were somewhat influenced by the good school environment in which they wrote their answers. The record is there-

[20] This represents only the reports giving this term instead of the names of the pieces.

fore a very challenging one to school music teachers and to parents, not complimentary. But the inclusion of " popular numbers," of which there is a still larger representation in the long list of pieces mentioned only once, shows an admirable freedom and sincerity on the part of the children, admirable especially for what it indicates of the teachers' attitudes toward them. Nothing could be worse for us musically than to feel obliged to speak praises of the best music when we do not know it and like it. This would be like making out checks with no money in the bank. In spite of its faults, including its sentimentalities, it is on the whole a cheering list. It points principally to the following needs:

1. *The cultivation of small groups in schools.* The large orchestra and band have little or nothing to contribute directly to the home and to other centers where small groups of players gather or might gather.
2. *The cultivation of small groups in homes.* A family of three that is at all musical is by right and privilege a trio, the family of four is a quartet, and so on; but it won't be that or be that very enjoyably if the members, including the parents, do not cultivate singing or playing together, or if they all sing the same part, play the same instrument or part, or play an uncongenial or uninteresting combination of instruments. A harp, banjo and piano make up one family group reported to us; a violin, saxophone, trombone, and guitar make up another, and a violin, piano, mandolin, and bass horn are pals in another home. Fortunately for these families, musical incompatibility is not recognized as a cause for divorce, but the man next door, even if he be a marital purist, must wish that it were. School music teachers should tactfully seek opportunities to advise children and parents in this kind of family adjustment.
   One or both parents were participants in each of 56% of the reported family groups.
3. *Provision of an ample supply of good, suitable music for all sorts of small groups, especially for the less advanced.* A committee of school music supervisors has been at

work on this, and a few publishing concerns have recently added effectively to the supply of simple chamber music or *haus-musik*. There should and doubtless will be more. But there is right now no end of delight to be found by any small, instrumentally well-balanced group, no matter how elementary it is, in the rich store of fine choral and other vocal part-music in the world — duets and trios by Bach, Handel, Mendelssohn, Schumann, Brahms; quartets and chorales by some of these and like composers; the priceless Tudor church music and Elizabethan madrigals, and much else that is " apt for voyces or viols " or woodwind or brass ensemble or a good mixture of the two, or for a combination of one or more voices and instruments. When a viola, clarinet, trumpet or horn is to be used, the part for it must be transposed by the player or written out in another clef or key, and sometimes it is desirable to have the entire composition in another key. But the reward is worth the effort.

Cultivating Chamber Music

The term " chamber music " usually suggests the string quartet and the trio of piano, violin and cello, but any small group of players may be worthy of the name, depending on the character of the music. Woodwind ensembles and brass ensembles are becoming less rare, and intermingling of two or all three families of instruments with or without piano occurs quite frequently, especially in homes and neighborhood centers. The performances of many of the latter groups would not be classified as chamber music because, aside from any considerations of balance and quality, the music is made up of a solo melody with mere accompaniment, not of fairly independent parts. There is not the fascinating interplay of coordinate parts. Not only is there no leader in chamber music, but no leading part.

Any kind of small group singing or playing with enjoyment is to be commended, but it was presumably in accordance with the accepted definition of chamber music, applied to singers as well as to players, that in 1930, of a total of 604 school music supervisors, 138 reported cultivation of vocal chamber music, and 110 reported cultivation of instrumental chamber music — all in high schools. (The definition was printed on the questionnaire.) The following table shows the distribution of most of these supervisors according to the population of their respective cities, and shows also the number of pupils participating: [21]

Population of Cities	Total Number Cities Replying	Number Reporting Chamber Music	(Percentage)	Total Number of Participants
	VOCAL CHAMBER MUSIC			
1–999	100	17	17	209
1,000–9,999	278	60	22	878
10,000–29,999	104	22	21	484
30,000–49,999	28	6	21	156
50,000–74,999	21	5	24	322
75,000–99,999	11	3	27	132
Over 100,000	62	12	19	636
Totals	604	125	21	2817
	INSTRUMENTAL CHAMBER MUSIC			
1–999	100	9	9	70
1,000–9,999	278	40	14	359
10,000–29,999	104	16	15	329
30,000–49,999	28	9	32	62
50,000–74,999	21	7	33	74
75,000–99,999	11	4	36	54
Over 100,000	62	17	28	515
Totals . . .	604	102	17	1463

The next table shows the cities distributed also according to the year in which chamber music was introduced in the schools of each one.

[21] Twenty-one supervisors did not report the number of participants.

The Number of Cities in Which Chamber Music Was Introduced in Each Year or Period

High School Vocal Chamber Music in 89 Cities

Population of Cities	1911	1915 to 1920	1921 to 1925	1926	1927	1928	1929	1930
1 — 999			1		2	2	3	3
1,000 — 9,999	1	2	2	3	5	12	9	5
10,000 — 29,999		2	2	2	1	3	4	3
30,000 — 49,999			1	1		2		1
50,000 — 74,999		2	2		1			
75,000 — 99,999		2						
Over 100,000		2			3		1	4
Totals	1	10	8	6	12	19	17	16

High School Instrumental Chamber Music in 80 Cities

Population of Cities	1911	1915 to 1920	1921 to 1925	1926	1927	1928	1929	1930
1 — 999				1	1		3	2
1,000 — 9,999	1	1	3	2	1	2	15	9
10,000 — 29,999			2		1	1	4	1
30,000 — 49,999			2	2	1		3	
50,000 — 74,999				2	1	1	4	1
75,000 — 99,999		1	1					
Over 100,000		4	2			5		1
Totals	1	6	10	7	5	9	29	14

The comparatively large growth in the last three years is shown also in the introduction of chamber music events in many state school music contests in the same years, and an early increase in the number of participants in them. The proportion of schools in which chamber music is being cultivated is still small, and the proportion of students enlisted is very small, but there is a rapidly growing interest in it among school music teachers, which at their 1930 National Conference was expressed in the following resolution:

Amateur Music

Whereas, the vocational aim has never been the primary aim of public school music, and

Whereas, the possibilities for the vocational use of music are now greatly lessened, due to mechanical reproduction and transmission of music: Therefore

Be it resolved, (1) That the Music Supervisors National Conference reassert the use of music as a grace in life that may add to the beauty and exaltation of spirit of our people. To this end be it further resolved:

(2) That we encourage and develop particularly all forms of musical interest and practice that tend to restore the use of music to the home and to neighborhood life as a rewarding activity for daily living. Specifically we would encourage the study of piano and other instruments, and the use of these instruments and the voice in small groups as well as in solo; and we would recommend that every effort be put forth to encourage self-initiated activity in this field;

(3) That in all music contests larger place be given to solo and small ensembles, both vocal and instrumental.

It will be observed that the term " chamber music " is not used in this resolution. For our present purpose it will be especially suitable similarly to expand our interest to include all small groups. " Haus-musik " or home-music is a better term for us, though where the music is performed is of subordinate importance so long as it is performed, not merely listened to, and is in the proper spirit. Before considering how it is cultivated, let us ask what the boys and girls think of it. Answers to the last inquiry on the questionnaire shown on pages 293–295 are, in summary, as follows:

	More Pleasure	Less Pleasure	About The Same Amount	No Opinion Given
Junior high school students	24%	29%	34%	13%
Senior high school students	26%	22%	20%	32%

Evidently, with regard to this interest, pupils improve with age and experience. But it is, after all, still a minority interest. It will undoubtedly grow when it is wisely and more largely cultivated in the schools.

How Is " Haus-musik " Cultivated in Schools?

In one Milwaukee high school there are two string quartets and one double string quartet, each coached once a week by one of the school music teachers. Two of these groups rehearse directly after school, each on a different day, and the other rehearses from 7:30 to 8:15 *in the morning.* Sometimes rehearsals take place in the home of one of the players. The music is owned and loaned by the school. No school credit is given for this work and there are few opportunities for public performances, almost all of these being at school assemblies. It is not surprising, then, to learn that when a young woman who had graduated from a quartet in this school became a student of nursing, she started a string quartet in the student nurses' quarters and sought the advice of her former school music teacher regarding choice of music.

Three string quartets in another Milwaukee high school all rehearse after school hours, quite often in the evenings in a home. In both of these schools ensembles of other instruments have also been formed but not for regular, persistent practice, because of lack of time.

In the Ventura (California) High School there is a string quartet which rehearses twice a week, once for an hour before school and again for an hour after school, under the direction of the High School music teacher whose enthusiasm for chamber music was bred at the New England Conservatory. These students receive school credit for the work, in addition to credit for playing in the school orchestra, and they play now and then at church services and midweek musicales and at parent-teacher association meetings. Haydn, Mozart, Schumann, and Dvorak have been supplying their musical sustenance.

Multiple Small Groups

So valuable an activity should be open to many students. Even five quartets, one for every afternoon of the school week, would involve only a very small proportion of the students in a large city high school. The good work should be carried on during school hours. But it would be regarded as being too expensive to engage a teacher or coach for such small groups. Moreover, it would probably be extremely difficult to arrange a school schedule for each of the students who might wish to play in them. One solution of these difficulties is the multiple small group. In one of Flint's high schools there is a multiple string quartet of 20 students (five complete quartets), a multiple brass sextet of 12, and a multiple woodwind quintet of 10, each group meeting on an average of two and a half hours a week. That is, they meet two hours one week and three hours the next week. The two lunch periods of each day are used. (Half of all the classes in the school take lunch in the fourth hour and half in the fifth hour.)

The string group rehearses during the fourth hour twice one week and three times the next week and the woodwind and the brass ensembles rehearse, in separate rooms, during the fifth hour three times in one week and twice the next. Thus:

	Mon.	Tues.	Wed.	Thurs.	Fri.		Mon.	Tues.	Wed.	Thurs.	Fri.
Fourth period	S		S		S		S		S		
Fifth period	W		W		W		W		W	

The same instructor coaches all three groups, attending to the string players throughout their period and alternating between the woodwind and brass groups during their period. This makes it possible for him to have a full period for lunch each day. In the other Flint high school the same arrangement of time is carried out with single, not multiple, groups: namely, a string quartet, a woodwind quintet, and a brass sextet; and there is a special teacher for the wind instruments and another for the strings. At this school there are also vocal ensembles arranged for in the same way — a boys' octet and a girls' sextet.

No academic credit is given for work in any of these ensembles, but it fulfills for the members of them the school requirement that every student take part in some extra-curricular activity. They perform quite often in churches and at meetings of parent-teacher associations, luncheon clubs, women's clubs, and fraternal organizations. Instrumental ensembles chosen from the multiple and other groups have taken part in state contests. Preparation for this choice has intensified the interest in playing by single groups separately at the school rehearsals and also outside of the schools. There are various other small groups in these schools which have no regular meetings but which receive help in finding suitable music and now and then some coaching.

One of the unforgettably delightful and significant endeavors in the National High School Orchestra and Band Camp in the summer of 1930 was the multiple string quartet of sixteen boys and girls who gathered regularly at 4:30 P.M. out-of-doors in a natural chamber music auditorium surrounded by trees. Each quartet practiced separately in leisure hours without coaching in preparation for the joint rehearsals which were coached by Mr. Vladimir Bakaleinikoff, assistant conductor of the Cincinnati Symphony Orchestra. But every conceivable sort of small ensemble was at some time formed in that camp. The distribution of the students among the dwelling places was so arranged that each cabin held a unified or well-balanced ensemble, and many occasions for chamber music were used, including chapel services and, now and then, good-night serenades immediately after " taps."

Developing Initiative

We have described ways of providing teacher-leadership for small groups, but what is also very much needed is development of the will to sing or play with others for the love and joy of it, a power of initiative that comes of good rehearsals held without a teacher. In Lincoln, Nebraska, the members of the senior high school orchestra (which won first place in the 1930 National Orchestra Contest) formed among themselves eight chamber music groups in response to their leader's suggestion. A list of the members and practice-times of each group was given to him, and he heard each one now and then. They practiced after school hours once a week. But the groups soon disbanded because of irregular attendance.

The leader then planned for the next year to have study periods used by small groups in schoolrooms, some meeting twice a week and others three times, depending on the pupils' class schedules. The groups could then be heard more often, though much of the time they would be on their own; they would make greater progress, gratifying to themselves, through the larger number of rehearsals; their energies would be fresher and better controlled by them than in the after-school hours; and attendance would be regular. They might be given school credit for this work, but the leader thought this unnecessary. The incentives for them would be the delight of it, the help that practice of small groups can be in improving the orchestra, occasional performances at school assemblies and the like, and preliminary contests for choice of entrants in the annual State Contest. The use of the school rooms in school time would be offered them as a delightful privilege needing no further reward.

Ensemble Playing in Instrumental Classes

Such playing is being valued more and more by teachers of instrumental classes. An especially significant use of it is in the work of the public school piano classes in Lincoln, Nebraska, which are held after school hours and on Saturday mornings. Besides piano duets and the like, and playing accompaniments for singing, there is playing with other instruments. An arrangement is made with leaders of school orchestras and with teachers of instrumental classes to have violinists and cellists from them come to piano classes now and then, where they are given music to play with the pianist. All the pupils are urged to form trios and duos among themselves and practice at home, a definite incentive being the opportunity to play at a later meeting of the class. Simple music such as Elizabeth Fyffe's " Team-work Tunes " is used.

" Haus-musik " in Elementary School Music Classes

The Lincoln plan just presented is especially well suited to the usual sort of singing classes in the grade school, resulting in what may be called " obligato " parts for one or more instruments to be played during some of the singing. There, too, small groups of the children will gladly undertake home practice of music to be performed later for the class. Parents, capable brothers or sisters in the high school or any high school student, or private music teachers in cooperation with the school music teacher, may provide all the coaching needed for such a project.

Choruses, Orchestras and Bands as Multiple Chamber Music Groups

Every chorus that is not too large may be regarded as made up of single groups in each of which there is but one singer for each voice-part in the music. For

four-part music, for instance, the chorus would consist of quartets, and were there time for it each quartet might sing a section of the music alone. In the
schools of Minneapolis and of many another city
whose music teaching is patterned after the methods
used in Minneapolis, the daily reading of music in
the upper grades is carried on so. For example, four
children in the last row, each representing a part, together sing the first phrase, followed immediately by
the four children in the next row singing the next
phrase, and so on.

But many choruses are too large and the music commonly sung by them is too dependent for its effect on
masses of sound, instrumental as well as vocal, to
favor such practice by quartets or to give any singer
even a suggestion that he and three others might alone
some time sing the music at home. And the Minneapolis plan, excellent for its purpose — independence
in sight-singing — may well provide skill valuable
in *haus-musik,* but it usually lacks the spirit and purpose of such music. The group most likely to serve our
desire in this regard is the *a cappella* choir.

Walking home after a Harvard Glee Club concert
in Boston's Symphony Hall one evening, the writer
overtook four of the members ambling along singing
softly Morley's " My Bonny Lass," with two parts
missing. (" Apt for voyces or viols " was said of the
parts of many a madrigal — why not apt also for
imagination?) The feasibility of singing such delightful music with only one on a part, anywhere, any time,
without accompaniment or conductor, is turned into
warm desire by the spirit of this glee club's endeavors
and by the quartet try-outs, not individual ones, that
determine eligibility to sing at a concert by the club.
So must it be with any *a cappella* or other chorus of
similar spirit in which each individual can hear his
own part interwoven with all the others as clearly and

intimately as though it were a quartet. Unaccompanied singing is naturally more favorable for this sort of experience than accompanied singing is, though the latter may be favorable for it also. The high school *a cappella* choir singing Gibbons' " The Silver Swan " or the like might well be regarded as consisting of as many madrigal teams as there are groups of five with an individual for each part. " Team " would be a good word for so good a sport.

Something like an *a cappella* movement has started in high schools, especially in the middle west where Dean Peter C. Lutkin of Northwestern University and Dr. F. Melius Christiansen of St. Olaf College have for many years been great leaders and advocates of such singing. Eighty-four out of 604 school music supervisors reported high school *a cappella* choirs of which all but fourteen were started since 1927. The excellent music and singing now being carried on by the best of these choirs is a development almost entirely of the past three years.

The sectional rehearsals of orchestras and bands frequently present opportunities for self-sufficient performance by the strings alone, woodwinds alone, or brasses alone, as though the section were a chamber music group. Even in the rehearsals of the entire band or orchestra there are such opportunities. Wise leaders often, in such rehearsals, call for brief periods of practice by a small group at a time especially where delicacy or fine tonal balance is very important. All of this if done well is likely to arouse interest in *haus-musik*.

Music Clubs in Schools

Last but not least among ways of cultivating *haus-musik* is the school music club. Good examples of this are in the New Trier (Illinois) High School, where a junior club of about 50 students meets once a month, and a senior club of the same size, of junior and senior class members, meets every two weeks. Dues of 50 cents per semester are paid. Every meeting takes place in a home of one of the members, and it consists of an hour's informal concert by some of the members followed by refreshments and joviality. The refreshments are provided by a committee of the club. A meeting at which three parents, two school music teachers, and the writer were guests had for music a Haydn Serenade for String Quartet, some piano solos, a vocal trio, the first movement of the Bach Concerto for Two Violins, and a vocal octet of boys. The members seek coaching before or after school hours from the school music supervisor.

This is a fine enterprise that brings *haus-musik* into its own habitat and spirit.

*   *   *   *   *   *

The hope that the generation of students now in good high school musical organizations will carry on such singing or playing in later life as a means of recreation, as a purposeful hobby, is one that may well concern not only music teachers but also all others who are engaged in any sort of education for leisure. In this respect school music is a model field of experiment. Its methods and outcomes have direct bearing on the whole philosophy of recreation and on our knowledge concerning what may be done in any field of activity to help carry out the bright prospects in that philosophy.

CHAPTER X

Colleges and Conservatories

WE have seen in public schools the promise of a rich development of musical understanding and performance among the American people. We have seen also the common obstacles to fulfillment of that promise. The main currents of life outside the schools, in leisure as in labor, go contrary to good amateur singing and playing. The conditions are beyond our control; we have often to struggle desperately to keep a chorus, orchestra, or any other musical group in the running. But in a college the conditions are in a large measure under control. The world may often intrude and college life obtrude, but the environment as a whole and in particular may to a large extent be molded to fit our ideals. Having this power, what we do with respect to music in college is especially important not only for the values of the activity itself, and also because it provides a possible means of conserving and advancing the musical gains made in high school, but most importantly because it is among college students that the largest proportion of future leaders and supporters in the cultural life of our communities are to be found.

The number of students in American colleges and universities has increased fivefold since 1900, and is likely to continue to increase as rapidly or nearly so for some time to come. A total of 863,793 had been reached by 1928, nearly one-fifth of the number in all the grades of our high schools. What is being done with respect to music in colleges and universities?

Glee Clubs and Choral Societies

As important as the best choral developments in high schools, and in some regions — most notably at Harvard — antedating them by many years, is the growth in college glee club singing. The richest source of information in this regard is the Intercollegiate Musical Council which grew out of the purposes of, and the intercollegiate singing contest brought about by, Mr. Albert S. Pickernell, formerly a member of the Harvard Glee Club, and a few other young college graduates in 1914. In that contest, the first of its kind in America, were represented only Harvard, Columbia, Dartmouth and the University of Pennsylvania; but in 1931 the Council was able to report similar contests in all parts of the country, enlisting altogether about 100 college glee clubs with a total membership of nearly 6000 singers.

The growth in quality is still more impressive and important. What the conditions were in the fifty years between the Civil War and the World War is aptly described by Mr. Marshall M. Bartholomew, present executive director of the Intercollegiate Musical Council, in an article in the *Yale Alumni Weekly* for December 19, 1930.

. . . College departments of music (in the few institutions where such departments existed) usually accepted the popular attitude that undergraduate glee clubs were largely social organizations and unworthy of serious attention. Consequently student music in its extra-curriculum phases was to a large degree left to the mercy of the mediocre musical environment out of which it grew.

. . . Following the line of the least resistance, it found its chief expression through the medium of small glee clubs and quartets, with occasional attempts at instrumental ensembles of banjo and mandolin clubs and, in the last few years, jazz orchestras. In order to make up a concert program it was frequently necessary to draw upon almost any talent of an entertainment nature which presented itself, such as monologues, tap dances, ventriloquism and whistling solos, so that the so-called college glee club concert resembled for many years a musical vaudeville. These activities, usually left in the hands of undergraduate leaders with little or no professional guidance, could seldom boast of excellence, and one need only study the programs of those lean years to become aware of the general poverty of the musical material involved.

Perhaps it was the apparently immovable weight of this tradition of mediocrity that suggested to Mr. Bartholomew a world-shaking war as the latter boundary of the period. But it would be difficult to trace any improvement in singing to the influence of the war. It was in 1918, however, that the Harvard Glee Club, then having only 40 members, resolved to drop the instrumental " acts " and all other trivialities from its programs and to devote itself to music. During several years before that time a good composition had been interpolated now and then, but it seemed out of place and was not welcomed by the singers. On concert trips, however, the applause for the better music was sometimes impressive. The " Hunters' Farewell " by Mendelssohn was the hit of an evening in St. Louis, and led to the question of whether the skillful and substantial should not be allowed to displace the mediocre and trivial, at least in concerts. The combination of the two did not seem good showmanship, to say nothing of questions of taste. A weight on the side of the best music was the enthusiasm of those members of the Glee Club who also sang in the Chapel Choir, in which music of Palestrina, Vittoria, Bach and their kind, was daily food. " Why can't we sing more such music in the Glee Club? " they asked.

The resulting development of the Harvard club in musical excellence, representing a rich variety of moods, not the loftiest alone, and in size (now 250 members), is too well known to need description. In

addition to its own concerts it has, in company with
the Radcliffe Choral Society sung the Brahms
Requiem, the choral parts of Beethoven's Ninth Symphony, the Holst " Hymn to Jesus " and other superb
music. Its performances in 1930–31 included a concert
of its own in New York City and one at the Boston
Art Museum attended by about 3,500 people, a joint
concert with the Princeton Glee Club and one with
the Smith College Chorus, the choral parts of Stravinsky's " Oedipus Rex " with the Philadelphia Symphony Orchestra, and greatest of all, the Bach B minor
Mass and the Magnificat with the Radcliffe Choral
Society and the Boston Symphony Orchestra — all
this in addition to less formal singing on a few social
and other occasions within the interests and domain
of the university itself. And in addition to the music
named, it has sung the best college songs, folk songs,
excerpts from Gilbert and Sullivan, and the like.

The quality of music and performance of the hundred glee clubs of the Intercollegiate Musical Council
varies greatly, but aside from the occasional protests
of some alumni against what they consider as " high-
brow," everything is in favor of general improvement.
The prize song for intercollegiate contests in all sections of the country, including the national contest, is
chosen by the Council, and the song chosen by each
college must be submitted to the sectional board of
directors or to the Council in order that a program
well-balanced and otherwise suitable can be arranged
for the audience at the regional or the national contest.
Thus a not unwelcome power, we hope, is gained and
democratically used for the gradual raising and maintenance of standards throughout the country. Each
contesting club sings also one of its college songs.

Very striking is the fact that this elevation of musical standards has been accompanied by a very large
growth in the size of most college glee clubs. Whereas

25 to 30 was the average number of members under the old regime, the present average is about 60, and in several of the larger colleges the number has risen above 200. At Yale the candidates for the Glee Club each year outnumber those for any other three recreational activities combined, including the major athletic teams. Mr. Bartholomew has stated that 130 more college clubs with a total membership of 10,000 singers have applied for admission to the Council and are waiting to be organized into regional groups.

Another striking consideration is the scope of influence of some glee clubs such as those of the Universities of Idaho, Arizona and Utah, whose annual trips bring their concerts to people in rural districts who hear no other music except the radio's reproductions. In a country where Puritanism and the stark realities of frontier life have set almost irrevocable standards of how a he-man should behave, there seem to be especially rich possibilities in, as there is great need for, the example of healthy young he-men singing first-class music with all the earnestness that has been expected only of long-haired foreigners, and often with greater spontaneity than those idolized professionals could maintain.

But the singing is not all good or spontaneous, because there are not nearly enough good leaders to go round. It is painful to watch and listen to the artificial endeavors of some leaders and their innocent singers to ape what they regard as the new cultivated sort of singing. The result is a soft, devitalized sort of refined crooning or a combination of this with a sudden breath-taking " swell " on almost every tone of a quarter-note or more in length. Distortion of the rhythm is also a means of " interpretation," of " putting the expression in." This sort of perversion is always likely to occur where an advance or renaissance in artistic expression which is the natural outgrowth of inner grace and learning in its leaders is imitated by others who have not yet achieved either the grace or the learning. Unfortunately, any sort of distortion may be defended as another interpretation, the misled individual being, according to professional ethics, not only entitled to his own, but also urged by his desire to establish himself as an " artist," a unique and superior person. But it is not difficult for anyone who has felt the essential sincerity and fitness of the best music to detect the insincerity, the fabrication, of such conducting. So it is not likely to go on long, especially when contests or other festival gatherings place the singing of the enlightened in telling proximity to the misdirected efforts of the unenlightened, and the judges not only know which deserves the greater honor, but also state tactfully and educatively the reasons for their decisions. Other tactics obstructive of the way to the most enjoyment can be similarly dealt with.

Alumni Objections

" This high-brow music doesn't express college life," says many an alumnus who recalls with pleasure " The Bulldog on the Bank " and other favorites of the old days, " and it ought to be stopped." " In my opinion," recently protested a Yale Alumnus in Chicago, " and I have hundreds out here who agree with me, the Yale Glee Club trip is for the purpose of reawakening (through the old college songs) the memories and enthusiasm of the graduates and instilling some of the glamor of College and the Yale spirit in our sons and others of the coming generation, who will make Yale what it should be." Following this statement, an editorial appearing in the New York *Evening Post* in January, 1931, took up the same cause and caustically likened the singing of the modern glee club to professionalized football which had at that time been vigorously attacked by many college authorities.

The editorial brought several responses, most of them from alumni who heartily, and some bitterly, agreed with the editor. But a reply from Mr. Henry Seidel Canby defended the new developments in college glee club singing, and so reasonably and delightfully did he do so, that we must quote all of it:

I profess no competence in musical criticism, but even so must question the analogy between college glee club singing and football in your editorial of January 6.

When you and I were at Yale (or wherever we were) the glee club sang "The Bulldog on the Bank" and "Upidee" and "Jingle Bells" and "Only a Bluebell" (with swipes) and had a darned good time at it, but I object to comparing these ginger ale ditties with the skillful game of football, which you do not wish to see professionalized. You feel that to sing Bach or the English madrigals is for the college glee club to progress out of undergraduate spheres into the area of professionalism. I submit that it may be only to move from childish music to adult music.

The comparison between " The Bullfrog on the Bank and the Bulldog in the Pool " (or was it the other way?) and an undergraduate sport would be closer if the sport were " rounders " or that " peel " which we used to play on ideal afternoons by bouncing golf balls against the stone steps of a dormitory. *There is an exact analogy between madrigal singing, which in the best age of English music was performed with skill and care by amateur singers of no great voice but with an intense love of fine music, and the best kind of skillful amateur football such as you wish to see preserved.*

The truth is that we reached reasonable maturity in our sports when you and I were in college, but we were still adolescent then (if that) in the arts. The college in this respect has grown up since our day. Mr. Davison at Harvard showed that with proper encouragement undergraduates could sing real music with intense delight and to the equal delight of an audience. Mr. Bartholomew at Yale and others elsewhere are following his precedent. It is not the undergraduate or the taste or competence of the undergraduate that makes their course still a little difficult; it is the musical juvenility of the middle-aged alumnus, who, like the correspondent of the *Yale Alumni Weekly* whom you quote, does not wish music to be too musical or to be taken as seriously as football.

I am no musician myself and should be sorry in any concert I attend not to hear *one* good old sentimental or humorous ballad sung for the sake of old associations. But if the boys want to sing good music, don't, for heaven's sake, let us oppose our nostalgias for an American day when only long-haired foreigners listened to "classical music"! When *we* sing we can sing "Bingo" and "We Meet Tonight to Celebrate," and so presumably will even the beerless assemblages of modern college rooms, but if voices are to be selected and trained (like a football team), don't prevent them from singing Purcell or even Bach if that seems more worth while to them. Do you ask that "campus baseball," as they used to knock it out in front of old Durfee, should be played on the Yale Field at Commencement?

Anyone who has attended a rehearsal of the Harvard Glee Club knows the intense delight and loyalty of its members. It is by no means certain that "Solomon Levi," "Bingo," and the others of their kind are any more expressive of college life than are, say, the finely romantic Brahms Rhapsody, the deep and forthright devotion and energy of Bach, the sheer beauty and mysticism of Palestrina, the rollicking humor of the best sea chanties, and every other sort of expansive feeling and fun to be found within the best music of each kind. And there is ample proof that such music, for those who sing it as it is sung by the best glee clubs, is as unforgettably and happily intertwined in memories of the "good old college days" as were any of the songs so much desired now by many of the older generation of alumni.

The Music of College Life

Two conditions are needed. First, the music sung by the glee club must find its way out of the rehearsal room and concert hall into the informal recreational life of the singers; and second, all the students — not only the three, five, or even ten per cent in the glee club — should be acquiring by use a heritage of songs which will enhance the meaning of their life in college and be everlasting reminders of its good fellowship, romance and fun. It may be that these two conditions, now apparently disjoined by the leap in standards of glee club singing, can be closely interrelated.

The first condition is being attained in at least a few colleges. For example, at Radcliffe house parties and at other social gatherings where there are any members of the Radcliffe Choral Society or the Harvard Glee Club, or of both organizations, there is usually spontaneous singing, by heart, of music sung at rehearsal or concert. Indeed, the rehearsals themselves at these colleges, fired as they are by the most alert endeavor, derive their warmth mainly from the very impulses and good fellowship that prompt the recreational singing at a party. This is due mainly to the attitude of the conductors. Bach is *great;* in his music we want often to bow our heads in deepest reverence or lift them high in fullest exaltation. But we will not, if we are sincere and wise, ever sing that or any other real music because it is virtuous to do so, or instructive, or " high-brow." For its essence, the impulses from which it has sprung, are as vital and natural as those that move and delight us in a folk song. And it is through those impulses — as simply and ardently as that — that we shall enter into all the music we sing, no matter how advanced it may be in other respects. Mastery of its substance is only to realize its meaning and beauty to the full. We don't get mountain-top views by sitting on the front porch. At Harvard and doubtless in many other colleges there will be as much camaraderie and gaiety in this climbing as in any other challenging sport.

For the second condition — singing throughout the college — there must be a body of songs which, by

their simplicity, universal appeal and relation to the
various phases and occasions of college life, have
found their way into meetings large or small of fraternities, clubs, other societies, Classes, dormitory or
other house groups, and into any other informal
gatherings of students in which singing may have a
place. There seems to be little or no use in trying to
bring back the Bulldog, Solomon Levi, and the like.
Aside from any other consideration, present-day students have heard too much first-class music, including
clever jazz, to enjoy them. " Are they vivid? Are they
done with distinction? Are they real? " — These, according to the introduction to the *American Student
Hymnal* (1928), are questions by which American
youth "measures the desirability of all its experiences, on the athletic field, over the radio, at the theatre, in the class-room, and in church and chapel."
What songs *are* sung on the informal occasions of
college life?

Personal investigation in a few colleges has shown
a marked decline in general student singing, and this
impression is confirmed by Mr. James Anderson
Hawes, who, as the first General Fraternity Secretary
of Delta Kappa Epsilon, has for twenty years devoted
most of his time to questions concerning student life.
Here is a paragraph from his book, " Twenty Years
Among the Twenty Year Olds."

It is with regret that I must note the fact that college fraternity
and club singing by students is rapidly declining. Of course this
may be laid in part to the more exclusive social gatherings forced
by prohibition, or to the great increase of the student body to
a point where the natural leaders only appear among the general population on certain occasions. We have the organized
cheering and singing at football games, but it must appear
forced to many, especially to those knowing how it is worked
up at "pep" meetings and regular drill for students for several
days before the big games. For instance, the singing on the
fence at Yale, or similar informal pleasant "get-togethers" has

almost entirely disappeared. Even in smaller gatherings where the men are supposed to know the songs, as at fraternity banquets and club meetings, there is just as little singing as possible. Since the earliest days of college life abroad and in this country, singing of the old " glees " and students' songs has been one of the most pleasant and vital facts and memories. Perhaps the young men of today are too sophisticated and embarrassed in public, at least when they are mixed with the great mass of whom they personally know but few. In any event it is too bad that this is so, and I consider it one of the greatest losses today in college life as compared with the past.

The Federal Office of Education received similar reports through its recent survey of land-grant colleges. One of the bulletins [1] having to do with this survey, after speaking of the apparent decline of interest in college class organizations, contains the following paragraph:

Music organizations, on the other hand, flourish on all the land-grant campuses, and are listed many times. In practically every case they seem to be under joint faculty and student control, and certain faculty members have a good deal of responsibility, both for the conduct of these organizations, and for any public appearance that the organizations may make. *Here, again, however, the emphasis is changed. The glee club is another disappearing group.* In its place we find such organizations as the orchestra, the band, the chorus, all of them decidedly more ambitious in the programs given and in the talent that they call forth than was the old-time glee club. The annuals reveal the really fine type of performance which these musical organizations give on many of the campuses. . . . The recognition of music as a proper field for academic endeavor is directly responsible for this change of emphasis, and the programs that these groups on land-grant campuses have presented in the past few years show a marked contrast to the light and popular type of singing called forth by the old college glee club. The signs of the times on the college campuses as regards these musical organizations are very bright indeed, and greater growth in this department may probably be looked for in the future.

[1] Section of Bulletin, 1930, No. 9, Vol. I, Part IV.

The contrast suggested in this report between "chorus" and "glee club," is not entirely true to the original meaning of the latter term, which meaning may offer part of the answer to our question regarding general student singing. That term is not at all in contrast with the word "chorus" with respect to standards of choice and performance, though it may be with respect to purposes and spirit. It was originally taken from the Anglo-Saxon *gligg,* meaning music. The first glee club was the outgrowth of some meetings commenced in 1783 at the home of an English gentleman, Mr. Robert Smith, at which motets, madrigals, glees, canons, and catches were sung after dinner. After four years of such meetings, it was decided to establish a society to be called "The Glee Club," which thereafter held "public meetings" now and then, but still combined conviviality with singing, at least in its private meetings, which were held at a coffee house or a tavern. The "rehearsal" was followed by dinner, and then Byrd's "Non Nobis, Domine" was sung. Another glee club was formed in 1793, a member of which, W. T. Parke, stated in his *Musical Memoirs* that its meetings were held on Sunday evenings at the Garrick's Head Coffee House in Bow Street, Covent Garden, once a fortnight, "when we amused ourselves by singing the works of *the old and modern masters,* after which we sat down to supper."

How Can General Informal Singing Be Revived?

This question is for the most part to be answered by the students themselves. That they are capable of doing so is sufficiently proved by their initiative and management in many other lines of activity outside of the curriculum, especially in the fraternities. At the University of Michigan the proportion of students who are members of fraternities or sororities increased from 22% in 1906 to 34% in 1926. These groups and others like them, the main carriers of college traditions, are in many colleges influential enough to make their members feel obliged to try out for extra-curricular activities and to strive for a career in them, even when doing so is against the interests of the individual. There is often rivalry between them with regard to securing or developing the largest number of men prominent in extra-curricular affairs. Of course, this interest runs strongly toward athletics. Musical organizations, outside of the annual opera, give very little opportunity for starring and no musical star in a concert ever receives the enormous amount of acclaim and prestige given to the heroes of athletics. But in some colleges this feeling of rivalry has been directed toward singing contests between fraternities or other student groups, and has caused more and better singing among them for the purpose.

Competition, however, may not bring about the sort of singing that is desired. Rather is that sort likely to come through endeavors, however simple and brief to begin with, to integrate it in the spontaneous social life of the fraternities and other college groups, especially those possessing their own houses and " home life." (Here is another incentive for the cultivation of informal singing, especially in small groups, in high schools, so as to establish a taste for it that will carry over into college life.[2]) The spirit of the original Glee Club in London may serve as a model. Some of the several *haus-musik* groups described in Chapter XIV, especially the University of Chicago one, may also be exemplary. When there was much more informal singing than there is now, there was also more eating and, we suppose, drinking, in company. Evidently, meals now are mostly meals and nothing else — it is said that good conversation is also often lacking —

[2] Cf. pages 307–314.

and drinking is done secretly in small groups. We can
very well dispense with the drinking, but we might
make more of eating together. The strong influence
exerted over the entire social life at Princeton by the
Eating Clubs of that University is regarded by
Mr. Hawes as perhaps bearing out his contention that
" eating together is really the basis of friendship and
the strongest element in creating a student organization." And it must be that music sublimates appetite
and is itself enhanced in doing so ; for as many a meal
otherwise dull has been made delightful by good dinner music (not counting those that have been ruined
by bad music), so, many a singing has been made unforgettably delightful by good talk and refreshments
before or after it.

If the fraternities and similar groups could arouse
in themselves as much interest in informal singing as
they have, by their own leadership, in other expressions of college life, the regrets and protests of the
older alumni might be turned to joy. The musical
leadership for the informal singing might well come
from the varsity glee club, which would cultivate especially suitable music for it in addition to the more
pretentious music for the major part of its concert
programs. It would also sing that and some of the
concert music, often employing only a small group of
its members, on many campus and fraternity house occasions ; and since its membership, influenced by the
interest of the fraternities and other college groups,
would include one or more representatives from each,
these students could bring to their respective groups
the inspiration and guidance that might be needed.
The director of the glee club would then become, unlike the football coach, a leader or source of leadership
for the entire student body. If the radio could be kept
silent long enough, one student's spontaneous playing of some songs on the piano after supper might be

all that is needed to start a habit of singing among his fellows.

All that has been said about fraternities might be applied to sororities and, with adaptation, to dormitory and other groups. And it is needless to point out the possibilities in class, college and other assemblies. At Barnard once a month the college assembly is devoted to general singing under the leadership of a member of the music faculty.

The choice of songs is, of course, of paramount importance. Among college songs there are already some that are in every way suited to modern youth, and it is likely that if interest in singing were revived through them and whatever other songs are suitable and attractive, more good songs would be written. Let the students choose, being sure that they hear and try out for the purpose a rich variety in addition to those already familiar to them.

At Radcliffe each year a song competition is held between the four classes, each class being judged not only by its singing of a given song, but also by the suitability for informal college uses of an original song written and composed by two or more of its members and sung by all of them. Perhaps some of the several sorts of occasions for which songs have been written in summer camps [3] could also inspire college students, faculty, or alumni; adaptation in subject and detail being necessary, of course, to fit college life.

Women's Glee Clubs

Undoubtedly there is no women's college or coeducational college that does not have a women's chorus. The greater musical interest and activity among women is well known. "Women and children first" has been the rule in music as well as on sinking ships and burning buildings. "Culture is in the hands of

[3] See Chapter XIX.

the women," said a professor of music at Smith College. But the men are now not far behind, and the new excellence and substantiality of their singing has undoubtedly had an influence on many of the college women's choruses, which have in the past been too much given to pretty music. Arrangements of many excellent compositions originally for mixed choruses have been added to the fine works written especially for treble voices by some of the madrigal composers, and by Purcell, Bach, Handel, Schumann, Brahms, César Franck, Holst and others. The choral society at Radcliffe College was said by President Comstock to be the livest activity in the place, enlisting about 200 of the 750 students — more than 25% ! Smith, Vassar, and Wellesley also are proud of their choruses. Joint concerts by Smith and Harvard in one year and Wellesley and Harvard in the next year, and those combining Radcliffe's chorus with that of its brother college, are exemplary of a way to enrich the musical experience of students who otherwise would be entirely confined to the limited repertoire and range of expression of men's voices alone or women's voices alone.

Choral Societies and Festivals

As the interest in singing turns more and more toward the experience of music as its chief goal, there is a growing tendency to combine men's and women's voices in a chorus, when that is possible. The range of experience in mixed choral singing is so much richer. At many of the coeducational colleges there is a permanent mixed chorus. For example, the Choral Union of over 300 young men and women in the University of Michigan, since its establishment in 1881, has presented all of the best larger choral works and many of the best smaller ones, in connection with the May Festival in which it takes part each year. It is said

that "many of its members have been so permeated
with the spirit of the work that they have been instrumental in organizing similar choruses in all parts of
the country." As great and famous as the superb May
Festivals of this University are the annual North
Shore Festivals in which about 400 students of Northwestern University join with about the same number
of townspeople in the Festival Chorus. The A Cappella
Choir of this University shares with that of St. Olaf
College the honor of highest excellence and of largest
influence in increasing and advancing *a cappella* singing by mixed choruses in the schools and colleges of
this country.

Since a festival may be the most inspiriting of all
musical enterprises, lifting even the dullest to a new
high level of expression and being, it is very gratifying
to note the number of colleges and universities whose
musical life finds such a climax each year. Among
these are the Universities of California, Kansas,
Maine, Missouri, and South Dakota; Cornell College
in Iowa; the College of Emporia; Bethany College in
the musically amazing town of Lindsborg, Kansas,
whose citizens are almost to a man either participants
or ardent supporters of the festival, now in its fiftieth
year; Smith College with its festival of opera, and several state teachers' colleges. Starting with a Brahms
Festival in 1930, then a Bach Festival in 1931, Harvard and Radcliffe have also set a superb precedent for
themselves. What of the hundreds of other colleges
and universities? But it must be remembered that the
festive spirit may enter and irradiate a single concert,
even a rehearsal.

International Musical Olympics

What seems in some respects the most important
development ever attempted in college singing, if not
in all musical endeavor of whatever sort, is the move-

ment now well toward fulfillment to enlist student choruses from all parts of Europe and America in an international festival that, like the Olympic games, will occur in every few years. At the first international conference on student music in Munich in July, 1931, the Intercollegiate Musical Council of this country invited the leading student singing societies of the world to a festival to be held in connection with the world's fair in Chicago in July, 1933. In addition to rejoicing at the promise that this holds of another very potent influence toward good will among nations, it is delightful to think of the interchange of ardors and standards of excellence that is likely to arise from it. The agenda of the conference included consideration of the formation of a permanent international union of student choruses and of the appointment of an international committee for the exchange and translation of the world's best choral music for men's voices.

How It Is Done in Germany

There could be no better proof and inspiring example of what students can do to revive singing among themselves, and indirectly among large numbers of other people, than have been given by the youth of Germany. In " Leisure and Education in Germany," a recent book compiled by the Reichsausschuss Der Deutschen Jugendverbande and by the Zentralinstitut für Erziehung und Unterricht in Berlin, Dr. Hermann Reichenbach has an article on " Folk Music and Leisure " from which we must quote very liberally, ardently hoping that a similar renewal or new attainment of joy in singing will come through our colleges.

Music is in danger. What can we do to protect it? To arouse the decaying interest every possible means is tried. The method in which the virtuosi are trained is developed in the most intense manner. To perform a masterpiece by Mozart is nowadays an indispensable condition for those who wish to enter a music academy, and for our high school graduates what was a technical problem for such a pianist as Beethoven or for an organist like Bach is simply a bagatelle. There is now no difficulty which our symphony orchestras cannot solve. Even glee clubs that have grown and developed from the household vocal quartets, afford in their gigantic choruses of many hundred voices, specimens of thorough vocally trained male and female singers, who are able to give the most astonishing artistic performances. Finally, in the modern domain of mechanical music reproduction such as the wireless and the gramophone, the most marvelous performances are possible. And yet, despite all this, the danger to which music is exposed is not thereby removed. Operas and concerts have still no doubt their audiences, but a distinctly marked decrease in the interest shown for these, proves that even the most perfect representation of musical performances is not able in the long run to supply the place of one's own inner musical feeling. At any rate one thing is certain, and that is, our modern popular songs are sure of a good market. But even the most cynical resident of a large city demands his right to higher spiritual and intellectual values. A way must again be found to enable the youth as well as the adult to acknowledge such ideals by being able to devote his leisure hours to music. . . .

In Germany, the young people have themselves found a way to this end. Within the limits of the love of nature movements and other cultural developments, that is to say, the so-called Jugendbewegung (Youth Associations) there has been from their very inception a most decided inclination to play and sing. Not by any means in the manner described above, that is to say, not in order to reproduce a musical work of art, but simply to give musical expression to their own inner feelings. They found also that in singing and playing together their own unity and comradeship could be more happily shown and expressed. This took place naturally and spontaneously without any preparation in advance. These young people sang of nature, of wandering, of life just as it was in the actual situation they happened to be in at the moment, and they played also at the same time some musical instrument. What did they sing? They found ready at hand in old books and in the country places songs, the so-called Volkslied, old melodies and old songs, street songs of a period when the street had not become debased, when it was still a pleasant and agreeable place in which to meet. In this manner songs with beautiful melodies suitable for all situations were collected and finally a song book written, the so-called "Zupfgeigenhanfel" — the Guitar Song Book — now published by Friedrich Hofmeister, Leipzig.

This spontaneous musical development in Germany has led gradually to the general cultivation of music amongst the young people who now devote to it a large part of their leisure time. . . .

In the course of time and by constant practice the young people became more perfect, and from singing spontaneous folk songs and songs suited to the immediate occasion they advanced to singing and rendering artistically ancient and modern melodies. These compositions are arranged for many voices but they are thoroughly understood by all, so that the singers can not alone sing the customary table songs, but take part in their leisure hours in serious polyphonic songs. . . . During a festival held in Baden-Baden in 1927, when a concert of modern chamber music was given for the first time, and when the people were waiting for the concert to begin, what astonished the foreign visitors most of all was the manner in which the audience began to sing extempore artistic madrigals by H. L. Hassler (1564–1612) and G. Gastoldi (1556–1622) uniting their voices in choral singing notwithstanding the fact that the audience was made up of people from all parts of Germany . . . the idea of a concert did not exist at all. The singing of the madrigals was simply due to the fact that each of the singers sang and practiced with strangers what he had already practiced and sung as a member of his local club. It is only in this way that the cultivation of music could be so rapidly developed.

This development made the production of suitable music a necessity. Many costly ancient treasures were preserved in the libraries; the early composers regarded it as a matter of honor to write something new for these purposes, so that after a time large music publishers developed from the smallest beginnings. I mention here as a sample the publishing firm of Georg Kallmeyer, Wolfenbuttel, and the Varenreiterverlag, Kassel, whose year books give the best information on the matters alluded to. The selection of the musical instruments suitable for such folk music was also a matter of the highest importance. The piano as an instrument for the layman remained in the background while the flute on the other hand became very popular and also other instruments such as the lute which is now in great favor.

From what has been stated above it can be seen that the question as to the musical education of the public can now be answered in a completely different manner. The old method of education both as regards the music and the instrumental technic proceeded from quite different standpoints. In many different cities music schools have been established, the so-called folk music schools, which are specially suitable to the modern demands of music amongst the people. (Fr. Jode: "Muskdienst am Volka," Publishers: G. Kallmeyer, Wolfenbuttel.) The cultivation of music in the schools was also directed to the general promotion of amateur music for which purpose numerous important reforms were introduced. Formerly, the object of musical instruction in the school was confined in the same manner as the glee clubs to the practice of special choral works for approaching school festivals. At the present day, however, the main problem is the education of the pupils to an understanding for music and preparing for occupation with music later on. If in this direction, the will of the younger generation, the lessons in the music schools, and the music lessons in the schools work in unison, a strong impulse will be given to an intelligent employment of their leisure time, and to a serious and cheerful cultivation of folk music.

Orchestras

The phenomenal new developments in high schools make one wish to inquire especially as to instrumental music at college. In only one college, so far as a brief survey has disclosed, is there such support for an orchestra as is more and more commonly given in high schools — with daily rehearsals and many school-owned instruments. Consequently, for many of the graduates of superb high school orchestras, most colleges can offer only a dwindling of their experience as players. Despite lesser support, however, there are a few very admirable college orchestras.

At the University of Wisconsin, the well-balanced orchestra of 60 students rehearses three times a week and gives three concerts a year which, at twenty-five cents for admission, attract large audiences of townspeople as well as students. Columbia University's orchestra is of the same size and, though it rehearses but twice a week, has an enviable record. Of its five public concerts each year — for which it engages a small number of expert players for greater excellence — three are included in the distinguished course of concerts and lectures given by the Institute of Arts and Sciences of the University. The chief aim of the orchestra, however, is to give students the opportunity to experience the best orchestral music. An example of this policy is to be found in its performance of the Brahms Third Symphony, which was at first regarded as too difficult and otherwise advanced a work for a public concert by the orchestra. But so inspired by this work were the students that it was included in a concert program, and was marked as one of the best performances ever given by the orchestra. Everything is done to make its playing a means of recreation for the students, and it is said to have a high place in the regard of the students generally as an extra-curricular activity. Its conductor is a distinguished member of the faculty, but its management is in the hands of the students themselves, who operate in the usual manner to be found in student activities.

What is probably the oldest musical organization in the United States is a college orchestra! It is the Harvard University Orchestra, or the Pierian Sodality, founded in 1808 by a small group of students interested in classical music, and continuing without break through all the years since then. A statement appearing on one of its recent programs gives most of the very facts in which we are interested.

The Harvard University Orchestra is made up entirely of students in Harvard University whose interest in music runs more to the classics than to popular music. It is open to all members of the University, and competitions are held twice each year to determine the placing of the men and to add to the personnel. The orchestra has the same standing in relation to the college as other outside organizations. Members of the orchestra who play regularly for one year are entitled to regular membership in the Pierian Sodality of 1808, which is the small group of elected men who organize and direct the activities of the orchestra proper. The membership in the orchestra has increased during the last few years. In the season of 1929–30 about fifty men played regularly. There is full symphony orchestration at all times.

The aim of the orchestra, as expressed in the preamble to its constitution, is "to maintain, encourage and advance orchestral music among the students of Harvard University." This orchestra is the only Harvard organization in which men have an opportunity to work on the best orchestral music and present it at concerts. It fills a very necessary place in the extracurricular activity of the University. But there is another purpose for the group: it endeavors to promote interest in good music not only among the students of Harvard University, but also among colleges and preparatory schools and in the community at large. The officers of the Sodality feel that a greater or less acquaintance with good music is a necessary part of each man's life, and that the programs given before preparatory school audiences and groups in neighboring towns and in various colleges do a great deal to promote that interest.

This orchestra also rehearses but twice a week. An especially important feature of its work is the choice of music which has kept its efforts within fields very happily suited to a good student orchestra of moderate size. There have been no heaven storming works, such as have lured some high school and community orchestras, in which fiery fiddling and the bombastic blowing of brasses or rumble of drums may stir to highest praise an audience for whose ears a lack of refinement, phrasing, or even of plain, honest accuracy is not a deprivation. Mozart serenades and overtures, Bach suites, the Schubert Overture to " Rosamunde," Grieg Norwegian dances and Dvorak Slavonic dances, a Haydn symphony, a Milhaud suite: these and the like of them have been its portion — a musical dining rather than feeding, so to speak, though the racy tang of common exuberance has not been lacking.

The University of Utah's orchestra of over 60 students rehearses on four days a week and plays at a

weekly student assembly on the fifth day. This unusually large provision of time is due to the fact that
there is in each week a faculty assembly on Tuesdays
and a student assembly on Fridays, both at 11:30, so
that hour is left free of curricular engagements all the
week. This university matches in another respect the
best support given to high school orchestras, in that it
owns and loans violas, cellos, string basses, an oboe,
bassoon, and an *A* clarinet, in addition to the band
instruments of its R.O.T.C. equipment. Evidently
largest of all and remarkably accomplished is the
University of Michigan orchestra which has the advantages of an unsurpassed corps of instructors in one
of the country's most successful music schools, now
amalgamated with the University, a public school
music department which attracts an especially large
number of persons interested in becoming supervisors
of instrumental music, and, most essential, an excellent conductor. It also rehearses four times a week,
though the schedules of some of the members do not
permit them to attend regularly.

Northwestern University, Yale and the University
of Miami are sponsors of community symphony
orchestras second only to our greatest professional
orchestras. They are, respectively, the Evanston Symphony Orchestra, the New Haven Symphony Orchestra, and the University of Miami Orchestra, the last
like the other two giving series of concerts in the community. The Evanston and the Miami Orchestras
each have a large proportion of students, the rest
being a few members of the faculty, professional players, and a few good adult amateurs from the town.
The New Haven Orchestra (of Yale) is more largely
professional. The sharing of orchestral labors and
pleasures by "town and gown," sometimes all amateurs, occurs also at Rollins and several other small
colleges. Unfortunately, where the number of profes-

sionals or townspeople is large, the satisfaction of a full or nearly full rehearsal is usually had only once a week.

Enough college orchestras have been cited to show what is possible. A fuller report would surely include similar achievements at Emory University and the Universities of Washington, California, Kansas, Nebraska, and Iowa; and there are doubtless other good examples of which the writer is uninformed. Such a report would undoubtedly also show that a large proportion of student players in all such orchestras, with the possible exception of Michigan's, which includes many prospective school music supervisors, have no intention of becoming professional musicians. For example, of 56 Columbia University orchestra members who noted their intentions, only 15 are turned toward music as a profession. The rest are divided among the fields of medicine, physics, architecture, business, pharmacy, missionary endeavor, teaching, engineering and law. Forty-two of them have been members of high school orchestras. At almost every college visited it was said that the new developments in high schools were bringing more and often better players to it.

Bands

The complete report in the book "College and University Bands" (Bureau of Publications, Teachers College, Columbia University, 1929) of a thorough study by Dr. L. V. Buckton of the organization and administration of these most pervasive of musical societies shows that in 1926–27 there were 3,565 men and 169 women, without duplication, in the bands of the 54 colleges and universities included in the study — an average of 69 for each college. The University of Illinois, which was not included, had over 300 students in four bands in 1930–31, and the first concert band a superb one! That the band may play a large part in the social and recreational life of the students, and in cultivating school spirit, is sufficiently indicated by Dr. Buckton's report of the numbers of performances by the bands of the 54 institutions studied, and the occasions on which they played in 1926–27.

FUNCTIONS AT WHICH COLLEGE AND UNIVERSITY BANDS PLAY — TOTAL APPEARANCES

Functions	Total
Football games	368
Basketball games	428
Wrestling meets	28
Track meets	69
Baseball games	133
Pep meetings	266
Pep parades — before and after games	201
Political meetings on campus	18
Convocations	91
Assemblies	114
Graduation exercises	35
Spring open-air concerts	152
Special concerts with paid admission	202
Dedication exercises — all kinds	89
Spring carnivals, camp fires, picnics, etc.	32
Receptions	13
Dinners	8
Water carnival	3
Radio broadcasting	16
Drill and R.O.T.C. functions	264
Miscellaneous playing	106
Total appearances	2,636

In a majority of the institutions studied, uniforms or some instruments, or both kinds of equipment are furnished in varying measure through government funds for the R.O.T.C.

The bands receive so much incentive from frequent appearances in connection with football and basketball games, that in many colleges there has been a slump in interest and effort after the seasons for these are over. Moreover, not a few students are inclined to transfer their interests from the band to some other student activity after a year or two of service in the former. Among the attitudes and devices that have been used to keep band members active throughout the year and all through the four years of college are the following, some of which may be helpful to community and other bands also:

School spirit

Pride in the band

Admirable traditions emphasized by an active band alumni association

Membership in a band fraternity or a college honorary society

The joy of accomplishment, through efficient rehearsing of music worthy of the best effort

Interesting social life, through parties, an annual banquet, or an annual college dance under the auspices of the band, or through all of these

Existence of two or more bands, graded according to ability, making it a sought-for honor to attain or maintain membership in the best band

Trips out of town for concerts or for performance at games

Making performance and free attendance at football and basketball games contingent on a good yearly record of attendance

An award such as a band " key," medal, pin, sweater, or a university blanket, for long, faithful membership

New uniforms every year

Rebate in tuition

Remuneration (in one university $50 for a year's work)

Increase in remuneration for each year of service

Chamber Music

There is evidently not as much chamber music playing as one would expect amidst large numbers of students sharing in the same home life in fraternity houses, dormitories and elsewhere. Even in the large music schools of Oberlin College and Northwestern

University it was said that after the compulsory musical work of the student's day is done, he is likely to
seek diversion in the prevailing leisure time activities
of the college or the town. The scarcity of recreational
trio and quartet playing and the like is doubtless,
however, largely due to the whole system of music
education from kindergarten on, which places too
much dependence on the work of the teacher or conductor, and on the receiving of credits or of some other
sort of external approval. Education in initiative,
spontaneous exercise of the will to sing or play without
teacher or assignment of any sort, is greatly needed.
It is especially gratifying therefore to find a Chamber
Music Society meeting weekly in the evening at Columbia University for exploration and enjoyment of
some of the large store of delightful music for string
quartet and related groups. Enough players there are
for three string quartets to play for each other, and
sometimes in an intimate public performance. The
leader in this society combines expertness as a coach
with the rare social attitude needed in a student organization whose activity is or should be peculiarly
free from domination by any individuals. There is also
a regularly accredited day course in ensemble playing
with an hour's meeting once a week at Columbia,
under the same leader, which in 1930–31 had two
string quartets for its explorations.

The University of Miami has been similarly fortunate in informal ensemble playing under the enthusiastic guidance of that prince of musical amateurs,
Mr. Arnold Volpe, who is by vocation one of our
most expert and best beloved orchestra conductors,
violin teachers and chamber music players. At Yale
the thing is done somewhat more formally, the students each paying $35 a year for one period of 45 min-
utes in a course under a prominent New York cellist
and chamber music player. The writer found three

string quartets of students and one of townswomen in this course in 1929. Equally interesting was a string quartet of members of the University's medical faculty, called by themselves the "Saw-bones Quartet." The universities of Washington, Utah and doubtless several others, also have courses in the playing of chamber music. Most enjoyable, of course, are the informal, self-initiated groups playing "out of course" for the sheer love of it. Nearly all that was said of informal singing in colleges, including means of providing leadership, might be applied to instrumental *haus-musik* as well.

The Music of Chapel Services

The college or university chapel, often a beautiful but neglected building, should, of course, be almost as vital a center of musical and religious life all through the year as it is during the Christmas carol services (such as are given at Harvard, Mt. Holyoke and many other institutions) when there is not enough room for all who wish to attend and not enough power in words to express the wonder and joy of it all. All that is said in the chapter on music "In Churches, Synagogues, and Religious Schools" (Chapter XV) with regard to congregational singing, choir singing and instrumental music, is applicable to the college or university chapel.

Theory

It is through this subject that music first found an accredited place in the college — in 1873 at Harvard — and, with the history and appreciation of music, it is still the most commonly accepted and emphasized in those institutions. This is not strange, because these three phases have to do with understanding and taste, which may be quite lacking in even a virtuoso performer, and which are in keeping with the general purposes of a liberal, not a vocational, college. The "theory of music," so called, including harmony, counterpoint, canon, fugue, instrumentation, etc., is carried in many of our colleges to the very practical extent of producing original compositions that, while often theoretical in the sense that many of them reach no outcomes in practice outside of the theory room, sometimes become beloved expressions in the repertoire of singers or players. In any event, the subject may be pursued with full academic credit by students purposing to become practical composers.

Nowhere is this — at its best — creative and supreme sort of musical activity cultivated more fully and effectively than at the Eastman School of Music of the University of Rochester, where every year since 1925 there has been a festival of music by American composers. A letter to Mr. Olin Downes from Dr. Howard Hanson, director of this school, appearing in the New York *Times* on May 31, 1931, gives an interesting report of the work in composition being done there, and of its purposes.

In order to explain the work that we have been undertaking it is perhaps necessary to begin with a statement of my own philosophy regarding musical creation. I have proceeded from the axiomatic truth that composition is the most important thing in music and that the composer is the hub of the musical wheel. . . . In spite of the obviousness of this fact I have been amazed to find again and again that intelligent people were placing almost their sole emphasis upon and devoting their chief thought to the performer rather than to the creator.

The corollary to my first theorem is that as the composer is of prime importance in music so is the national composer important in the development of a national musical culture. . . .

Coming to the practical matter of determining how such concentration on the development of American music can be guided to produce the best results, I have come to two conclusions. The first is that it is not possible for one man, no matter how great he may be, to produce a significant national development. Such a development must be the work not of one composer but of many composers. Some of these men will have great talent and some will be of lesser talent, but it will be the combined efforts of all of these men that will be fruitful.

* * * * * *

In the second place, I believe that it is equally imperative to foster spiritual atmosphere that is favorable to creation. In other words, the subsoil must also be tilled so that we develop among those interested in music a feeling of interest in and sympathy toward creation. . . .

. . . it was possible as early as the spring of 1925 to begin this work by the inauguration of the American Composers' Concerts. The original aim of these concerts was to furnish a laboratory where young composers of talent might come and hear their orchestral works for the first time. . . . After a comparatively short time, however, I found, to my amazement, that apparently many of the older and well-known composers wished to avail themselves of performances at these concerts, and accordingly the number of concerts per season was increased. The programs, at the present time, are therefore very eclectic in character, consisting of works from the pens of totally unknown composers side by side with the new works from the pens of America's most distinguished creators.

* * * * * *

Since the first concert we have given in all twenty-two symphonic programs of American compositions, not to mention many performances of choral and chamber music works. Altogether sixty-three composers have been represented on these programs and ninety-seven works have been performed, many of which have been first performances. . . .

These concerts have been generally attended by the composers whose works were performed, and out of this has come an important and rather unexpected development. Composers from all over the country have gathered together from time to time and have come to know each other. They have discussed their problems and their philosophies of music and in doing so have developed a sympathetic understanding of one another. They have found that the American composer is trying to do a distinctive piece of work in expressing through music the life of his own country. This resulted in a certain consolidation of purpose, a sort of communism of artistic endeavor.

Along with this development, which has been in a sense an " extra-curricular " activity of the school, there has been a similar development within the institution itself. When I arrived in the fall of 1924, there was one student majoring in composition. At the present time there are eighteen students majoring in composition, of which number seven are undergraduate and eleven are graduate students. These students are motivated by the same desire, not only to express themselves, but to add something to the development of American music. This month, for example, there will be three composition concerts of works written by students. One of these programs will consist of ten symphonic works! . . . I can say, furthermore, that all of these works indicate both technical ability in the handling of the orchestra and, in many cases, indicate as well the possession of distinct creative talent. . . .

* * * * * *

. . . the entire theory department, from the first year classes in theory and dictation up to the advanced study of orchestration, has been imbued with the creative ideal. The members of these departments are themselves composers and are themselves working constantly on the development of their own creative work.

In conclusion perhaps the most gratifying thing of all has been the development in the Eastman School, as a whole, of enthusiasm for creation. The festival of American music which we have just concluded . . . called forth from the entire faculty and the student body the greatest zeal and enthusiasm. It is impossible to live in the midst of such an atmosphere without feeling its stimulus and essential productivity.

Surely the establishment of an environment so wholesomely conducive to creativity is of great importance to music in American life. Not greater, perhaps, but still more important would it be, could it result not only in symphonic and other ambitious works, but also in the creation of songs and other music good in every way for the development of the informal singing and playing for which we long.

Appreciation

The development of acquaintanceship with, and of a love and understanding of, the best that has been thought and said in music is the primary purpose of all music education in colleges, and is likely to affect the greatest number of students. It is after all the basic need and richest means of delight in all types of musical activity, professional as well as amateur. Yet — and despite its long history as a college subject — the methods of cultivating it are subject to more questioning and debate than those of any other course. This is because it cannot be *taught* at all, but only *caught* through enlightened but unobstructed experience of music itself. The ardent but mysterious play of the spirit, or intuition, by which we apprehend the meanings of music, "those essences of which even ideas and concepts are projections," is too often obstructed by earnest lectures that turn out to be only small talk. Analytical study and explanation are to a degree necessary for adequate growth in appreciation, and so is appropriate knowledge of the social, spiritual and personal background of the composer and his period; but often the most widely effective teaching of appreciation in a college is the unconscious influence of its general environment, the kind of attitudes and interests to which it silently shapes its students. The many faculty concerts, organ recitals, and the series of concerts by great professionals, at an increasing number of colleges and universities — many of them free to the students — are a very important feature of college life. A device that has brought many a student to concerts that he has considered too " highbrow " is the " activity ticket," for which a moderate fee is required of him. The series of events to which this ticket gives admission includes concerts as well as drama, forensics, lectures by celebrities and, sometimes, athletic events.

Especially notable are the *All-Musical Vespers* at the University of Kansas, which through the variety of media possible for each program where the musical staff and best student organizations of the Univer-

sity's School of Fine Arts are excellent, have attracted
large numbers of students to the best music. Four
such Vespers are given each year during the months
of November, December, February and March. At
the December Vesper the Painting and Design Departments of the Fine Arts School participate with a
series of Christmas tableaux which, with the choral
and instrumental music in keeping with the Christmas
spirit, make a service of great beauty.

The University of Missouri has provided an excellent example of " music in industry." " At four o'clock
each afternoon during examination week (in 1929) an
organ recital was given to offer relaxation through
music from the strain of the examination period. The
average attendance was over a thousand — about 25
per cent of the student body — and it was evident
from the way the same students returned each afternoon, that the purpose of the recitals was being accomplished." [4] The same purpose and means have
been carried out at Harvard and, doubtless, at some
other colleges.

*   *   *   *   *   *

Credit or No Credit?

In commencing this chapter we asked whether the
colleges offer better and more opportunity for carrying on the good work of the best high schools than
does the world outside. Apparently many of them do,
though in greatly varying degree. But read the report
of a recent brief survey made by Mr. Osbourne Mc-
Conathy for the Federal Office of Education: [5]

While . . . the musical student who surveys the field [of
the musical offerings of different colleges] with care may find
opportunities to pursue his college studies with due considera-

[4] From an address by Dean James T. Quarles printed in the Music
Teachers' National Association Proceedings for 1930.
[5] Bulletin, 1931, No. 20.

tion to his musical interests, there is nevertheless a wide gap in our music system which the colleges still leave open. This gap is found in the failure of colleges to provide adequate opportunities for the large number of students who found cultural pleasure in playing in high school orchestras and bands. Few colleges assume direct supervision of their bands and orchestras, and still fewer offer credit for this form of applied music. *The amount of time necessary to keep in practice on an instrument seriously handicaps the student who gives this time without credit.*

The last sentence, which we have italicized, is a protest frequently made by musicians and others. At least 500 American colleges and universities have admitted music theory, history and appreciation among accredited courses. Why keep out singing and playing, as the majority of those colleges do? Why give credit toward the A.B. degree for listening to the music of Bach or a lecture about him or it and none for playing it?

"The study of applied music," says Dr. Davison,[6] "differs from other subjects of the academic curriculum. . . . [It] aims primarily to supply a physical facility, which is the result of mechanical motion. . . . It is not unlike the tracing of designs through tissue paper. The only contribution made by the student apart from his performance is emotional, not intellectual; and even his interpretation, when there is one, often comes directly from the teacher. . . . With the amount of time ordinarily accorded music practice by the average American there is little opportunity for attention to anything other than technique. . . . Thus the powers of memory and of ratiocination, so fundamental to the kind of knowledge generally required of the A.B. degree, are almost entirely lacking."

Quite to the contrary, in an address delivered before the Association of American Colleges in January, 1931, Dr. John Erskine says:

The amount of practice necessary for a weekly or fortnightly lesson in music involves two or three times the moral and intel-

[6] Music Education in America, by A. T. Davison, Harpers, 1926.

lectual effort which the average student expends on any other course. Two hours a day of practice demand absolute concentration in order to produce results, and they can be crammed into nothing short of a hundred and twenty minutes. Music practice cannot be surreptitiously worked up, as many a history lesson is, during morning chapel or the Sunday sermon. Musical performance differs from any other recitation now encouraged in our classrooms, in that it must be good as a whole as well as in detail, and the student can expect no lucky break in the question he draws from the instructor.

But other difficulties are in the way of inclusion of singing and playing among subjects accredited toward the A.B. degree. For example, how are the results of practice to be measured? To what extent shall progress in mere dexterity be accredited? The best interpretation may be the result of the best mimicry of a teacher or other performer. We cannot here go into all the questions and discussion aroused by the increasing pressure from many quarters to give performance equal place with the theory, history and appreciation of music in colleges. A thorough study of the situation is now being contemplated by officials of the Association of American Colleges, and if it is shown that large numbers of students previously trained in music have been forced to give it up because of the pressure of other studies, the increase in the number of colleges accrediting musical performance will probably be even more rapid than it has been in the past decade.

Over one third of the 594 colleges and universities included in the report of *A Survey of College Entrance Credits and College Courses in Music*,[7] now allow credit in varying measure for singing and playing. The members of every orchestra mentioned in this chapter, except the Harvard one, receive some credit, though usually comparatively little, for their performance.

[7] Prepared by the research council of the Music Supervisors National Conference in cooperation with the National Bureau for the Advancement of Music, 1930.

There is unquestionably a growing regard for the importance of musical skill as a phase of education. This is strikingly shown also by the fact that, according to the survey just mentioned, of 452 colleges now granting entrance credit for music — a gain of 166 in ten years — 359 include applied music as an entrance subject.

But Are Not Singing and Playing for Leisure?

Whatever differences of opinion exist regarding the status of music in a liberal college, all parties are agreed that its purpose in such a college is as a·leisure time pursuit, not a profession. The protests against the pressure of other studies sound very much like the protest dealt with in Chapter IV regarding obstacles to community musical endeavors, that there are " too many other things going on." But out in the community it is directed against the too many other things, the lack of purposefulness in leisure time life. One might argue that if college life is such that an individual has not sufficient leisure or interest to practice an art as a means of recreation, then it must be failing in its main purpose, which is to educate for life, especially avocational life, rather than for a vocation. Can we expect the business or professional man in the world outside to play in an orchestra or chamber music group or alone, in leisure hours, without " credit," if in the model world of the college he has not time or inclination or opportunity to do so? Or is the college still only preparing for life by obliging or paying its students (with credits) to do that through which they will find most satisfaction in real life?

It might also be argued that if credits and the like could be valued for what they are intended — as tokens of what William Orton has called " the initiation of the mind to ever new and finer types of experience " — there could be no question as to granting full credit for intelligent experience of the best music through playing it; but they are often, in effect, only the currency of a bargain relation between pupil and teacher, each trying to get as much as possible from the other for the least return. In other words, it might be said that the curricular activities of the college are often the equivalent of labor in the outside world, and all the rest of college life the equivalent of leisure. Though this is not true for many a student, whose instructors, courses and inclinations make even compulsory studies a way of fine, full living, it is generally enough true, in varying degree, to make the question of how the periods of labor and leisure are to be apportioned and enhanced or changed in character more important than that of how good amateur playing of music is to be included among the gainful occupations of the labor period.

The supreme test of the worth of any cultural music study is whether or not it does have a vital place in the self-propulsive life of the individual outside of all the business of degree-getting. We have noted the large numbers of students who strive as valiantly as any credit-seeker, but much more ardently and happily than most, to help produce first-rate singing by glee clubs at Yale, Princeton, Harvard and other colleges, where no academic credit for the effort is given at all. Three times a week, we said, the Harvard club rehearses, but it has rehearsed as many as six times in a week, and nearly as many times in two or three preceding weeks, just before a fine performance such as it gave with the Radcliffe Choral Society in a Bach Festival in 1931. The writer heard the members hiss their displeasure in a rehearsal one evening; it was when their leader announced that a regularly scheduled rehearsal in the following week would have to be given up!

True, instrumental music requires outside practice,

especially to be equal to present-day standards even of amateur performance. But a handicap greater than the lack of credits is the lack of adequate leadership in many places. Indeed, in not a few colleges the students themselves must provide the funds for purchase of the music and even for engaging a leader. The glee club of one of our oldest and leading colleges has in each of a number of years appeared at a vaudeville theatre for a week's engagement to gain funds. If no other source of support is available, a small appropriation from the hundreds of thousands of dollars collected at the gate of the football field might be awarded to extra-curricular musical organizations for helping to preserve a balance in the leisure time life of the college.

The Study of Music Through Performance

All are agreed also that actual participation in the music being studied greatly enhances the value of the study. Ideally, in every course in appreciation the students would sing or play much of the music rather than merely listen to it, absorb lectures about it, and then write about it. A chorus, orchestra, chamber music society, or group of pianoforte players whose purpose was not public performance, or that alone, but a practical study of music, would surely be as worthy of credit, and rightly so from every point of view, as a class in English Literature or in a laboratory science. But the credit would be given for the study of the music, which would be chosen to provide the richest opportunities for growth in musical understanding and delight, and there would be time for comments, discussion and outside readings and practice. Unfortunately, the proportion of students who could play well enough to carry on such a course is still very small, though it is growing. But a large proportion could sing their way through such a course. At Northwestern University, the University of Michigan, Harvard, and, commencing this year, at Columbia, there are courses in the history of choral music in which much of the time is given to actual singing of the most significant examples of the music being studied.

How Provide for Professionally-bent Music Students?

Now we come to conservatories, which the title of this chapter announced as bravely as it did colleges. But we must be brief. Dr. Erskine, in the address already quoted, makes a clear distinction between the liberal college and the conservatory:

A number of colleges, particularly colleges for women, are . . . organizing what are practically conservatories associated with the colleges. From the point of view of the musical educator this is a questionable move. A conservatory ought to be first rate or it ought not to exist, and it can't be first rate unless it aims at professional standards. The moment a college sets up a conservatory of music in association with its college course, it undertakes something which will almost certainly be better done elsewhere, and in the end it exposes itself to comparisons which are unfortunate and unnecessary.

When the reader remembers some of the many conservatories that are to be seen in almost every city and town, the idea that they are to be distinguished from college music departments by their higher, professional standards will amaze him. But he doubtless also knows of the Juilliard School of Music, the Curtis Institute, the Eastman School and a few other such institutions that give impressive warrant for Dr. Erskine's statement. The reader should know also that in 1927 the National Association of Schools of Music adopted standards for admission to its membership that only 46 such schools in the entire country have thus far passed. These standards are expressed through minimum curricula for the degrees Bachelor of Music and Master of Music, and thus exclude the excellent

Juilliard School and Curtis Institute because they offer no degrees. And this leads us to the first of four considerations with which we wish to close this chapter:

1. There seems no good reason why a conservatory of high rank could not be effectively associated with a college or university. The recent " Report on Proposed Expansion of the Department of Music, Columbia University " gives the principal obstacle.

. . . it is a mistake for a university to emulate the work of a conservatory, perhaps neglecting its own work in order to do so. Certain universities [less fortunate than Columbia in the near proximity of a first-rate conservatory with which to co-operate], afford us useful lessons of what not to do . . . in maintaining conservatories as schools of their universities. [They] tend to produce a body of students who have no relation to the intellectual life of the university, and take no interest in such activities as college orchestra and glee club. Where advanced training in piano playing or singing is offered, the popularity of such studies tends to upset the balance of the educational program, and produce narrow specialists with no sense of the wider and deeper values of music.

The presence of an unassimilable body of students, at its worst an exotic parasite on the university tree, is gravely objectionable, and ought not to be tolerated. But we are sick of having this exoticism, this disease, in our musical life in the world outside. Where are we to begin the cure if not in the conservatories? It may be unfair and even prove unwise to inoculate the universities with the disease, but the chance of gaining immunity so may be worth taking. In any event, at least 150 American colleges and universities are now offering professional along with liberal arts courses leading to a Bachelor of Music degree. In most of the states, the college or university is evidently the only agency through which musical education worthy of the attention of talented music students is being, or could be, given. Even the independent conservatories are trying to be colleges, offering liberal arts courses of varying quality in addition to the professional music courses, and having the right to confer music degrees. The unfortunate attitude of some professionally minded music students is largely due to contagion from teachers who were themselves deprived of the broadening and humanizing influences of a good college or its equivalent. The production of a larger proportion of excellent teachers than now exists is likely to be the most valuable outcome of the association of a conservatory with a college or university.

2. If the music student tends to isolate himself, a contributory cause may be found in the narrowness and inadaptability of college life in many places. The strong tendency of college students in those places to conform to a narrow range of extra-curricular interest and behavior is well known. The mingling among them of a good proportion of students with a frank, wholesome passion for beauty in the arts, and skill in one or more of them, might be very beneficial; and this would be likely to occur if the college were to give full recognition and perceptible support to artistic expression by its own students enrolled in a not too large school of music in the hands of a cultivated and wise faculty. At Yale, which has for many years maintained a conservatory, "the change in the attitude towards the arts in recent years has been quite remarkable," says Dean David Stanley Smith. This change, which is doubtless felt in many colleges, is, of course, partly due to developments in the world outside.

3. It must be remembered that preparation for professional performance or composition, even for teaching, requires intensive study and practice of music during many of the hours of the day. The distinction between the purposes of a department and a school of music in a college is therefore clear, as is the distinc-

tion between the A.B. and the Mus.B. degrees. To state this distinction is, perhaps, only to be confronted by the chief obstacle again, in another form. Professional courses of every sort should, it is said, be reserved entirely for graduate schools; the college at its best is purely a cultural institution. But the study of music, with all the literary, historical and scientific interests to which it is or should be a natural introduction, may be entirely cultural even for prospective professionals. Surely, the persons pursuing it with the intention of becoming professional performers in these days should, with the exception of singers, who need not and cannot give so much time to technical practice anyway, have acquired advanced technical skill and the ability to maintain or advance it efficiently before entering college. The fully accredited high school orchestras rehearsing daily, and the example, say, of the highly ranked University of Wisconsin accepting four out of fifteen units of entrance credit for music, give promise of the possibility, at least, of adequate provision at that stage of the process. Pianoforte students are not so well off, though credit for outside study is given in some high schools, but the trend is in their favor also.

Even if we grant that the future Kreislers and Paderewskis cannot be adequately provided for in the undergraduate college, there is still ground for associating a conservatory with it. Let those top-notch geniuses go for graduate work or without any previous college training to such independent conservatories as the Juilliard School and the Curtis Institute where the greatest teachers are gathered. Let there be good independent conservatories open to lesser folk also, in all parts of the country. We need them for their greater adaptability to individuals with special needs or desires, and for their possible contributions to the musical life of the cities and towns in which they are.

But what of the many fine craftsmen in music destined to play in our great symphony orchestras, who could profit very happily from studies in a good college? And most important of all, what of those who will teach music in our public schools and colleges? In many positions in those schools the teachers must possess advanced skill in musical performance as well as cultural and pedagogical training given by a good college. Shall they be obliged to acquire that skill in outside conservatories or studios in which there is the least likelihood of there being any relation to the intellectual life of the university or to the general educational and social life and needs of the schools or colleges in which they will teach?

The writer has for several years had a part in giving a graduate course in the teaching of music in which there have been students whose own musical education was so contrary in spirit and detail that they found it almost or entirely impossible to teach *music*. Some of them had evidently experienced only as performance what music of the masters had been assigned to them; and though technically advanced, they could not sing or play a simple song naturally and musically. An increasingly large proportion of students in independent and college schools of music are intending to be teachers, and it would be well if all their musical training could be exemplary of a fine sort of cultural education such as they themselves will later be asked to administer to children or young men and women.

4. Even the good professional must first of all, and always, be a good amateur. When one of the greatest pianists and composers of the day, Rachmaninoff, was asked through an application blank of the Society for the Publication of American Music to state his interest or status in music, his answer was " amateur." A musical education that does not include much student-

initiated (though faculty-inspired) singing and playing for the love of it " out of course," especially
in small groups, may produce world beating virtuosi,
but they are likely to be of the sort that only intensify
what has been called the curse of professionalism in
our music. The cultivation of the amateur spirit among
future professionals may be one of the most effective
things to be done for what we have already said is the
most important need in American musical life — example and leadership in good amateur singing and
playing among the people. The mingling of vocational
and avocational music students and these, in turn,
with the other students in a college or university is for
this reason, also, a good thing.

CHAPTER XI

Settlement and Community Music Schools

A " red cassock and a sky-blue cymar " [1] were worn by Pergolesi and his fellows in the *Collegio de' poveri di Gesu Cristo* in Naples. This was one of the eight *Collegii di musica,* four in Naples and four in Venice, famous in the early days of the eighteenth century for their musical prowess. All eight were primarily orphan asylums, although in Venice children having parents were admitted — if they had good voices! Were they animated, these ancient *collegii,* like their successors, the settlement and community schools of today, by the desire to share one of the greatest joys in life? Ask some of their pupils: Domenico Scarlatti, Porpora, Paisiello, Pergolesi!

Settlement and community schools partake of the purpose of the young Oxford men who originated the settlement idea in London in the early eighties of the last century. These young college graduates appreciated keenly the advantages and delights that life had brought them, and felt that they wanted to share these things with people who had never enjoyed such opportunities. They took some rooms in the slums of London and started keeping " open house " for their neighbors. Suspicious at first that a lurking string might be attached to this hospitality, the slum-dwellers approached the young men with becoming caution. But when they found that nobody wanted to " uplift " them or dissect them, physically or mentally, they took courage — and the settlement movement was launched.

[1] Rolland, Romain. " A Musical Tour Through the Land of the Past," page 172.

COMMUNITY MUSIC SCHOOLS   361

So England. In the United States, Miss Jane Addams was the first to found a settlement, Hull House in Chicago. The first music school connected with a settlement was established at Hull House in 1892 by Miss Eleanor Smith. It is still a very active center, the first of thirty-five such schools now active in this country.

How a School Begins and Grows

Let us trace the growth of a typical settlement music school, drawing freely on actual history. The scene opens in the front hall of a settlement house, with the reception secretary at her desk regarding two earnest-eyed boys of about nine years of age.

" Teacher! " exclaims Paul, and pauses in dismay at his own temerity. Silence.

" What can I do for you? " inquires the secretary.

Paul looks at Peter; Peter shuffles and prepares his thumb for immediate use.

" Him and me " — the prepared thumb indicates the presence of Paul — " we wants music lessons."

" But we don't give music lessons here."

" No, I know. But we wants 'em. And there's a lot of kids down our block as wants 'em too."

And so music lessons are forthcoming. Five pupils presently increase to twenty, twenty to a hundred. Then the music department forges ahead of the other departments — dramatics, arts and crafts, gymnasium, athletics. Its head insists on having teaching studios that do not serve as highways from one part of the house to another. Soon so many children come trooping in for music that the department overweights the settlement, attracting numbers who are not interested in the other activities offered.

The next step is to split off from the settlement, form a board of directors, find or build a new home and move in. The building should be located within easy reach of main lines of travel, or else in the heart of a poor neighborhood. Schools flourish in both situations.

Although the aims and purposes remain the same as those of the settlement music department, our original unit is not an independent music school, self-governing, financially responsible. It has, let us say, 267 pupils, 34 teachers including the director who takes a few pupils in piano. Lessons are given in voice and all respectable instruments except the tuba. The only requirement for entrance is a desire to learn to make music well. Absence of talent bars none except students who cannot afford to pay anything at all toward their lessons. Such scholarship students are accepted when the school can afford it, each case being judged on its merits.

The new building has a small auditorium, airy studios, a students' library and lounge, a faculty lounge, plenty of room for the executive offices, possibly living quarters for resident staff members as well as the janitor, a pleasant office for the director to interview faculty or students in and make them feel at ease and a reception desk near the front door. The furnishings, while simple, are in excellent taste. Outside the door a handsome sign announces the presence of The Heavenly Harp Community Music School.

September 29: Registration Day for new pupils, after two days of registering old pupils. Yes, your registration fee amounts to two lesson fees, and you'll have your last two lessons in May without paying for them. Yes, I know the Black Hand Music School charges a $7.50 registration fee that you never see again, but that doesn't mean that we have to. Now, Mr. Sbzrko, I've told you four times that Sylvia must take one hour of theory a week, and she can't have so much as an ocarina lesson in this school if she doesn't. Everybody must take theory and I'm not making rules against Sylvia.

On October 6 The Heavenly Harp Music School is astonishing the neighborhood with the sounds that issue from it. Before long it will be giving informal monthly students' concerts; its ensembles, chorus and orchestras will be famous in the city and in demand for various kinds of affairs; the roster of pupils will contain 862 names; a trained social worker will be engaged on full time to look after the pupils and their families; Heavenly Harp neighborhood gatherings will be considered Occasions!

Finances

Financial habits differ in various schools. In general the budget divides itself Gaulishly into three parts, of which one is covered by tuition fees, one by contributions from annual members, and one by efforts on the part of the board of directors and other friends of the school. In cities where music schools are financed by community chest funds, roughly two-thirds of the budget will come from the chest.

Salaries of directors — meaning the head of the School, not members of the board — range from $2,000 to $5,000; heads of departments (violin, piano, voice, wind instruments) are usually paid by the year, from $1,500 up. Lesser teachers receive from $1.25 an hour up, though pupil teachers sometimes receive less. Twenty-five hours of teaching a week is the usual maximum, since schools do not open until after public school closes in the afternoon.

Tuition fees may be fixed or sliding, and range from nothing at all to about $4 a week, according to the policy of the individual school. Children usually pay less than adults. One school in New York asks $1.25 a week from children for a half-hour instrumental lesson and an hour of theory, and $1.75 from adults. It is assumed that adults can earn something toward their tuition, which the young children should not do.

Expenses of maintenance also vary. Taking an average for sixteen schools from New York to San Francisco, we find that in 1926 the total cost per pupil per year was $65.81. Later figures are not available. The cost includes faculty salaries, executive salaries, office expenses, house expenses, all overhead.

Some critics accuse settlement music schools of harming private teachers by filching pupils. While the criticism may be just in some individual cases, it is broadly untrue. A really good private teacher fears no competition, partly because of the results that build his reputation, partly because he draws on another section of the community and is not interested in teaching at two dollars an hour or thereabouts. A poor teacher ought to be put out of business anyway. Certain teachers in settlement music schools accept two dollars an hour downtown for the fun of it and get ten dollars an hour uptown to pay the rent!

We have considered the establishment of a typical school. Others have started differently. The oldest in New York City, the Music School Settlement on East Third Street near the Bowery, grew from the devotion of Miss Emily Wagner, who in 1894 gave piano lessons to as many East Side children as came for them. The Cleveland Settlement Music School had its germ in the piano salesroom of a department store. Lessons were given at twenty-five cents each to swell piano sales — until thirteen hundred pupils a week came clamoring in!

Why Settlement School Music in Addition to Public School Music?

Certain differences between the approach to music in public schools and in settlement music schools may be briefly considered:

1. All or nearly all children who study music in settlement schools do so because they themselves want music. No credits, contests, or any other ulterior pressures bring them. It rarely happens that parents bring a child to study for the gratification of parental pride. One youngster's mother complained bitterly that Lena, having decided that she wished piano lessons, would not let her family sleep but beat on the furniture with a stick, chanting the while, " You think you're going to sleep, but you're not going to sleep till you get me a music teacher! "

Naturally this attitude on the part of the children, their eagerness to lap up every grace imparted, simplifies the situation for all concerned.

2. Being organized for one specific activity, the teaching of music, the settlement music school has a freedom unknown in many public schools. It does not need to feed the child history and physical exercise and geography and spelling and arithmetic in huge classes. The pupils do not have to be ground out of a hopper, all more or less alike because the pressure of numbers prevents individual attention. The settlement music school can pick its teachers, limit intake, experiment with pedagogical methods and various ways of stimulating interest in the whole field of music as well as in one's chosen instrument.

To this end the Greenwich House Music School sent last fall to every student over fourteen years of age a searching questionnaire. Their range of interest, their tastes in music, history, literature, foreign travel were ascertained. Based on the answers to the questionnaire, cooperative programs were made up in which both faculty and students participated. French music, Brahms, opera, acoustics, Bach were among the topics considered, with short papers, discussion, musical illustrations. Although serious work is done, the atmosphere is one of having a good time, so that the " Co-ops " have continued bi-weekly throughout the winter with undiminished ardor.

Furthermore, there is a degree of intimacy, a fellowship born of single-hearted devotion to music, between pupil and teacher and the school as a whole that must be very rare in public schools. At its largest, the difference between a settlement music school and a public school must be to the child like that between a beloved club or home and a busy department store.

3. " After school — what? " a question propounded elsewhere in this volume, is answered in varying measure by settlement music schools and departments which accept adults as well as children. Instruction, opportunity to play in ensembles, bands,

orchestras, to sing in choruses, to take part in " Co-ops " — whatever is desired can be had so far as the budget permits.

Settlement school graduates can be found in every one of the major orchestras in this country. Nevertheless, the schools do not aim to turn out professional musicians into an already over-crowded field. They offer music of professional quality for non-professionals as a delight that belongs in life, as comfort, emotional outlet, inspiration, recreation. Music, as they see it, is a joy for leisure time, and only in exceptional cases do they encourage a student to enter the professional world. Special emphasis is given to singing or playing in small groups, as in *hausmusik*.

4. Being partly supported by charity — as are our best colleges! — the settlement music school must perforce maintain the highest possible standards of material and performance. This is not always possible in the public schools, although certain of them leave nothing to be desired in excellence.

5. The essential difference, however, between music as taught in the public schools and in settlement music schools, lies in the ability of the latter to take the child as a whole and make music minister to his individual needs. Practically all its students belong to the ranks of the underprivileged, and, as mentioned above, they crave music because it makes up for many of the miseries of their daily lives. The wise teacher can do much to mold her pupils, to make the " vainglorious ones " realize the value of team-work, to establish self-confidence in the timid, to awaken dormant powers, to set up standards of performance in life as well as in " pieces."

For good teaching of music there is always a place in public schools and settlement music schools alike. Can they not join hands in giving the students the very best that is available? And then, perhaps, the time might come when together they could turn out a second Pergolesi — even though he be not clad in " a red cassock and a sky-blue cymar! "

CHAPTER XII

Schools of Leadership

"LEADERS are born, not made," it has been said, and surely birth has much to do with it. But that a great deal is being done about the making end of the business of musical leadership is plainly shown in the increasing length of courses in the teaching of music given in normal schools, colleges, universities and conservatories, and in the number of institutions giving them. (Teaching is itself, of course, a mode of leadership; and school music teaching usually involves some conducting.) Of the 594 colleges and universities represented in *A Survey of College Entrance Credits and College Courses in Music* referred to in the last chapter, 208 are providing such courses. It is a difficult and uncertain business, with outcomes varying from failure to great success, and there has been much criticism of how it is carried on. "Too much *method*," many a speaker and writer has said, " and not enough music." Others have pleaded for still more emphasis on the teaching of methods.

From our point of view, looking toward better and more amateurs, the love and understanding of music which comes of direct and full experience of the best of it, from the simplest to the greatest of each kind, is so important that we are with the first rather than the second group of critics. Professionalized leading, which goes assiduously through all the steps and motions of leadership but has lost or never possessed the true impulses for them — like empty courtesy — is as ruinous to the amateur spirit as any effort to gain wealth through singing or playing. And how can one know how far an individual can be taken in *methods* of leading without losing him in that kind of professionalism? In other words, the made part of his leadership may be disjoined from the born part of it, instead of being an outgrowth of it.

In most of the few (only eight) normal schools and colleges visited, where classes in teaching and conducting were observed, there seemed to be this disjunction. This is perhaps not strange, considering that both the number of teachers or leaders needed and the number of young people who desire to enter so attractive a field of work are apparently a good deal larger than can be provided for through the born end of the business. But whatever capacities for musical leadership are born in an individual are nourished mainly by the best music *as music;* and in most of the schools and courses observed, the work of the students and faculty as a whole showed symptoms of malnutrition in this regard. There would be little or no use in describing the courses or whole curricula that gave this impression, for it came mainly of actually being where they are carried on, in the classes and elsewhere, and of chatting before or afterwards with students and their teachers.

There is undoubtedly marked improvement, in general, over what is said to have been the prevailing sort of teacher-training of an earlier day, which often left nothing to the student's intelligence and musical nature. Students are now usually obliged to conceive and carry out some projects of their own, and in other ways to learn through experience and thinking, not merely memory; and in many a normal school and teachers' college there are a very proficient chorus and orchestra whose repertories include a large proportion of excellent music. But the purposes and spirit of the projects and even of the beautiful music seem rarely to escape the watchful eye of pedagogy. Somehow, the professional aspects of the work, combined with the effects on faculty and students of the whole business of examinations and credits, seem to shallow or dry up the springs of musical insight and beauty. We should not look for high enthusiasm or even the glow of simple pleasure in all the study and performance. Music has its necessary and rigorous disciplines and so has the art of teaching and conducting. The trouble is not too much discipline, but that it is not thorough-going enough and really educative. It lacks the depth and validity that enough real, unobstructed musical experience could have given it for at least some of the students and teachers. "You should start with their great-grandmothers," said one teacher of teachers to another who had complained of the difficulties of his job. That is to say, if the musical life in the homes, churches, and lower schools of the prospective teachers could have been what it would likely have been, say, in Germany, at least in the past or among the present-day Wandervögel, the present curricula of the normal schools could be carried on with fewer defeats. All power, then, to the school music supervisors responsible for the best work now being done in the public schools; and to the growing number of teachers whose efforts are admirably in keeping with the best music itself, though often handicapped by students who have never had the benefit of adequate musical experience in the public schools! The demands of some state boards of education for too great a preponderance of educational theory have also been a handicap in the normal schools and colleges governed by them.

A Unique School

A remarkable school for teachers that is entirely free from all external demands, even from the credits and degrees system, is the Concord (Massachusetts) Summer School of Music which has grown out of a

small group of teachers who gathered in the summer of
1915 for a series of conferences with Mr. Thomas
Whitney Surette on the teaching of music. A chief
cause of their coming to Concord was a series of articles in the " Atlantic Monthly " by Mr. Surette,
which were a kind of declaration of independence for
children and music from the mass of vacuous, made-
to-order songs and other pedagogical devices of the
time. So a chief purpose, even in that first year, was the
re-orientation of the teachers in *music* — through
singing and playing the best music not for some future
performance, or for the virtue of doing so, or for sight-
reading, or for any other purpose outside of the music itself.

The School consists each year of from 100 to 150
carefully chosen people who are teachers or prospective teachers, and a few others who come because they
have children of their own or simply because they value
the experience as a means of education and recreation
in the fullest sense. What goes on here in a short period
of four weeks seems vastly more valuable than all the
doings of a year in some other schools. But we are perhaps prejudiced, having taught there during several
summers. Let Mr. Edward Yeomans, a student of the
school, describe the best part of a day there.[1] He can do
so with authority because he is a very knowing musical
amateur and a cellist, a well known writer on, and
worker in, education and the head of a family whose
principal recreations are string quartet playing, various handcrafts and sailing.

Mr. Yeomans begins at the opening of a school day.

" The orchestra has tuned, Mr. Surette disentangles
himself from groups or individuals, suggesting, as he
walks to the desk, that we sing, first, the choral by
Bach, ' Deck Thyself, My Soul, with Gladness.'

" There is a slight pause — the baton comes down

---

[1] In an article in " The Survey Graphic " for September, 1926.

and the room floods with the tide from that mysterious ocean of which music is the most perfect expression — and in Bach the great majesty of that ocean is always evident.

" In the singing of this and similar chorals in the radiant mornings of these July days, and again in the afternoon, you see where transformations in tastes and standards begin. . . .

" We sing, for instance, part of the Brahms Requiem and the Song of Fate. Listen to the orchestra beginning this — the first bars are a challenge to everything in you that is aware of the tragic sense of life.

" Then there are things from the Russian Church — Rachmaninoff's Hymn to the Cherubim, for instance, or the English Holst's Psalm CXLVIII, and 'Turn Back O Man' or Parry's 'Jerusalem' and 'There Is an Old Belief,' the solo and chorus from the last act of 'Die Meistersinger' with the orchestra filled with contending voices until it suddenly takes the stride of that thrilling march to the rhythm of which your pulse leaps again, as it has always done. The Bach Mass in B minor, the St. Matthew Passion, with that most profoundly moving chorus 'Here Yet Awhile.'

" These things are sung and they are sung exceedingly well, because these are musical people. But never have they sung with such obeisance of the whole heart that is the influence of the music and the leader.

" After a half-hour's singing, involving repetitions to secure just the emphasis, enunciation, and quality desired, the discussion of some subject pertaining to the business of teaching music begins. Let us say that, this morning, it is the question of music in the primary grades.

" Nothing could prepare the atmosphere better than this sort of singing, and it is frequently the idiosyncrasy of Mr. Surette to pull this to a focus by reading a poem or part of one, or some piece of great prose, which also bears directly on the subject he proposes to talk about. On this day — this day of primary grades, it was this sonnet of Wordsworth he read:

It is a beauteous evening, calm and free,
The holy time is quiet as a nun
Breathless with adoration; the broad sun
Is sinking down in its tranquillity;
The gentleness of heaven is on the sea;
Listen! the mighty Being is awake,
And doth with his eternal motion make
A sound like thunder — everlastingly.
Dear child! dear girl! that walkest with me here,
If thou appear untouched by solemn thought,
Thy nature is not therefore less divine;
Thou liest in Abraham's bosom all the year;
And worship'st at the temple's inner shrine,
God being with thee when we know it not.

" And so the lecture begins, and after an hour of discussing method and content, the responsibilities and privileges, joys and sorrows of this very delicate art of starting little children toward the expression of their divinity we sing again — and one can see how values begin to take their proper and relative places under these influences.

" The business of teaching music begins to be involved with a great many things besides a ' system ' and a ' book ' and a necessity for satisfying a ' supervisor ' . . . it seems to require more than ' knowing ' and ' doing ' — it seems to involve ' being,' and how to ' become ' is the question — how to spin out of yourself the sort of web that will not entangle you and lots of other people with you — how to spin the filament upon which you climb out of yourself and out of all entanglements of your own or others' devising, to a higher place and a more intelligent and sympathetic point of view.

"Music, understood as this teacher of teachers understands it, keeps its relationship with the other arts intact, and especially its relationship with literature. So there is much talk of books.

"For a music teacher must be a reader and a discriminating one, not one of these newspaper and magazine receptacles — waste baskets — not while you can find something by Conrad, Tolstoy, Rolland, James Stephens, Knut Hamsun — and how many others — and then Blake, Poe, Thompson, Whitman, Keats! . . .

"We don't want people that are merely impressive anatomically, or vocally, or dextrously — the scheming, ' getting-on ' sort — we want real people.

"In order to illustrate anything he may be discussing, whether in music or literature, painting, sculpture, or architecture, this man can sit down at the piano and play from memory any musical composition he may require for his purpose, whether symphony, sonata, string quartet, opera or what not, talking and playing, talking and playing, until this fabric which all art makes together is woven there before you. And you may clothe yourself in it if you will."

The most remarkable thing about all this is the challenge it gives, the implicit demand of the music itself for excellence in all things, for which no pressure of credit-getting can ever be substituted. Mr. Yeomans is quoting Mr. Surette when he says, "Whatever you may mean by Education, by learning and the laws of learning, this is what I mean by it: to secure and establish a set of trustworthy emotions based on a clear perception of the difference between what is good and what is not so good, between what is great and what is less than great, and ' little,' in things and in conduct — between the best things men have done on the earth, and the second and third best. From that you can go on with the years to any kind of specializing and to any technique; without that, you go on to a mere series of illusions about yourself and this world and the next."

A complete account of this school would include the instruction in choral conducting given by Dr. Davison of the Harvard Glee Club; and other courses. It would also include the sense of intellectual and spiritual comradeship which is especially strong and delightful here because of the high adventurousness of exploring unhampered so much fine music, and because of weekly " revels " and such other extra-curricular experiences as the annual visit or pilgrimage, of which Mr. Yeoman tells, to " a beautiful Norman chapel built by Ralph Adams Cram on his own place near Concord. The students fill it full. It is evening — the little candles flicker above their heads, the strings are in a secluded balcony, the church is packed with one hundred and fifty singers. Nothing in America is quite equal to Palestrina's *Tenebrae factae sunt* and Parry's 'There is an old belief,' under the spell of this setting."

Why are there not more schools like this one? There are, of course, many things needed in the training of a music teacher that it does not provide — important but minor things that in a four weeks' course cannot be given. But why not spread the benefits of such a school over the year, two years, or four years, of the training given in so many normal schools and colleges? Or if the curriculum, because of traditions, of demands from higher up, or lack of adequate leadership, makes this impossible, why not have an extra four or six weeks' course of the Concord kind offered by persons — imported if necessary — who can direct it well for the students who have the good sense to respond to the offer even if it bring them no credits?

In all institutions for school music leaders there might very profitably be at least one course for the purpose of acquainting the students with the conditions and possibilities for musical activity in each of the channels of life outside of schools, and ways of making the most of them. In a few such institutions, notably the universities of Wisconsin and of Southern California, and Teachers' College of Columbia University, there already are valuable courses in community music.

* * * * * *

Other Schools

Mention has already been made, in Chapter XVI, of the course of training under the auspices of the Music Division of the National Federation of Settlements; our Chapter XV on music in religious institutions gives attention to schools for choir leaders; and in dealing with leadership in Chapter VII we had occasion to describe the main processes of institutes for the purpose. Institutes for rural leaders in musical as well as other kinds of recreational activity are held in every state. These are under the auspices of the state university or agricultural college or the National Recreation Association, often with the aid of the federal Department of Agriculture; or — as in Utah where unusually effective work is done through the Mormons — they are carried on by some church association. And they are frequently associated with the work of farm bureaus, farm and home conventions, or 4-H clubs.

Mr. John Bradford, of the National Recreation Association, whose ability in conducting such institutes has taken him to every state in the Union, distributed at each one during a few months in 1930 a questionnaire asking in which of 19 different recreational activities the members wished leadership training; 700

of a thousand persons, the largest proportion, named community singing.

Musical leadership is an important subject in the curriculum of the National Recreation School in New York, which is conducted by the National Recreation Association. This school is attended each year by about 40 carefully chosen college graduates from many parts of the country, who intend to be recreation leaders, usually in positions connected with municipal recreation departments. The music course includes as much singing, playing, and song-leading as the time and the students' abilities will permit — most of it carried on with the informality and the delight in the activity itself that are characteristic of recreation. But its emphasis, so far as leadership is concerned, is on the opportunities that recreation executives may have to initiate and support provision for music in the community.

Training in Orchestra Leadership

Orchestral conducting is taught in almost all schools and colleges in which there are courses in public school music, but we wish especially to describe the work of the National Orchestral Society of New York. This Society maintains a large symphony orchestra composed mainly of advanced students being trained as professional symphony players. Very importantly, for each kind of instrument in the orchestra there is an expert who acts as coach to all those playing his kind of instrument. Thus, there is a core of artistry in the orchestra which not only makes its several public performances remarkably excellent, but it also is the best possible tonic for the playing of the students. The latter take turns in sitting beside their respective coaches. The Society also maintains a course in conducting, and this is the orchestra that is used for practice in that art when the students in the course are ready for it.

It is the work of this organization and of the Civic Orchestra of Chicago that is probably mainly responsible for the growth in the proportion of native-born American players in our great orchestras. Of the 1140 players in the 13 major symphony orchestras in the United States in 1931, five hundred and thirteen were native born, undoubtedly a larger proportion than at any time in the past. And we may expect a similar growth among native-born orchestra conductors. But the most important expectation or hope suggested to us is the establishment in state universities of the plan of training adopted by the National Orchestral Society and the Chicago Civic Orchestra, where, given adequate leadership, it would be likely to be effective in ways impossible to those two organizations, and could be used in choral as well as in instrumental music.

A Tonic for School and Community Music

Applied, let us say, to the university of any of our middle western states, the plan would be as follows:

To Be Provided by the University

I An Expert Orchestral Player for Each Kind of Instrument of the Orchestra (namely, concert master, principal 2nd violin, viola, cello, bass, flute, oboe, clarinet, bassoon, horn, trumpet, trombone, tympani — 13 in all), Who Is Capable of the Following Duties:

A. To act as teacher of his kind of instrument at the university.

It has become a common requirement that students preparing to become public school music teachers shall learn to play at least two orchestral instruments. Furthermore, it is likely that more and more high school graduates who have played in school orchestras will wish to continue study of their respective instruments, even if only as an avocation, a means of playing more satisfyingly in the university orchestra and later in a civic orchestra or in chamber music groups. (The wind instrument teachers are likely to have fewer pupils than the string instrument teachers, but they will have the added duty of occasionally playing and coaching in the university band and in civic bands.)

B. To act as a player and coach for his kind of instrument or section in the university orchestra.

This orchestra to give concerts at the university and, during the spring vacation and other vacant intervals in the university year, to make a concert tour of cities and towns of the state which are not now provided with such concerts. The students in the orchestra will consist of three groups:

1. A small group who wish to become professional symphony orchestra players.
2. A larger group who wish to use music only as an avocation.
3. A still larger group who wish to become teachers of music in schools, colleges, or conservatories, or in their own studios.

In each of these groups there may be some who are well suited by nature to becoming leaders of adult orchestras.

C. To act, where asked for, as an additional player and coach in the final rehearsals and concerts of adult civic orchestras in the state, or to act so only in a rehearsal occurring at any other stage of preparation for a concert.

The concert dates of orchestras wishing him or one or more of his colleagues would be so arranged as to provide a convenient "circuit" for them. The university man might act as a first-chair man if it is desired that he do so, but that honored position would better be reserved for the local player. The usual prerogatives of a superior and professional guest player with an orchestra are not to be expected. The university man is, above all, an educator.

D. To take part in chamber music or chamber-symphony performances at the university and in public schools in the state, and in conjunction with concerts given by civic orchestras.

For example, the 13 expert players constituting, as they do, a little symphony orchestra, might twice a year make a brief tour of cities and towns of the state, giving morning or afternoon concerts for children in the schools, these tours being in addition to those made by the entire university orchestra. Having arrived in time for dinner in a city or town where there is a community orchestra, some or all of them will take part in the final rehearsal, stay in the city overnight, and on the following day, after giving one or more concerts for school children, will take part in the evening concert of the community orchestra. Besides playing in this orchestra, a small ensemble of them might present alone some chamber music on the program. A pianist or singers or both, also on the University staff, might also be members of the touring group and take part in both the children's concerts and the adult one. Other possible arrangements will occur to the reader.

E. To act as a coach to chamber music groups at the university and in cities and towns of the state.

Groups outside of the university could directly or through a local authority apply for such assistance to be given them if any when the teacher is conveniently in or near their town and has time to help them.

The expert players needed in this whole plan might be secured from one, two, or all of the following groups:

1. Professional orchestra musicians who are equipped to be permanent members of the university staff.

2. Professional orchestra musicians who wish to become teachers and leaders of public school and community orchestras and bands, but have not had the academic training required by school authorities. While giving the services suggested in this plan, they could be pursuing special university courses designed to give them that required training. They would agree to take full, faithful part in the plan here outlined for at least one or two years, according to circumstances, before accepting any positions outside of the university.

3. Graduates of the best music schools and of the National Orchestral Society, the Chicago Civic Orchestra, and similar institutions.

II An Expert Conductor Capable of the Following Duties:

   A. To act as teacher in courses in conducting at the university.

     Such courses to take into account the possibilities of adult amateur groups and of festivals as well as those of school, university, and professional groups. (If it is impossible to make an adequate salary possible for such work as we have assigned to the conductor, he might instruct in other courses also, or be dean of the music department or of the music bureau of the state extension division.)

   B. To act as conductor of the university orchestra and possibly of the university choruses also.

     His relation to the university band, with all its football observances, might be as supervisor, only occasionally as conductor, his influence being to help the official band conductor to make a fine " symphonic band " of the organization after the last goal has been kicked.

   C. To act as coach to conductors of orchestras, bands, and, possibly, choruses, in cities and towns of the state, holding institutes for groups of them, consultation with individuals of them, and demonstrations, if desired, at rehearsals of their choruses, orchestras, or bands.

   D. To act, in so far as his other duties will permit, as conductor of county, district, and state festivals in which his services are needed and desired.

     His chief interest, however, will be to help in finding and developing local leaders in the counties and other districts of the state.

*   *   *   *   *   *

Such a plan is applicable to choral music also. So we go on with the university's provision of leadership.

III An Expert Singer for Each Kind of Part in Choral Music (namely, soprano, mezzo soprano, contralto, tenor, baritone, bass, or only a quartet or quintet of these) who is capable of the same range of duties as have been prescribed for the orchestra musicians. The organizations in which he or she will coach or sing or do both could be the university chorus and, possibly, glee clubs;

the university *a cappella* choir; a vocal chamber music group, like the English Singers, made up of the expert singers; student vocal chamber music groups; and choruses, *a cappella* choirs, and vocal chamber music groups in the cities and towns of the State.

These expert singers and some of the choral groups mentioned could join with university or civic orchestras or smaller instrumental ensembles in great oratorios and other fine choral works. If anybody wanted it, they might produce opera also. The expert singers might well take part in some performances of Gilbert and Sullivan works and other good light operas to be given by civic groups in cities and towns of the state. A suitable grand opera might be undertaken with an advanced group now and then. But the singers' time and energies would have to be conserved for the best uses, which are likely to be in choral music.

If the university orchestra conductor is not entirely capable of directing choruses, one of the expert singers should have that power.

*   *   *   *   *   *

A list of benefits that are likely to result from fulfillment of such a plan would at the same time be a summary of the most important needs in American musical life. The persons who are going to teach music or direct choruses, orchestras or bands in schools and colleges would receive very good individual instruction in singing and playing; and, even more valuably, they would have the stimulating experience of performing the best music in the company of excellent musicians. The conditions of time and equipment for music instruction in the schools of many cities are right but there is danger of making the musical picture for which they are the frame only a mediocre one. We may, by a process of inbreeding, develop a mediocre quality of performance in the schools — a public school kind of playing that is different from the good musicians' kind of playing. But here in our plan there is a blending of the fresh blood and vigor of musical excellence with that of public school education.

The same tonic effects would be felt in the singing and playing of adult amateurs who would perform in the company of experts and receive desired coaching from them. The concerts of community choruses, orchestras and bands would achieve a new radiance that would increase the enjoyment of performers and audience. The rows of empty seats which have so often been a cause of failure would probably be amply filled. These happy changes would be due also to the influence on the conductors of the coaching or conferences or generally higher standards of leadership brought about by the university's conductor.

There could be excellent and inexpensive professional concerts of various kinds and, if desired, opera also, for cities and towns now lacking in this advantage. But the university is not to go into the entertainment or concert managing business. Its concerts are for education at its best.

There would be increased employment of excellent musicians, and a fortunate distribution of them throughout the country, instead of the present concentration of most of them in a few of our largest cities.

Of course, all these values are contingent on the qualities of the musicians engaged, and of those who direct the fulfillments of the plan. They are contingent also on the cooperation of those in charge of the public schools and of musical organizations in the state. In many instances, civic, religious, industrial or social organizations would play a supporting part, among these being municipal recreation departments, parent-teacher associations, music clubs, farm bureaus, 4-H clubs, federations of churches, industrial and commercial companies, service clubs, and chambers of commerce. The city, county, state or university extension libraries could together, in connection with such a plan, arrange economically for the lending of scores and parts for the various kinds of musical activity.

Costs of the Plan

The amount of money needed to put the plan into effect would depend on present musical resources and conditions in the state university and the communities of the state. It would also depend on distances, the mode of transportation, and the arrangement of tours to the cities and towns to be visited, and on the status of the musicians employed. These matters cannot be adequately dealt with in this book. It is encouraging to know that most of the many excellent concerts for children arranged by the National Music League have been self-supporting with respect to the traveling expenses as well as the remuneration of the artists. The examples given in Chapter VIII of various sources of financial aid may also be encouraging. The plan may, of course, be carried out only in part.

After one or two years' successful demonstration in a given state, it is probable that the costs of continuing the plan there and of establishing it in other states would be willingly and jointly borne by all concerned in it, including the state itself — through its university — the municipalities, and some or all of the organizations mentioned above. But it is also probable that a special donation from the state or from one or more foundations would be needed in the first year to make an adequate demonstration possible.

CHAPTER XIII

Music in Adult Education

IN a recent announcement of home study courses being offered by Columbia University it is stated that such courses, given by many colleges, universities and other institutions, were in 1930–31 being taken by about 1,500,000 people. From a report of the Federal Office of Education (Bulletin 1930, No. 10) we learn that in 1928–29 over 250,000 persons attended extension classes for adults offered by 291 colleges and universities. No one knows how many grown-ups are in public evening school classes in hundreds of cities and towns, or in institutes and other short courses, or how many are pursuing courses given by radio or recommended by public library officials. Almost every sort of club or society — even a rural one known to the writer, for the preservation of a cemetery — has annually a unified course or a miscellaneous series of lectures or speeches for the edification of its members. The hunger for education of one sort or another, always quite common and strong among adults as well as children, has evidently become more so in recent years. And much of it has been directed at cultural studies. For example, of 6,400 women from 20 to 60 years of age enrolled in the Hunter College (New York) summer evening session in 1930, the largest proportion took courses in literature, art, music and history, though by their vocations they were housewives, cashiers, factory hands, nurses, milliners and clerks or stenographers, and the studies offered included many vocational courses.

In the evening schools of Long Beach, California, it

has been a custom to ask the students at the close of the year to state their principal impressions of the work of the school, especially as to its value to them. Eight years ago when a Mr. Elmer C. Jones became superintendent of those schools, the responses of the students had almost invariably to do with the commercial value of their studies. While encouraging interest in subjects making for better workmanship, Mr. Jones has succeeded in bringing more and more people into avocational courses. This he has done mainly through two agencies: one, a small, well-printed periodical of the school containing interesting reviews of cultural books, concerts and lectures, as well as special articles on adult education and witty and other comments on the life of the school; and the other, a school council composed of about 60 students chosen by their classmates as representatives, who meet every Friday evening with the superintendent to discuss objectives and other matters affecting the work of the school. In 1929–30 there were 48 students in a mixed chorus and 36 in a well-balanced orchestra; 39 in beginners' classes in piano playing, 29 in a second year's class, and 10 in an advanced course in this subject; and 30 in violin classes; all these classes and other groups meeting twice a week. All music lessons are free (beyond the $1.00 entrance fee required of all students), except for the advanced lessons in pianoforte, for which a charge of $10 for 10 lessons is made. Needless to say, the chorus and orchestra and, sometimes, the best pianists and violinists are active in integrating music in school functions of various kinds, as well as in learning to sing or play better. In addition, the school sponsors an annual artist series of five concerts for which a season ticket costs only $1.50.

Choruses, orchestras, bands, and vocal and instrumental classes or individual lessons — that is, some or all of such musical activities — are to be found in the evening schools of some other cities also, notably in Los Angeles, St. Louis and Milwaukee; and many a conservatory and settlement music school has some adult students. In Boston the Massachusetts State Department of Education offers an elementary and an advanced course in piano playing for adults, one given in the lecture hall of the main public library, and the other in a room at Boston University. In Wisconsin the local Boards of Industrial Education, of which there is one in every community of 5,000 or more people, are empowered to establish any classes desired by 25 or more persons. It is said that " a prospective student can have whatever he wants, provided he can find a sufficient number of others who also want it." This has resulted in various kinds of avocational music classes and organizations in what are presumably vocational schools.

In Madison's Vocational School, for example, the classes include Piano I, II, and III, a male chorus, music appreciation, violin, harmony, a band, and fretted instruments, in addition to a chorus and a symphony orchestra which were started and are still partly supported by an independent Civic Music Association. The School contributes to the maintenance of the chorus and orchestra a good place to rehearse and a salary of $5,000 a year to the leader of both, who also gives a course in music appreciation. This orchestra is especially interesting in showing how valuable socially as well as personally and musically an evening school group can be. Its personnel, listed according to vocation, was in 1930 as follows: six music teachers, a bookbinder, nine clerks, two bond salesmen, a dentist, a housewife, seven high school students, five instrument makers, a housemaid, a laundress, three clothiers, a university professor, a watchmaker, two insurance agents, a station master, a drug store woman clerk, a reporter, a grocer, three

In a Delaware Adult Education Center Parents May Bring Their Children

machinists, a carpenter, three barbers, a realtor, three music merchants, a mail carrier, a manufacturer, a rug cleaner, an accountant, a printer, a laborer and a minister.

This list is sufficient proof of the present universality of evening school education. For immigrants, and for natives who have somehow missed the common schooling given to children, such a school has been an elementary school; to some people it has been a high school or college in which to continue the traditional studies of such institutions; to others it has been a vocational school. And now to an increasing number of people it is also a school for avocational practice of an art.

Another example of this development is the work of the Delaware State Bureau of Adult Education under Miss Marguerite H. Burnett, who in 1926 established six adult education centers in the State. The courses here, too, are arranged in response to the interests of adult residents of the community, the local Parent-Teacher Association usually taking the initiative in determining what these are. By January 1931, there were 65 such centers, and the largest number of requests were for music, handcrafts and home decoration. Six hundred of the 1,600 white students were in choruses. Seventy-one per cent of all the persons enrolled in the centers were parents, a fact which points to an especially valuable possibility with regard to adult education in music.

To the fortunate parent who knows the satisfaction of family singing or playing at home, and to the multitude of unfortunate ones whose families, despite their desire, rarely join in any undertaking — even in breakfast — the richest results of the musical training given in schools and elsewhere must be those obtainable in homes. But family music is not likely to commence or flourish without leadership and example from parents.

Evening schools and other suitable adult education agencies should therefore offer to parents instruction in singing and in playing, with the express purpose of making it possible for them to do these things with their children at home. Expense is no longer an obstacle, nor is age or the self-consciousness that may arise in individual lessons; for class-teaching of singing or playing has become common and effective and is inexpensive to each student, and we have Professor Thorndike's often-quoted word of encouragement to oldsters.[1]

*   *   *   *   *   *

Outside Agencies of Adult Education in Music

Schools for adults could have a much larger part than most of them have thus far taken in the musical life of their respective communities; but every sort of adult musical endeavor, outside of schools, referred to in this book is also a field of adult education in music. How to fill it with greater delight and understanding is a question having as much to do with adult education as any consideration of evening school music may have. So we commend this whole book to the adult educationists who are interested in music; especially the last section of the preceding chapter, because the plan therein proposed has directly to do with university extension service.

*   *   *   *   *   *

Appreciation through Participation

What can be done through the agencies of adult education to help make the most of the many opportunities, open to all, to listen to excellent music? Obviously, there should be courses in music apprecia-

[1] A book on "Adult Learning" by Edward L. Thorndike, Elsie O. Bregman, J. Warren Tilton and Ella Woodyard, Macmillan, New York, 1928.

tion. There already are many such courses, and there is no end of books, articles and lectures on the same subject, the large number of which is indicative of how general is the interest in gaining greater insight into music. Our question would better be, how can the most be made of that interest? In answering, we shall be wise if we seek ways in which even the novice or the person apparently incapable of singing or playing well may actually participate in some measure in the music to be studied. Not mere story-telling about the music or setting little jingles to its themes; these, for good or ill, are already being supplied through the radio. Not a series of lectures on the forms of music or its history, with music used merely to illustrate the theories of the lecturer or of his masters; these are likely to be to would-be listeners of little more use than stories of the sea and lectures and observations regarding its density and motions could be to would-be swimmers.

It is necessary to get into the music and there feel its motions of rhythm and harmony, its significant rises and falls of melody, its correspondences and balances, and apprehend its inner meaning deeply personal and unique to each listener. Swimming is a far-fetched analogy to listening, but it points to the dynamic factor in esthetic experience of any kind — the response of the whole organism — which is exceptionally vital to music appreciation and yet in that art is more remote from ordinary experiences than it is in any other art.

Sing the themes and other significant portions of suitable instrumental compositions that are being studied, and also sing some of the best folk songs and chorales, and composed songs and choruses. The best music to start with in a course in appreciation is that which you can perform, however simple it be and however elementary your performance of it. The singing of folk songs is especially valuable, for not only are all the secrets of musical form and development to be found in such songs, but many of them or parts of them or tunes like them have been used as themes in magnificent music wherein, like acorns, they grow into expansive trees. And nothing could be more revealing of the magical inner harmonic and melodic stuff of music than the singing in chorus, with all four parts, of simple Bach chorales. Even the singing in unison of one inner part while the other parts are being played on a piano may be revealing.

Whether or not the student can sing, let him beat time to the music now and then with the large free motions used by Dalcroze, so that he can feel more deeply not only the beats but also the deep, forward, changing motion of the music toward and away from climactic points; or let him walk to it freely, changing his direction at the end of each phrase (if the music is suitable for this). This method is especially useful in connection with unusually slow music and other music in which the pulsating flow of the rhythm is not obvious and is likely to be missed. Let him tap or step its most significant rhythms, or dance to it. The best music for this dancing, at least in the beginning — for self-conscious and sedentary or jazz-strutting adults — is folk-dance music, especially the music of the English country dances and some of the old American country dances. These dances are comparatively easy and he-mannish and she-womanish to do, and much of the music and the delightful musical designs made visual in the dancing of it are worth some study in no matter how serious an elementary course in appreciation. Such dancing is very likely to make the individual more responsive in listening to any other kind of music. Could he later engage in a gavotte, a minuet, and a saraband, or the like, one of the richest fields of beautiful music by great masters would thereby be much more fully revealed to him than it could be through lectures and listening to music alone. All the dancing could be carried on in a supplementary period. Of course, if for any reason dancing is very difficult or distasteful to an individual, it would become an impediment for him instead of an aid to music appreciation.

Eyes can help ears. It is not hard to learn to follow a printed score of music while listening to a performance of it, and for most people the doing of this provides a rare grasp of the music itself. Starting with piano music, followed by string quartets or duos (e.g., the slow movement of the well-known Bach Concerto for Two Violins), and going then to a symphony by Haydn or Mozart and to the fifth symphony of Beethoven (because it is the most familiar), the student is soon competent enough to adventure score-guided, with much firmer step than he could otherwise have, into any symphony. (Inexpensive miniature scores are used for chamber and orchestra music.) There are measures that the teacher and students will wish to hear again or to talk about. The pianist or phonograph readily provides repetition or silence. There are red-letter passages here and there for horns or violins or some other instrument, which the student will find and perhaps mark in his score, and other great moments to be equally well observed, such as when, in the Prelude to "Die Meistersinger," three magnificent tunes march along together amidst a radiance of all the voices of the orchestra that is quite blinding to the uninitiated, unguided listener. The teacher will, of course, clarify such "scenes" by revealing parts of them through the piano and by having the students sing the tunes as far as they can.

The cost of the scores may be an obstacle. This is being overcome in at least one class by the payment of fifty cents by each student for the use of scores throughout the course. In the beginning only a large enough number of scores was purchased to provide one score of each of a few compositions for every three persons. But the library is growing, and before long will be entirely adequate and entirely in possession of the school.

Some or all the above activities carried on in conjunction with quiet listening to music (without scores), and in addition to brief explanatory talks, demonstrations of orchestral instruments and an excursion now and then to a fine chamber music or orchestra rehearsal or concert which has been prepared for in the class, would leave little time for the instructor to unload books of history and of other information *about* music. But who cares? The music itself can be so chosen as to present as fully as the time will permit, though not necessarily in chronological order, not only a history of the art but also a history of the human spirit from medieval times to the present.

The more and better the music instruction in schools for youth, the more important and worth while does it become to provide corresponding opportunities for adults. This is true not only because the musical gains of youth should not be lost in adult life, but also because the minds and emotions and life experiences of adults call for expansion of those gains. They call for a music of their own and new insights into it. A whole world of such music, either closed or only dimly perceivable to youth, invites adults to a lifetime of happy exploration in it. Guides are wanted.

CHAPTER XIV

Home Music

We are looking for a few serious minded amateur musicians living in the vicinity of Rye, New York, who would be interested in forming a small informal music club.

The purpose is to get together socially and make music. We are not music teachers or professional musicians.

THUS appeared a notice posted on a public library bulletin board in New York City. There are many flourishing music clubs whose meetings usually give opportunity for performance by small groups, if there are any; but the writer of this notice wanted a small, informal music club whose meetings would always take place at home and consist only of *haus-musik,* good talk, and perhaps simple refreshments — no chairman, audience, "club business," or any other appendages. "Serious minded amateurs" were wanted, which is to say eager lovers of the art and of the happiness of taking a good part in it — no mere pleasure seekers or stage minded professionals. That the writer and his wife are not music teachers (he is an architect) was stated perhaps to avoid the impression that they might wish, as one of those who answered the appeal wished to do, to add to a pupils' orchestra or to make the playing or singing mainly a means of adding to their own stock of knowledge and skill as pedagogs.

This search for fellow-adventurers in music has not been successful. One probable reason is the distance of about 20 miles from New York City to Rye. But though such a search might well bring a few like-spirited singers or players together, a more promising means of doing so is through the usual processes of neighborliness. Among one's neighbors and the other persons one comes to know through the day's work or the evening's sociability there may be only one person who is suited to your sort of home music and personality, but he may know other persons who with himself and yourself might make a good team. So you start with him and let sociability and watchful waiting find the others.

A Kammersymphonie

It was in this way that a home company of amateurs came into being in Spokane, and in the home of a music teacher — contrary to the fear of the architect from Rye. One evening when the writer visited the home of this violin teacher and ardent chamber music "fan," he and ten other musical explorers were well started among the romantic hills and dales of a Wolf-Ferrari Kammersymphonie for solo strings, wood winds, horn and piano. Earlier in the evening the Beethoven Septet had been played. These eleven, or a smaller group of them, meet regularly to play just for the love and joy of it. The string bass player, seventy-five years old, is a janitor in a dance hall. "It's all that I live for," he said, holding out his instrument as we conversed after the "rehearsal." The oboe player is a letter-carrier, the flutist a waitress in a restaurant, and the others, with the exception of the violin teacher, are similarly innocent of any professional intentions. The reader can readily imagine the keen delight of this company even when somebody lost the place or some other mishap sent them back to a safe valley whence to start a climb all over again. An especially memorable moment on that evening was after such a climb to a fine climax, when a beautiful, expansive flute melody soared out of all reach of circumstance and the mundane needs of a restaurant. No boy who has just knocked out a homer on the baseball lot ever looked freer and more radiant than did that otherwise frail-looking waitress behind the flute.

All Outsiders inside a Home

Many a beautiful room in a home now musically mute except for a radio or the like could be blessed with *haus-musik* could it be used now and then by an invited group of musical amateurs, boys and girls or men and women, even if no member of the home is able to take part in the singing or playing. One is especially impressed by this possibility when observing beautiful private residences in our large apartment-housed cities. Made for chamber music they seem to be. Visions of Charleston, South Carolina, of Coral Gables, Florida, and of Santa Barbara also come to mind, with their exquisite, romantic-looking houses. In the eighteenth century no home of a European family of the nobility was regarded as complete without its small orchestra, and in an earlier time the singing of madrigals was as common a home activity as the playing of cards has become in our own day. Why should not more of the many otherwise beautiful homes conceived by our excellent architects be designed, in another sense, by their owners for living music as they are designed for hearth-fires, books, conversation and reproduced music? The effect of such music on the children of the home would be more than reason enough for such designing to say nothing of the delight and inspiration to all the adults concerned in it. Of course, the room should be simple in spirit and decoration, as the host and guests should be. Simple refreshments at some of the " rehearsals," though not necessary, would add still further to the camaraderie and delight, and doubtless to the quality of the singing or playing also.

It is in the best sort of fine American home that by invitation the Billings, Montana, Ladies' Ensemble of 20 players rehearses twice a week. Children in the Brookline (Mass.) Music School, a kind of settlement school, have likewise been invited to play together in the drawing room of a lovely home; and similar kindnesses have been extended to pupils in other music school settlements and the like. Of course, the best place for anyone to sing or play, other things being equal or nearly so, is in his own home.

Itinerant Home Groups

For a number of years a group of about twenty congenial men and women of Concord, Massachusetts, have, every fortnight through the winter, met for singing and sociability at the home of one of their number, but never the same one twice in succession. They are all amateurs and they sing folk songs, some in unison and some in choral arrangement, simple madrigals, and other good choral music. Sometimes one of them or a duo will play two or three piano compositions, or a violinist will provide the diversion from singing.

The very name Concord takes one to colonial times when in Philadelphia our first American composer, Francis Hopkinson, was the center of a similar group of itinerant home music-makers. Hopkinson was one of the signers of the Declaration of Independence, an intimate friend of George Washington, and the first Secretary of the Navy. He was also a poet, painter, and inventor, and the very best sort of musical amateur. Mr. John Tasker Howard's account of the home group of which Hopkinson was a member should place home music among the traditions upheld by the D.A.R., and by many others of us.

From his own correspondence we may guess that Hopkinson was the center of the musical life in Philadelphia. A talented harpsichordist, he was a member of a group of amateurs and professionals who met at each other's houses, and also gave subscription concerts in public. Hopkinson conducted at the harpsichord; James Bremner, Stephen Forrage and John Schneider would play the strings in company with Governor John Penn; and wind instruments were furnished by Schneider, Ernst Barnard, George D'Eissenberg (French horn) and John Stadler (German flute). From Hopkinson's library, which is still in the possession of his descendants in Philadelphia, we learn something of the music played at these concerts. The works of Handel were well represented. The Italians: Pergolesi, Giardini, Scarlatti, Corelli, Vivaldi, and the English Arne and Purcell were favorites. The group was familiar with the best music of its day.

Philadelphia enjoyed a musical life that extended to the home; households that wished to enjoy music could do so undisturbed by Quaker influences. In this respect the Pennsylvania capital was distinctive. Soirées of chamber music were frequent occurrences, and music for its own sake was not disturbed by the *virtuoso* influence that was later to dominate America's musical life.[1]

A Philadelphia Tradition Maintained

Mr. Hopkinson would be a delighted guest in the home of a prominent attorney of his native city, especially on one of the four or five winter evenings each year when an informal musicale brings a score of congenial people to that home. He would probably arrive promptly at five on a Sunday afternoon and after greeting the members of the family, all of whom, including the three children, sing or play, and meeting the other guests, he would join with them in singing folk songs and other very enjoyable music such as we found being sung by the Concord group. Mere listening to the songs is permitted — this is a courteous household — but regretfully, and only because wives are allowed to come with their singing husbands, and vice versa. Supper at 7:30, and then some special fea-

[1] From "Our American Music," by John Tasker Howard, Thomas Y. Crowell Co., New York.

ture is given by one or more of the family or guests.
On the evening we have in mind, Mr. Hopkinson
would have heard the two songs for alto and viola by
Brahms and would probably have played a short piano
duet with the host, or a trio with two of the latter's
children, they providing the violin and cello parts. He
would have taken a happy part in the good talk between musical expressions and in the two or three
choice songs that closed the evening's pleasure at about
10 o'clock. An important thing about the musical
evenings in this home is that the music to be sung or
played is all chosen and gathered beforehand. Of
course, changes in choice may be made during the
evening, but the possibilities for delight that there are
in a few hours and a group of people gathered for
music are so rich that it would be a pity to spend even
ten minutes on a song or other composition that does
not give nearly so much pleasure as some other would
give. The pleasure given often depends largely on the
relation to one another of the selections sung or played.
Full, wise preparation for such a " red letter " time —
with allowance for mood and immediate desire of
the guests — is certainly worth while.

From Bridge to Madrigals

A recent national conference of public school music
supervisors meeting in Chicago gave the writer occasion to seek assistance from his friend the choirmaster of the University of Chicago. There was special
interest in small groups such as meet in homes and
neighborhood centers. So a month or more in advance we asked the choirmaster whether he could
provide a small group of young men and women who
would sing some madrigals or the like in the spirit and
style of Elizabethan times. " This is a coincidence," he
replied. " Only a few days ago a group of students
came to me saying that they wished to gather on Sun-

day evenings for coffee and — instead of bridge — madrigals. 'What shall we sing?' they asked. . . ."

They sang at the conference some madrigals and a specially arranged folk song; all without accompaniment, of course, and without a leader. They sat, the twelve of them, in a semi-circle as though grouped about a dinner table at home, with appropriate ease and geniality, and their singing was said to be the most lovely and delightful of any heard during the musically full week of the conference.

It is amazing, how widely popular the game of bridge has become. Could home singing and playing ever gain such popularity and devotion? If half or even one hundredth of the 400,000 members of the Federation of Music Clubs were themselves in their own homes to cultivate home music to the extent that bridge has been cultivated in thousands of homes, they would probably accomplish more than is possible in any other way. One thing about bridge that accounts largely for its spread, and which can be applied to music, is that it is played in "teams." If you happen to drop into a home when a bridge game is going on, you are likely to be invited to "take a hand." You and the other players will have an engrossing and therefore a pleasant evening full of activity (mental activity). When your turn comes to have a social gathering — or before your turn comes — you, knowing of the success of the bridge evening, will likewise have cards and table ready for a game. And so the thing spreads, by example, from home to home. No federation or association or national bureau is needed. The radio model bridge games and the newspaper articles have undoubtedly added to the interest, but the newspapers can have as much influence in music. Of course, bridge has competition in it. Almost everyone likes the challenge of a contest, and growth in skill is a happy result of it. But it is the opportunity to take a hand in a small group that if applied happily to suitable music in your home is likely to cause a spread of home music in the way that bridge has spread. The schools are giving some musical skill to almost every child, which is more than can be said about bridge.

Music Clubs and Chamber Music Societies

The home meetings of the Junior Music Club referred to near the close of Chapter VIII are exemplary of what the best of all the music clubs are doing. Another type of association for *haus-musik* is the society of chamber music players who, having no national or state outlook and little or no interest in who's who among the members, have more time than do the music clubs for actual playing — it might be singing. They are usually in small enough groups to meet in a home, and generous enough to admit a few persons who only listen. Where there are dues to defray expenses for music, the value of having listeners does not consist alone in the stimulus that a small, sympathetic audience can give and the increased range of sociability that they may bring.

Family Instrumental Groups

As was shown in Chapter VIII, an average of about 20% of the members of school orchestras and bands play in family groups. That is, of the 3,200 boys and girls in such organizations who were questioned, 640 sometimes make music at home with one or more members of their families. Eighty out of every hundred, according to the reports, do not. It was further shown in that chapter that many of the combinations of instruments in family groups show a lack of planning for home music. Let us repeat that " a family of three that is at all musical is by right and privilege a trio, the family of four is a quartet, and so on." It

would be very unwise to force any individual to learn
to play an instrument unsuited to him simply because that instrument is well suited to those played
by the other members of his family. But the field of
choice is wide. Personal liberty need not result in the
coupling of a mandolin with a tuba as it did in one
family. Indeed, it is probable that not personal liberty
but the needs of a school band produced that tuba
player. Now bands must have tubas and other instruments that may not find suitable company in a home;
and orchestras are in the same fix. When for the sake
of the school orchestra or band as well as for the individual's own sake as a possible member of one or
the other organization, the playing of such an instrument falls to the lot of your son or daughter, must his
or her possibilities as a member of a family musical
group be sacrificed to the school?

Evidently, in many instances there is no sacrifice
because nothing has been done about the home possibilities anyway. Drums, a horn, a string bass, any
instrument needed in the school orchestra or band
may be the single effective opportunity of a lifetime
for the boy or girl to enter the rich field of instrumental music. But surely there should be as much
care and planning for the music of a home as there is
for the music of a school. Adjustments can be made.
(1) Our bass horn player may learn to play an additional instrument. Many boys and girls have done this.
(2) The horn may be an additional instrument, his
first love being the piano. (3) The horn can fit beautifully in a family brass ensemble. There is a suitable
small ensemble also for every other not outlandish
but often outhomish instrument. (4) Almost any
combination of instruments is musically possible if
one of them is a piano or an organ. (5) There is always the possibility of singing, everyone singing or
some singing while others are playing.

The happy balance of instruments in some family ensembles makes one suppose that on the birth of a child in one of those families, only the question as to whether it is a boy or a girl is more eager than the question as to what instrument it will play. Indeed, judging from the talk of some parents, one might suspect that many a child has been brought into this world simply because another player was needed in the family. But interest in the musical possibilities of a home is all too rare.

The family "orchestra" may start as a so-called toy symphony, a rhythm band, even when the children are still very young. The drum, triangle, tambourine, and cymbals — all in miniature — are the polite society of such a band and their company should be cultivated. But cereal boxes, a small dinner gong without definite pitch, any other musically friendly object already available, even pat-a-caking hands, may serve with well-played simple music on the piano, violin, flute, or phonograph, or with singing, for the first steps of family instrumental music-making. Water tumblers, the xylophone, the psaltery, and the flageolet — all of them of simple sort but true — may one by one or in rotation be added to the band or substituted for one or more of the purely percussive instruments. Such lovely folk music and guidance as are given in the "Rhythmic Ensemble Band-books for Children" by Diller and Page [2] and the many suggestions in Mrs. Satis Coleman's book, "Creative Music in the Home," [3] are especially helpful. No home where there are children resident or invited, and a piano or phonograph, is completely equipped without a set of rhythm band and other simple instruments, enough for guests big and little as well as for the family.

[2] G. Schirmer, Inc., New York City.
[3] Lewis S. Myers and Co., Valparaiso, Indiana.

The interest in having a family ensemble may arise when the children are older. In the family of the superintendent of schools in Cedar Rapids there were a boy of 10, another boy of 12, a girl of 13, and another girl of 15. Shortly after the teaching of instrumental music had been introduced in his schools, the superintendent one breakfast time proposed that every member of the family learn to play an instrument. The proposal was at first received as a joke. But he was serious. He himself would learn to play, and his wife would refurbish her piano playing. The school director of instrumental music was invited to a family conference on the subject and he helped to determine the kind of instrument that each would learn to play — violin and cello respectively for the girls, clarinet and cornet for the boys and flute for the father. The fun and the deeper values of this project in the life of the family can readily be imagined. They grew up musically together, stimulated and nourished by group playing to which they came much sooner in the process than used to be thought possible or desirable, and, thanks to the mother's piano playing, with considerable musical satisfaction even in the beginning.

How Do You Get Him to Practice?

Family music is the best incentive for practicing. It leads the parent to say to the child, " Let *us* play (or study) this," instead of having to say, " *You* play or study this." The social interest and sense of responsibility, of team-work, that has been so influential in the development of school orchestras and bands may be made operative — and still more favorably so — in the home. Perhaps there will be guests for a social evening before long, or the family are looking forward to visiting the home of friends or relatives, and they wish to be ready to contribute some lovely music, however simple, to the pleasures of the occasion. Or the motive for practicing may be the playing by the family without guests on a certain evening soon to come, or whenever the opportunity arises. The interest in taking good part in the group performance is likely to carry over into the necessary practice of solo music and studies. But what a lonesome, detached sort of activity practice must be for a girl or boy in a home where no one else plays with the devotion and delight that are expected of him or her! It is no wonder that some parents themselves take lessons and practice an instrument in order to be more helpful to their children.

Another thing to be remembered about children's practicing is that while regular periods of practice are very desirable, to force them on the child or nag him into them may utterly defeat the whole purpose. He ought to have frequent lessons in the beginning that nourish his interest and start him well into good habits of attitude as well as procedure. If expense is an obstacle to this, the parent might act as friend and assistant teacher. Attaining strong enough and rightly directed interest, though it be slow in growing, to practice regularly without compulsion is worth more than the skill that might be gained through any amount of uninterested practice. Through encouragement and social interest, as has been suggested, and through the skill and good graces of his teacher, he should be brought to as high a level of achievement as is commensurate with a well-rounded life. But if with such treatment he does no more than maintain a happy connection with real music, along with baseball and all the other interests of a healthy boy, the gain is still worth the price and effort. He is likely then in his early adolescent years to develop a passion for playing or singing that will relieve you of all your concern about his part in a musical education.

A good instrument and a quiet, cheerful, and otherwise suitable environment for practice are also, of course, important factors. But nothing in this regard is so effective as the tendency of the child to emulate the persons he loves. A playing mother, other things being equal, is much more influential than one who can only talk about it. Next to her in power comes the mother who loves to sing and does so to simple accompaniments that the child can easily learn to play; and then, not far behind, comes the mother who is a good listener even to a child's music. The influence of a family's listening to good music together is shown later in this chapter.

Family Vocal Groups

In the Third Annual Tompkins County (N. Y.) Rural Musical Festival in 1930 there were eight family groups, five of whom were in the vocal contest and two in both the vocal and instrumental contests. In the Munson family there were the grandmother, mother and father, and five children plus a baby, the oldest of the children being thirteen. From thirteen to two or three, the youngsters all sang the soprano of two hymns, the mother alto, the grandmother tenor, and the father bass. The Dorn family consisted of the mother, four sons, and two daughters, all of them grown up, and all of them singing while the mother played the accompaniments of two other hymns. Two high school girls accompanied by their mother at the piano made up the Dawson family. The Steenberg family was represented by the mother and a son singing an alto and tenor duet with another son at the piano. A duet by mother and father while their son played the piano represented the Daughintai family; and the four daughters of the Westlake family sang a four-part secular song.

There, in a single county gathering you had almost every sort of family singing group imaginable;

and common sense as well as sentiment will tell you that in-so-far as everyday living is concerned, those groups were of more importance than your largest city festival. There were village and rural choirs and school choruses also at that county festival, and they might have been joined in impressive and exemplary singing under a fine leader; or some other means of providing stimulating but not too remote models of admirable music and musical performance might have been found. That, perhaps, would justify having a contest of families, though it would be better if a non-competitive festival could attract the people. But the start that those families have made, perhaps away back in a forgotten generation, is the most important thing of all.

The best time to start is when the children are still small. Time was when children were rocked to sleep with lullabies, but the doctors and psychologists have stopped that, and economy and other factors in a more and more urbanized world have in many a home stopped the custom of having children. There may be other difficulties. The members of some families are rarely together, even at breakfast time; and when they are, the children may each be separately engaged in what is miscalled "home work" (it has nothing to do with the home), the mother in washing the dishes or sewing or perhaps attending a meeting of a music club or the like, and the father in reading the newspaper or in doing *his* home work. Or the radio has been turned on, let come what may, and no one has sufficient initiative toward any sort of constructive family activity to turn the thing off.

Evidently, homes need leaders as much as clubs and communities need them, a person who sees to it that there are times for group play by the family and that nothing interferes with full, happy participation by children and their parents. Some congenial neighbors or friends may be invited also. Some families have such a time on a certain evening each week, some daily or whenever opportunity and mood arise. A good time for singing is next in importance to the will to sing, which is usually caught from someone, often the mother or father, who sings or plays spontaneously for the love of it. The beginning of the day, grace before meals, and fireside time are common occasions. Almost all homes have carols, at least by radio, at Christmas time. Why not have appropriate songs for Columbus Day, Thanksgiving, the birthdays that the nation celebrates, as well as birthdays of members of the family and of well-known authors and composers in whom the family are interested, for St. Valentine's day, a lovely autumn day, the first snow of winter, and surely for May Day? Related pictures or other simple and appropriate decorations or table tokens may also be provided for each occasion.

"Where can such songs be secured, and how are they learned?" is asked. Thousands of public school music teachers are giving their lives to teaching such songs in the schools; and millions of dollars are spent in support of the process. If the children do not sing school-learned songs at home, why do they not? The parent-teacher association or even the individual parent might help through friendly conference with the school music teachers, and in other ways,[4] to answer that question or, better still, to make it unnecessary. No matter how good the school music teaching is, it needs the quickening association with real life that singing in the home can give it. And if the children do not wish to make that association, some change in conditions at the school, in the home, or in the music or methods of its performance may change their attitude very gratifyingly.

It is said that the school singing is carried into the

[4] See page 302.

homes when the children are in the kindergarten and the primary grades, but as they grow older they seem to lose interest in making this carry-over. Is this because the music used and the methods of teaching it are less vital in the upper grades? Is it because parents' interest in the school life of their children, made strong by the novelty of it in the beginning, dwindles through the years? Many new interests are acquired and new needs felt by older children. Do these make the need or desire for musical expression less strong? Whatever the reasons for a decline in musical interest in the upper grades, it must be admitted that the possibilities in home music increase as the children grow older, because part singing is possible then, one of the best of all sports as well as means of beauty.

And it is during those years, when children may easily drift away in interest from their parents, that any such unifying influence as family singing is most valuable. Differences in age, sex, interests, and attitudes toward one another are likely all to be dissolved in the flow of the song. At the same time each individual is made more wholly himself or herself. For the ordinary experiences of life and the stresses of adolescence tend not only to divide the interests of the family, but also the interests of the individual, to disintegrate him. But in singing or playing he is made whole again, good to live with. For older boys and girls the larger home group that includes guests as well as the family in the singing is likely to be attractive even when the family singing alone is not.

How Is Singing Improved?

If the family singing is poor, the children, at least, are likely to shun it when their standards of judgment are raised by school and radio. The parents would do well to have some lessons in singing from a good, sensible teacher. There never was a better purpose for doing so. But much can be done, even without lessons, by listening to good singing, by striving to make one's own sounds blend with those of the other singers, and by cultivating in simple ways the natural expressiveness of the voice. Even in ordinary speech, how faithfully and naturally the voice can express what we feel as well as what we think. Only compare your " Good Morning " to a neighbor's little child with the one you give to the bank president. It is this natural power of the voice that should be found and cultivated in singing, and that may be beautiful even in a voice that is lacking in sensuous beauty.

The first essential for this is a good song, a real song, excellent and convincing, that must itself have arisen out of a warm desire for expression. Songs of this kind are to be found among the hundreds of folk songs and the songs of Schubert, Schumann and Brahms and the like; that is, among the songs that have been beloved and sung again and again by generations of people. The rich experience that such a song can give becomes a standard by which, consciously or unconsciously, we determine the worth of other songs, including new, modern ones. And so, instead of giving ourselves and our time to any song that is attractively published and advertised and thus accustoming ourselves to a low degree of enjoyment, we turn naturally to the best songs and make of them and ourselves sources of enjoyment hardly dreamed of until our first rich experience of a fine song.

The second essential is the endeavor of the singer to get into the song, as we say, to come as nearly as possible to the thought and feeling of the composer or the folk; that is, in a way, becoming the fervent home-loving old Negro in " The Old Folks at Home," or the loving mother in the Brahms " Lullaby," the strong, toiling Russian boatman in " The Volga Boatmen's Song," or the radiantly merry lass or lad danc-

ing on the green in the old English " Maypole Song."
This needs only desire and imagination and the ability
to carry a tune. It is helpful to speak the words of the
song in the rhythm of the music as easily, clearly, and
interestingly as intelligence can make them, and then
to sing them just as easily and clearly and interestingly, but with tones smoothly sustained or light and
dance-like, or in whatever other quality the character
of the song suggests. To try to sing simple, slow songs
with steady but easily sustained tones — with smooth
lines of tone — is very good practice.

There is much else to be said about singing, but this
much may help a good deal. The possible value of
good song records for a good phonograph should not
be forgotten, both for learning songs and acquiring
models of good singing. A list of such records suitable
for homes as well as community centers is given on
page 467.

Home Dancing and Acting

The home is an ideal place for the kind of dancing described on pages 94–98. The children can be
barefooted and clothed in simplest garments allowing a maximum of freedom. It is impossible to speak
too enthusiastically about this full, happiest sort of
play. Nothing pretty or spectacular is wanted, no
exhibitions. It is as though the dancing were a part
of the music itself, the individual entirely forgetful
of himself. Becoming butterflies, horses, giants, or
fairies in the music is of the same free, wholesome
character. As to this and the acting out of songs
and ballads, the reader is urged to review the brief
section on Acting on pages 98–100. Every home should
have a costume closet, even if it be filled only with old,
discarded clothes that may be suitable for such acting.
What can be done in this regard with curtains or
draperies, tablecloths, scarfs, colored cheesecloth and

other common properties of a household, it is not for this book to say.

Listening in the Home

The rocking cradle and the rocking arms are now out of fashion, but there is still the rocking music to carry the child off to sleep. How many adults have awaited the radio's " Slumber Music " for themselves at bed-time each evening? And is there not music for every mood, for curing the bad ones, and summoning the good ones?

Much has been said and written about the therapeutic values of music, and Dr. Willem van de Wall and others have turned these good words into admirable deeds, and vice versa.[5] But the most common and effective cures are made in those diseases or " ill-at-eases " of daily life in the home. " The Musical Pharmacy," Mr. Robert Haven Schauffler entitled his delightful chapter of remedies and tonics for the spirit.[6] And later, in "The Poetry Cure," he gave a whole book of literary specifics:

Mental Cocktails and Spiritual Pick-me-ups
(Poems of Laughter)

Sedatives for Impatience
(Poems of Reassurance)

For Hardening of the Heart
(Poems of Sympathy)

Hasheesh for a Torpid Imagination
(Magic Carpet Poems)

Stimulants for a Faint Heart
(Poems of Courage)

[5] " The Utilization of Music in Prisons and Mental Hospitals — Its Application in the Treatment and Care of the Morally and Mentally Afflicted " by Willem van de Wall, National Bureau for the Advancement of Music, New York City.

[6] In " The Musical Amateur," by Robert Haven Schauffler, Houghton Mifflin Company, Boston, Mass.

Poppy Juice for Insomnia
(Soothers and Soporifics)

Accelerators for Sluggish Blood
(Poems of High Voltage)

There you have a new classification for your music
shelves and phonograph record albums, in place of the
meaningless alphabet. Where will you put the third
movement of the Beethoven Seventh or the Schubert
Waltzes, the Bach so-called "Air for the G String,"
the Schumann, "Du bist wie eine Blume" or the
Dance of the Happy Spirits from Gluck's "Orpheus,"
the "Midsummer Night's Dream" Overture or the
Scheherazade, the slow movement of the Franck Symphony, and the "Ride of the Valkyries"? — all of
them and hundreds of others to choose from the
phonograph studios. If you are wise, you will choose
equally excellent but simple ones for the children, as
well as some of the biggest and greatest, and you will
practice economy in their use.

The home is better suited than any other agency
for this, in a sense, therapeutic use of music. If it were
to lead to a mere pandering to moods or to what a
disgusted music critic has called "sitting in a stew of
emotion," it would be quite the contrary to therapeutic
and a very foolish if not tragic waste of the true values
of music. But amidst the fabulous wealth of music
now available to almost everyone, why not choose
carefully not only for purely aesthetic qualities, but
also for the musical capacities of the children, for the
different occasions for music in a day and in a year,
and especially for the varied qualities of feeling and
attitude that may be realized in the music.

"I am not so Pollyanesque," said Mr. Schauffler,
"as to feel that the medicated use of poetry (or music)
can work any sudden, radical change in character.
But it undoubtedly exercises a powerful effect on

mood. And is not the persistent correction of adverse moods bound in time to have a permanent effect on character?" Quite aside, if you like, from character and therapeutics, let us use listening to music as a way of experiencing more fully, delightfully or valorously the common flow of life in a home. And let us have good home-made music, if we can, as well as, or without any, reproduced music.

In one New York home the children and parents on Sundays look together over the New York *Times* publication of the radio programs of the following week, and choose tentatively and sparingly which ones they wish to hear. Among the chosen ones are likely to be two or three compositions which the ten- and twelve-year-old children will enjoy all the more for having their father, who plays the piano moderately well, lead them in a little exploring of the music at a good time beforehand. This father knows that music is a personal affair and easily spoiled by too much talk about it and about what it means to the talker. His main interest is in letting it have its own way with the children with the help that comes of some familiarity with its outstanding musical characteristics — its important rhythms, tunes, some of the adventures through which these are taken by the composer, and its general character or changes in character. Singing the tunes and dancing to its rhythms, even the slow ones, are part of the game, and questions from the children are not only welcomed and eagerly answered, but they are sought for. Sometimes, in these days of school culture, one of the children can herself be a guide to the party. She may be urged to ask her music teacher or to go to a book for some information desired by the family. There are now many books on music appreciation that may be very helpful to the family. A good phonograph can be almost as obliging as a piano-playing mother or father.

Similar family preparations for a children's or young people's concert in a school or concert hall is made possible by distribution of the programs long in advance and by inclusion in them of music that is available for phonographs. "Keep pace with your child," says a circular of the Cleveland Orchestra inviting adults to hear its concerts for children or young people. Music memory contests in many cities, towns, and some counties, have enlisted parents as well as children.

Arousing Interest in Having Home Music

The most potent organization for the promotion of home music is the parent-teacher association with its primary interest in relations between the school and the home. Reference has already been made in this chapter to the ways in which such an association can — and many of them do — help to increase or improve the music in homes. An additional way is through the choruses of mothersingers that have in recent years been formed in almost all parts of the country, and are ardently encouraged by the National Congress of Parents and Teachers. At the 1931 meeting of this Congress a widely representative chorus of these amateur singers sang from memory a substantial program of part-music including a cantata by the American composer, Joseph Clokey, which chorus was a model not only for the 800 or more delegates of the Congress from every state in the Union, but also for the countless numbers who listen to a national radio broadcast.

There are values in this mothersinging beyond the delight and liberation of spirit that in many of the choruses it must give, though these would be more than enough to warrant full support of them. Many a mother who appears singing in an admired concert must gain a new kind of distinction in the minds of her children, which is good for them and her. Children easily fall into the habit of taking their mothers for granted, as persons dearly beloved but having very little relation to the vital interests of " real life " outside the home. But there she is, enthroned with her chorus mates before an admiring audience, a person of romance and happy potentialities that the habitual round of household chores had not revealed. Moreover, the chorus makes more likely the cultivation of singing, playing, and listening to worth while music in the homes of the members. " The music in my heart I bore long after it was heard no more."

When family groups perform at meetings of music clubs and women's clubs, there must be many in the audience who feel urged to have their own families do likewise. The same effect is gained through family musical groups in community night programs on playgrounds and community centers, as in Los Angeles, Jacksonville, and other cities; and in a Home Night program during Music Week as in Flint. For the latter the family groups were secured through the community and school music director's acquaintance with school boys and girls who are members of such groups. Some did not perform well at the concert, but the audience was enthusiastic nevertheless. No preliminary hearing was given to any of the groups. The principal desire was to encourage enough to come and face the audience. But with a larger number of entries in the future, there will be a very obvious reason for selection — the program must not be too long. Another reason for selection might be the need for having a varied, well-balanced program.

The National Better Homes Week observances have in many cities and towns included demonstrations and discussions of home music. Better Homes in America, which is the national educational organization responsible for these observances, has, with the National

Recreation Association, recently sponsored the publication of a new " Home and Community Song Book " that by the efforts of these two organizations is likely to find its way into a very large number of homes.

Public libraries in Evanston (Illinois), Indianapolis, Cleveland, Chicago, Detroit, Philadelphia, New York, and in an increasing though still small number of cities, have for circulation vocal and instrumental part-music suitable for homes, and almost every public library makes various collections of songs available.

*   *   *   *   *   *

This chapter started with quite skillful home music groups. There are also the old-fashioned sort of singing-parties to be found in homes here and there, when all gather about the piano for the simplest sort of informal singing. The closing blessing of the chapter is given to them!

CHAPTER XV

In Churches, Synagogues, and Religious Schools

AT no other time during the week can such a large part of America's population be found singing as between eleven o'clock and noon on Sunday morning — millions of them — singing hymns in church. Among adults there is more group singing here than anywhere else at any time. Among children the church as a place of music is second only to the week-day school. And if one asks what melodies are most familiar to America as a whole, one will find the largest number are hymn tunes.

The church has in the past been the most important single agency for developing the musical consciousness and activity of the peoples of many countries ; and the American church, with its 54,000,000 members — Jewish, Catholic and Protestant — still has, through its various Sabbath and week-day activities, a very great opportunity in this regard. It is important therefore for us to consider what happens to people through the medium of church music, and, ideally, what should be happening. That many persons have been greatly inspired by it is universally recognized. That many have been aesthetically revolted thereby is equally true.

At present we are in a period of musical reform which some are inclined to say is trying hard to make up in good taste and earnestness what it lacks in emotional fervor. The movement is too complex, however, for simple generalizations. But on the importance of two questions all parties seem agreed, namely,

1. By whom should church music be performed?
2. What kind of music is most desirable?

A third question, implied in the first two, but regarding which, strangely enough, many church musicians seem helplessly inarticulate, is,

3. Just what is the ultimate purpose and function of church music? In a word, these three might be called the who, what and why of church music.

For centuries, wherever choirs have been introduced, conflicts have arisen between two theories — the artistic and the congregational. Is music to be primarily an aesthetic adornment of worship? Then let its performance as well as choice be restricted to those with special ability or training. Is it rather a means of devotional expression for those who sing? Then let all the people join and sing whatever they feel most deeply. As in most church conflicts much confusion has resulted from ignorance or disregard of original meanings and their history, and from the failure of each party fully to appreciate the value in the faith of the other.

Let us therefore glance backward over the ways by which we have come into our present situation, observe some of the various experiments and projects now going on in American church music, and then consider paths worth traveling toward the future.

*   *   *   *   *   *

Music As White Magic

From the earliest times music has been intimately connected with practically every form of religious observance. So far as we have been able to discover, mankind has not known any completely unmusical religion. Whenever man's consciousness has been exalted, his outward behavior has become increasingly rhythmical and ordered, and the musical principle, except when definitely interfered with by certain social conventions and inhibitions (which are themselves rooted in fear and contrary to the freest spiritual expression), has taken increasing control of the two chief aspects of his outward activity — doing and speaking. The religious dance and the religious chant therefore are practically as universal as religion itself.

It is true, of course, that in the interest of a supposed simplicity or modesty both forms of expression have often been suppressed as much as possible. This is especially true of the dance in our Western churches. But even in them we are unable completely to crush all sense of the significance and symbolism of bodily posture and movement, as witness such scattered survivals as kneeling, standing, or bowing heads in prayer, procession of choirs, the minister's lifting of hands in benediction, and in Catholic or Episcopal churches the elevation of the host at mass or communion service. The ordered march of ushers, bearing the collected offerings of the people to the chancel and the lifting of these by the priest or pastor in a prayer of consecration are also outcroppings of the same instinct which, in many ages and civilizations, has flowered in the religious or liturgical dance. The making of the sign of the cross is another gesture with a history, and furnishes an interesting link with the magical aspects of early religious music and rhythmical movement.

For as James Frazer,[1] Dane Rudhyar,[2] and others have pointed out, art was for primitive man not always so much a means of adornment as a means of magic. The African savage carving the features of a demon on the handle of his weapon, the New Mexico Indian seeking to bring down rain by the magical power of his ceremonial, or the Hindu aspirant chanting his mantrams as a means of invoking spiritual illumination, were all alike using forms of art —

[1] " The Golden Bough " (Macmillan).
[2] " Art as Release of Power " — Hansa Publications.

sculpture, dance, or song—not primarily for their aesthetic but for their magical virtues, to conjure up or release some desired power for a very practical end. The medieval Christian dispelling the power of evil spirits by the sign of the cross was employing a pattern of movement in the same way. It was a " charm." And this word, interestingly enough, retains some of the dual connotations of beauty and power involved in early art forms, its older meaning having far more rugged strength than is usually implied in our present-day usage.

The attainment or release of power is by no means, however, an exclusively primitive conception of the function of religious music, nor is it necessarily connected with a superstitious belief. Mrs. Justine Ward, for example, founder of the Pius X School of Liturgical Music in New York and a leader in Catholic music reform, especially through the revival of the Gregorian chant, voices the conviction of many Jewish and Protestant as well as of Catholic thinkers when she says that all church music at its best should be musical prayer. And by prayer, she explains, is meant not merely petition, but all that is involved in " lifting the mind and heart to God." If this is not religious power at its height, what is? At least it indicates the true spirit of much of the finest music of worship.

The Coming of Choirs

At first in synagogue and church everybody sang. Except for the chanting of the cantor, music was always congregational. Then, as a means of supporting and leading the congregation, instruments were introduced for accompaniment, and some of the better singers or those particularly interested began to have extra practice and to sit together in the place of meeting. Thus choirs came into existence.

But these efforts to encourage the congregation to

sing, often resulted in silencing them altogether! For as choir members became more proficient they became interested in doing more elaborate music in which not everyone could join, and the people began to adopt the passivity characteristic of any laity. The choir became to the church, in short, what a prize football team has become to many a college — a highly specialized group in which the rest of the institution may take pride and whose performances they may enjoy, but in whose activities they do not share. The musical director of many a modern church, like the athletic director of too many a college, takes as his function the intensive training of this specialized group through which the citizenry of the institution express themselves, musically or athletically, by proxy.

Colleges and churches are awakening to the evils of the situation in which they have found themselves, and in some of the former we find moves to substitute physical directors for specialized team coaches, while among the latter an encouraging number are displacing or supplementing their quartet choirs by ministers of music, whose function is to cultivate the musical resources of the entire parish. It must by no means be supposed, however, that the specialization of choral interests was an unmitigated detriment to the musical experience of congregations. For it was precisely this divergence of interest which opened the way for the creation of some of the most inspiring works of religious art that humanity has produced.

The Three Branches of Church Music

At present, then, we are concerned with three distinct branches of church music, all of which have grown out of the ordinary service, and which now contribute to it, each in its own way. First is what may be called the religious folk music — chorales, hymns and gospel songs. For in spite of the growth of choirs, congregations were not entirely suppressible, and some have continued to sing, really sing, even to this day. Second are the choral works — masses, cantatas, oratorios, anthems — and solos, duets, trios, etc. Associated with these is to be found, third, often by the same composers, a rich instrumental literature, chiefly for orchestra or organ. Let us now consider each of these in turn.

Congregational Singing

If a church can afford a good choir, is there any reason for asking the congregation to sing? If beauty and refinement in the service are to be maintained, is it not absurd to invite a " miscellaneous crowd, trained and untrained, capable and incapable, careless and careful, to lift up their voices together? "[3] Moreover, even apart from artistic considerations, does not the physical activity involved act as a hindrance to the fullest inner experience of worship? Samuel Sebastian Wesley, in a tract on cathedral music published in 1849, argues against the congregation's taking a prominent part in the ceremonial of religion, " considering that persons who take part in and perform a public ceremony can never be so thoroughly imbued with its spirit as those who preserve a silent attention."

On the other hand every great popular church reform or revival has been carried forward on a tide of mass singing. One of Luther's distinctive tasks in 16th century Germany was to restore singing to the people, from whom it had practically disappeared so far as church worship was concerned, owing to the choral elaboration of the mass. Some of our finest old chorales are continuing testimony to the vitality and strength of his work. Huss, Calvin, and Zwingli were

[3] " Studies in Worship Music," First Series — J. Curwen & Sons, London, 1880, J. S. Curwen.

likewise active in this respect, the first two establishing singing schools in Prague and Geneva, respectively.

The Methodist revival was so strongly a musical movement in 18th century England that to sing hymns was tantamount to being a Methodist. There was a whole-hearted sincerity in their singing that drew crowds to their meetings and touched many hearts with the message of a new life, just as Wesley himself had been touched by the singing of the Moravians. In the process of religious awakening, hymn singing not only accompanied, but apparently quite generally preceded, preaching and the reading of Scripture. A letter to Wesley from one of his preachers in 1759 describes his work as follows:

> As soon as three or four receive convictions in a village, they are desired to meet together two or three nights in a week, which they readily comply with. At first they only sing, afterwards they join reading and prayer to singing.

He then quotes instances in which numbers of people were "broken down" and "seized with strong conviction" only by hearing hymns sung. More recently the Moody and Sankey and the Billy Sunday and Rodeheaver movements have carried on the tradition of singing evangelism.

Today we may not sing hymns as heartily as we once did, but it is quite clear that we still believe in hymn singing. For are we not spending millions of dollars in revising hymn books and in printing the full musical score for all the congregation? It is true, of course, that often we do not know what to do with the new books after we get them. We discard many of the gospel hymns because they seem cheap or undignified, and commission our experts to provide better ones which we buy and approve but often do not learn. We know that most of the congregation cannot read the tunes we give them. But we are at least providing

better hymn collections, and some day serious efforts
may more generally be made to use them adequately.
Since the vitality of congregational singing is partly
determined by the meaning and quality of the words
sung, let us examine some recent endeavors to provide
better and more fitting hymn verse.

Romantic Hymns and Social Service

The 19th century on its arrival discovered a hymnody prosaic and full of worms (for the same divines
who presently objected most violently to Mr. Darwin's
suggestions that we might have a remote cousinship
with highly evolved anthropoids, had with cheerful enthusiasm long sung to the Almighty that they were
really but worms crawling in the dust). The romantic
spirit of the 19th century asserted itself by admitting
that it could put up with the worms, but not with the
prose! Presently Reginald Heber, Bishop of Calcutta,
published a small collection of new hymns which were
destined to mold the mind of a century. He insisted
that the words sung should have color and literary
value. "From Greenland's Icy Mountains" and
"Holy, Holy, Holy," are two well-known samples,
abounding in the picturesque geography of coral
strands and glassy seas. The characteristic passions
were personal salvation and missionary zeal. Man,
however, was still "vile."

The twentieth century has a fondness for good
poetry, but it draws the line at worms! It believes
man, however disagreeable at times, is not vile — or
at least should not be called so in church. And as for
crawling in the dust, it would be quaint to remark
that the extravagance of the present American temper
is not particularly in the direction of self-abasement.
The good bishop's missionary hymn has therefore been
retired, and there appears a small collection, "Social
Hymns" (A. S. Barnes and Company), expressing the

social service gospel of its day, and like Heber's work, a hundred years before, exerting a profound effect upon its contemporaries. Its influence has reached the public chiefly via the editors and revisers of other hymn books, which because of their more general purposes have achieved wider circulation, but which dare not neglect the new note.

These hymns are in obvious contrast to those of the Moody and Sankey variety. The latter were concomitants of a movement marked by much zeal, sincerity, and emotional fervor, but they often contained cheap sentiment and a great deal of what one irreverent critic has called "slaughter house theology." "There is a fountain filled with blood," and "washed in the blood" are phrases typical of the "nice gory hymns for children " on which some of us now living were nourished as youngsters. Erotic songs such as "In a garden," and those affecting an easy familiarity with God are also being omitted from most of the newer publications.

The Hymn Society and New Revisions

Nearly all the leading denominations have become involved in the epidemic of hymn book revision, which began in the Episcopal Church with the "New Hymnal" (1916) — still the best of all musically. The Hymn Society, founded in 1922, took up the cause of raising literary and musical standards, and through its prize contests has stimulated the writing of a considerable amount of good poetry and music for hymns. It has also been largely responsible for the appointment of music commissions by several denominational boards. The Central Conference of American Rabbis, whose "Union Hymnal " of some years ago was modeled on the best traditions of Christian church music (and which contained many fine Jewish hymns that alert Christian churches would do well to study and adopt) is issuing a revision which gives more space to traditional Jewish music in the old modes, including the "Jewish Phrygian" mode represented by the scale e f g♯ a b c d e. It likewise includes hymns emphasizing peace, social justice and world brotherhood.

Young people, especially those who have been influenced by student groups, are among the leaders in their demand for the finer type of hymn, responsive reading, and worship service. The "Hymnal for American Youth" (Century Company), while not the last word in this field, helped to set new standards at the time of its publication in 1919. A million copies were sold during the next eleven years, by the end of which period advancing taste and changing attitudes had necessitated a revision. (Of the new version 35,000 copies were sold during the first winter.)

The contrast between the old and new is well illustrated by the following excerpts from two prefaces to interdenominational hymn books published by the same company in 1865 and 1928 respectively. From the first: [4]

The History and purpose of the following Collection of Hymns and Tunes may be sufficiently set forth in a few words. It has been prepared by a PASTOR; for the use, primarily, of the Church to which it is his privilege to minister, in their public and private worship of Almighty God. . . .

The compiler presents the humble result, of what has been to him very serious labor, to his own beloved people, and to the Church at large, with unaffected pleasure, in the simple hope that it may be used by our Divine Redeemer in building up His chosen in the most holy faith; and that it may be so accompanied by the grace of His Spirit — would that it might be even so honored! — as to be as the sound of silver bells calling those who know not our Lord to His most joyful feasts of love. So may it advance, in its own measure, the worship of our KING, till our eyes shall see Him in His beauty, and behold the land that is very far off!

[4] Preface to First Edition — "Songs for the Sanctuary" by Charles S. Robinson, 1865.

and from the second: [5]

If Whitman was speaking for all the arts rather than for poetry alone when he wrote, " To have great poets there must be great audiences, too," the present hour is most opportune for the publication of the American Student Hymnal. Its appeal is to an audience as ruthlessly scornful of the shoddy or pretentious as it is sincerely appreciative of the genuine. Young intelligence in the United States accepts the traditional or the novel only if they meet the double test of finesse and livingness. These are the standards by which it measures the desirability of all its experiences, on the athletic field, over the radio, at the theater, in the classroom and in church and chapel. Are they vivid? Are they done with distinction? Are they real? . . .

That the devotional element is not overlooked is indicated in the concluding paragraph:

It is not too much to hope that the American Student Hymnal . . . will become a cathedral of song, capable of providing a quietly colorful atmosphere for the most varied services and of voicing, through modern lyrics and melodies, the medieval aspiration of vaulted ceilings and spires against the sky.

It is true that these two examples are in some senses not strictly comparable, since the former occurs in a book designed for general church use and the latter in one especially for students and young people. On the other hand, they reflect the obvious difference in the whole mental and spiritual outlook of two groups of religious leaders not atypical of the best of their day.

In general we may say that the present renaissance, for it amounts to that, involves, as do all such movements:

1. A fresh appreciation of the best in the old — Jewish chant, Gregorian plainsong, Lutheran chorales, and the " fine old hymns of the Christian Church."
2. An adoption of materials not in the direct line of tradition. This is marked by the inclusion in the " American

[5] From the Preface of the " American Student Hymnal," Century Company, New York, 1928.

Student Hymnal " of twenty-one hymns in foreign lan-
guages for students from other countries, the increasing
use of Negro spirituals (which in spite of their American
origin often seem exotic in churches whose traditions
reflect a different racial culture), and the adoption of
much good secular poetry of ethical value.

3. A new literature expressing the aspiration and feeling of
the new leadership.

The tendency is toward greater dignity in both
words and music. There is less emphasis on privilege
and more on responsibility. Heaven-longing hymns
are giving place to a larger number expressing ideals
of present living. Sentimental tunes are giving place
to sturdy melodies, many of them culled from the
best survivals of previous centuries, and to the refined mysticism of plainsong. The social gospel, while
emphasized, is by no means regarded as a complete
one and there is also a demand for better hymns of
personal devotion. In short there is an aroused conviction that if our churches are to have a hymnody
intellectually, artistically, and spiritually worthy of
the worship of God, it must be constituted of good
poetry, good music and good religion.

Our Difficulties with Singing

When we turn from the publishing of hymns to the
singing of them, we have a different picture. Some of
the congregation do not sing at all, others often sing
half-heartedly, perfunctorily, not to say unmusically,
and with scant attention to any of the words beyond
the first stanza. Yet most people enjoy singing, and
some churches have excellent congregational music.
What, then, are some of the chief obstacles in the way
of equally good singing elsewhere, and how may they
best be overcome?

1. *A careless or irreverent attitude.* This is not
wholly new. In 1791 Dr. Edward Miller in his

"Thoughts on the present performance of Psalmody in the Established Church of England," gives a depressing picture of Anglican psalmody:

> If any one would step into the parish church while the psalm is singing, would he not find the greater part of the congregation totally inattentive, irreverently sitting, talking to each other, taking snuff, winding up their watches, or adjusting their apparel?

Today we may not indulge in taking snuff and winding our watches during the singing, but all too often we show a mental blankness which is not much better. Too often music has been treated as an accessory to a meeting rather than as a vital act of worship. Hymns are used as stretching exercises, as a cover for disorder and as a filler of gaps. In Sunday school, if the leader wishes to have a private conversation with an assistant, the hymn is not uncommonly regarded as legitimate "time out" from the serious business of conducting worship. During prayer, Scripture reading, or the delivery of a sermon or talk, we have been accustomed to preserve a reverent decorum as befits our approach to God, our listening to His word, or to the voice of instruction. But while we enjoy music, and should be disturbed at its deletion from the service, we are often very fuzzy-minded as to its real function, and our conduct during the musical parts of the service is apt to be correspondingly vague.

This condition, happily not universal, is usually the result of sheer neglect on the part of leaders rather than of any determined opposition on the part of a group. Thoughtful consideration of the meaning of worship, as much care given to music as to other aspects of it, and a positive, constructive program of developing musical worship to its best will very probably win the respect it deserves.

2. *The reluctance of the masses to learn new hymns.* Give them songs worth learning, and the conditions

of learning, and one will find no innate antagonism to new music. Why are new popular songs constantly being sung on Saturday night by people who in church on Sunday are dumb? One reason is that the popular song is heard effectively sung by a favorite in theatre, on radio, or in social group, and it is heard repeatedly. Often people dance to it, the tune is heard at meals, on the street, and in a variety of ways. By contrast, it is not uncommon that an unfamiliar hymn will be sprung on the congregation almost without warning, and if they do not respond heartily on the first or second attempt, it is assumed they are incapable or unwilling. The same hymn may not be tried again for weeks or months.

The experience of the 18th century Methodists in this field is illuminating. An English Churchman of the day (Rev. Dr. Vincent, in " Considerations on Parochial Music," 1787) admits that "for one who has been drawn away from the Established Church by preaching, ten have been induced by music." He goes on to say:

That the harmony arising from the voices of a well-regulated Methodist congregation is delightful, no one who has heard it can deny. Let us not envy them the enjoyment of it, but draw our own instruction — by examining in what points their excellence consists. . . . It will be generally acknowledged that the effect is produced first by the *union of every voice in the assembly,* secondly, by *practice,* and thirdly, by *moderating the voice to the most harmonious pitch.*

Four years later Dr. Edward Miller, in the tract above cited, described an example of good Methodist congregational training:

A singing master of sense and judgment selected ten persons with good tenor voices, and having instructed these in a certain number of plain melodies till they sang in 'time and tune, he placed them in different parts of the church. He next proceeded in the same manner with basses and countertenors. By degrees the whole congregation came to join with them, so as to approach as near as possible to perfection.

It may be of interest here to note that even as late as 1900 a similar method was employed in so fashionable a church as the Fifth Avenue Presbyterian in New York. According to Mr. Harry Gilbert, the present organist in this church, it has been only during the last thirty years that the paid singers have consistently sat together as a choir instead of being distributed through the congregation.

A church in Palo Alto, California, with a reputation for a singing congregation, is still carrying on a tradition which began over twenty-five years ago as a result of a period of special congregational training. A man was engaged for a series of meetings in which to teach the people to sing. There was ample time allowed for practice, and for the repetition necessary to gain familiarity with many of the hymns. At present the personnel of the church membership has almost entirely changed, but the new members have come into a singing church, and like new cells in a body, have acquired the characteristics of the body of which they have become a part.

Similar to this project in the opportunities they offer for gaining familiarity with hymns are the Sunday evening or mid-week song services held in some Protestant churches in all parts of the country. These are primarily for the purpose of immediate devotional expression, not for practice, but where a fine freedom of spirit, a wise choice of hymns, and brief, well-chosen comments on some of them give the proper setting, there may be as effective a learning of new hymns as could be gained through more formal instruction and drill. What was said on pages 409–410 about learning to sing better can be applied in such a service. There may be good though simple endeavor

to achieve accuracy, better diction, good phrasing,
and the like, in a hymn worth the effort, all as means
to greater satisfaction in the singing.

3. *Emotional attachments to words and music intellectually and artistically outgrown.* It is legitimately complained that such sentimental attachment
to songs which no longer express the best of one's religious thinking or aesthetic feeling, may, if allowed
to continue their use in worship, be a serious hindrance to spiritual growth; for they may serve merely
to produce a certain pleasure gained by the repetition
of relatively infantile experiences. Nothing is more
calculated to produce insincerity in worship than the
humoring of such an appetite, for it tends to disso-
ciate religious expression from a man's most mature
thought and seasoned judgment. Instead of worship-
ping with his best and fullest self, he may be merely
indulging in what serves as a pious lullaby, even
though the tune be as stirring as " Onward Christian
Soldiers."

The answer to this difficulty would seem to lie
partly in a more frankly critical approach to both
words and music of hymns. Here again an active
cultivation of the appreciation and use of the best
is one of the most effective means of eliminating the
inferior.

4. *The high register of hymns.* This is another evidence that our attack on the problem of congregational music has often been a singularly uncoordi-
nated affair. Congregational rehearsals are rare, and
when they occur are apt to consist in the practicing
of a few hymns sung only in unison. But if we expect
hymns to be sung in unison, why do we score them for
four voices, pitching the melody so high in the soprano
that most lower voices, especially the men, have to
squeak, yell, or drop out altogether in their effort
to reach the higher climaxes? We cannot blame this

practice entirely upon the bad example set by our national anthem.

If, on the other hand, we wish to encourage part-singing, as our spending such sums on printing parts would seem to imply, could we not make an effort to train a larger number in this art of worship? It is true that many of the younger people are learning part-singing in day schools, but others of the congregation may have no opportunity in this direction except that provided by the church. We might also consider a re-arrangement of many hymns so that whether sung in unison or in parts, the melody could be brought within the middle register most conducive to mass participation. Fortunately, some of the newer publications are doing this very successfully.

5. *Lack of musical understanding on the part of ministers.* This is a deficiency to which many theological seminaries have awakened, and which they are trying to rectify. Some are giving courses in hymnody in which the history and development of church music are discussed, and special attention given to literary and the theological standards in hymn verse. Considering the importance of the hymnal as a tool-book in the minister's library kit, it seems not unreasonable to ask that, as a professional leader of public worship, he should at least be able to read it. Reading the words only is, of course, not reading the song.

If a minister has been denied the advantages of special musical training, however, two courses may be open. First, he may undertake a private study of both words and music of the church's great hymn literature. Secondly, if he has a competent organist or musical director on his staff he may consult him freely, and possibly trust him even more freely to guide the musical policy of the church.

6. *Lack of interest in congregational singing on the*

part of the music director. Where this exists, it is a
serious situation calling for conference. The trouble
may not be entirely with the musical director, who
may have been given but little responsibility for developing congregational singing. Such a person has
usually been engaged to play the organ or direct the
choir and may have little direct contact with the congregation. If a church wants to use its musical resources for improving its congregational singing, a
way can usually be found to enlist the interest of those
primarily concerned. Some other member of the choir
than the director may have a superior gift for leading
mass singing, in which case a way should be found to
call him into this service.

7. *The general lack of ability to read music.* If we
do not believe that a goodly proportion of the congregation should be able to read music, why do we spend
such sums in printing the musical score for all of
them? Would it not be more reasonable to return to
the less bulky, less expensive books which, except in
copies for choir and organist, omitted the musical
score? But if the church wants its members to make
full use of the hymnals it has been at such pains to
provide, why should it not revive its educational philosophy, its memories of singing schools, and help
them learn to read the music, or to revive the skill
therein which some of them must have acquired in
school?

This might conceivably add not one whit to the devotional quality of their singing. No one who has felt
the power of a Negro spiritual sweep through a vast
colored congregation in the South would be so aca-
demically naïve as to suggest that the ability to read
musical notation is essential to all effective mass singing. Many people who have this ability often sing
just as mechanically as others read the Scripture in
the responsive readings, or, let it be confessed, as

ministers have been known to read the prayers in the prayer book.

But the ability to read bestows upon one a great freedom in any literature. And if, in addition to this mastery of the language and letter, there could be an awakening of spirit which uses the newly won freedom for full-hearted expression, might we not have congregational singing such as would give great vitality to the entire church service, and inspiration to all taking part in it?

If we believe this a goal worth striving toward, it may be encouraging to realize that with modern methods of teaching it is by no means a very difficult task to learn the rudiments of sight reading. The author has in a single evening seen adults taught enough of the principles involved for them to recognize and follow simple folk tunes written on a blackboard and to detect errors purposely written in the score. Any seriously interested group willing to devote eight or ten evenings to such a project, should, under able leadership, be able to " catch on " enough to make the musical score intelligible, and its use a genuine pleasure. Further facility would, of course, come with practice. A series of such evenings, arranged for those in the congregation who might desire it, could include some actual practicing of fine hymns, together with a brief study of their origin and history. This would result in at least a small nucleus — perhaps a large one — of persons in the congregation who have a welcome sense of responsibility with regard to singing heartily and well in the church services. Their attitude would likely be contagious.

Cooperation with Home, School, and Neighbor Churches

Apart from the above considerations, let us look at a few general aspects of the question. The practice of singing hymns at home was at one time a strong factor in developing congregational singing. An anti-Methodist clergyman of 1805 evidently regarded it as an extremely pernicious habit! He says:

A consequence attends the very devotions of this sect, so injurious to the domestic economy of the poor, that it may be almost considered a political evil. I allude to the almost daily practice of singing their divine hymns. The labourer of this class returns from his day's work as others do, nearly exhausted by it; but instead of taking rest so much wanted in his chimney corner, he immediately takes his wife and family from the wheel, and other useful employments in the house, to hear or join him in this religious exercise; which is not unfrequently kept up at the expense of fire and candle to an unseasonable hour. I have often heard this singing in some of our poorest cottages at so late an hour as nine, and sometimes later of a winter's evening.

Today we find hymn singing outside the church decreasing in homes and, while being maintained in varying measure in schools, it is in the latter often but a means of providing for part singing. But practically all school song books contain a number of good hymns, and in a few places definite cooperation between public school and Sunday school leaders is correlating the music of the two schools. In Durham, North Carolina, a young people's choir school has resulted from such team work. The successive steps in its formation were, first, a demonstration of child voice training for those in charge of the Sunday school music; second, a standardization of Sunday school music material with a view toward eliminating unworthy texts and melodies; third, the formation of a junior choir. This process led to the choir school, with each church sending representatives as members of a model choir. Two weekly rehearsals were required, after school hours. By the second season the choristers were already furnishing musical leadership in about twenty churches of the vicinity.

The National Federation of Music Clubs has endeavored to stimulate better hymn singing by the promotion of hymn memory, hymn singing, and hymn playing contests. Educators are not all agreed as to the values of the contest as a method of developing interest in the thing itself, but it is significant to note the spread of the idea. It is said that 400,000 children took written examinations on the eight hymns chosen for the contest of 1923–24. This represented 42 states, with 5,000 to 12,000 children participating in each state. In Virginia about twelve hundred children have recently taken part in these contests, the two largest gatherings being in Roanoke (300) and Danville (500), both conducted in public schools by their music supervisors.

Cooperation between the various churches of a community can be a great help in developing spirit and enthusiasm in mass singing. An effective means is the Sunday evening union musical service, for which a number of ministers and congregations forego the services in their own church in order to come together in one church chiefly for united hymn singing. Such meetings can contribute much not only to the improvement of music in the churches involved but also to the development of conscious spiritual unity among the various denominations. A joint committee may agree on a certain list of hymns in advance and have these used frequently in each of the several churches for some weeks preceding such a union sing.

Such a community hymn festival may well serve as the occasion for a pastor's devoting a preparatory series of Sunday evening or mid-week services in his own church to the study and singing of hymns. Stories of hymn writers, of occasions on which certain hymns have been used with particular significance, and of circumstances surrounding their origin may give hymns richer associations for those who sing. The religious implications of their content may also be discussed or interpreted.

All that has so far been said with reference to cultivating the possibilities of hymn singing may be in principle applied to the use of chant, plainsong, and chorale. While Catholic, Anglican, and Lutheran churches have a stronger tradition than most others in these fields, the grandeur of old German chorales and the exquisite spirituality of Gregorian chant are musical heritages of Christian worship too fine not to be explored by any seriously interested group. The resources of Jewish chant are also rich in emotional warmth and dramatic power.

Choral Music

The present outlook for church choral music is one to arouse enthusiasm. There are many communities, still struggling through the banalities of " the quartet school," which have not yet been touched by the revival of choral society and choir festival interest, but the vitality of the revival, where it flourishes, is encouraging, and its spread seems imminent.

Concerts and Festivals

The tours of college and church choirs, such as the St. Olaf College Choir, the Northwestern University A Cappella Choir, the Westminster Choir, and of imported choral organizations such as The Russian Symphonic Choir, have unquestionably had a profound effect upon public opinion by giving excellent performances of the best religious choral music. The Harvard University Glee Club, though less directly a model for church choirs, has also been an inspiring influence through its excellent performances of such music. Practically all of the larger music festivals, such as those of Cincinnati, Westchester County (N. Y.) and many smaller ones in various parts of the country, include choral programs of oratorio and other religious music. The Bach " B minor Mass," "St. Matthew's Passion," the " Messiah," " Elijah," and the Brahms " Requiem," though still unknown to many, have now been heard by a larger number of America's population than ever before. It is probably safe to say that there is hardly any choral organization of significant size or musical standing, whether organized under church or secular auspices, that does not include in its repertoire at least some of the world's best religious music; and as the number of such organizations is increasing, we have scattered through the country hundreds of places where excerpts from the best musical literature can be heard. The broadcasting of choral programs by radio is, of course, a further significant factor in acquainting a large number of the American public with higher standards of choral performance.

The fact that most of the festival choruses include large numbers of church choir singers, even though the choruses be organized quite independently of any church, means that many church choirs are feeling the influence of this training and are consequently less satisfied with mediocre standards. Still more direct in influence are the festivals participated in only by church choirs. In some of these, as in one held annually in Boston, the Synagogue as well as Catholic and Protestant churches are represented. The music chosen is often in large part such as can be used in each choir's own weekly services, and it is rehearsed by each choir separately for from six weeks to three months before the two or three joint rehearsals of all the choirs are held, within a week or two of the festival. Performances of the " Messiah " and other oratorios are in many communities given by a combination of choirs.

These festivals and other special performances

growing in large measure out of the already organized choirs' own rehearsals are usually easier to achieve than the formation of a new chorus for the purpose, but additional singers unattached to any choir may very well be admitted into the work, in which event there will be a larger number of rehearsals for the entire festival chorus. Needless to say, there must be full agreement and cooperation between the choirmasters and other church authorities; and if the music is worthy and a great leader can be secured — from out of town if necessary or otherwise desirable — to join in the original planning and to be a guide in the interpretation and other phases of the separate and the joint rehearsals, a long step forward in the church music of the city can be achieved.

A Cappella Singing

In all of these festivals the finest music on the programs, when well done, is usually the unaccompanied singing of polyphonic music of the old masters and of the present Russian school. The increased interest in this difficult but exquisite art has been largely brought about through the example of such choirs as have already been mentioned. To quote Dr. Peter C. Lutkin, Dean of the Northwestern University School of Music, and a pioneer in the development of American A Cappella singing:

A cappella music is to choral singing what the string quartet is to instrumental music. It deals essentially with fineness of feeling and delicacy of nuance. Poor *a cappella* singing is intolerable. Each part must be solid and impeccable as to pitch, tone quality, rhythm and dynamics. The singers must really feel the purport of both words and music, and the highest results are attained only when the music is memorized. Memorizing accounts for the greater part of the marvelous singing of the St. Olaf College Choir under that prince of choir masters, F. Melius Christiansen. The absorbed attention his choristers give him leaves him free to produce new effects upon the impulse of the moment. It goes without saying that the conductor who aspires to *a cappella* singing must thoroughly know his business and have a clear mental concept of what he wants to do. The organ surely has its place in church music. Its dignity and grandeur, both as a solo instrument and in conjunction with choir or congregation are indispensable. Its dominating volume, however, has had a detrimental effect on choral standards. After all, the human voice is the most expressive of all instruments, and ambitious choir leaders should see to it that a certain amount of unaccompanied singing should be part and parcel of their programs. It will place their offerings of prayer and praise upon a distinctly higher plane.[6]

Vested Choirs and Village Choirs

The increasing use of vestments for choirs, even in so-called non-liturgical churches, is significant as a symptom of the growing dignification of church music. When the Prince of Wales visited New York in 1860 and attended a service in Trinity Church, the choir on that occasion sang for the first time in chancel, robed in cassocks and cottas. The boys and men had formerly sung in citizens' dress, outside the chancel.[7] The practice thus begun at Trinity, and about the same time in a few other churches (even earlier in Boston) was gradually adopted in other parts of the country. About 1886 there began a revival of choral music in Episcopal churches — soon spreading to other denominations and continuing in varying degrees to the present — in which the direct and indirect influence of Trinity Choir was enormous. Quartets gave place to boys' choirs and mixed choruses. Intoning and chanting came into more general use, church libraries increased in number and size, and enlarged and improved hymn books, already mentioned, went through various editions.

[6] Article in " Music in Religious Education " January, 1929.

[7] See Stubbs in Gardner and Nicholson's, " A Manual of English Church Music."

If we look at this period as a whole, we find it marked by three strangely contrasting movements:

1. The development of vested choirs
2. The gospel hymns of the later Victorian revivalists (see pages 424–425)
3. The growth of the "quartet school"

The latter, from which some communities have not yet recovered was an outgrowth of the old time village choir on the one hand and budding virtuosity on the other. To understand it, and to appreciate more fully our present developments, we should glance back a few years.

George Eliot, in "Scenes of Clerical Life" has given us a vivid picture of the village choir:

And the singing was no mechanical affair of official routine; it had a drama. As the moment of psalmody approached, by some process to me as mysterious and untraceable as the opening of the flowers or the breaking out of the stars, a slate appeared in the front of the gallery, advertising in bold characters the psalm about to be sung, lest the sonorous announcement of the clerk should still leave the bucolic mind in doubt on that head. Then followed the migration of the clerk to the gallery, where, in company with a bassoon, two key-bugles, a carpenter understood to have an amazing power of singing "counter," and two lesser musical stars, he formed the complement of a choir regarded in Shepperton as one of distinguished attraction, occasionally known to draw hearers from the next parish. The innovation of hymn books was as yet undreamt of; even the new version was regarded with a sort of melancholy tolerance, as part of the common degeneracy in a time when prices had dwindled, and a cotton gown was no longer stout enough to last a lifetime; for the lyrical taste of the best heads in Shepperton had been formed on Sternhold and Hopkins. But the greatest triumphs of the Shepperton choir were reserved for the Sundays when the slate announced an anthem, with a dignified abstinence from particularisation, both words and music lying far beyond the reach of the most ambitious amateur in the congregation — an anthem in which the key-bugles always ran away at a great pace, while the bassoon every now and then boomed a flying shot after them.

An amusing account is also found in Fraser's Magazine for September 1860:

The particular choir in our own church we recollect well to this day, and some of their most striking tunes. We used to listen with mingled awe and admiration to the performance of the 18th Psalm in particular. Take two lines as an illustration of their style:

> " And snatched me from the furious rage
> Of threatening waves that proudly swelled."

The words, " And snatched me from " were repeated severally by the trebles, the altos, the tenors, and the bass voices; then all together sang the words two or three times over; in like manner did they toss and tumble over " the furious rage," apparently enjoying the whirligig scurrying of their fugues, like so many kittens chasing their own tails; till at length, after they had torn and worried that single line even to the exhaustion of the most powerful lungs — after a very red-faced bass, who kept the village inn, had become perceptibly apoplectic about the eyes, and the bassoon was evidently blown, and a tall, thin man, with a long nose, which was his principal vocal organ, and which sang tenor, was getting out of wind — they all, clarionet, bassoon, violoncello, the red-faced man, the tall tenor, and the rest, rushed pell-mell into " the threatening waves that proudly swelled." We have not forgotten the importance with which they used to walk up the church path in a body with their instruments, after this effort; and our childish fancy revelled in the impression that, after the clergyman, and the Duke of Wellington, who had won the battle of Waterloo a few years before, these singers were the most notable public characters in being.

While not all choirs were as ludicrous as these, the first half of the nineteenth century can hardly be regarded as the golden age of church music, viewed from any angle, Jewish, Catholic, or Protestant. It was not essentially an artistic age. Architecture was at a low ebb, and good taste was somewhat sparsely scattered. It is not surprising, therefore, that we should find the latter part of the century blossoming with a fair crop of fussy little anthems — fluted and starched and done up in curl papers. Music was often as heavily upholstered as the women's clothes. It was a day of the sentimental and pretentious, of fancy architectural gingerbread and of brownstone fronts.

When we turn, therefore, to the revival of Palestrina and plainsong, and to the new music of Vaughan Williams, Gustav Holst and others, we realize what a long way we have had to travel. Along the line we had a train of organists, choirmasters, composers, teachers, choral conductors and others who have worked at the task of simplifying, purifying and strengthening our taste. Among directors of Catholic Church music the Motu Proprio of Pius X in 1903, a document calling for finer and simpler standards of liturgical music, has exerted a strong influence. So far has their outlook changed that a leading publisher of Catholic church music finds seventy-five per cent of his business altered in character, the operatic best sellers of the nineties having given place to more austere and devotional music, with a new demand for plainsong and Palestrina.

Training the Choir and Its Leaders

If training, practice and able leadership are necessary for the development of good singing by congregations, this is even more true of choirs. Irregular attendance at rehearsals; slipshod discipline; perfunctory practice; leadership without alertness, devotion, and sound musicianship — these are only some of the devils which may at times infest the choir loft. Their presence usually means death to the spirit of musical worship at its best. In some churches the interest and loyalty of the choir are deepened through providing social life in addition to the singing. For example, in the First Congregational Church of Los Angeles, each rehearsal of the volunteer choir of 80 men and women is preceded by a supper especially prepared for them by the Women's Society of the church, at a cost of 35 cents to each singer. About 75% of the choir members attend the supper and enjoy the best sort of sociability as well as being entertained now and then by a speaker, singer or group, or more rarely through a general round of play for all. The same practice is carried on at the First Baptist Church of that city, where a choir from some other church is sometimes invited to join in the supper. There is quite frequent interchange of choirs among the churches of Los Angeles. The Federation of Church Musicians there meets once a month and arrangements are made for such interchanges, the small costs of transportation sometimes being defrayed through the proceeds of a special concert given by one of the choirs. Choirmasters have occasionally exchanged positions for a week's rehearsal and services. Such means of expanding interest among the choir members — especially the interchange of choirs or of choirmasters — are conducive to better workmanship also.

The American Guild of Organists, National Association of Organists and other organizations have helped to improve matters by focusing the attention of organists and choirmasters on artistic and professional standards. Even more basically constructive, however, are the various schools for training choir members and leaders, and the movement to have ministers of music.

Choir schools for children are still limited for the most part to a few Episcopal churches, but there is a definite increase in the number of junior choirs in other denominations. (Reference has already been made to the school at Durham, North Carolina, page 436.) One of the most extraordinary efforts in this field is the Children's Choir School at Flemington, New Jersey, directed by Elizabeth Van Fleet Vosseller. This school, organized at the very end of the last century, admits boys and girls of the community, from the fourth grade up, to its training. The following brief account is taken from an article by the director published in "Music in Religious Education" for May, 1929.

Every child must work in the Probation Class a year to become a chorister in the choir; and a chorister of the school must earn sixty credits to receive a diploma admitting him to the Senior Choir of his particular church. This takes six or seven years, and no one is permitted to graduate under four years' training.

The village has five churches: Presbyterian, Methodist, Baptist, Catholic, and Episcopal. These five churches are all represented in the school; and as the work is done by grades, the denominations mingle in rehearsals, save once a week, when a rehearsal is held specially for each individual choir.

Each of the five churches has a splendid Senior Choir, nearly all graduates from the Choir School, who serve their churches almost 100 per cent in attendance and spirit, voluntarily, from September to June, inclusive. There are no paid choristers among the Seniors. The children have a small salary, ranging from three to twenty-five cents a month, in order to make the discipline easy. (Good work brings a full envelope, while poor work fines the offender.) Prizes are offered also for fine work, and a special prize night is held one week previous to the graduation each spring, when a vocal contest, a piano contest, and yearly prizes (amounting to more than eighty individual ones last season) are presented. The prizes are voluntary gifts from the community, and the money for them pours into the school each spring without a request being made by the directors.

The graduation occurs the third Friday in May and is one of the most unique services one could imagine. People come from far and near each season to see and hear it, and hundreds are turned away because of no more room. The entire Choir School of nearly 200 choristers and a group of about 150 from the Chorus of the Alumni, sing at this festival. Every one is vested, and the great processional with its crosses and banners is a thrilling pageant.

The ministers of the five churches are in the procession, and the organists of the five churches participate in playing the service made up of beautiful music, well executed. The diplomas are presented to the Seniors and the class kneels as the gold hoods are placed on their shoulders. The Alumni do an anthem in a most finished style; the Choir School also sings a fine anthem, and the little Probationers carol their hymn and are formally received into the choir when one of their members is vested with a surplice. Service stripes are put on the hoods of the Alumni each stripe indicating 150 rehearsals and 300 services attended, and the earnestness of their purpose is summed up in the following creed, to which each young graduate must pledge himself before he receives his certificate admitting him to the upper choir and membership in the Chorus of the Alumni.

The Alumni Creed

We, the Chorus of the Alumni of the Flemington Children's Choirs, believe music to be God's gift to His children, and as ministers of song do give ourselves by our service, enthusiasm and means to aid the music of the church; to raise the standard of music in the community; to respect by perfect silence the art of music during its performance, nor to suffer disturbances from others. Thus do we give our utmost support to this cause of good music in any community, in which we live.

Ministry and Ministers of Music

The recognition of song as a ministry, so obviously fundamental in the above creed, is at the root of all the finest church music development. A weekly service at four o'clock Sunday afternoons in the new Riverside Church, New York,[8] is called the " Ministry of Music." This is one of the churches where music is by no means limited to its Sunday services. Its calendar recently listed twenty-one musical affairs during a single week, including rehearsals and performances of various choirs, men's chorus, " tower sing," orchestras and instrumental trios. The Riverside Guild, a young people's organization, has Sunday evening worship services chiefly composed of music, drama and dance.

Not long ago the Central Presbyterian Church of Montclair, New Jersey, had an impressive service for the installation of two new ministers, a minister of religious education and a minister of music. The

[8] Where the Rev. Harry Emerson Fosdick is the minister.

latter is now responsible, with some assistance, for the training of four choirs: primary, junior, high school and adult, with a total membership of 135. Each choir has its own schedule of services for which it sings, and once or twice a month the combined choirs sing together. The church also provides free individual instruction in singing, for the members of the various choirs. This plan, not original with the Montclair church, is now being tried in an increasing number of communities in various parts of the country. The expense of having such a highly trained person who will devote his whole time to developing the music of the church, and to training as large a number of the congregation as possible in musical worship, is often no more than that of a paid quartet and organist. The educational value to the church is usually vastly superior.

This movement has received great impetus from the various schools for training choir leaders. Among these may be mentioned the department of sacred music in the Northwestern University School of Music, St. Dunstan's College (Episcopal) at Providence, Rhode Island; the Westminster Choir School at Ithaca, New York; the Pius X School of Liturgical Music (Roman Catholic), and the School of Sacred Music at Union Theological Seminary; the last two both in New York City.

Westminster Choir School

At present the most internationally famous of these is the Westminster Choir School, organized in 1926 in Dayton, Ohio, under the direction of John Finley Williamson and sponsored by Mrs. H. E. Talbott. During the 1927–28 concert season the Westminster Choir sang before 110,000 persons outside of Dayton. Some of the audiences were the largest ever assembled in their localities for a musical event. In St. Louis there were 9,004 paid admissions, the next night in Kansas City, 7,600. This tour was followed by one through principal cities of Europe. In Albert Hall, London, two concerts were given a week apart. At the first there were 3,500, at the second 7,000.

A feature of the school has been the "Westminster Plan" by which churches in the vicinity of the school, first at Dayton, then moved to Ithaca, make arrangements for musical leadership to be furnished by the school under Dr. Williamson's supervision. The minister of music is responsible for organizing and directing three choirs, junior, high school, and adult. The rapidity of the growth of this movement has been phenomenal. In the 1930 June choir festival at Ithaca forty such choirs took part. In 1931 the festival was made up of about eighty choirs, all directed by students and graduates of the Westminster Choir School. They represented the area of Indiana, Ohio, North Carolina, Maryland, Pennsylvania and New York. A recent survey shows that whereas in the sixty-seven churches now being served directly from the choir school there were formerly but 800 persons active in choirs, there are now, since the adoption of the plan, 4,078. Even this number, however, does not represent the attainment of a final goal, for the development of chorus choirs is from one angle but a step toward training the whole church to sing.

Pius X School

Another school with a similar ideal is the Pius X School of Liturgical Music established in connection with the College of the Sacred Heart, New York City, in 1918. To step into its gardens is to leave the bustle of the metropolis and twentieth century for an air of old Europe. Electric lights seem almost blatantly anachronistic in the mellowness of its Romanesque architecture. The eighty-odd choir boys, however, who are brought in for rehearsal twice per week by bus from various parochial schools are thoroughly healthy, modern, American youngsters. They come to sing and obviously have a good time doing it. If the director asks "who would like to sing the next verse alone?" a flock of hands go up eagerly. The boys also often take turns for a few minutes in conducting. To the uninitiated it may be a surprise to find that all of this enthusiasm is not for jazzy tunes, but for the finest of old plainsong, sung in Latin!

The school was founded for the purpose of concentrating on "the systematic working out of the reform in church music decreed by Pope Pius X in the Motu Proprio of 1903," which had urged that music be restored to the people as a means of sanctification, and that such music as was used by the church must adequately express the content of her message. Mrs. Justine Ward, the founder, felt that such a reform as was contemplated could be achieved only by means of a thorough musical education in parochial schools. The Pius X school has therefore become a center not only for the training of children in near-by parochial schools, but also for training choirmasters and teachers. A four-year course is offered with special emphasis on Gregorian chant and classic polyphony.

Those not fortunate enough to be within reach of New York City can now hear some of these beautiful ancient melodies sung by the children of the Pius X Choir in Victor recordings. The subtle rhythms of dignified prose, and the exquisitely mystical, soaring quality of this music when properly sung provide a transparent tonal garment for devotional aspiration that is unequalled by any other music in the world. It is not the music for our modern social service hymns. It is not a complete expression of twentieth century religious thought and feeling. Neither, on the other hand, should it be regarded merely as the expression of an early European phase of Christianity. For, like the art of Greece and the music of Bach, it is one of the perfect and timeless arts.

Union Theological Seminary School of Music

One of the most recently established schools of sacred music, and the highest of all in its academic standing, is that connected with Union Theological Seminary, New York City. A college degree or its equivalent, in addition to certain musical training, is required for entrance and a two-year graduate course offered which leads to the degree of Master of Sacred Music. Outstanding men in various aspects of musical work, drawn from New York's exceptionally rich resources in this field, constitute its faculty. Its association with the theological seminary affords an exceptional opportunity for breeding an intelligent understanding between future clergymen and ministers of music. Theological students are given certain musical courses, and all students in the school of music are required to take at least ten credit hours in theological subjects. Considerable attention is given not only to organ playing and conducting but also to the philosophy of music and its creation. One feature of the year is a spring concert of instrumental and vocal music composed by the students, the chief emphasis being on original choral works.

Instrumental Music

As we have seen in descriptions of choirs of the past century the organ was by no means the only instrument known to the choir loft. In some churches the bass viol was at one time the only one tolerated, as this gave support to the singers, " without interfering with the air." Small orchestras were more common, but that they were not always entirely captivating may be gleaned from such disgruntled remarks as those of William Mason, precentor of York (the situation in America was much like that in England) in 1795:

Psalmody is become not only despicable to persons of a refined musical taste, but is now hardly tolerable to our village practitioners, if they either can, or what does as well, fancy they can sing at sight. For these, since the rage of oratorios has spread from the capital to every market town in the kingdom, can by no means be satisfied unless they introduce chants, services, and anthems into their parish churches, and accompany them with what an old author calls scolding fiddles, squalling hautboys, false-stopped violoncellos, buzzing bassoons, all ill-tuned and worse played upon, in place of an organ, which if they had one, they would probably wish to improve by such instrumental assistance.

Oddly enough Mason adds that he "prefers the cylindrical or barrel organ to one played by hand, as more likely to keep time." The barrel organ was especially popular in towns for accompanying the psalms as sung by the "screaming charity children."

The pipe organ, however, was destined to become the accepted church instrument, though not without sturdy opposition. For as the choir, brought in to aid congregational singing, soon developed its own literature, even at the expense of discouraging the congregation's participation altogether, so the organ, brought in for a similar purpose, was at times felt to be defeating its own end. Robert Druitt in his tract on church music (1848) laments the intrusion of this new enemy, then becoming more common in small towns as well as cities. Writing with a greater fondness for the village choir instruments than that displayed by Mason, he says:

As things stand, we have no hesitation in saying that the organ has contributed as much as anything to the decay of congregational singing; for, in the first place, after the organ has been set up, and the organist appointed with a salary, the parish authorities imagine that all has been done that there is any need for, and never think of engaging a choir, either for love or money; and in the next place, fifteen or twenty stops of the full organ render it a matter of perfect indifference as to how people sing, or whether, in fact, they sing at all. Often and often has the writer been in a church where, with an overpowering organ, not three persons in the whole church opened their mouths. Truly, if a foreigner entered some of our churches he might imagine that, as a great manufacturing community, we employed machinery in the service of God, as well as in other things. They who really love our old English virtues and customs must have frequent occasion to lament the gradual progress of degeneracy in the substitution of these odious machines for the ancient village choir with their simple instruments. Badly enough, perhaps, they sing; time and tune may suffer rude encounters, and shocking may the old blacksmith's bassoon sound in the ears of the squire's daughters, on their return from a London visit, filled with fine ideas of 'pictures, taste, Shakespeare, and the musical glasses.' *But surely these men are made of the right stuff; their hearts are in the work; their occupation gave them a tie to the church which it were unwise to sever; and with patience and encouragement and instruction, they might be made the nucleus of a true congregational choir.*

The Organ's Message

But the organ has, under proper hands, not only developed a technique of leading choir and congregation: it has a message of its own to offer. Dr. William Merrill, pastor of the Brick Church, New York, in describing the daily noon service there, remarks that

Attendants will unite in testifying that one of the most helpful and uplifting features of that service is the organ interlude which immediately follows the prayer, when the organ plays a complete little theme, soft, always melodious and worshipful, planned as carefully as is any other feature of the service, a means of silent communion often richer than the fellowship with God through spoken word of prayer.[9]

He adds that the practice of sitting quietly through the postlude "lends itself to this use of music as an

---

[9] "Music in Worship" — National Bureau for the Advancement of Music, New York.

incentive to meditation, almost a lost art in many Evangelical Churches."

Needless to say, the organ prelude may be an exceedingly important part of the worship service, during which cares and preoccupations of the outer world may be somewhat laid aside or brought consciously into the presence of God. When a thoughtless minister therefore rises at the close of the prelude with the remark, " Let us *begin* our worship by singing hymn Number 246," he is practically serving notice on the organist that the preliminary music doesn't count. On the other hand it is too often a habit of organists to open a service with a serenade or lullaby, or, as one prophet has remarked, " with some fanciful pretty little trifle that has nothing whatever to do with the worship of Almighty God."

But just as a masterful choral work may bring out a wealth of meaning in words not always rendered in the mere reading, so instrumental music, without words, may in sheer tone reveal depths and heights and subtleties which even the singing of words do not always convey.

Orchestral Instruments

The possibilities of stringed instruments and small chamber orchestras in church are far greater than most of us have attempted to realize. We have for the most part left orchestras to the Sunday schools, and here, all too often, the playing has been limited to playing of hymns and marches.

With the increasing development of high school orchestras and choral societies, the question is often asked, " why do not more of these high school musicians become active in church choirs and orchestras? " The answer is that many of them do, but many are not challenged by sufficiently good music in the church organizations to hold their interest. If a boy or girl has developed a taste for solid work in a high school symphony orchestra, it is not surprising if he is not enthusiastic about an opportunity to play musical rubbish, or in the loosely organized, poorly trained style of ensemble often characteristic of the Sunday school. Here again, however, we are dealing with a situation which varies so widely in different communities that hardly any single statement would apply to all cases. As a matter of information, some surveys have been made in various communities to discover the actual proportion of high school orchestra and band players who also play in Sunday school. (See Chapter IX p. 296.) Of these groups herein recorded, we find the highest percentage among players in the Kansas State Contest of 1930, 42 per cent of whom also played in Sunday schools. Flint Senior High School shows 31 per cent, the National Orchestra Contest at Lincoln, Nebraska, 23 per cent, Milwaukee 6 per cent, Yonkers 3 per cent and White Plains, New York, 2 per cent. (See also last note on p. 297 of Chapter IX.)

Brass

Brass instruments, usually too blatant for indoor use, may under certain circumstances be quite thrilling. Perhaps the two most striking and dignified examples are among the Moravians. One case is that of the Bach Festival at Bethlehem, Pennsylvania, in which, as a prelude, the trombone choir plays chorales from the church tower on the Lehigh University campus. The other is the amazing Easter dawn service in the cemetery at Winston-Salem, North Carolina. Here a large band of 300 players, of all ages from childhood to old age, a combination of the bands of the city's eight Moravian churches, gather at an unbelievably early hour under the direction of a man who has led them for half a century, to play chorales. Later, the band divides in four sections which go separately through the streets, playing chorales. Then, at dawn, the sections are stationed at opposite quarters of the cemetery and play chorales antiphonally. Perhaps an ancient psalmist had experienced some equally inspiring ceremony when he wrote, " Praise ye the Lord! Praise him with the sound of the trumpet! "

FUNDAMENTAL NEEDS

The Unified Service

If congregational, choral, and instrumental music are to contribute their utmost to enriching the service of worship, the service itself must have a certain unity, with music, prayer, Scripture, and sermon focusing toward one central idea or experience. Fragments of music, no matter how beautiful in themselves, if sandwiched into the interstices of a haphazard assortment of reading, prayers, exhortation and announcements of the week's events, tend to lose their meaning. It is like having a few finely wrought pieces of furniture in a cluttered and disorderly room. It is essential, therefore, that there should be as thorough an understanding as possible between minister and music director. In some churches these two confer early each week so that music may be chosen appropriate to the theme of sermon and service. Anyone interested in this phase of the problem would do well to read the excellent and brief pamphlet by Rev. William P. Merrill, D.D. previously quoted. ("Music in Worship, and the Relation of Minister and Organist," National Bureau for the Advancement of Music.)

The Educational Task

For the best results, however, it is not only necessary that minister and organist cooperate intelligently, but also that the congregation as a whole develop a sympathetic understanding of all parts of the service. It is usually assumed that church members need training and instruction in prayer, in Bible study, in giving, in personal ethics and in social service. During the course of a year one may hear many sermons on these subjects. But how rarely does one hear of any serious educational efforts being made by the clergy to enhance the meaning of the music of devotion or praise! In many churches this might legitimately be undertaken as a task to be worked out by the music committee. But too often the church music committee conceives its function to be the provision of special equipment or performance rather than the leading of the entire congregation into the fullest possible experience of musical worship. If a music committee would see the greatest progress, it must abandon any conception of church music as a species of entertainment, and undertake its work as one of education in the largest sense. It needs to clarify its ideals, discover the needs and resources, and develop a policy accordingly.

Music in Church Budget

In many cases this may demand a fresh consideration of budget. Church music committees, possibly through no fault of their own, have failed to realize what is involved in the professional preparation of a good organist. The following is a pertinent extract from an open letter " To the Clergy of America " issued by the National Association of Organists:

The organist must possess high intelligence, and, having secured a good general education, must thoroughly master the various subjects which are essential to his work. He must keep abreast of the times by constantly studying the best new music.

As the organist of a church is nearly always the choirmaster, he must have a knowledge of voice training, and a wide acquaintance with vocal literature.

He must not only be in full sympathy with the devotional function of religious music, but must be trained in its use and be familiar with its history.

It is obvious that this work involves as much preparation and equipment as that of a person entering any other profession. The music of the church cannot be adequately rendered by those who have not the requisite qualifications.

In view of these facts the Association asks you to consider whether the organists who are serving your churches receive the recognition and encouragement they deserve.

It is true that relatively few organists meet all of these requirements adequately. Some have a knowledge of music in general rather than of religious music in particular. They may play the organ well, yet add little or nothing to the devotional power of the service. On the other hand the low salaries paid organists in many churches have acted as a strong deterrent in discouraging many of the ablest musicians from concentrating on church music. Again to quote Dr. Merrill:

There are good and sufficient reasons why a church should spend on its music more than on most of the other departments of its life. To be satisfactory, music must be presented by artists who have spent time and money on training, and are dependent on their art for a livelihood. I believe that no money in a church budget is better appropriated, with a view to bringing the souls of the people into the consciousness of God than is the money spent on the music, provided it is spent to secure music that is worshipful in spirit and in truth.

He then concludes a few words of counsel to the organist by saying

Keep up your religious life. Only a man of prayer can play a church organ as it ought to be played. One ought to come to the choir loft as to the pulpit, from the secret place of the Most High.

Music in the Educational and Social Life of the Church

The securing of an able organist or minister of music may, however, be only the first step toward adequately developing the possibilities in a parish. One may survey the various activities of the church, such as mid-week suppers, men's club, young people's society, dramatics, etc., with a view to discovering opportunities for increasing the ministry of tone. Not all the music need be sacred in the usual sense. For in the social life of the church practically all phases of community music may have a place. Group singing and folk-dancing are important. The dance of ritual or pantomime may also be used to good purposes in dramatic presentations. The Church of St. Mark in the Bowery, New York, has for a number of years made this a feature of their Sunday afternoon services. For an excellent discussion of some of the possibilities in this field the reader is referred to the chapters on "The Spiritual Basis" and "Dancing in Church" in Ted Shawn's "American Ballet" (Henry Holt & Company, New York).

Special musical services in which choral and instrumental works are given may be of great value. And apart from the distinctive worship music in the programs and such equally religious music as slow movements from the best string quartets, and the like, there are wide possibilities in programs of music devoted to the study of other nations and cultures, in connection with education for peace and world brotherhood.

The newer talking machines, such as the Electrola, may be valuable if properly used. The Victor and Columbia companies are recording excellent choral works. One large city church has been using this equipment for a series of Wednesday evenings devoted to studying the history and development of church music.

This may be combined with studies of great characters in church history, music of the period being used, e.g., plainsong with a study of St. Francis of Assisi, and chorales with Luther. But the chief value of such a project is to be found in its effect on the singing of the choir and the congregation themselves.

* * * * * *

From much of the rhapsodizing one hears about the power of music, one might be in doubt, as a modern writer has remarked, whether to regard it most satisfactorily as " a police regulation, an educational rule, or a medical prescription." But surely, at its highest music is at least a sacrament, a vehicle through which order, beauty, and strength are brought into life.

Listen to the vast tramping of armies to the throb of drums, watch the faces of children at their May dances, or hear the majestic roll of a great morning hymn, and one knows there is here a solemn mystery, radiant and alive. He who controls the currents of music that play on and through a race of people may effect their destiny far more than he realizes. For he who yields to music develops a texture of soul that is grained by its tone and pattern.

In education for peace, in energizing for work, in liberating man's spirit from the immediate into the infinite, and in uniting worshippers into a spiritual brotherhood music has an endless mission. Pretty triviality has no more place in it than ostentatious virtuosity. Sincerity and directness are as essential to good music as to good preaching or good praying. Dignity without formalism, sympathy without sentimentality, relaxation of spirit without drowsiness, passion and fire — but purified of all vanity or self seeking, richness without luxury, simplicity without barrenness, profundity, not bombast, and often silence — these are to be desired in the music of worship.

One seeks the sun in daylight — yet the greatest suns are visible only at night. And largest thoughts may come not through speech, but in quiet. Let music therefore wash the silence, as the rain the air, that through its night may be clearly seen those points of light by which our planet steers, that in the pause one hears those soundless tones that are the Voice.

CHAPTER XVI

Social Music in Settlements and Community Centers

THERE is scarcely a term regarding musical attitudes or experience that has not been abused out of its original meaning. What shall we call the musical activity at Union Settlement in New York City that is such as to cause the head resident to write as follows about it?

The greatest results have been observed in the changed attitudes of all ages and conditions of those who have come in contact with the activity. . . . This method of social approach through music has helped greatly to break down race and language barriers. . . . We are conscious of a degree of friendliness hitherto not experienced. . . . (The music) has brought a fineness of culture to groups of boys and men as well as of girls and women. It has brought to our whole work a richness and depth which is very apparent.

Recreational it is, but though entirely worthy, that term is not customarily associated with fineness of culture and richness and depth. Is the activity, then, educational? Indeed it is, profoundly and happily so. But as a description of some of it later will show, it has very little relation to ordinary music lessons and other practices often associated with education. Community music it certainly is, but this noble name lost the better part of its meaning during the war. What shall we call it? From the Music Division of the National Federation of Settlements has come the term Social Music; and while it is in their hands, it will very likely continue to mean musical activity that is recreational and educational both, in the best sense of each. The chief danger, of which they are fully aware, is that its social and musical purposes will both be defeated by subordination of the latter to the former. The music's the thing! Without the fresh, unobstructed delight of it all, no social philosophy or procedure — so valuable with it — can save it.

The full intent of this social music which has found its way into an increasingly large number of settlements is most significantly shown in the curriculum and requirements of a new school known as the Training Course, "organized to prepare those who enlist to fill music positions in settlements, and recreation and community centers." It is given under the auspices of the Music Division of the National Federation of Settlements, and as a phase of the work of the New York School of Social Work. Its year's course includes studies in "The Nature and Varieties of Human Behavior," "The Family," "Methods of Community Organization," "The Administration of Social Agencies," and "The Application of Psychology to the Teaching of Music," as well as studies and practice in all phases of musical endeavor in settlements, community centers and music schools. Matriculated students must have attained a baccalaureate degree from a college of recognized standard or a minimum of two years of college work plus enough experience or training in other fields to make up for the lack in regular college work, and they must have received advanced musical training in schools or under teachers of recognized standing and have had at least one year of experience in teaching and dealing with groups. Only seventeen students are enrolled in this training course in its second year (1930–31), the same number as in its first year, but anyone who knows how much higher its standards are than those now prevailing in its field, and how low the remuneration now usually is for work in that field, must regard seventeen as a gratifying and promising number.

Settlements, being concerned with all phases of social welfare in the poorest neighborhoods of cities, customarily reach deeper levels of life than are sought in the usual sort of community centers, social centers or recreation centers. But in all such centers and in settlements there is the wish to provide opportunity for the people to find in their neighborhood such ways of leisure time life as are lastingly satisfying and delightful. Therefore almost all that may be said about music in one sort of them may be applied to every sort, and we may regard all of them, settlements included, as community centers.

What Is Done in Community Centers?

To determine the place of music in any institution, one must know what other interests are carried out in it. Here is a brief composite list of the kinds of activities other than musical ones that are to be found in a survey of community centers:

> Lectures and forums
> Small discussion groups
> Plays and pantomimes
> Festivals
> Story-telling
> Dancing of all kinds
> Physical games of all kinds
> Quiet games
> Tournaments
> Meetings of many kinds of clubs
> Handcrafts of all kinds
> Shop work
> Classes in painting, modeling, etc.
> Motion pictures

What Place Has Music in This Company?

At eight o'clock every Monday evening in one of the community centers of a large mid-western city a community sing was offered. The elective and volunteer council of citizens in charge of the center felt responsibility in making this endeavor successful. They wanted their center to have music as well as many other things, and some of them could be seen at almost every sing. One of them acted as press agent and they all felt urged to attract people in any way they could to these Monday evening gatherings. But after eight weeks of such effort, the Council voted emphatically to drop community singing. The number participating in it, only about forty in the beginning, had dwindled to eight or ten.

Now a tonic of good, lastingly palatable food for singing and some for listening, an interest in dramatizing some of the witty old ballads, the stimulus of a project such as singing between the acts of a play, or some other vitalizing influences might have made this musical patient flourish very happily. But there were many other opportunities for community singing in that community center that might have had a tonic effect.

A visitor going through the building one evening found young men in a gymnasium class marching around in silence with orderly, vigorous step, but without the liberating buoyancy and swing of movement that marching should have. A good brass band would have helped enormously if the place were larger, and almost as helpful would have been the piano if it were well played and if it were in tune. But a good hiking song sung by the boys themselves would have been best of all.

In the auditorium on the same evening a group of women, some of them middle-aged, were engaged in what was evidently one of the last rehearsals of a sort of burlesque show. The leader, locally famous for his radio " jazz patters," was playing " That's My Weakness Now " and shouting directions to the women, who were wriggling or strutting around the stage or in a row in the front of it and yowling the chorus. A pathetic sight it was, without laughter; apparently a desperate but vain effort to be gay. One thought of the really gay singing and dancing they might be having, and thought of other deeper and romantical things about womanhood; and he very soon turned away from that show.

In a classroom near by a small group were rehearsing Barrie's "The Old Lady Shows Her Medals," a delightful antidote to what the auditorium was forced to hold. This and two other short plays were later to be given to the folk of the center. There was to be music between the plays, which was to be provided by the jazz patter man! But why not have a group of men sing the Scottish *Bonnie Dundee* or *The Hundred Pipers*, before or after that Barrie play, and have them followed by a chorus of women in another good Scottish or an English folk song, and then the men and women together in such a song as *Ay Waukin, O,* or *The Blue Bells of Scotland?* This singing might be all the more intertwined in the thread of the Barrie tale if it were behind the scenes. Why struggle to attract people to community singing on Monday evenings and then have "jazz patters" when the people *are* attracted to a play that, like many other plays, can be very happily wedded to music that is appropriate both to itself and to the community singers or players? The whole audience might well have sung *Annie Laurie* or the like.

There were several other activities scheduled for that evening in the center. A mothers' club had a sewing bee which was also very much of a talking bee and might have included some informal singing. Lacking someone to start a song and help to keep it going, a good phonograph sparingly used might very well have done the trick with only the help of one of the mothers to start it off. Here is a list of songs that have been recorded for the very purpose of persuading and otherwise helping people of all ages to sing them:

Victor
Records

1. Spring Song (Chopin) 2. Spring's Messenger (Schumann) 3. Autumn (Franz) 4. Greeting (Mendelssohn)   20343
1. Morning Song (Grieg) 2. The Rose (Franz) 3. The Jolly Miller (Schubert) 4. The Brooklet (Schubert)   20343

1. Lavender's Blue (English) 2. I Had a Little Nut Tree (English) 3. Golden Slumbers (English) 4. Sweet Nightingale (English) 5. The Spanish Gypsy (Spanish)   20986
1. Going Through Lorraine (French) 2. Praise to the Father (Dutch) 3. La Cachucha (Spanish) 4. Bosnian Shepherd Song (Bosnia)   20986

1. Lullaby (Cradle Song) (arr. Brahms) 2. Little Dustman (Brahms)   20737
1. Hey Baloo (Schumann) 2. The Linden Tree (Schubert)   20737

1. Away for Rio (Sailor's Chantey) 2. Blow the Man Down (Sailor's Chantey) 3. Sourwood Mountain (Kentucky Folk) 4. Billy Boy (Old English) 5. Be Gone, Dull Care (Old English)   21751
1. Sweet Kitty Clover (Knight-Kean) 2. Bendemeer's Stream (Moore) (Old Tune) 3. Frog Went a-Courting (Kentucky Folk) 4. Spanish Guitar (College Song)   21751

1. Flow Gently Sweet Afton (Burns-Spilman) 2. Sally in Our Alley (Old English) 3. Ye Banks and Braes of Bonnie Doon (Burns) (Old Scotch)   4083
1. John Peel (Border Song) 2. Scots Wha' Hae (Old Scotch) 3. Jock O'Hazeldean (Old Scotch) . . .   4083

Home, Sweet Home (Payne-Bishop)   21949
Sweet and Low (Tennyson-Barnby)   21949

Old Folks at Home (Foster)   21950
Dixie (Emmett)   21950

Drink to Me Only With Thine Eyes (Old English) .   22081
Believe Me, If All Those Endearing Young Charms (Old Irish)   22081

1. All Through the Night (Old Welsh) 2. Love's Old
Sweet Song (Molloy)   22082
1. Annie Laurie (Old Scotch) 2. Auld Lang Syne (Old
Scotch)   22082

A Plowing Song — Dreaming — The Keeper (English)
— Kye Song of St. Bride (Clokey) — Music in
the Air (Root)   22455

Alleluia (German) — Tiritomba (Italian) — Morning
Comes Early (Slovakian) — A Song of Seasons
(Hungarian)   22457

Song of the Volga Boatmen — Going Through Lorraine
— Andulko (Slovakian) — Rada Song (Slovakian)   22456

Any of those songs is likely to set people humming
if not singing it, and it is very likely to remain in the
memory for many a day, a very enjoyable accompaniment not only to sewing but also to other chores of
housekeeping at home. Having the words of the song
or songs on the blackboard will add to the urge to sing,
and a mimeographed copy of them for each mother
would be likely to find its way to her home, there to
do likewise, perhaps for her family as well as for herself.

It would be very foolish to try to introduce music
into every activity or meeting. That is not the intention. There were quiet games of cards and checkers in
that center, and saws, hammers and planes kept ears
and minds full in the shop. But it is equally foolish
to neglect or misuse opportunities to bring music into
what are natural settings for it.

In many community centers a special community
night is held once a month or every two months, in
some, once a week, when the whole evening is given
to some kind or kinds of activity or exhibition which
everyone at the center can participate in or observe.
Music almost always has some part in such a program,
and sometimes occupies all of it. Harvest, Christmas,
spring, and folk festivals and other celebrations also

offer fortunate opportunities for singing and playing. Some of the many uses of music in summer camps, described in Chapter XIX, may be made happily suited to community centers.

At this point it should be emphatically repeated that musical groups from the public and private schools and music schools of the neighborhood should now and then be given opportunity to take part in community center affairs. The importance of this was shown in Chapter IX. Such a relationship to the schools is especially suited to the many community centers that are in school buildings.

Special Musical Activities

Every sort of singing, playing, or listening group mentioned in the composite plans given in Chapter III is suitable to a community center. And the acting out of songs and the dancing suggested in that chapter are also suitable. We need now only to describe a few of the examples found in our survey, and to add a few suggestions.

Singing

One of the most pleasant memories of a two-year itinerancy throughout the country is of a group of 35 boys, girls, and young grown-ups in Howell Neighborhood House, Chicago, singing Bach chorales and other lovely substantial music in parts with rare expressiveness and delight. The youngest one was a lass of six and the oldest a man of about twenty-five, with all ages between, and together they constituted the choir for Sunday chapel services at this Presbyterian Neighborhood House in a poor neighborhood. They were also a chorus for some week-day evenings when parents and children gathered for dancing and playing or other activities as well as for singing. After the chorus on a certain Friday evening in April came a group of six Croatian mothers dancing as gaily as the colors on their native costumes. They were followed by three Croatian boys, brothers, playing spirited folk dance music on a tiny, a somewhat larger, and a very large tambouritza, the smallest boy playing the largest instrument, which properly should be played standing, but which he plucked as it lay with its neck across his lap.

A striking thing about that choir, aside from its lovely singing and eagerness, was the social ideal that it embodied. The older singers with their greater powers of voice and mind must have had to be patient while the youngest ones learned their parts, and then they had to sing in such a way as to make the most of the little ones' efforts, while the latter had to bear their welcome responsibility bravely and well. Mutual responsibility and mutual respect glorified by the music — a perfect society it was. Many a church boy choir might be similarly characterized, but the informality and general spirit of the community center had much to do with the peculiarly blessed qualities of the Howell Neighborhood House group.

The musician, Miss Martha M. Cruikshank, who formed and developed that group was also the leader in the very important experiment in Union Settlement, New York City, referred to in the beginning of this chapter. Her report in the magazine " Neighborhood," for July 1929,[1] is well worth quoting at length:

An Experiment in Fostering Social Music
By
Martha M. Cruikshank

Since in recent years, the use of music in the program of the Settlement has to some been increasingly evident, The Music Division of the National Federation of Settlements determined to conduct an experiment to discover, if possible, the value of music in the program of the Settlement and as a social force

[1] Quoted with the kind permission of the editor.

in the neighborhood. Two questions were asked of the experiment: First — Can a department of social music be a means of serving the work of other departments in a Settlement; and second — Is music a sufficiently vital social force to warrant the establishment by other Settlements of social music departments with full time directors?

Following is a brief survey of the procedure and the findings of this project which was developed at Union Settlement, New York City.

Equipment

Upon being assigned to this work in the fall of 1927, the first problem was that of the location and equipment of the social music room.

With a view to making the social music room a place easily available to all the various clubs and classes meeting in the Settlement, a room was chosen on the corridor, situated just off the lobby through which the members of all the clubs and classes have to pass. The room was made as attractive as possible with a grand piano, a gift of the Woman's Auxiliary of the Union Settlement Board, gaily colored benches constructed under the direction of the boys' worker by one of the boys' clubs, an Orthophonic Victrola, and some colored prints and curtains at the windows.

. . . Sometimes the feeling of the headworker or the board of a settlement is that if the music group is established, and proves worth while, some money may then be expended for making attractive its permanent surroundings; but it needs to be borne in mind that it is just at the beginning before there can be much that is beautiful in the work done by the group, that the building up of an esprit de corps is greatly aided by having an orderly and beautiful meeting place and good equipment.

. . . the music director, deprived of a room set aside for the particular work of her department, loses the opportunity of getting together certain groups that can be of the greatest help to the social music department. . . . It has not been an uncommon thing for the adult members of a nutrition class to drop in to sing with their own children; or for a club of Italian girls to join with a club of Jewish girls in preparation for a Festival program.

Organization

. . . the children enrolled in the Music Department were those who had made music their choice of one of the three activities allowed each member. Of these children, there were formed the following groups meeting weekly: one pre-school group, two groups of junior girls, two of junior boys, one of intermediate girls, two of intermediate boys, totaling 112 children; 74, or 66%, of which number carried over into the second year's registration.

During the two years these groups had to be several times rescheduled to meet the requirements of the projects of the other departments. So keen was the interest of the children, however, that at the end of four months they presented a program in conjunction with the dancing classes in which were sung folk songs of the various nationalities, selections from simple operettas, and a Bach chorale. During the two years the various singing groups have taken part in the productions of one Thanksgiving Play, presented with music and dancing, two Christmas programs, the Pageants " The Pied Piper of Hamelin " and " Hansel and Gretel."

Fully as important as work with the children's clubs were the weekly and bi-weekly meetings of the English classes (for adults). There has been informal singing in the Music Room for sixty mothers, and weekly and bi-monthly meetings of mothers' clubs in which music and folk dancing have been a regular part of the programs. Further opportunity for this type of expression was offered by the monthly community nights.

During the summer months community nights were held out-of-doors every week, and a small string orchestra, under volunteer leadership, presented programs, and accompanied the community singing which on each occasion formed a major part of the evening's entertainment.

It is generally conceded that the boys of the 'teen age are not so interested in music as the girls. However, if the right type of music is presented in the right way, they respond equally well, as is evidenced by the fact that there have been four successful boys' groups meeting weekly for music. . . . there was a group of ten boys who composed a typical East Side gang the members of which became so interested in Schubert that at the end of a year they presented a program portraying the life of the composer through a play written by the group, illustrated with Schubert songs of which they had a repertoire of eighteen, and closing with what must be confessed was a startlingly original analysis of the B Minor Symphony.

To prove that boys not only want music, but good music,

another case in point is that of " Nickie's Gang," reckoned the toughest of the younger gangs of 104th Street. The boys came into the Settlement with a request to be taught some sea songs for a " sailor's minstrel." After about six meetings of practicing the sea songs, one, " Jo-Jo," suddenly asked: "Miss Cruikshank, please sing something soft." With another year's leadership this group will be able to present a program as musical as that presented by the Schubert club.

Music in the Neighborhood

Since the work was instituted in a community strange to the Director, the work of the first year was largely confined to getting acquainted with the musical possibilities of the neighborhood through the Settlement. Thus the first year's work was largely an attempt to answer the question asked of the experiment: Can a music department be a means of serving other departments? By the second year, it became apparent that if music was to be a social force in the neighborhood, we must first discover what material the neighborhood itself had to offer — and on that rebuild the music program of the settlement. The fall of the year was accordingly devoted to making contacts with neighborhood groups, and at Christmas six national groups presented Christmas eve scenes with Christmas carols from their own country and in their own language.

After Christmas there was formed a Neighborhood Social Music Committee, which sponsored a series of five national programs, an International program and an International ball. Great care was exercised that the personnel of this committee should represent each national group with members on an equal footing with each other.

In preparing and presenting these programs, the Committee not only developed a line of activity highly useful to the Settlement, but unconsciously demonstrated what one of the worthy by-products of social music may be. The very fact that Soviet and Nationalist groups among the Russians and Polish and Jewish peoples could work together selling tickets for each other's programs is in itself a significant item in the social development of a neighborhood.

Among other interesting results of the Music Department's work in Union Settlement are to be noted that the Jewish neighbors have made increased use of the auditorium as have also the Ukrainians; the Russians have organized a balalaika orchestra for their own children; sixty Polish children have been

organized into a folk-dancing society on the initiative of the
Polish members of the committee, which in turn resulted in
the organization for the first time of the Polish parents of the
neighborhood. Finally, of their own initiative, the Neighborhood Social Music Committee has requested a series of talks
on American history, and a program of American and English
songs to be presented in the fall.

Not only were the existing national groups in the neighborhood sought out and utilized in the program, but an effort was
also made wherever possible to utilize the musical material
available. A collection of 120 folk songs and dances was made,
and in the development of the project these songs will be para-
phrased and orchestrated with a view to their being brought
back into the settlement to be a part of the common musical
library for all the different groups.[2]

This kind of twofold program contributes to the double need
of the members of the settlement. Bringing in these songs and
dances gives them an opportunity for self-expression hardly
equalled elsewhere in their humdrum daily economic struggles.
But sharing these old world treasures and learning to know
and appreciate those which their neighbors of a different racial
background have also contributed, is an exercise on which the
bones and sinews of a social nature are strengthened. In what
more socially valuable project could a settlement engage than
one in which the members of different races and creeds can
unite in a common love of a beautiful thing.

*   *   *   *   *   *

To one on the outside, or to one first entering such a work
as this, the strong appeal of the task tends to hide its inherent
difficulties. The challenge of the opportunity to serve neighborhood people in an enduring way tends to conceal the fact that
there is a long severe discipline necessary to the fulfillment. To
retain one's interest in things of the highest artistic merit, and
at the same time keep alive one's appreciation for humbler
contributions; to rigorously maintain one's standards and at
the same time to be constantly on the qui vive of the expectation of finding talent and appreciation of the highest type
among the (musically lowliest) people of the neighborhood; to
be ruthless with one's self and tender and understanding of the

[2] These songs and dances were collected by Miss Cruikshank from the
children and adults of the neighborhood, who sang or played them for her.

humble efforts of others; these will always be the supreme tasks of a Director of Social Music.

Music for Boys

Miss Cruikshank's work has been done in settlements amid some conditions and challenging purposes of social welfare that are seldom operative in the usual sort of community center. But it is nevertheless exemplary of what might be done in many such centers. Further encouragement for musical endeavors with boys may be found in the great success of boys' glee clubs in an increasing number of schools. For instance, in Minneapolis there are junior high school boys' glee clubs that meet voluntarily three times a week during club periods when there are meetings of many other kinds of clubs that any boy might enter. The principal of a school in which there are 70 boys in a glee club said that there could be three more such clubs if there were teachers enough. Those 70 boys sing four-part music admirably and are able to read such music at sight with remarkable skill. This ability to play the game well is, of course, an important factor, but the process of acquiring ability, if carried on effectively, without waste of time or effort, is also interesting. In Seattle there is an extracurricular Junior High School Glee Club of 90 boys who come regularly at 7:45 A.M. for their rehearsals.

A very remarkable example of the potential effectiveness of music among boys is the singing in the Cook County Juvenile Detention Home in Chicago. Though the psychological conditions are necessarily very different from those in a community center, the musical conditions throw further light on possibilities in such a center. The boys, in their teens, are apparently as tough as can be, but they learn to sing first-class folk songs with admirable refinement, and seek the privilege. They are led by a woman whose fine presence is itself a challenge to be a gentleman. When she speaks or sings to them, very well and with all the courtesy and respect and yet ease of manner that mark a fine lady anywhere, it would be hard for them not to listen. Moreover, they have to listen in order to learn the words and then the tune, for there are no books or song sheets. Especially helpful in learning the words was the leader's speaking them in rhythm while the accompanist played the song. A sparkling Mexican song and the Volga Boatmen's Song, both sung in unison, were most effective. It is very important to let the choice of songs and the keys in which they are to be performed depend on the range of the boys' voices. The Volga Boatmen's Song, for instance, is only an octave in range and should be in the key of E or F for the basses and A for tenor boys. The best key for all to sing it at the same time would probably be G, for boys of that age.

* * * * * *

Choral Groups

In the Y.W.C.A. in Washington, D. C., there has been a Madrigal Club of 18 men and women whose weekly rehearsal from 8 to 9 o'clock is always followed by a social hour. In respect to the social hour, this is similar to the large Cincinnati chorus of young men and women which is described on page 136 of this book, and which is also exemplary of what might be done in a community center. During Music Week in San Francisco last year three leaders of working girls' choruses in different centers combined them in a single concert. In Baltimore fourteen women's clubs with about 600 members, and ten girls' clubs with a membership of about 200, all of them community center groups, came together at the recreation pier for a song contest in which each club presented a song and tableau and was judged for its singing.

A festival combining the community center choral groups of a city, or a quota from each group, could be a fine, stimulating project; all the better if it could combine orchestral groups in the same way for the same event. In the Washington Y.W.C.A., a glee club was formed of a quota from each of several clubs meeting in the building. This suggests the possibility of an all-community center chorus similarly formed.

An all-city or an all-neighborhood choir of boys alone, girls alone, or one of boys and girls together, formed of the most faithful and capable singers, could be most easily attained in the schools — and this has been done in a number of cities. If adequate leadership and cooperation with the school music teachers could be gained for it, having it outside of the schools would be even more likely to integrate it in the life of the community and in the real, lasting life of the boy or girl, especially if it could grow genuinely out of the entirely self-propulsive living in one or more community centers. An excellent example of such a choir is that of the Chicago Civic Music Association, described in the next chapter.

Such a choir might be formed only for special occasions, including visits to the city by very distinguished persons. It might have only three or four rehearsals before each occasion, using worthy music made familiar, perhaps, in the schools. It might be led by the school music supervisor. A select choir of unchanged voices — boys or girls of 11 to about 14 years of age — would be the easiest to gather and train, but a choir including also good tenor and bass voices of boys would have even greater social and personal value.

*   *   *   *   *   *

Playing

From the toy orchestra or rhythm band to the symphony orchestra there is no kind of instrumental group that cannot be found in some community center or settlement. Most of what has been said in this chapter about possible relationships between singing and other activities, and all that has been said about relationships between the schools and the community centers may be applied to playing.

The municipal and school centers of Long Beach, California, shelter two boys' bands, several harmonica bands enlisting together about 500 children, ukulele groups of a similar number, a band of 40 old troupers — all of them veterans of professional circus or troupers' bands — , a Civic Orchestra of men and women, and a Woman's Symphony Orchestra of 50, all sponsored and supported by the Playground and Recreation Commission of the city, which does likewise for two large choruses and for weekly community sings at which there is always a brief concert also. A recent program given jointly by the Long Beach Civic Chorus and the Woman's Symphony Orchestra is not only impressive for its content — Handel's " Messiah " — and for its list of eight instead of four soloists, three of whom are members of the chorus, but it is also enlightening as to one potent cause of the large extent and success of community music in Long Beach, for the following notice appears on the program:

Clyde Doyle, President of the Playground and Recreation Commission, will present Mayor Asa Fickling, who will speak on Community Music.

*   *   *   *   *   *

The social centers of Milwaukee have an unsurpassed example of community playing by orchestras to which any player is admissible without try-out. The meaning of these orchestras cannot be better stated than it was in an editorial by Mr. Richard S. Davis for a June 1930 issue of the Milwaukee *Journal*.

Herewith is ammunition that seems to the writer to be the best possible corrective for the musically despondent. It has to do with the work done by the extension department of the Milwaukee public schools, a work begun this last season in the various social centers of the city.

The other night a program was given in the Lapham Park social center by the orchestras of the Grant Street, Dover Street, Clarke Street, Third Street and Fourth Street centers and the glee club of the Thirty-seventh Street center. The smallest orchestra had 17 members, the biggest 35. In all 129 instrumental musicians were assembled and the united glee club had 145 singers.

Now the writer was not there to hear the program, but a far more competent witness and listener has come in to tell all about it. She has reported, this witness, that the evening was one of the most encouraging experiences of her musical life, which has been eager and active. She has told of the radiance of the players and singers as they paid their devoted respects to Bizet, Weber and Mozart. She has made a picture of it, a picture revealing the expansion of souls, not less than that.

At least one man has been convinced that no better work for music is being done in the town. The people making up the orchestras, you understand, are not the people who go to all the concerts and idly listen to expensive music. They cannot afford it. Most of them can afford very little in the way of entertainment. But they have the spirit and the devotion to make music of their own, now that the opportunity is provided.

Many nationalities are represented in the various social center groups and the ages range from lively youth to grave maturity. In one orchestra there are four members of one family doing noble service to winds and strings. In another a father plays the cornet, while his daughter manages the cello. In still another a father is one of the leading fiddlers, while his son concentrates on the bassoon.

The glee club is made up largely of women who are getting along in years. They are women who know all the intricacies of keeping house from mop to masher and back again. But they want to sing and sing they will. They have divided into groups that meet once a week in one home or another, for the sole purpose of keeping in vocal trim. If that is not genuine, you are asked what is.

Each one of the orchestras and the glee club has a competent director. For each there is training. And for each, undoubtedly, there is the immense satisfaction of steady progress in musical ability and musical appreciation.

Much is said about "good music" and the tone of the talk is frequently so unctuous that independent folk are driven into scoffing. But to the musicians who gather to play in the social centers good music is good music, with no slightest trace of buncombe about it.

All of which is most refreshing.

Of course, the possibility of having an all-city community center orchestra for a special occasion is no less attractive than an all-city chorus.

* * * * * *

Chamber Music

The small group needing, if anything, only coaching now and then is especially well suited to community centers. In every city there are lone players who would like to find one another at such a place and play together for the love of it, especially if some coaching (the coach usually playing a part himself) and a supply of music suited to their abilities were available. Once gathered, they would willingly together purchase more music and even, perhaps, contribute to the cost of the coaching. But there have been good volunteer coaches, and some public libraries have suitable music for free circulation. A chamber music society in which groups perform for one another and sometimes together, and have time also for sociability, can be a rich source of pleasure and more.

Listening

Informal Music Hours have been very successfully held on Sundays at five o'clock in the Washington (D. C.) Y.W.C.A. Each series of hours has been enriched in meaning through being unified by a single subject. For instance, in October the series was confined to " Native Music," in November to " What Men

Live By — Work, Play, Love, and Worship," and in December to Christmas carols. At each concert the music secretary introduced the artist of the afternoon, who gave a brief explanatory talk about each composition or section of the program. The attendance increased from 18 for the first concert to 125 for the concerts of the third month.

Such informal periods of listening offer opportunity for all kinds of worthy groups of amateur singers and players to have the incentive and satisfaction of giving a concert; and in these days there is many a soloist amateur or a budding professional accomplished enough to give pleasure to everyone concerned.

In some centers notices of concerts anywhere in the city are posted, and tickets distributed for those that are free or for which some free seats are available. The Community Center Department of Washington, D. C., directs a Community Institute which brings to the city a series of excellent concerts, lectures, and other events, two each month from November to March, that cost the subscriber only 30 cents each.

Two Further Suggestions

That "nothing succeeds like success" is especially true of musical endeavors. In every field of music, among amateurs as among professionals, there may be found groups whose achievements and resulting prestige have been a great stimulus to other groups and individuals. There are millions of people engaging in singing and playing, and having a fairly good time at it, but one has only to hear a group like the Czechoslovakian children led by Bakule, who were in this country a few years ago, to realize how much more vital and joyous a thing music can be than it is as it comes from most choruses, orchestras and the like. If the community center officials could find anywhere in the city a person who would be likely to induce children or grown-ups to sing or play in this vital way, let them engage him even if only for one group. For those who hear this group will say, "Why can't we sing (or play) like that?" or "Why can't our community center have music like that?" and half the battle will be already won.

The other suggestion is that there be effort to interest and develop promising individuals to be leaders of their groups, insofar as this can be done without impairing the progress or delight of the groups. "Institutes" in music-leading followed by actual leading under gradually lessening guidance by the instructor is the usual method.

Shall Music Instruction Be Given?

A rehearsal of any sort of musical group should, of course, itself be instructive, but many an individual in such a group realizes in a short time that his enjoyment would be increased if he could have special lessons in "voice" (as it is called) or in playing some instrument. Moreover, it is likely that there are persons in the neighborhood who are not in any musical group who would welcome opportunity to have such lessons inexpensively. In many community centers and the like, free instruction is given in playing the harmonica or the ukulele, and in handcrafts of various kinds. There seems to be no fundamental reason why instruction in any sort of musical expression or craftsmanship should not be offered, especially since class lessons in voice or an instrument have become an accepted means even by some of the best teachers. The only admissible objection is that good instruction at sufficiently low cost is already available for all who might wish it, in the day schools, evening schools, music schools or private teachers' studios; and even that objection might be denied if the general life and activities at the community center were such as to make music study there more truly educative and delightful than it might be elsewhere. It is a question first of all of the quality of experience, musical and personal, that can be given. As Mr. Bruno Lasker has said in an article in the *Survey,* " where means are very small, it may be wiser to have good singing . . . under a competent leader, and good victrola records for social dancing, than to have teachers of mediocre ability teach more youngsters to pound out sickly *pièces de salon* on pianos so poor that they could not be traded in by their erstwhile suburban owners."

As has been shown in Chapter XI, many settlements have provided music instruction, and there are very important matters to be considered with regard to it. Since the summer time offers the most common and persistent challenge to all agencies having to do with children, the summer music schools described in Chapter XII should commend themselves with special force as possible ways of service by such agencies.

CHAPTER XVII

Playground Music

REPORTS from 766 cities in 1930 gave a total of 7,677 outdoor playgrounds conducted under leadership. Nearly 25,000 men and women were employed as recreation leaders, most of them on the playgrounds. The largest proportion of the average daily summer attendance of 3,722,358 was by children from 7 to 14 years of age. Naturally, games and sports are the principal activities on playgrounds, but there is among recreation leaders everywhere an increasing interest in cultivating in simple ways the arts, notably dramatics, handcrafts, and music. "How can music be used as a mode of play?" is the question.

The usual sort of community centers are primarily for adults, with often some special provision for children. Playgrounds have precisely the opposite relation to the people of a neighborhood. But in other respects most of what has been said about music in settlements and community centers, and much of what will be said in another chapter about music in summer camps, may be applied to playground music. This is especially true for those playgrounds, about ten per cent of the total number, on which there are buildings containing one or more rooms for recreational activities. The main purpose of this whole book is to answer the question, "How can music be used as a mode of play?" — play in the fullest sense. But there are some distinctive considerations and examples to be drawn from conditions and musical activities on playgrounds; and some to be drawn therefrom that are in turn applicable to settlements, community centers and summer camps.

Playing with Music

By play we mean what anyone does when he is following freely a whole-hearted desire of his own, without thought of the reward of what he is doing, or the virtue of it, or the social value of it, or anything else of it except the doing of it. How do children play with music or, rather, in music? How do they get eagerly into it as they get into playing volley ball or into making a promising model aeroplane?

Our first thought in answer to this question is likely to be of singing games — " Looby Loo," " Roman soldiers " and the like — best for children under ten; and of folk dances like the Swedish clap dance and carrousel for the younger children, and the Irish Washerwoman, Kamariskaia, and the English country dances for the older ones. Rhythmic motion is what we think of first, perhaps, as suited to playgrounds. For the true response to rhythm is a response of the whole organism. The whole personality is enlisted. Conversely, when feeling takes complete hold of us — joy, but even sorrow or rage — we tend strongly to act or speak rhythmically. Who has not seen children come bounding out of school and go skipping down the street, or heard them singing as they skip, with that apparently universal though unwritten tune of children's joy, " We're going to the playground! " or whatever else they are going to, or going to do?

This mood of most eager living is surely a boon surpassed by no other; and music can bring it to us, especially to children, even when that mood has been far away. But the rhythmic motion must be free and spontaneous for the magic to be performed. Even better for it than singing-games or folk-dancing, though these are excellent and almost indispensable, is the free skipping, galloping, marching, swaying, running, or whatever else the music calls for, that is the very essence of the English " Come, Lasses and Lads," the Schumann " Reiterstuck" in his " Album for the Young," the Schubert " Moment Musical " in F minor, and no end of other good music. The reader is urged to review what was said of this sort of dancing on pages 94–98. All that is needed to begin with is suitable music played on a piano or a violin or flute or on a phonograph, and even singing may be amply effective for it. A simple drum accompaniment to the singing would insure its effectiveness. Our Indians give ample proof of that.

Singing is, of course, another mode of music-play, and so are playing, whistling, acting out music, and listening. The most magical of all effects of music in this regard is in its power to set us dancing as merrily or grandly as can be, even when we are sitting perfectly still — or seeming to do so, for there is no telling what is going on inside of us. Whatever kind of music-play we choose, the freer and the more musically effective it is, the more's the satisfaction; and that means free, expressive voices or, for an instrument, free and skillful fingers, arms or tongue, and, of course, a free, alert mind.

Playing with music, in our sense, does not mean being careless and foolish about it. The word is frequently used as though it were the opposite of taking a thing seriously — and that use makes " seriously " a solemn word, which it need not be at all — but the definition of play that we have given fits every beloved performance of music from singing in a Bach festival or playing in a symphony to the child's crooning himself to sleep. It becomes play when it *is* beloved, when it comes of inner desire, of that urge of life that makes an unspoiled child the wonderfully expansive and creative creature he is at his best. The playground music leader's main job and privilege is, then, to provide a total environment, the music and himself included, that will arouse that urge for expression and nourish it on the most suitable best; for that way lies the most fun and deeper satisfactions. Now let us not be solemn or dogmatic about it. There are times when "a little nonsense . . . is relished by the best of men." But let us remember, with Emerson, that "Art is the record of 'good days,'" and give children as many a taste as we can of what is meant by "good days."

Now it would be fine to present actual demonstrations of what is meant by the foregoing. This being impossible in a book, we shall describe a variety of demonstrations, not all of them as good as they might be, commencing with the entire program of playground musical activities in each of two cities.

Music on Salt Lake City's Playgrounds

Imagine a city's twenty best story-tellers distributed about on a park meadow and in among neighboring trees at sunset-time, each telling a certain kind of tales unlike all the others, and each appropriately distinguished by his or her costume and by a handsome, illustrated poster that betokens the kind of stories to be told at that spot. Irish stories, says one; Oriental, another; Mother Goose, Japanese, Negro, Indian, Scandinavian, Russian, German, Fairy Tales, Nonsense, Persian, Gypsy, Patriotic, Believe It Or Not, King Arthur, Chinese, Pioneer, Frontier, "Our Gang" — all these seen in a few minutes' walk. The annual Midsummer-eve story-telling festival it was, which, ending for children just before night-fall, was later resumed for adults, this time by the light of fusees purchased from the railroad company, each one burning for about eight minutes.

This was not a musical activity, but we are reporting it as one because it is the very stuff of which not only dreams but also music is made. With the possible exceptions of "Believe It Or Not" and "Our Gang," each kind of stories is related to songs, one or two of which might have been sung by one or more persons capable of singing them well at the beginning or close of the period or between stories, to add still more to the atmosphere and delight of the occasion. Small groups of children from the various playgrounds of the city might each have gladly prepared to sing in whatever country or subject gave them the happiest prospect. Of course, the singing would have to be so good and so true to the spirit of the occasion and subject as to blend happily in the spell of the stories, meadow, trees and sky. The singers would have to forget themselves and be forgotten, and thus enjoy the music all the more. Simple costumes would help. A ballad or other simple story-telling or picture-giving song might have been sung and acted out as one story for each of the Western nationalities, including our own Negroes, Indians, and Cowboys, and also for Mother Goose, Fairy Tales and Nonsense stories. One or more costumed and singing, playing, or dancing natives of the country represented in the story-telling, and represented also in the population of the city, might have given still greater reality to the occasion. Of course, in this festival the story's the thing, and music would be suitable only insofar as it made the telling still more delightful and gripping, and did not take too much time.

Fortunate Circumstances

Nibley Park in Salt Lake City has a lake, at an end of which there is a small island very near the shore. On this island there is an outdoor stage that is connected to the shore, for actors and orchestra, by a simple, low bridge. Twenty-five hundred seats on the shore complete the conversion of a gift of nature into a very good theatre. Here for six nights every summer a light opera is given under the direction of the Recreation Department by a chorus, cast and orchestra who, with the exception of a few of the orchestra players, are all amateurs. Here the "Pirates of Penzance," the "Gondoliers," the "Chocolate Soldier," "Robin Hood" and Victor Herbert's "Fortune Teller" have brought as many people as could see the stage — two thousand each night finding free seats, five hundred paying 25 or 50 cents for a seat, and others standing. And it is here, with these happy associations added to the lure of the lovely out-of-doors, that the best playground groups also perform at different times in connection with the weekly Friday evening art programs given from mid-June through August.

The printed programs of one summer name three small orchestras, each from a different playground, a number of high school students in vocal solos, a harmonica band and solos, A Boy Scouts' Chorus and a Boy Scouts' Band, an operetta given by playground children, and various groups of dancers. Among the other items on the programs is Shakespeare's "Twelfth Night" given in abbreviated form by a playground dramatic group. This is especially important for us, though not musical, because of its relation to the schools. Junior high school boys and girls are organized and trained in the spring, with assistance from the director of recreation, to give a play in the summer. Why could there not be similar provision for summertime singing and playing by groups of children expecting to remain in the city during at least a certain part of that season? The very good and extensive musical work done in the schools of an increasing number of cities makes this a very pertinent question, especially in those cities. We shall refer to it still more practically later in this chapter.

On each playground in Salt Lake City there is a piano and a phonograph, one or the other of which aids valiantly in general singing, singing games, rhythm bands, in music appreciation meetings now and then, and in the preparation and performance of simple operettas. The three playground orchestras play for operettas on other playgrounds of the city as well as on their own. These orchestras and all other playground musical activities were in charge of regular play leaders who are musical.

A Recreation Music Supervisor Works

On pages 138–139 of this book there is a brief account of musical accomplishment in San Francisco which the reader is urged to review before continuing on this page. It is very interesting to go with the Recreation Commission's music supervisor in that city to her various playground groups. On Monday at 3:30 she will appear at one of the 25 municipal playgrounds, ten of which have pianos, to direct a chorus of little girls whom she gathered for the first time shortly before Christmas for a radio singing of a Christmas carol. While the supervisor is there, one of three accompanists engaged regularly on part time is at another playground directing 35 children from six to ten years of age in a rhythm band. Some mothers in that neighborhood heard such a band at the Shriners' Hospital for crippled children, and very soon thereafter asked whether their own children might have a similar opportunity. On next Monday the supervisor herself will probably lead this group, leaving her chorus to an accompanist for that day. A little later today she will go to another playground to take charge of a singing group of camp fire girls who also got their start in a Christmas celebration, their part having been the singing connected with a series of tableaux given at the playground.

On Monday evening between 7 and 10 she will go to two or three playgrounds, directing a glee club of older girls at each one. One of these clubs of working girls is also a social and dramatic club and sings only

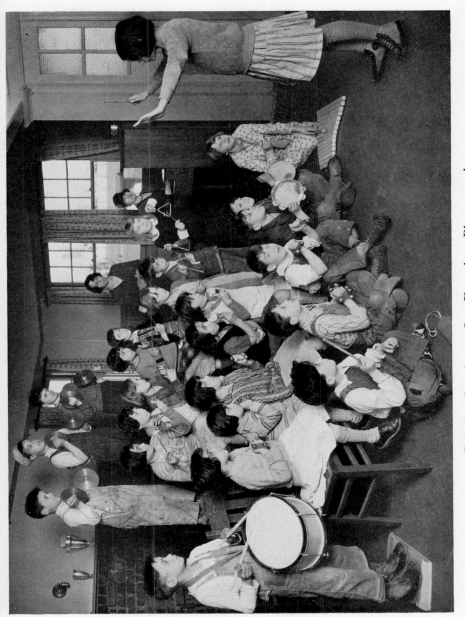

Rhythm Band on a San Francisco Playground

North Beach Playground Boys Singing Group, San Francisco

twice a month. They gave a play not long ago, between the acts of which they appeared before the curtain without their play costumes and sang. They are especially fond of a two-part arrangement of Rimsky-Korsakoff's "Song of India" and of the Brahms "Lullaby." Another of the clubs is composed of 30 girls recently graduated from high school. As high school students they had been loyal playground participants in games and sports and the playground director was eager for some sort of activity and organization that would hold them together after graduation. They, too, started with Christmas caroling. Now they sing a delightful variety of excellent two- and three-part songs as well as unison ones. They have sung enough folk and other songs of different character to be unusually quick and happy in appropriating new songs, especially folk songs of any western European nation, of Russia, and of our own country. Each member pays dues of 10 cents a month, and the money is devoted once every fortnight to simple refreshments after the rehearsal. Last spring they joined with a Y.W.C.A. chorus in giving a concert at the latter's auditorium, assisted by a string ensemble and solos from the conservatory — a very special event.

On Tuesday afternoon there will be two rhythm bands to take care of; then in the evening, very importantly, a singing group of 21 Italian boys from sixteen to nineteen years of age, and at another playground a harmonica band of 25 boys, also Italian, from twelve to twenty years of age. Both these groups are typical boys' clubs, without any frills at all. The singing group wanted only popular songs, which the supervisor promptly agreed to provide, she adding that she would like them in return to sing an Italian song for her and to prepare to sing it at the next festival. They agreed to her proposal as promptly as she did to theirs. On the next Tuesday, after she and they had sung popular songs for nearly an hour, they wanted to know what Italian song she wished them to sing. The harmonica band is in charge of a young man engaged at $2.50 a session, usually about an hour and a half. He has three other such playground groups which, with some unattached players on almost every playground, will soon be drawn into a city harmonica contest.

Another rhythm band will meet on Wednesday afternoon, of 35 boys and girls aged from five to twelve who are especially skillful in remembering the carefully worked out orchestrations; and in the evening another singing group of Italian boys, 30 of them from sixteen to twenty years of age, whose history starts exactly like that of the Tuesday group. At the second meeting of these boys one of them asked permission to sing alone, and got it, and the supervisor later gave him quietly and encouragingly a helpful hint or two. For the first two meetings the boys wanted only unison singing of popular songs in which their ears played no part whatever, only their mouths and their good, hefty lungs. But this supervisor sings very well and does so freely in introducing a song and in responding to a request; and the boys soon desire to sing better. Listening to her, their ears and feelings tell them that there is a quiet but gripping sort of pleasure in this singing business that they had not bargained for, and her easy, spontaneous way of singing tells them that it isn't hard to do likewise. That boy standing up there to sing a solo probably had a good effect on them also. They listened to him as one of them — listening to themselves is what they mainly need — and that very likely made many of them wonder a little about their own vocal possibilities. Now they won't turn into angels at once; there will still be some bellowing. But the urge is aroused; the wind is up and a wise lady is at the rudder.

This very night at their first meeting, she steers them by her own singing into the smooth-flowing current of "Carry Me Back to Old Virginny." After they have sung it through once, in unison, she having demonstrated how smooth and flowing it can be, she has the accompanist play the simplest sort of tenor part above the melody of the first two phrases of the refrain and then asks four or five of the more musical boys with lighter voices to sit together and sing it fully while the rest sing or hum the melody softly. The result is very pleasing. More tenors are found and part-singing's begun, for the fun of which not only the pitches but also the tone-qualities wished for are such as to blend. The rest of that evening is given to the rounds " Row, Row, Row Your Boat " and " O How Lovely Is the Evening," a spirited popular song, and to a few folk songs including the familiar Volga Boatmen's Song — in which physical energy once more had a full chance — and " O Sole Mio." This group had been gathered by the playground director and organized with officers before the music supervisor came for the first time to lead it. Its stated purpose was just to have singing and a socially good time. In the following spring it took a happy part in the Music Week Festival.

So the week goes, the rest of it presenting more rhythm bands and choruses, including among the latter a mothers' club and on Saturday morning a group of 30 boys ten to twelve years old.

We have given so detailed an account of San Francisco's playground music because it is a record of a modest but durable beginning made by a capable person of good taste and personality left free to expand her work quietly among playground groups. There is nothing here of which to make striking newspaper publicity, though one of the city's and nation's best music critics wrote a long editorial about it. No statement like "two million people participated last year in musical activities under the direction of ————" brought the writer to San Francisco, as it did to another city, there to find that a marked deflation had occurred. But the factual report of the San Francisco Playground Commission for 1930, the year following after the week just chronicled, shows admirable growth.

Amateur Groups Organized	No. Groups	Total No. Enrolled	No. Public Performances	Total Attendance at Performances
Bands, Harmonica	9	75	2	1,500
Orchestras	1	12	1	200
Toy Symphonies	12	300	12	11,500
Choral Groups	26	815	25	12,850

Number of special paid music workers *9*: Year round *1*, Seasonal *8*.

*   *   *   *   *   *

We may now describe single musical activities found here and there, commencing with

Singing

Choruses, glee clubs, quartets, or any other singing activity may be carried on outdoors where or when it is not too noisy. Instrumental accompaniment is not essential, though often desirable. Where its chief value consists in suggesting and upholding the rhythm, this may be secured almost as well through a tastefully managed drum or rhythm band as through a piano, and sometimes, as in Indian songs, it is preferable to the piano. A guitar, violin, mandolin, ukulele or a phonograph can be made to give support to both pitch and rhythm. It is "in the evening by the moonlight," out-of-doors, that many a "barber shop" quartet or other singing group is at its best. Of all singing times and places in camps, camp fire time on beach, field, or hillside is the most fruitful of songs. But any other time in a fairly quiet outdoor place may hold enjoyable singing.

Playground Choruses in a Festival

On the first Sunday afternoon in May each year there occurs in Chicago's Orchestra Hall a music festival, the culmination of a year's singing by children that is in almost every respect the most admirable playground musical enterprise found in the United States. The single respect in which it is not so admirable is its failure to enlist more boys. In the 1930 festival less than ten per cent of the children were boys. But the music used was all of the best that is enjoyable to children, it was very well sung, the children were extremely happy to be taking part (especially evident was this in the final rehearsal), and there they were, many of them from the poorest sections of the city, singing with a symphony orchestra in the abode of all that is best in Chicago's musical life.

There were 500 of them from 5 to 15 years of age — most of them about eleven — all the stage could hold. Three hundred more wished to sing, it was said, and were prevented only by the limited capacity of Orchestra Hall, which for some reason must be used rather than some more capacious place. It must be keenly disappointing to be kept out of the festival for such a reason. Even singing a while from the balcony, if well directed — perhaps in antiphony with the main chorus — might give the extra children a good deal of satisfaction. However, having limited space may make many of the children strive more faithfully than they might otherwise to be worthy of a place in the festival. Moreover, concerts of Christmas carols at the Art Institute, Lyon and Healy's, the Stevens Hotel, the Fine Arts Building, and over the radio, and one or more neighborhood concerts given by the individual playground groups, give additional opportunities for public performances.

As far as its funds permit, the Civic Music Association of Chicago, which is responsible for this good work, will provide a leader for each group of from 30 to 50 children that can be gathered for singing on any Chicago playground where there is a piano. All children between the ages of 4 and 14 who can carry a tune are eligible. Each chorus rehearses twice a week in the field house of the playground. There is also a group in an orphan asylum and one in the County Detention Home. In 1929–30 there were altogether 24 choruses in charge of 10 musically trained leaders under the direction of a full-time supervisor. The well-known musician who is superintendent of the Association holds a conference with the leaders and the supervisor once a month. The songs are taught by rote.

The songs to be used are carefully chosen in each preceding spring, and the words of them mimeographed. In the 1930 festival there were four groups of songs — folk songs, sacred songs, including Bach's "My Heart Ever Faithful" and one of his chorales, operatic songs — a sprightly aria from "Mignon," and the Sandman's Song and Children's Prayer from "Hansel and Gretel," the alto part of the Prayer learned separately by a few carefully chosen groups — and songs by Schubert and Brahms. The free, delightful singing of all these songs was impressive proof of the natural capacities of many, if not all, children for singing and loving the best music. A very important factor in this was the prospect of the festival with its honored setting and its orchestra accompaniment.

It was the Civic Orchestra, also a project of the Civic Music Association, that played the accompaniments, many of them especially arranged for the festival. It also played three orchestral compositions of moderate length. This orchestra is composed of about

75 advanced students and a small corps of Chicago Symphony Orchestra players who act as coaches of their respective sections of the orchestra. It was founded by the conductor of the great Chicago orchestra to give first-class training in symphonic performance to American musicians, and its playing at the festival was, very importantly, adjusted in every way to the songs and the singing of the children, a task not easy for men accustomed to the often far-flung ardors of a symphony orchestra. The children have only one rehearsal with the orchestra.

The total cost of maintaining the children's choruses for the year 1928–29 was $7,141, which included all expenditures for leadership, accompanying, and $300 spent for music and printing. Each leader receives $250 a year for each chorus in her charge, and no leader is allowed more than four. The Civic Music Association is supported through contributory memberships ranging in amount from one dollar to a thousand dollars; through special contributions from the South Park Commissioners for Free Artist Concerts in the parks, from private individuals for the children's choruses, and from the city ($450) for summer-time community singing at Navy Pier; through entrance fees ($25) paid by members of the Civic Orchestra; and through sales of tickets for this orchestra's three concerts each year and for the festival.

The cost of maintaining these children's choruses would make them impossible in most cities, but the most important features of the whole enterprise could be attained at much less expense in any city where there is or could be made available a good music leader and a good, well-balanced orchestra of, say, fifteen or more players. In the increasingly large number of communities having good community orchestras composed mainly or entirely of amateurs, the possibility of such a festival as we have just described, even where such excellence in performance is impossible, should be especially attractive. In many a city the public schools achieve a similar festival every year, usually using a high school orchestra, but even in those cities there is distinct value in having a playground music festival, an expression of purely voluntary, leisure-time interest. A miscellaneous though unified program such as they have in the Chicago festival seems especially well suited to such interest, more suitable than the cantata or operetta which is often the form given to school festivals. The songs are, of course, completely memorized by the children, and they are such as to be remembered and often resung or whistled in all sorts of places throughout many a year. It is a great advantage to have a trained music leader for every rehearsal of each group, but many a playground leader could be trained to do very well with the periodical aid of a music supervisor in charge of all the singing. More boys could be enlisted if there were opportunity to join boys' choirs or glee clubs. The success and some resulting renown of even one such group would very likely attract many boys to similar groups, each of which could maintain a full life of its own, Christmas caroling and singing at other good occasions, as well as taking part in the festival with the girls' groups.

Other Occasions and Incentives for Singing

On many of the Philadelphia playgrounds an assembly is held every morning at 9:30. After a song by all to start the day, there is often a short program of music, story-telling, dramatics, or dancing, or a brief exhibition of some sort which is followed by one or more songs and, perhaps, by announcements or discussion of playground activities or management. These programs are often in charge of children appointed beforehand to prepare them. Some of the best community singing at the assemblies occurs when one of the children, called forward to do so, has sung part or all of a song chosen by him or her and is then joined in singing it by all the other children — about 40 of them, including, in two groups observed, as many boys of all ages as there were girls. The opportunity for initiative and leadership by the children must account largely for the success of these assemblies.

In Cedar Rapids, Iowa, there has been on each playground a glee club of from 15 to 35 children whose ages range from seven to fifteen, mostly girls. They have sung familiar songs, rehearsing once a week, and have often performed at the weekly Community Nights on the playgrounds. Medals are awarded upon acquisition of enough points of credit for participation in playground activities, and singing is one of those activities.

The recreation commissioner of Jersey City, wishing to avoid losing contact with the children of the city after the summer playground season, asked a playground leader who could sing to form a chorus of boys and girls in the fall. An accompanist was engaged to help him. Only eighteen children came in the beginning, but the lure of the radio has increased the enrollment to nearly 1,200, distributed in several loosely organized choruses. The local broadcasting station officials agreed to have the first small group sing over their radio, and the number of favorable responses to the singing persuaded them to set every Wednesday evening at eight as the children's hour. The city is for this purpose divided into eight sections, one section only being represented by its chorus at each broadcast. There is still only one leader, and he rehearses each chorus only during the week before its radio performance, holding five rehearsals during that time in a school building of the neighborhood. Once when an adult singer was substituted for the children there were many protests from listeners-in. The children are evidently enjoyed by many people. Whichever chorus broadcasts is expected to sing and sometimes entertain in other ways at the city hospital on the following Saturday afternoon. The recreation commissioner goes with the children to radio station and hospital and often attends rehearsals. He announces over the radio the chorus that is next to perform and the place and times of rehearsal. The newspapers also make these announcements.

Where such an enterprise is carried on there must, of course, be careful avoidance of exploitation of the children. They should as far as possible be led to forget themselves in the music and in the desire to sing it well enough to please their listeners and represent their neighborhood worthily. The more interested they are in the music itself, which should be of the character and vitality of the best folk songs, the most valuable in every way will the enterprise be. For that reason and others that are obvious, it would be better to have each chorus enjoy longer periods than one week for rehearsals, and to have two instead of five rehearsals in a week. The only advantage of having all the rehearsing in one week is that it obviates the forgetfulness and loss of interest that are likely to occur in a play activity when its goal is remote.

* * * * * *

We must again refer the reader to the references made to singing in community centers and in camps in Chapters XVI and XIX respectively. There he will find other occasions and incentives for singing, most of which may be used on playgrounds also. The making of new camp words for old tunes or of tunes as well as words will suggest another playground possibility.

Before leaving playground singing, let us be reminded again of the possibility of providing for small groups of junior and senior high school students who, trained in school to sing first-class music in parts, might enjoy meeting on the playground for singing in the twilight or early morning, or in the moonlight or starlight. They could be guided by occasional visits from the playground music director or some other musically capable person — an advanced high school or normal school student, or the like, might do very well — and be offered music and suitable occasions for performing it for other people.

PLAYING

Bands

The accounts of playground music in Salt Lake City and San Francisco have already indicated each of the various kinds of instrumental music that are being found suitable. Most satisfying of all in the out-of-doors is a well-managed band. Indeed, the summer time with its opportunity for outdoor performance is the best time of all for a band, for the performers and the listeners. Knowing of the increasingly large number of school bands, one wishes that during that season of warmth and leisure there could be one or more bands of boys and girls in every city that would be to the playgrounds what adult bands are to the parks in hundreds of cities, but without pay to the boys and girls.

With very capable leadership, frequent rehearsals, an adequate supply of instruments and a quiet, private place for rehearsals, a group of interested and faithful boys or girls or both, all beginners, gathered for a band in June, could before the end of the playground season in September play very simple but real music well enough to be worthy of their own ears and of their listeners. But this combination of ideal conditions is yet to be found on any playground. Summer time playground bands have had to borrow skills gained in the winter or else, started in the summer, they have been given means and opportunity to continue after the summer.

The Schools Help

For example, the 45 members of the Boys' Band of the Irvington, New Jersey, Department of Recreation received most of their training in school bands, 35 of them still playing in those bands, and the remainder having recently graduated from school or left it to go to work. Their ages are from 12 to 18. The director of instrumental music in the public schools is engaged by the Recreation Department to conduct this band, which throughout the summer rehearses once a week and gives one or two concerts a week in the parks. It also frequently plays for playground folk-dancing, marching, circuses and other events, doing without some of the older boys if they have to be at work at the time of such an activity or event. The boys receive no remuneration. Three Union bands are engaged, also by the Recreation Department, each to give a certain number of summer concerts in the parks, and it is agreed in connection with their engagement that the Boys' Band will without any protest from them give as many supplementary concerts as may be desired.

Civic Spirit on Playgrounds

A band like this one not only provides a delightful play activity but it also goes far toward doing for all the children of the city what a school band does for the children of the school. That is, it tends to develop civic spirit that is essentially like school spirit, without which an educational institution can scarcely if at all carry out its main purposes. Even adults must be proud of, and have a fine feeling of moral obligation toward, a community that has a city boys' band. It was the Kiwanis Club that furnished the uniforms for the Irvington band, and this band is sometimes called to perform at civic functions during the winter. The 60 members of Detroit's Recreation Department Boys' Band have played in civic receptions to Lindbergh and other distinguished visitors. The Los Angeles Playground Boys' Band has helped to greet President Hoover. No matter how many and how fine the school bands may be, there is always reason for having a city band also, of boys or girls or both. Surely the school and the recreation officials should arrange for the best possible mode of providing band leadership and performances for as many as possible of the boys and girls of a city who want to play in a band during the summer. If necessary, some school-owned instruments and music should be loaned for the purpose, under supervision.

A Playground Band Independent of Schools

The Wilkes-Barre Playground and Recreation Association has a boys' band which in origin (in January 1924) as well as present training is its very own. This band's 60 members rehearse once a week throughout the year, and besides playing for the playground circus, lantern fête and other activities, they take active part in Christmas celebrations — including concerts at the Old Ladies' Home, the children's wards in the hospital, and the jail on Christmas Day — the Memorial Day parade and other civic occasions, and they give two or three formal concerts during each winter for which 35 cents admission is charged to help defray the cost of the band. A bandmaster from a near-by city organized them in the beginning and taught them to play, they paying 50 cents a lesson, upon which he depended entirely for his remuneration. All the instruments except three bass horns and a bass drum, which were purchased by the Association, were acquired by the boys through an easy payment plan arranged for by the bandmaster. This placing of almost the entire financial as well as the musical and social responsibilities of such an organization into the hands of one person is a dangerous though very convenient way of getting a band started. But the Association's director of recreation saw to it that the bandmaster and all the conditions were such as to be entirely dependable.

During the first year there were 100 members, then 125, then 80, and now 60. The decline in number has been mainly due to the starting of other bands in near-by towns which were at first represented in the Wilkes-Barre band, and to the development of free bands in the public schools. But some who play in school still continue to play in the Recreation Association city band. About once a year a dinner is given for the boys, and now and then there is a parents' gathering, with refreshments, in a room at the Fire Engine House where the boys rehearse. Additional helps to morale are the good uniforms worn by the boys, the privilege of leading the band occasionally given to worthy boys, and the personal interest and presence, at each rehearsal, of the band "mother" who is a member of the Association's music committee. The present leader, succeeding the out-of-town bandmaster after the latter had led the band for two years, is paid ten dollars a rehearsal, and the boys now pay dues of 50 cents a month. The band mother, who is also its secretary-treasurer, sees to it that no boy whose family cannot afford even that small sum is therefore deprived of membership and full respect. The total yearly cost of the band is about $600, four hundred of which is given from the community chest and the rest is gained through dues and the sale of tickets for the special concerts for the purpose. These concerts are attended by from 200 to 500 parents and friends of the boys, the latter selling most of the tickets themselves.

Small Groups and Some Lesser Cousins of the Band

There is also the possibility of having small groups of agreeably mated band instruments played on the playgrounds, and of the appeal and often pre-band training of a bugle and drum corps or a fife and drum corps. In Jacksonville, Florida, the Recreation Department offers bugle practice on one day, drum practice on another, and the two together in a parade on a third day each week. If learned properly, a bugle is a direct introduction to the playing of any brass instrument, and no one can doubt its appeal to boys and also to many girls, especially in these days of scouting and summer camping when buglers are needed even more than most of us need band and orchestra players. The drum well played is, of course, the main "life of the party" in musical as well as plain rhythmic accompaniment to such common playground and camp activities as are set to rhythm, to say nothing of its value in band or orchestra concerts.

*   *   *   *   *   *

Chapters XIV and XVI contain suggestions for maintaining orchestras, rhythm bands, and other instrumental as well as vocal groups that are suitable also to playgrounds.

CHAPTER XVIII

In Art Museums

ONE of the most favorable tokens of the coming status of music in American cities is its inclusion in the offerings of at least nineteen of our art museums. When the prevailing interests in music divide it between brilliant concert hall and opera house performers, often surrounded by salesmanship and hocuspocus, and the showmen of Tin Pan Alley and its outlets, there is great need but little likelihood of its finding a haven in the temples of the Muses. But there must be an increasing number of people who seek living performances of excellent music — as views of great painting, sculpture, or architecture have usually been sought — without sensational lures of "personalities" or of mere amusement. Music is after all an art, and one which by its most nearly universal appeal and its embodiment in purest form of the essential qualities of all art is peculiarly well suited to an institution seeking to cultivate appreciation of these qualities as they appear in the several other arts. And the art museum is peculiarly well suited to cultivating love and understanding of the best music.

Eleven museums offered 89 orchestra concerts for which the average attendance was 1,555. But 8,000 is the average number and 11,000 the largest number of persons per concert for the eight concerts given by an orchestra of sixty-five at the Metropolitan Art Museum in New York City. The character and meaning of these eight concerts may be seen in the following excerpts from an informal address given by the conductor of them, Mr. David Mannes, at the 1930 convention of the American Federation of Arts:

Of course, there must be many of you who have not been to the Metropolitan Museum on such a night in January or in March, so just let us make an excursion up Fifth Avenue to Central Park and Eighty-second Street. We ascend a broad staircase. We get into the hall. People are seated on a few of the benches that are there. It being early in the afternoon, we go around and look at the pictures, and at five fifteen we come down to the lecture hall where we find about two hundred people listening to a lecture on the program. We come up at six o'clock and find that all of the three thousand seats have been taken. We go out and get dinner. We come back to the Museum at eight o'clock and find that there is hardly standing room. For you who do not know the size of the great hall at the Metropolitan Museum, I will tell you that it is comparable to the railroad station of a great city. Around the gallery is a rail, back of which is the orchestra. At eight o'clock the conductor steps forward. There is no time to applaud him and the program begins — perhaps with an overture by Beethoven, followed by the César Franck symphony.

The extraordinary part of it is that whereas at the symphony concerts in Washington, New York, Chicago, Philadelphia and other large cities the conductors have to contend with noise and confusion between the numbers, this great audience at the Museum could not be persuaded to make a sound — there is absolute silence. The number of this audience is eleven thousand people. As I look down I cannot see the floor, it is packed so tightly with people. Nobody moves. They do not go out and look at the pictures. Some of these people have been standing there since six o'clock.

The program begins again — a chorale of Bach; then follows a symphonic poem, *The Afternoon of a Faun,* by Debussy. Then comes an excerpt from a String Quartet followed by excerpts from *Die Meistersinger* — the introduction to the third act — and so the thing ends. It is ten o'clock. The people still stand there. There is a great deal of applause. It is such a well-mannered audience that the applause comes in the right places. They are not likely to applaud on the chord of a dominant seventh, as often happens in Carnegie Hall. It is really a highly intelligent audience.

Then at ten o'clock people go around the galleries and see the pictures. That is what the concerts have developed into. . . .

There must be a tremendous field for this sort of thing when people will come at four o'clock in the afternoon and wait four hours for music — music must have a tremendous appeal. . . .

Why should you not have as high a standard in music as you have for the works of art which line the walls of a Museum? You will probably be amazed when I tell you that in twelve years, with a total each year of eight concerts, reaching sixty-eight thousand people, nothing in the Museum has been hurt, nothing has been broken. There are no police in the building and no guards. There are no signs to keep still. If you should move about, your neighbors would tell you to please be quiet. There is no talking, no whispering. If you have ever " heard " silence, it is on these occasions.

If you need faith in the human race, if you need faith in the aspiration, in the aristocracy of our democracy, come next January and March and renew your faith, because you will never doubt again.

At the Art Institute of Chicago a small orchestra has given fifty concerts on twenty-five Sunday afternoons from October to May, each program being given twice, at three o'clock and at four fifteen. Twenty-five cents was charged for admission to these concerts, the programs of which have been comparatively light in character, and the average attendance was 358. Four of the eleven orchestras that performed in museums were comprised mainly of amateurs. The fees for professional orchestras have ranged from $100 for a group of twenty to $1,730 for the sixty-five players and conductor of the Metropolitan Art Museum concerts.

In fifteen art museums a total of sixty-nine free concerts of chamber music were given in 1929–30 and attracted an average attendance of 368 for each concert. The yearly series of five or six such concerts at one of these museums — the Pennsylvania Museum of Art in Philadelphia — have, however, been attended by about 3,000 persons at each concert. About one-third of the sixty-nine concerts were given by amateurs who played without remuneration. The fees given to professional groups ranged from $20 for a group of young performers to $300 for an established string quartet.

The lowest average attendance for all museum concerts — 310 persons — was for the fifty-nine vocal and instrumental solo recitals held in thirteen museums. About one-seventh of the vocal soloists were amateurs, but all the instrumentalists were professionals. The fees for the paid soloists ranged from $50 to $200, the latter fee including the accompanist.

Thirty choral concerts were offered in ten museums. The average attendance at these concerts was 720, but about 2,500 persons attended the annual performance given by the Harvard Glee Club at the Boston Museum of Fine Arts. About two-thirds of all the choral concerts were given by amateurs, including a small number of local " foreign " groups, and almost all of the concerts were given without charge.

One hundred and sixty-five organ recitals were given in five museums attracting an average attendance of 318. All of the organists were professionals, and their fees ranged from $25 to $150.

In one museum three concerts by choruses of public school children were given, in another a number of high school orchestras each gave a concert, and in a third the junior orchestra of a local music school performed. Four museums each offer a course in music appreciation and four others a series of talks explanatory of the museum concerts.

Two museums each have a regularly organized music department in charge of a curator of music, a third one has assigned the supervision of its concert-giving to a local music club, and the musical destiny of another is in the hands of a civic music association. In one museum this work is delegated to a music committee of six representing that number of the city's musical organizations. Music in the Fogg Art Museum of Harvard University is under the direction of the Music Department of the University.

The cost of the concerts in three museums was provided through gifts from one or two individuals. In another, a special endowment for music is a perennial blessing. An appropriation from the city, several private voluntary subscriptions, and an Educational Fund were, respectively, the means of support in three other museums.

Purposes and Values

Music returned to her rightful estate beside the other " daughters of enthusiasm," as Emerson called the arts! — How came this to be? What purposes have the museum directors in providing concerts in the museum and what values do these concerts seem to have? Here are excerpts from directors' own answers to these questions:

1. To develop an appreciation for and an understanding of the finest in music as the other departments of the museum do in the other arts.
2. To supply good music free to all who desire it.[1]
3. To intensify art appreciation.
4. To relate as far as possible all the arts.
5. To bring people to the museum where one art could help in the appreciation of the other.
6. We find it decidedly worth while. In listening to music and then visiting museum exhibits or vice versa our visitors have an increased range of aesthetic experience.
7. People attending seemed to feel that they had experienced an even greater pleasure because of the beauty of the setting.
8. It was interesting to note the number who lingered after the concerts and visited the different galleries, apparently appreciating, many of them for the first time, the beauty

[1] It is said that at all public museum concerts there are people who do not attend the usual professional concerts, and at nine museums it is believed that most of each audience is comprised of such people.

and attractiveness of works of art, of which previously they had no conception.

9. Get a closer affiliation between the music lovers and the lovers of the other fine arts.

10. The concerts have brought many who were not before visitors to the Gallery. Their enjoyment and appreciation were very genuine, and many of them could not afford paid concerts.

The directors of a number of museums in which no concerts have been held have stated their belief in the value of art museum concerts and given as their reason for not having any, either that facilities and funds are lacking or that an adequate number of concerts is being provided by other agencies in the city. The latter reason is not entirely justifiable because a concert in an art museum is likely to provide an experience quite different from that derived from a concert in any other place.

Closer Views

It will be interesting to review the musical activities in some of the art museums in greater detail. The Cleveland Museum of Art was the first to give music a place equal to that given to painting and to sculpture in a large city museum, its Department of Musical Arts having been established in 1918. Organ recitals at this museum are held in the beautiful rotunda, and all other concerts in the Lecture Hall seating 500. Many more people wish to attend the concerts than can be accommodated in this hall.

What is most significant in the endeavors of this museum is the great wealth and range of the musical experience that has been offered, all within the fields of the best music, and the educational ways in which this has been done. In addition to many separate, independent concerts, complete series of concerts have been given of the string quartets of Beethoven and of

Brahms, the greater organ works of Bach, the pianoforte sonatas of Beethoven, and the best German lieder. Such concerts, preceded as they are by brief expository talks given by the Curator of Music to those who wish to come a half-hour earlier to receive them, provide for the kind of accumulative progress that makes for deeper insight and therefore deeper enjoyment than is ordinarily possible through a succession of unrelated programs. Furthermore, many a Sunday afternoon program of fine substantial organ music played by the curator has been repeated by him on three succeeding Sundays " so that those who wish may become more familiar with it."

The range of interest, extending back as far as Gregorian chants and 16th century choral music sung by a local choir, has reached forward to music of contemporary composers of Europe and America, and has given sanction to worthy folk music sung by competent though amateur foreign-born groups of the city, as well as to the most advanced music performed by professional players or singers of the first rank. Once each year a whole concert is devoted to music by Cleveland composers.

There have also been a few musical programs involving the dance as a kindred art, and in 1925 the music of Stravinsky's ballet " Petrouchka " was accompanied by a pantomime of marionettes made by Cleveland children. There are two classes in singing and music appreciation held every Saturday morning for the children of members of the museum. These, like the concerts for adults, are devoted to music as music and as a means of education, not as a mind trainer or a mere diversion. At Christmas time each year these children have presented an appropriate play with music, the latter consisting largely of old folk carols. Once each year a concert is given by the Junior Orchestra of the Cleveland Institute of Music.

The Detroit Institute of Arts also has a Department of Music in charge of a curator. A distinctive feature of the musical offerings of this museum in 1929–30 was a series of eight monthly lectures given by the Curator on the History of Music, each of which lectures is followed two weeks later by a pianoforte recital, also by the curator, of the music referred to in the lectures. Another interesting feature of this museum's service to the community is the use that is made of its auditorium for concerts by local chamber music groups and other musical societies, under their own auspices.

From the Worcester (Massachusetts) Art Museum has come the following report:

The Worcester Art Museum began in the winter of 1919–20, giving free concerts every Sunday from 3:00 to 4:30, from November 30 to February, with two additional concerts in March and April. The average attendance was 1085. Owing to the extra work which these concerts entailed, during the second season they were given on every other Sunday. The average attendance for the ten concerts was 1185.

With eight concerts in the third season the average attendance was 1475, the largest on any one Sunday being 2233, which taxed the seating and standing capacity of the museum to the limit. The program was given by the Harvard Glee Club.

As the attendance at the concerts began to decrease after 1925, only four concerts were given in 1926–27, with an average attendance of 810. We have gradually increased the number of concerts again, and in 1929–30 we had an average attendance of over 1000 at the seven concerts.

We feel that there are a number of reasons to account for the decrease in attendance. Many people are satisfied to get their music from the radio without being obliged to go outside in winter weather. Others object to the crowds that they find at concerts and dislike to run the risk of having to stand if they arrive too late to get a seat, and the Movie Houses which were not open on Sundays when we began our concerts, are a very serious rival.

We might say that the majority of our concerts are given by the various groups made up of Boston Symphony men, varying in number of performers from quartets to fifteen or sixteen men, the average cost per concert being $300. Of course, we vary the attractions somewhat, and each season have one concert in which we feature a pianist, violinist, and a vocalist, which is arranged by a local musician who is in touch with musicians all over the country.

With one exception we have avoided local organizations. The exception was a very creditable concert by the Worcester High School Symphony Ensemble, which was given as our last concert in 1929–30.

The Baltimore Museum of Art is fortunate in having the cooperation of different musical groups in Baltimore, all of them of importance in the city's cultural life. The Johns Hopkins' Orchestra, consisting mainly of amateurs, gives an annual concert. Excellent programs are also presented by students of the Peabody Conservatory, by the choruses of two music clubs and the Choir Choral Club and by choral and orchestral groups from the public schools.

The Parrish Memorial Art Museum of Southampton, Long Island, has provided concerts of one sort or another since its foundation in 1899. It has had a pipe organ since 1902, and besides offering many concerts and recitals to its small responsive community it has provided a rehearsal place for, and an annual concert by, the Southampton Choral Society which has been in existence for about thirty years.

The following report has come from the Isabella Stewart Gardner Museum in Boston:

The conditions at this museum are peculiar; no additions are made to the collection and we make no changes in exhibition. We are open on Tuesdays, Thursdays and Saturdays from 10 A.M. to 4 P.M., and on Sundays from 1 P.M. to 4 P.M. (We are closed during the month of August.)

For the last three seasons, on week-days we have had a half-hour of music each morning and each afternoon. Two days a week the music is furnished by two young men who are museum guards. One of them is a tenor, a graduate of the New England Conservatory of Music, but he also conducts a suburban church choir. The other is a pianist, still a student at the Conservatory. On the third week-day we have the same pianist, and a very good young soprano who graduates from the Conservatory this month. Generally only a few people take the time to sit through the half-hour of music, but the idea is very often commended and we feel that the music animates the museum.

On Sundays at 2 o'clock we have a slightly longer program, lasting generally about three-quarters of an hour. We regularly have two young soloists. Our young soprano sings every other Sunday, and with her we have either a pianist, violinist or cellist. On the intermediate Sundays we have a combination of two of the following: male singer, pianist, violinist, cellist. One Sunday we had a harp and flute, and one Sunday we had a local amateur Women's Chorus. Admission to the museum on Sunday is free, and these brief sessions of music have become an important element in the pleasure of our Sunday visitors. We provide chairs for about 100 people and generally from 50 to 100 stand. Many of our Sunday visitors come over and over again on purpose to hear the music; most of them, I imagine, cannot afford to go to other concerts.

As our musicians are all young people making a professional start, the fees we pay are small, ranging from $10 to $20. This next season on week-days we may give up the morning music, as we find that most of our visitors come in the afternoon.

An interesting event in the Brooklyn Museum was a ballet performance given by Ruth St. Denis in connection with the opening of an exhibition of Dutch East Indian Art, attended by 1,300 persons.

The especially rich variety of 26 concerts given on Sunday at the Toledo Museum of Art, including choruses, vocal and instrumental soloists, chamber music groups and high school orchestras, has been largely due to the fact that there is no other place in the city so well suited to the giving of public concerts as is the museum lecture hall. Moreover, there is a pipe organ in this hall.

Exploratory Singing

There is one other kind of musical activity, not yet mentioned, that may be suited to art museums and be of especially great value. It is informal singing, such as was carried on for a little while in the Cleveland Museum of Art several years ago. Excellent folk songs, Bach chorales and other simple choral works were sung by everyone present and were interestingly commented upon by the leader. The goodly number who came for this experience — anyone was welcome — seemed to find delight and profit in it, but it was protested against by some professional musicians and by a few patrons and officials of the museum as being unsuited to an art museum because of the crudity of the singing. Consequently, an attempt was made to substitute for it a chorus which, though free and inclusive as the informal singing had been, would prepare by systematic rehearsals to sing a few things very well and give a concert. But the chorus was too much weighted with inferior voices to rise so high in the time allowed, and it was given up.

The obvious moral to be drawn from this, that in art museums there should be no attempt to have choral singing except by admirably accomplished choruses, is not necessarily true. Might there not be as much justification for a kind of singing whose purpose is only to provide direct experience of the best music, as there is for the copying of great drawing, painting, and design in order to appreciate them the more? That the copying is crude makes it little if any the less educational. Singing, unlike copying, has the great disadvantage of usually being unavoidably public — we cannot close or turn away our ears as we can our eyes — and of therefore being judged as the picture or design itself, not the copying, is judged. Or else it is judged — as in what is commonly regarded as community singing — according to its social or other ulterior value with which an art museum cannot concern itself when the music or the singing seems to have no aesthetic value.

But exploratory singing such as is described in Chapter XIII does or should escape both these pitfalls. It may well be that the art museum, with its freedom from professional and scholastic conventions and with its implicit and welcome demand for excellence, is the ideal place for such singing. There might be opportunities for the members of the course to find in the museum's paintings and architecture of a given period or character the same inner qualities that they have found in the music of that period or character. Surely it would be much more inspiring to sing or listen to Palestrina, Lassus, or Byrd in the presence of old religious paintings than to do so in the common sorts of rehearsal places; and the paintings might be infinitely more meaningful to the singers or listeners than they would have been through silent staring alone.

CHAPTER XIX

In Summer Camps

EVEN a group gathered from different families and places for only an hour's work or play needs the feeling of fellowship that music better than anything else can give. How is it then with a group of boys or girls and counselors who are to live together for two months? It is no wonder that music in some form is welcomed or sought by every camp director, even in camps where physical education or "back to nature" is the sole aim. But more and more camps are dedicated primarily to development of richer, fuller living, to mental and emotional health and growth as well as to physical welfare. Music in such camps should find the very impulses from which the best of it has always sprung. The opportunities to integrate it in the life of the individual or group, which have often been lost or overlooked in schools, are at their most inviting best in camps.

Consider the environment and the many occasions and activities that may call for singing. For example, at a girls' camp in Vermont a bugle call ordinarily sounds the beginning of the day, but on Sunday mornings and sometimes on other days also a small chorus of campers goes about the camp singing in canon the inspiring Zuni Sunrise Song with its "Wake ye, arise, Life is calling thee." The grace at breakfast is spoken, but there will very likely be a song to welcome a visitor, or perhaps one to banter a tardy camper, sung to an old chantey tune,

> Oh! Wake her,
> Oh! Shake her,
> Oh! Shake that girl with the bloomers on.
> You can't be late for breakfast
> At Camp Hanoum.

Someone will start a good old tune with words in serious or laughing praise of a counselor or of the camp, or "Summer Is A-Coming In" or some other round will be sung. At morning assembly, after such a song as the Zuni Invocation to the Sun, commencing,

> Rouse, O Spirit, our endeavors,
> Keep our thoughts free, our hearts eager,

there will be good talk about plans for the day or the experiences of yesterday, followed by a half-hour or so of delightful singing led by "Throstle," whose superbly musical and free spirit and singing would liberate even a monotone-bound grandfather. It is then that the everlasting songs of previous camp seasons are happily learned by new campers, and new songs — some of them with verses made by one or more of the campers to commemorate a trip or for some other vital purpose — are heard and the best of them learned by all. A grace will be sung at midday dinner and another one at supper, and other songs will grace those meal-times also. Best of all occasions perhaps is fireside time when, as a favorite good-night song has it,

> Round the camp-fire's ruddy glow
> Tales are told in voices low,

and the listening to beautiful music well played adds still more to the urge to sing. Fun, romance, beauty, adventure, pass before minds and hearts like images in the flames while breezes from the mountains play upon cheeks and bring the trees with their gentle rustling into the singing fellowship. The handsome

open building, "Three Gables" it is called, that holds
these gatherings is set high on the hillside overlooking
the friendly Lake Abenaki and facing the east where
Nature starts all her magic of moon and stars. Will
the spirit of such an evening woven into unforgettable
music ever be entirely lost to those campers?

Before parting for the night they sing an invocation,
perhaps this one written by a counselor:

> As night comes stealing over hill and lake,
> Spirit, to thee our evening prayer we make.
> O thou who guides us, thy gifts release,
> Refresh and bless us, keep us in peace.
>
> Keep our hearts free to love the best in all,
> Guard those we love from danger, great or small.
> O thou who guides us, thy gifts release,
> Refresh and bless us, keep us in peace.

"Taps" is soon sounded, and on a clear evening it
is likely to be followed by the music of a small serenad-
ing party in canoes or by a duet sung from the other
side of the lake by "Throstle" and "Nunkie Bill,"
who sings with equally superb freedom and genuineness. A favorite song for this is the folk tune, "Du, du,
liegst mir im Herzen" sung to verses made by Nunkie
Bill himself.

> Lake, hill, valley and meadow,
> Brown road winding along,
> Friendships, hearts of gladness —
> These are Hanoum's song
>   Hanoum, Hanoum,
> These are Hanoum's song.
>
> Brown limbs flashing in water,
> Swift prow cleaving the tide,
> Strong stride climbing the mountain —
> These are Hanoum's pride.
>   Hanoum, Hanoum,
> These are Hanoum's pride.

But there are many other occasions for singing in this and other camps, including those for boys. A complete list of occasions, activities and other interests of camp life that are often motives or subjects for singing would include the following:

CAMP ACTIVITIES AND OCCASIONS

Rising-time

Meal-time (grace and during and after meals)

Assemblies

Riding

Dancing, including folk dancing

Rest-hour and "good-night time"

Swimming

Canoeing

Camp-fire gatherings

Listening to music (some or all of it performed by groups of campers)

Sunday services

Devotion to, or good-humored bantering of counselors

Devotion to the camp

Praising honor-winners

Hiking

Plays and festivals

Story-telling (a good time for "acting out" ballads)

Intercamp meetings of any kind

Welcoming guests

Games (singing games and team songs)

Singing in a choir or glee club

Song contests

Fourth of July celebration

Weaving

Puppetry plays

The beauty of surrounding country

Water carnivals

Serenades

Stunt nights and other evening programs

Truck trips

Minstrel shows

Flag raising or lowering

Birthday celebrations

"Star parties"

Operettas

Camp-made Verses for Songs

The verses of many of the songs for these occasions and interests are made by the campers or counselors themselves. In a questionnaire recently sent to 700 camp directors they were asked to state the proportion of such songs used in their camps. Of 137 directors who answered this question:

5 reported 5% and under
9 reported 10%
34 reported 25%
37 reported 50%
52 reported 75–100%

A very large proportion of the tunes used for these original verses are from popular songs or college ones. In many cases only a word here and there is changed in a college song to make it fit the camp. After seeing what admirable poetry boys and girls associated with Mr. Hughes Mearns in a city school can write, as shown in his books, " Creative Youth " and " Creative Power," it seems strange that young campers out under summer skies produce so little that is good or even merely clever. Some fine folk tunes have also been used for camp-made verses, but even a musician eager for better music in camps must wonder whether poor, trivial tunes with inferior words would not be better than fine tunes with such words. Which is most damaging to potential capacities for musical enjoyment and taste? After all, the delight of a good tune is at least as dependent on the manner and meaning of the singing of it as it is on the succession of tones and rhythmic shape of it.

However, it is evident that camp-made songs are often the most enjoyed. The making of them should be encouraged for other reasons as well, and the best ones for their respective purposes be heartily welcomed. The contests held in several camps in this regard between tent groups, table groups, or " song teams " may be useful, though the song books from those camps give no evidence of resulting benefit. The good, passing fun of such contests is perhaps often the chief or only gain. One of the most commonly used motives for song-making is the expectation that a group of campers returned from a long hike or other trip will bring a new song with them, made on the way. Another motive is the idea that each tent or cabin group should have at least one good song of its own. But in addition to these, the same kind of desire that sends many campers happily to the handcrafts or art shacks may be naturally directed now and then to the making of poetry, sung or not.

Camp-made Tunes

For some camp songs the tunes as well as the words are originated by campers or counselors. The proportions of these are shown in the following summary of replies to an inquiry:

Proportions of Songs Having Camp-made Tunes

5 reported 5% and under
43 reported 10%
14 reported 25%
1 reported 50%
2 reported 75%

What Songs Are Liked in Camps?

One question in our inquiry of camp directors had to do with the choice of songs used in camps:

Which, if any, of the following songs were sung this summer? (Please check *once* those sung seldom, *twice* those sung quite often, and *three times* those sung very often and most liked.)

The given list of songs is here shown with a summary of the answers to this question.[1] (See next page for list.)

[1] Answers from camps composed of both boys and girls are omitted because, while equally interesting, they do not differ sufficiently from those sent from other camps to warrant printing them.

	Boys			Girls		
	No. checking once	No. checking twice	No. checking three times	No. checking once	No. checking twice	No. checking three times
American Patriotic Songs	27	15	12	28	20	7
Stephen Foster Songs	7	8	—	10	12	2
Sea Chanties	17	3	1	13	5	3
Rounds	18	11	4	16	25	17
O, No, John	1	—	—	14	4	—
The Keeper	1	1	—	10	7	4
Londonderry Air	2	—	1	8	6	4
Volga Boatmen Song	16	2	5	12	10	4
The Hundred Pipers	1	—	—	—	1	—
All Through the Night	11	2	—	19	8	—
Aloha Oe	8	3	1	15	4	7
Annie Laurie	18	4	—	23	6	1
Auld Lang Syne	23	3	—	18	7	2
The Bear Went over the Mountain	24	5	3	10	7	3
Believe Me If All Those, etc.	10	2	1	21	2	3
Carry Me Back to Old Virginny	35	13	2	29	14	2
Drink to Me Only With Thine Eyes	11	3	1	22	9	2
Flow Gently, Sweet Afton	12	1	2	16	5	—
Good Night, Ladies	26	6	5	16	7	8
Jingle Bells	21	3	6	15	7	3
Juanita	18	4	1	22	12	5
Levee Song	12	7	4	7	1	2
Loch Lomond	5	2	—	4	4	—
Long, Long Ago	6	1	1	11	5	1
Love's Old Sweet Song	19	5	7	22	19	3
A Merry Life	2	—	2	5	2	1
My Bonnie Lies Over the Ocean	22	6	5	12	7	4
Nancy Lee	5	2	5	10	2	7
On O Thou Soul!	2	—	—	—	3	1
Our Boys Will Shine Tonite	18	6	4	16	1	3
Sailing	9	7	6	15	6	1
Santa Lucia	13	6	1	27	8	5
Smiles	22	11	5	15	15	4
Stars of the Summer Night	11	2	—	12	9	1
Steal Away	5	1	—	5	4	—
The Sun Worshippers	2	—	—	3	—	1
Sweet Adeline	26	10	8	15	7	—
Sweet and Low	16	3	1	21	10	6
Sweet Genevieve	7	—	1	4	2	1
Swing Low, Sweet Chariot	16	8	1	20	7	4
Tavern in the Town	5	1	1	7	3	—
There's a Long, Long Trail	33	12	13	22	20	9
Today is Monday	13	15	11	13	7	5
Till We Meet Again	12	3	4	16	6	8

	BOYS			GIRLS		
	No. checking once	No. checking twice	No. checking three times	No. checking once	No. checking twice	No. checking three times
When You and I Were Young, Maggie	4	2	1	8	—	—
Yankee Doodle	9	2	3	7	4	2
Alouette	13	12	12	17	8	9
John Brown's Baby	15	7	7	22	14	10
Mistress Shady	9	3	2	4	6	2
The Tree in the Wood	4	1	—	3	2	4
Clementine	12	8	12	11	5	1
Dogie Song	3	4	5	2	5	6
The Far Northland	2	2	—	7	3	8
Follow the Trail to the Open Air	7	3	1	13	11	11
Caisson Song	7	4	7	4	5	4

The following lists show the songs or kind of songs that received the largest number of " votes " as being *most liked* in camps.

IN BOYS' CAMPS

Song or kind of song	No. camps " voting " for it
There's a Long, Long Trail	13
Alouette	12
Clementine	12
American Patriotic Songs	12
Today is Monday	11
Sweet Adeline	8
John Brown's Baby	7
Caisson Song	7
Love's Old Sweet Song	7
Jingle Bells	6
Sailing	6
Volga Boatmen Song	5
Good Night, Ladies	5
My Bonnie Lies Over the Ocean	5
Nancy Lee	5

IN GIRLS' CAMPS

Song or kind of song	No. camps " voting " for it
Rounds	17
Follow the Trail to the Open Air	11
John Brown's Baby	10
Alouette	9
There's a Long, Long Trail	9
The Far Northland	8
Till We Meet Again	8
Good Night, Ladies	8
Nancy Lee	7
American Patriotic Songs	7
Aloha Oe	7
Sweet and Low	6
Dogie Song	6
Today is Monday	5
Santa Lucia	5

The songs or kinds of songs mentioned most often — including single and double checks as well as triple ones — are as follows (see top of next page) :

In Boys' Camps	No. camps singing it	In Girls' Camps	No. camps singing it
Song or kind of song		Song or kind of song	
There's a Long, Long Trail	58	Rounds	58
American Patriotic Songs	54	American Patriotic Songs	55
Carry Me Back to Old Virginny	50	Carry Me Back to Old Virginny	55
Sweet Adeline	44	There's a Long, Long Trail	51
Today is Monday	39	John Brown's Baby	46
Smiles	38	Love's Old Sweet Song	44
Good Night, Ladies	37	Santa Lucia	40
Alouette	37	Juanita	39
My Bonnie Lies Over the Ocean	33	Sweet and Low	37
Rounds	33	Alouette	34
The Bear Went Over the Mountain	32	Smiles	34
Clementine	32	Drink to Me Only with Thine Eyes	33
Love's Old Sweet Song	31	Swing Low, Sweet Chariot	31
Jingle Bells	30	Good Night, Ladies	31
John Brown's Baby	29	Annie Laurie	30

Answers to the question "What other songs are favorites?" brought the names of about 200 other songs showing a variety of tastes similar to that of the given list.

Surely there is no cause in these lists for complacency with regard to musical possibilities. There is all the room in the world for growth in taste and for corresponding growth in enjoyment. The girls have a better record than the boys. Aside from any considerations of quality, one must wonder what right "Sweet Adeline," "John Brown's Baby," "Today is Monday," and some of the others can have to first place in a camp, after all that we have been thinking about the occasions and other motives for singing that may arise in two months' full living in the out-of-doors. The presence of "The Far Northland," the "Caisson Song," and "Follow the Trail" in high places in the lists is token enough of the possibilities. The honor given to "There's a Long, Long Trail," "Love's Old Sweet Song," and "Carry Me Back to Old Virginny" betokens a common love of slow, sentimental songs, by boys as well as girls, and probably has much to do with many camp-fire "sings" in camps.

Various Special Musical Activities

Evidently all camps have general singing, and almost all have listening periods, but along with the growth in special musical endeavors in the schools, especially in instrumental music, there is likely to be more attention to such endeavors in many a camp. A list of most of them and the number of camps having each one is here given:

SPECIAL MUSICAL ACTIVITIES

Activity	84 Boys' Camps	71 Girls' Camps	11 Camps for Boys and Girls
Glee Club	8	26	2
Choir	18	28	4
Vocal Quartet	33	18	1
Orchestra	32	16	3
Band	11	7	2
Chamber Music [2]	9	10	—
Light Opera	13	28	2
Folk Dancing	9	35	6
Singing Games	9	29	8
Harmonica Bands	18	3	2
Ukulele Groups	8	8	1

At a camp for about 180 boys there are two bands: a senior band of 30 players and a junior one (junior in musical advancement, not in age) of 20. The senior band has three beginners, for the sake of completing the instrumentation, and it also has two or three counselors. These bands rehearse daily for about 40 minutes, but the members are not compelled to come regularly and there are often interfering activities for individuals, due to special trips or the like. The bands play at stunt nights, sometimes at the daily chapel

[2] In most cases this is provided by counselors or special musical assistants.

exercises, on some visiting days, and sometimes on short trips. Thirty of the instruments belong to the camp, having been given by a friend. There is also an orchestra of 21 players that performs nearly as often as the bands. These three organizations are primarily for the musical satisfaction of the players, not for performances. There are two full-time music instructors in addition to the leader of the orchestra, who also has charge of a tent group. The leader of the band (one of the two instructors) is a public school supervisor of instrumental music. Private half-hour lessons in piano, violin, and band instruments are given twice a week without extra charge. The playing of an instrument is in keeping with the emphatic policy of this camp, which seeks artistic or other creative work from each boy, in modeling, drawing, painting, pottery, dramatics, shop-work or music. Though no one is under compulsion in this regard, a boy soon feels out of things if he is not engaged in some such activity, no matter how simply.

Unfortunately, this policy has not been carried out in the singing. The only occasion used for singing by all members of the camp is at chapel every morning at 9 o'clock, when there is a prayer, Bible or other inspirational reading, announcements, an account of the latest news as received by radio, usually only one song, and a special performance of vocal or instrumental music by an individual or a small group of boys. The song for the general singing is chosen by one of the tent groups, which is told the day before that it will have that honor. This group sings the first verse of the song, the rest joining in the other verses. There is emphasis on developing each tent group as a community in itself, its counselor, called a "master," being responsible for cultivating suitable interests and activities, some of which, like the choice and good singing of part of a chapel song, contribute directly to the life of the whole camp. In past years there has been a professional singer at camp who has sung at chapel. But there is more singing by boys this year because of his absence. Even the singing of a masters' double quartet has been curtailed in order to provide opportunity for more singing and other musical performance by the boys.

*　　*　　*　　*　　*　　*

An admirable small *music camp* is carried on by a trio of well-known musicians. Here the best music is freely entered into as music and as recreation in the best sense. The activities offered in 1930 were: (1) singing — usually about an hour a day — of folk songs and ballads and songs by Schubert, Schumann, and Brahms, including part songs by these composers (e. g., 3-part Gypsy Song by Schumann) ; (2) playing — in small groups or the orchestra; (3) dramatics — the acting out of ballads, helping to prepare and taking part in simple festivals or pageants as well as in short plays; (4) puppetry — closely allied, of course, to dramatics, but involving the making of the puppets as well as the dramatic manipulation of them; (5) sculpture of a simple, real sort; (6) painting, sketching, and design; (7) Dalcroze eurythmics; (8) outdoor sports including swimming, riding, tennis, tramping, and archery.

There were 22 girls at the camp in 1930, ranging in age from 9 to 19, all of them evidently living a full, satisfying life at the camp. Among these girls there were eleven who play the violin, three the cello, one the harp, and nine the piano. The main musical purpose of the camp is to provide opportunities for ensemble playing, and every kind of group possible has formed itself — duos, trios, quartets, quintets and small orchestra. Some of the groups have consisted of singers as well as players, that delightful combination practiced so commonly in Germany, at least in the old days, as *haus-musik*. It was delightful to hear two string groups and later an orchestra play admirable though simple music out under the trees.

The orchestra is supposed to rehearse every day, but it and the smaller ensembles may meet at any time in response to desire or may not meet at all if other special activities are going forward, the camp program being flexible though by no means uncontrolled. It was not intended that private lessons on instruments should be given, but a few of the students have appealed for such lessons. It is probable that ensemble playing, under the conditions in such a camp as this, provides the strongest possible incentive to improving one's musical skill, to go more deeply and fully into music-making. In such a camp instrumental as well as vocal music seems to be much more nearly integrated in real life than it usually is in the studio, the concert hall or the practice room. The hills, stars, the running brook, the abounding health that comes of living fully in the out-of-doors, all seem to call for wholesome musical expression which is then entered into as naturally and delightfully as possible. It is under such conditions that individuals are most responsive to the best in music. Given proper leadership, there seem to be no insurmountable obstacles to having the main musical conditions of such a camp set up not only in other camps but in cities, on playgrounds, in school buildings wastefully closed for a whole summer, and in homes.

*   *   *   *   *   *

An especially promising kind of endeavor is represented in the " Music Interest Group " provided for in some Y.W.C.A. camps. Its purpose is to give opportunity to individuals to carry out as far as possible whatever musical interests they have. In Camp

Maqua, for instance, a meeting-time for the group was held from four to five o'clock every afternoon except Sunday, the attendance varying from three members to twenty-five. Miss Imogene Ireland, in charge of the music in the Y.W.C.A. camp, reported as follows regarding the work of these groups: [3]

In the period July 10–21 we made the beginning of organizing the groups, learning their interests, preparing for the Sunday services, and getting ready for our part in Robinson Crusoe Day. We were asked to learn and teach the whole group several sea chanteys, and to learn bird calls. The latter were particularly successful. Two of the "Sammies" whistled the bird calls as given in Olds' "Twenty-five Bird Songs for Children."

In the period July 23–August 4, a group came together who wished to do the following things: study the piano, the ukulele, play in the toy symphony, learn folk songs, camp songs, part songs, the principles of song leading, learn more about good music. We talked over their various interests and how they might be worked into a project with the result later that we gave an evening of Czech music into which came the learning of folk music, the use of the toy symphony for the folk dances, the learning of several compositions of the Czech composer Dvorak — two of these in the form of part songs. As we studied the folk songs we found they naturally formed themselves into a dramatic tale, so with the help of Myska Palentova, a Czech "Sammie," the dramatics counselor and group, and the dancing counselors, a little play was evolved for which the music group furnished the musical setting. This was probably the best example of a "project" undertaken by the music group during the summer. The program for it was as follows:

Evening of Czech Music, August 2
    Short sketch of the history of the country Myska Palentova
    Sketch of Dvorak's life .... Ellen Jones
    Four of Dvorak's selections:
        Humoresque .... Elizabeth Higgins (piano)
        Songs My Mother Taught Me
                        Ellen Jones, Joyce Caldewell,
                        Mary Ball (vocal trio)

[3] In such a camp the girls come for periods of only ten days or two weeks.

Indian Lament .... Ellen Jones (violin)

Massa Dear .... Music Group (3-part chorus)

Play:

Scene located in Czech village

Four characters: Marenka, Andulko, Maminka, Sedlak

Action takes place to accompaniment of the following songs: (from Folk Songs of Many People, G. Schirmer, sung by music group) All Joy Is Gone; Andulko; Little Dove; Rada Song; Sedlak; I'll Have No Other One; Weeding Flax Fields Blue; Good Night (in Y.W.C.A. Song Book). Folk dances played by Toy Symphony Orchestra: Bag-pipes Sounded in the Village; Tripping Maidens.

In the period August 6–18, a camper taught the members of the group who wished to learn to play the harmonica, so that they performed with credit to their teacher at the camp fire on Friday night, the 17th. The other main interest of the group during this period seemed to be in the learning of part songs, so time was given to learning about seven part songs in the Y. W. C. A. Song Book. These were sung on the same evening.

In the final period, August 20–31, the first week was devoted to learning the principles of song leading, to working on selections for the Sunday vesper service, and to learning pirate songs and sea chanteys. During the second week the group learned about eight folk songs which were sung with guitar accompaniment on the afternoon that the Japanese Tea House was introduced to the camp at Pine Grove.

Despite these good accomplishments, Miss Ireland doubts whether the campers should be urged to attend an indoor activity day after day. She would prefer an arrangement by which the music counselor would be available for a certain number of hours each day to give help to any individual or group desiring it, on as many days as it is desired. If the daily period for the same group is maintained throughout the season, it should be from five to six o'clock, not earlier.

Another project as interesting as the Czech program was the " Peasants' Festival " presented after two

weeks' preparation by a music interest group at the
Y.W.C.A. Kamp Kahlert. Poland, Russia, Czecho-
Slovakia and Germany were represented by music of
outstanding composers from these countries and by
folk songs and dances performed by the girls in costumes, ending grandly with the whole camp taking part
in the polonaise. The episodes in the festival were
based on the diary of Countess Françoise Krasinka.

* * * * * *

Rhythm bands have been mentioned. In a few
camps there is interest in the making as well as playing of elementary instruments such as drums, xylophones, psalteries, and crude violins and cellos.

* * * * * *

In one camp three types of musical evenings are
planned, all of which are said to be very popular.

(1) Music appreciation period
   a. Comments on some famous composer
   b. Explanatory comments on certain of his compositions
   c. Performance of these compositions
(2) Request programs (voluntary attendance)
   Anyone may come and ask for any selection to be
   played or sung by the music counselors. (Excellent
   judgment is shown in this, it is said.)
(3) Musicales
   A program prepared beforehand is performed by
   campers and counselors. Solos for piano, violin, or
   voice; and duets, four-hand piano music and other
   concerted selections are enjoyed.

* * * * * *

In another camp each girl has an accomplishment
book mentioning goals toward which she may strive in
each kind of camp activity, the goals being arranged
in three classes; namely, Beginners', Intermediate
and Advanced. The advanced goal sheet is as follows:

Music

Accomplishment	*Year*	*Counselor*

Lead camp songs to the satisfaction of the music counselor for two weeks.

Show originality along some musical line approved by the counselor in charge of music.

Construct or contribute to a musical program.

Sing acceptably in the camp chorus.

Sing acceptably in the camp choir.

Play an instrument acceptably in a duet or other small ensemble good enough for a camp " musical evening."

Know by heart 25 folk songs.

Know by heart 50 folk songs.

Be intelligently familiar with 25 compositions to which you have listened.

Act as leader to a group of campers who need someone to help them to pass some of their Beginners' or Intermediate tests in Music.

Attend regularly some class in music for the summer.

Remarks:

Those Operettas!

There can be no question as to the fun to be got from performing in a good operetta — a rarity amidst hundreds of poor ones. But how many precious summer hours will be taken in preparation of it? What will be left in the memory of it that is worth remembering? What other singing or playing might the campers have enjoyed in the time given to the operetta? Here is a boys' camp in which an organist who spends his summers near-by " put on [through the campers] his own original musical comedy which was a big hit." The only other music in that camp, according to the director's report, was some singing now and then of Rounds, the Caisson Song, and a few college songs with camp words. There is no camp song book and no mention of favorite songs. In another camp two operettas " have been done each year, a junior one for little fellows, and another for the older fellows "; and though the music counselor is a Doctor of Music, the favorite songs of the camp are the Levee Song, " Today is Monday," and " Let Me Call You Sweetheart " ! The only possible excuse for such conditions is the presence among the boys of opposition to songs expressive of the full, adventurous life of a good camp, and the absence of leadership capable of winning them over. The operettas may then be a last resort.

Now it is not intended to condemn all operetta performance in summer camps, but to suggest criteria for determining its value in such places. Most of the tunes in the Gilbert and Sullivan operas are worth a lifetime of remembrance, and where there is the abundant energy of youth, an enjoyable performance may be got ready without taking too much time from other things. But it would seem that the acting out of ballads, a more or less spontaneous festival, or the like, that takes comparatively little time, is a better sort of musico-dramatic activity for a camp than the sustained operetta.

When Are Songs Learned?

Fifty-one out of 84 boys' camps have a daily scheduled period for singing, and one camp has a weekly period; 57 out of 71 girls' camps have such a daily scheduled period. In other camps the campers acquire songs mainly through the folk way of learning: e.g., when a natural occasion for singing, like a camp-fire gathering, arises, those unfamiliar with a song sung by some of their camp mates learn it by trying to join in. Someone, to help in this, may speak the words. In at least one camp there is frequently a learning period after lunch or supper and on rainy days. In a Y.W.C.A. many a girl has learned songs while wash-

ing dishes. After supper on many days in a camp
for boys and girls six to twelve years of age there is a
free period of 45 minutes during which time a camper
may choose between singing, a reading circle (reading
aloud in turn), and boating. Usually about one-third
of the children choose singing, and frequently all the
rest of the children come in at the end of the 45-
minute period and sing until bed-time. "The children
always welcome such an evening," it is said. "At the
end of an hour and a half they are still asking for
other camp favorites that have not been sung."

The very valuable advantage of having a daily singing and song-learning period is in the cultivation of
familiarity and skill in the songs, including Rounds
and other good, suitable music for part-singing. How
often the reason given for not taking part in a song
is "I don't know it." And ability to sing well is an
additional incentive to take part. In one camp every
camper has in the beginning of the season a tactfully
conducted test of her voice before the music leader,
who keeps a record of the resulting information and
is thus much better able to adjust her own aims and
efforts to the specific abilities and needs of the individual campers. This also tends to give the camper a
sense of value with regard to her voice and her singing, and a sense of craftsmanship in the development
of them. Such test would be even more valuable in a
boys' camp. There is certainly no loss in the social and
other values of camp singing if the campers can say
with deserved pride, "You ought to hear Camp ──
sing! We sing many kinds of songs; sea songs, humorous songs, songs of heroism, fine love songs, songs for
hiking, paddling, and weaving, quiet songs, and great
hymns that make you dream of being a very fine person,
every sort of song, most of them sung and loved by real
red-blooded people for a long time. You ought to hear
us. Our leader loves the songs himself and his main

question about how we sing them is whether we are big enough in imagination and sympathy to make them real, to sing each one well and according to what it means." This is a kind of team spirit that can be as strong as that bred in any game, though, fortunately, it may lack the competitive attitude altogether. In other words, singing may become another sport and another creative or exploratory activity like the best of the handcrafts or the best sort of nature study.

But the success of the regular daily period depends very largely on the leader and there is evidently a scarcity of good camp music leaders. Compulsion in singing may be more irksome than in any other activity, because the desire to sing is itself ninety per cent of the doing of it. It is in these regular singing periods that, we suppose, most of the damage of too much teaching, about which many camp directors have complained, is done. However, given a good leader, the daily music period is likely to be of great benefit.

The Leader

No need in camp music is so urgent and apparently so difficult to fulfill as that for good leadership. Only forty-five out of eighty-four boys' camps have persons engaged especially to take charge of musical activities, and some of these are in charge of a tent group or of some other activities also. The proportion among girls' camps is larger, as it is in all other things musical, there being fifty out of seventy-one camps that have special music leaders.

" In eight years I have had but one successful music counselor," said one girls' camp director. From the director of a boys' camp comes another report of disappointment: " So far most of them [music counselors] have been no additions to the camp even in their ability — or lack of it — to get the group to sing, even excepting any emphasis on quality. . . . [They] have failed in personality traits or in understanding of camp music objectives as different from school music objectives." Many directors have made similar complaints, most of them concerned mainly with these lacks of personality traits and understanding of camp music objectives.

There is no test of personality so revealing as camping. Many a leader can shine and evoke full, satisfying responses in his first hour's singing with a group. That is very easy compared with the task of getting such responses every day, sometimes several times a day, for two months, and during the same time living with the singers day after day. It is no wonder that many camp directors place much more emphasis on personality and all-round manhood or womanhood than on musical ability when they are seeking a music leader.

The development of leaders having all the necessary traits is a matter for parents, schools, and still more for the individuals themselves. Institutes such as have been held now and then for camp music leaders may also be very helpful. All that a book can do is to suggest ways of making the most of whatever leadership is available.

What the Leader Can Do

To begin with, let us consider what the leader himself can do in this regard. First, he should be a good camper himself, growing in health and spirit, and a good comrade growing in sympathetic understanding of the people about him and also, in another sense, of sun, rain, hills, lake, sea, stars, and all else of beauty or challenge that nature can provide for him — doing these things through giving himself freely and self-forgetfully to the life about him, of people and of nature.

Secondly, he should know and appreciate the possible scope of his job — the large variety of occasions and musical activities already referred to in this chapter through which music may enrich the life of the camp and of individual campers. In connection with this, he should be happily familiar with a large quantity of first-class music of all kinds suitable for each sort of occasion and activity, and be able to sing or play this music with genuine love and spontaneity. There is altogether too much dependence on scintillating personality traits in this business of music leading. Minimize this dependence. Shift as much of it as possible to the propulsion to sing that comes of relating music to such vital interests and situations as have been described in this chapter. The " project " idea is a good one, setting goals desirable and largely initiated by the campers themselves. It is very good, too, to quicken the imagination by word, manner, costume or pantomime, so that the full meaning of the song is realized, however simply, in the singing of it. Especially fortunate is the camp in which there are two or more people who can sing or play *haus-musik* beautifully together. At least three camps engage a string quartet or trio for the camp season. A single good violinist may be a great boon. Experience of beauty shapes the spirit and even the voice to its welcome demands, so that the responsive listener to such music will without any other urging sing better than he knows how to do.

Let the music have its way. Even a good phonograph reproduction of a first-class folk song or the like has been known to set large or small groups to singing. A real, spontaneous, and handsome singing of such a song by a person will have its royal way with them if it is just given a good chance, especially if it has a refrain of any kind for them to start with. All the " pepping up " tactics will only get in its way. A leader need not be a showman. Ultimately it will be much better if he is not. Some of the best camp sing-

ing observed by the writer has been done with the use
of stereopticon slides showing words and music. The
leader could scarcely be seen. His presence and his
love of the song were felt, and this with an occasional
brief remark or happy demonstration was enough.
Of course, the accompaniment must be in keeping, or
else left out.

Thirdly, the camp music leader should give frequent opportunity and help to individuals among the
campers to lead their tent-mates, table-mates or
larger groups. In one camp there are Sunday evening
sings at which each group of eight campers is led alone
by its own leader and then the entire camp is led in a
number of songs by the camp song leader. The idea
again is to provide for as much willing initiative as is
possible and effective from the campers themselves. Of
course, for the sake of the led, these opportunities
must not be turned into practice periods for the young
song leaders.

Fourthly, the camp music leader must be a well integrated member of the camp staff, cooperating with
all the other counselors, and quick to see ways of fitting his musical resources into the life of the camp
which they and he are together molding. He should be
eager also to learn from their experiences and knowledge of dealing with campers.

*   *   *   *   *   *

What the Camp Officials Can Do

Now let us consider what the camp officials can do
to help make the most of the possibilities and leadership available. First, they must see to it that the music
leader can live fully and well in the camp, that he is
not overloaded by, or overconfined to, camp tasks. In
what impressed the writer as the best singing camp,
the music leader lives outside the camp proper, though
on camp property, and is with the campers only at

singing times of all kinds. She keeps in touch with the other counselors through staff meetings, informal chats and through occasional observation. If personality is a more important factor in music leading than in any other sort of camp leadership, the music person better not be compelled to be in the midst of camp activities all the time. Even the almost hypnotic hold of a Paderewski on his audiences would soon weaken if he had to live with them all the time and perhaps help them to be good, occupied, healthy and clean.

Secondly, the officials and the counselors in general and particular should, as far as they genuinely can, show interest in the musical endeavors and possibilities of the camp, best of all through taking eager part themselves. In a large measure, the singing may be regarded as a barometer of the general spirit of the camp. The good fellowship, enthusiasm, imagination, expressiveness and freedom of body, spirit and voice that are looked for in the singing are not likely to be found there if they do not exist in other activities or among the counselors themselves.

Thirdly, a person not leading in the music may often learn more about the effects of the leading than the leader himself can perceive in the midst of his efforts. The camp director or a counselor may be able to help the music leader greatly by friendly counsel. Many directors are evidently either fearful of offending the leader by talking things over with him or else it does not occur to them that as supervisory officers they have the duty to help their counselors in any respectful way that they can to carry out the latter's best purposes. The director should in this regard be to the counselors what each one of the best of them is to the children in her charge. His duty and privilege it is to discover the best possibilities of that counselor and to act in such a way as to lead her, with freedom on her own part, to fulfill them as richly and effectively as may be. When a counselor fails, it is partly a failure on the director's part also. Of course, he must be sufficiently learned and wise to do this, or else he should engage someone to do it for him — that is, if the camp music is not as good as it might be. Ideally, that person would, of course, be an expert music leader familiar with camp possibilities and capable of supervision as we have defined it, and such a person should be sought, but many a camp music counselor could profit very much from the help that a good music-loving educator in any field could give. Two or three visits from him in a season, even one visit, might be of great benefit to the camp.

*   *   *   *   *   *

It has been estimated that 1,117,000 boys and girls were in summer camps in 1930, a very large proportion of them in so-called public or semi-public camps which are supported wholly or in part by municipalities, national organizations such as the Boy Scouts, child welfare agencies, and other groups and individuals. And the number will surely increase. No phase of American life gives greater opportunity for cultivation of the natural, everyday love and expression of music that we have admired and enjoyed so much in the peoples of Germany, Italy, Czecho-Slovakia and other nations.

From another point of view the most significant camp development of all is the National High School Orchestra and Band Camp in Michigan, and the recently established Eastern Music Camp (1931) in Maine. But we have already referred to this development several times in this book, and it has been made widely known through the radio and in other ways.

Postlude

WHEN the national study, of which this book is an outcome, was started, the nation was at the height of a period of prosperity. It was not unreasonable to expect financial support for any good plans of musical development in our schools and communities. True it was that most of the amazingly large profits being gained were left in the growing stream of business, and much of the rest was going to the purchase of material luxuries, the sale of which constituted a very large proportion of the business. But unprecedentedly large sums were being given for music in the schools and for the support of our greatest symphony orchestras and opera companies. Apparently, all that was needed for further expansion of musical activity was the growing appreciation of music among the people everywhere and good plans and leaders.

But the whole outer structure of our prosperity has crashed beneath us like Sinbad's ship, and no one will venture to say when, if ever, it can be recovered. What is the use of proposing musical developments now? Should not all the labor and money asked for them rather go to physical relief of the unemployed?

It should not. For the need is greater than ever to hold fast to the things that make life worth living, while we at the same time provide for the bare sustenance of life. The greatest danger is not starvation but degradation.

The work of making the national capital more beautiful than ever is a model relief measure. A nonproductive investment, it is called; but we cannot now afford any other kind. We are already suffering from too much productive investment. We as a people have, so to speak, added to our spare time all the working hours of 7,000,000 men and women. What better than to employ it in enriching American life?

But the construction of fine buildings and other means of beautifying a city is not the only way to do this. Even more beneficial would be an increased development of cultural activities, of vocational and avocational skills and appreciations among us. " Build thee more stately mansions, O my soul." For example, what would be the effect if such a chorus as the Bethlehem Bach Choir or of any other good sort in every city could attract many of the unemployed to its ranks now, when rehearsals could be held in the day time and frequently? No matter how simple or crude the beginning would have to be, the growth in appreciation, skill, and morale could be great. Group instruction in singing and playing might also be offered, and orchestras, bands and smaller playing or singing groups be formed — all without charge, and instruments loaned. Could we do these things and provide also for development in the other arts and crafts, literature, drama and the dance among the people, we might turn calamity into good fortune. Incidentally, many more people would find employment because of the need for books, music, instruments and other materials, and for leaders and teachers. Best of all, we would be progressing toward a permanently better social order, through a better sense of values: not merely through a political system for artificially enforcing economic changes, but through a welcome realization by many more people of what men live best by, of the things that are of most worth and that increase in the sharing of them.

This is another dream, but not so fantastic as the dream we called prosperity until the crash came. The millions of men and women who in idleness are walk-

ing the streets, lounging on park benches, or seeking
shelter — the less proud of them — in municipal lodg-
ing houses, can think of nothing but getting the bare
necessities of life for themselves or their families, it is
said. They are in no mind to be singing or playing or
doing any of those other cultural things. But their
demoralizing worry and disaffection and worse are
the primary evils of the situation, needing desperately
to be changed. Most of the unemployed evidently
cannot find jobs to cure these ills. Why could they not
rise to the point of using their time and energies to
learn and use new skills and appreciations or enhance
old ones for the joy of doing something, anything,
well, or of growing in it? If it is music, real music, the
joy of what is done will more than double the joy of
the doing.

The truth is, as Dr. Frederick P. Keppel recently
said, " that the great field, the potential realm, for providing continued excitement and thereby continued
stimulation for the mature mind is the realm of the
arts." The romance of riches, of undiscovered natural
resources, booming stocks and growing cities has
heretofore engaged most of our best creative power.
Until the crash in 1929, the daily matin of almost
everyone, it seemed, from the bootblack to the banker,
was said over the financial page of the newspaper. But
here in the arts is a new, endlessly rich continent which
exists within the minds and hearts of the people and
may be realized through such adventuring as is proposed in this book. Here is pioneering and enrichment
for everyone, and increased leisure for it.

There are encouraging signs, as we have shown.
Especially significant is the fact that the large increase
in the amount of high grade music being heard over
the radio has come about through the ordinary processes of democracy; that is, through growing popular interest in such music, opportunities for education

with regard to it, and through the choices of independent concerns sponsoring the broadcasts, not through government domination. The remarkable progress from the din of low grade music that was received almost everywhere with apparently unchangeable complacency in the beginning of the radio's popularity gives new assurance of the innate capacity of almost all people to grow in responsiveness to what is excellent and inspiring in music. Still more important is the assurance, given by the schools, of potential capacities for musical skill of greater or lesser degree existing almost universally among the people.

There is evidence that the new prosperity which will follow our present disillusionment will be — *must* be — noted principally for the development of our best human resources rather than principally for the exploitation of natural resources and human frailties!

Bibliography

Musical Values and Musical Taste

Buck, P. C., The Scope of Music, Oxford University Press, 1927.

Caxton Institute, New York, The Fundamentals of Musical Art, 20 vols., Vol. 19 Music as a Social Force.

Dickinson, Edward, The Spirit of Music, Chas. Scribner's Sons.

Diserens, C. M., The Influence of Music on Behavior, Princeton Univ. Press, 1926.

Henderson, W. J., What Is Good Music?, Chas. Scribner's Sons.

Mason, D. G., Artistic Ideals, W. W. Norton and Company, Inc., N. Y.

Parker, DeWitt H., Principles of Aesthetics, Silver, Burdett and Co., 1920.

Schauffler, Robert Haven, The Musical Amateur, Houghton Mifflin Co., 1911.

Schenck, Janet D., Music, Youth and Opportunity, pub. by National Federation of Settlements, Boston, Mass.

Smith, C. T., Music of Life: education for leisure and culture, P. S. King and Son, Ltd., London.

Surette, T. W., Music and Life, Houghton Mifflin Co., 1917.

Dalcroze, E. Jaques-, Eurhythmics, Art and Education, Chatto and Windus, London, 1930.

Music Education

Birge, E. B., History of Public School Music in the United States, Oliver Ditson Co., Boston, 1928.

Dalcroze, E. Jaques-, Eurhythmics, Art and Education, Chatto and Windus, London, 1930.

Davison, A. T., Music Education in America, Harper and Bros., 1926.

Dykema, Peter W., Music for Public School Administrators, Bureau of Publications, Teachers College, 1931.

Mursell and Glenn, The Psychology of School Music Teaching, Silver, Burdett and Co., 1931.

National Bureau for the Advancement of Music, N. Y. Survey of College Entrance Credits and College Courses in Music, 1929.

Pennington, Jo, The Importance of Being Rhythmic (Based on Dalcroze's book), G. P. Putnam's Sons.

Rossman, Floy A., Pre-school Music, C. C. Birchard and Co., Boston, 1928.

Schenck, Janet D., Music, Youth and Opportunity, pub. by National Federation of Settlements, Boston, Mass.

Surette, T. W., Music and Life, Houghton Mifflin Co., 1917.

Thorn, Alice G., Music for Young Children, Chas. Scribner's Sons.

Storr, M., Music for Children, E. C. Schirmer Music Co., Boston, 1925.

Singing

Scott, Charles Kennedy, Madrigal Singing, Oxford Univ. Press, 1931.

Coward, Henry, Choral Technic and Interpretation, Novello and Co., Ltd., London, 1914.

Greene, H. P., Interpretation in Song, The Macmillan Company, London.

Proschowsky, Franz, The Way to Sing, C. C. Birchard and Co., 1923.

Wood, Sir Henry, The Gentle Art of Singing, Oxford Univ. Press, 1931.

Playing

Goldman, E. F., The Amateur Band Guide and Aid to Leaders, pub. by Carl Fischer, Inc., N. Y.

Maddy and Giddings, Instrumental Technique for Orchestra and Band, Willis Music Co., Cincinnati, Ohio.

Mason, D. G., Orchestral Instruments and What They Do, H. W. Gray Co., N. Y.

Leadership

Coward, Henry, Choral Technic and Interpretation, Novello and Co., Ltd., 1914.

Earhart, Will, The Eloquent Baton, M. Witmark and Sons, N. Y.

Gehrkens, Karl W., Essentials in Conducting, Oliver Ditson Co., 1919.

Kendrie, F., History of Conducting, H. W. Gray Co., 1929.

Stoessel, Albert, Technic of the Baton (Revised) Carl Fischer, Inc., 1931.

Church Music

Benson, Louis F., Hymnody of the Christian Church, Doubleday, Doran and Co., 1926.

Benson, Louis F., Studies of Familiar Hymns, Westminster Press, N. Y., 1903.

Curwen, John S., Studies in Worship Music, First Series, J. Curwen & Sons, Ltd., London, 1888.

Gardner, Geo., and Nicholson, Sydney H., A Manual of English Church Music, S. P. C. K., London, 1923.

Gillman, F. J., The Evolution of the English Hymn, The Macmillan Company, 1927.

Hughes, Edwin Holt and others, Worship in Music, Abingdon Press, N. Y., 1929.

Hunter, Stanley A., editor, Music and Religion, Abingdon Press, 1930.

Lightwood, J. T., Hymn-Tunes and Their Story, Epworth Press, London, 1923.

Merrill, Rev. Wm. P., Music and Worship, and the Relation of Minister and Organist, National Bureau for Advancement of Music.

Price, Carl F., 101 Hymn Stories, and More Hymn Stories, Abingdon Press.

Reeves, Jeremiah Bascom, The Hymn in History and Literature, Century Co., N. Y., 1924.

Home Music

Child Study Association of America, Music and the Child, 221 West 57th St. N. Y.

Coleman, S. N., Creative Music in the Home, Lewis E. Myers, Valparaiso, Indiana.

Thorn, Alice G., Music for Young Children, Chas. Scribner's Sons, 1929.

Miscellaneous

Beach, F. A., Preparation and Presentation of the Operetta, Oliver Ditson Co., 1930.

Chubb and Others, Festivals and Plays, Harper and Brothers, 1912.

Clark, K. S., Municipal Aid to Music in America, Nat'l Bureau for Advancement of Music, 1925.

Clark, K. S., Music in Industry, Nat'l Bureau for Advancement of Music, 1929.

Holt, Roland, List of Music for Plays and Pageants, D. Appleton and Co., 1925.

National Recreation Association, Community Music, C. C. Birchard and Co., 1926.

Odum and Johnson, The Negro and His Songs, University of North Carolina Press, 1925.

Phillips, W. J., Carols, Their Origin, Music, etc., E. P. Dutton and Co., Inc., 1928.

Tremaine, C. M., Nat'l Music Week Celebrations, Nat'l Bureau for Advancement of Music.

Umfleet, Kenneth, Staging School Operettas, C. C. Birchard and Co., 1929.

van de Wall, W., Utilization of Music in Prisons and Mental Hospitals, Nat'l Bureau for the Advancement of Music, 1924.

Watson, F. R., Acoustics of Buildings, John Wiley & Sons, Inc., N. Y., 1930.

Linnell, Adelaide, The School Festival, Chas. Scribner's Sons, 1931.

Collections of Songs *

Bach, J. S., 25 Chorales, E. C. Schirmer Music Co., Boston.

Bantock, G., One Hundred Folk Songs of All Nations, Oliver Ditson Co., Boston, 1911.

Botsford, F., Collection of Folk Songs (3 vols.), G. Schirmer, N. Y.

Colcord, " Roll and Go " (sea chanties), Bobbs-Merrill Company, Indianapolis, Indiana.

Davies, Sir Walford, Choral Songs for Male Voices, Oxford University Press (Carl Fischer, Inc., Cooper Square, N. Y.).

Davison, A. T., Harvard University Glee Club Collections for Male Voices, 3 vols., E. C. Schirmer Music Co., Boston, 1925–30.

Davison and Surette, Home and Community Music Book, E. C. Schirmer Music Co., 1931.

Davison and Surette, Concord Series, 140 Folk Tunes (for young children), E. C. Schirmer Music Co.

Davison, Surette and Zanzig, Concord Series, Book of Songs (for older children), E. C. Schirmer Music Co.

* Ampler lists of music for all kinds of musical activities will be procurable from Music Service of the National Recreation Association, 315 Fourth Ave., N. Y. C.

Davison, Surette and Zanzig, Junior Song and Chorus Book (including parts for changed voices), E. C. Schirmer Music Co.

Dearmer, Williams, Shaw and Martin, Oxford Book of Carols, Oxford University Press, N. Y., 1928.

Farnsworth and Sharp, Folk Songs, Chanties, and Singing Games, H. W. Gray Co., N. Y.

Gibbon, J. Murray, Canadian Folk Songs, E. P. Dutton and Co., Inc., N. Y.

Gilbert, H. F., One Hundred Folk Songs from Many Countries, C. C. Birchard and Co., Boston, 1910.

Girl Scout Song Book, Girl Scouts, Inc., N. Y.

Niles, John J., Kentucky Mountain Songs, G. Schirmer.

Sandburg, Carl, The American Song Bag, Harcourt, Brace and Co., N. Y.

Ten Folk Songs and Ballads, E. C. Schirmer Music Co., 1931.

*Collections of Instrumental Music for Home Groups.**

A Bach Suite for Strings with optional parts for wind instruments, Oxford University Press (Carl Fischer).

Bach, String Suites, 1, 2, 3, 4, and 5, published separately, Oxford University Press (Carl Fischer).

Bach, J. S., Sleepers Wake, No. 4 of Cantata 160, for strings with optional parts for wind instruments, Oxford University Press (Carl Fischer).

Brahms, J., Op. 52, Liebeslieder for Piano Duet, Violin and Cello, N. Simrock (Associated Music Publishers, 25 West 45th St., N. Y.).

Burmester, Willy, Pieces by Old Masters (for violin and piano), 5 vols., G. Schirmer.

Cheyette and Roberts, Fourtone Folio (for any combination of strings, woodwinds, or brasses), Carl Fischer, Inc.

Diller and Quaile, Piano Duets, 3 vols., G. Schirmer.

Fyffe, Elizabeth, Team-work Tunes (for violins, cello, and piano), Carl Fischer, Inc.

Glossner, Chamber Music Album for School and Home (Trios by Mozart and Haydn), Vol. I, Universal Edition, No. 458 (Associated Music Publishers, N. Y.).

Handel, F., Five Short Pieces for String Orchestra, Oxford University Press (Carl Fischer).

* Ampler lists of music for all kinds of musical activities will be procurable from Music Service of the National Recreation Association, 315 Fourth Ave., N. Y. C.

Hermann, Ed., String Quartet Album for the Young, G. Schirmer, 1901.

Lake, M. L., Best Select Album of Brass Quartets, Carl Fischer, Inc.

Moffat, A., Op. 41, First Pieces for Ensemble Players (for 3 violins), N. Simrock (Associated Music Publishers, N. Y.).

Pochon, Alfred, Flonzaley Quartet Favorite Encore Albums, 4 vols., Carl Fischer, Inc.

Pochon, Alfred, Progressive Method of String-Quartet Playing, G. Schirmer, 1928.

Pochon, Alfred, Schirmer's Melody Gems, G. Schirmer, 1924.

Wilson, M., Pipes and Reeds (woodwind sextet), J. Fischer and Bro., N. Y.

Wilson, M., Tubulariana (brass sextet), J. Fischer and Bro.

Winslow, R., Sixteen Simple String Quartets, C. C. Birchard and Co., Boston.

Index